RADIANT

TONY VALENTE

CONTENTS

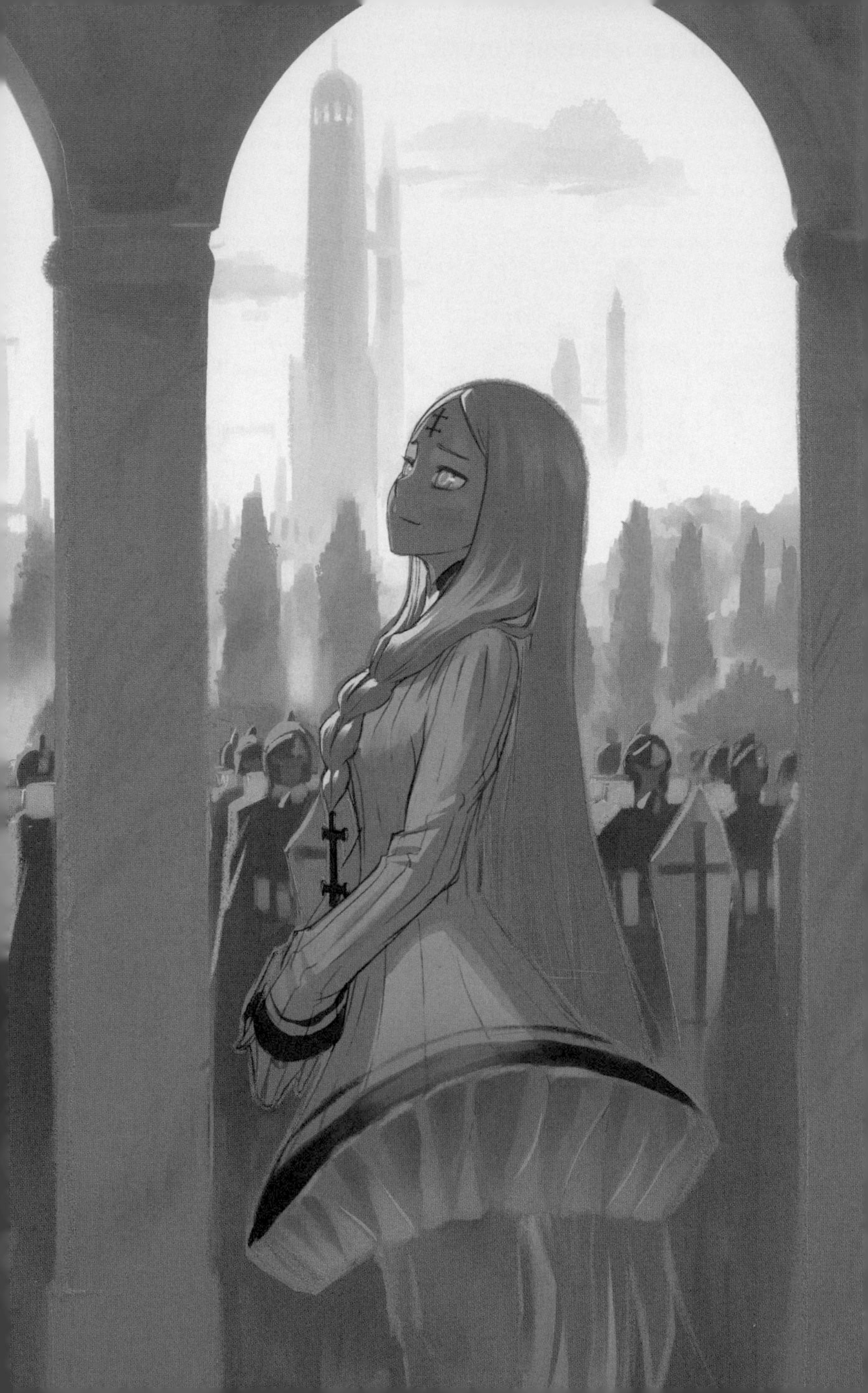

Synopsis of the previous volume:

After coming to Bôme in an attempt to find Grimm, Seth and his gang are split up upon arrival. Thanks to Dragunov, Seth manages to escape Adriel. Mélie, Ocoho and Yaga in the meantime are about to get crushed inside Yaga's cauldron, when Ocoho has Mélie book them. Locked inside the memory of Vénélope's disappearance, our little group is saved by the "Droplet Gang." Doc, meanwhile, pretends to be a victim of the Horned Wizard's group and is saved by the Inquisition...
That's when Seth, forced to keep a low profile due to the presence of a group of high-ranking Inquisitors in Bôme, gets hunted down by two Domitors–Lupa Lycco and Kamagoe.

Seth | Ocoho | Mélie | Doc | Myr | Yaga

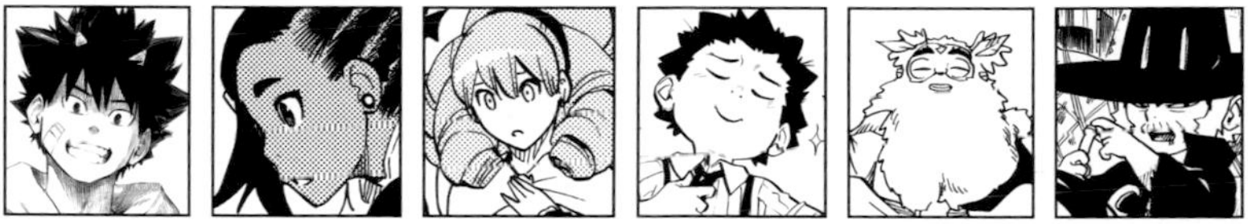

Hürla | Droplet Gang | Herklès VII

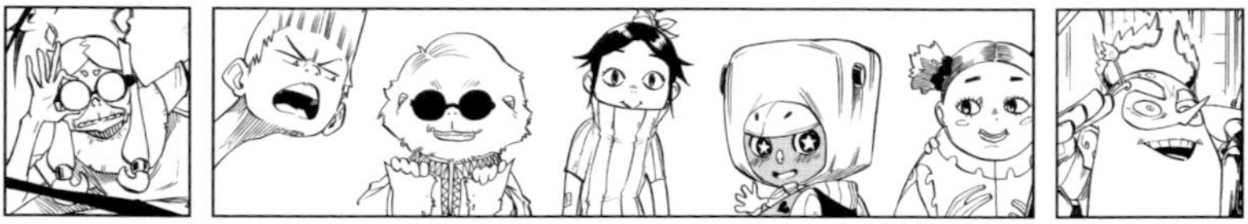

Shoan | Alcille | Lupa Lycco | Adhès | Kamagoe | Torque

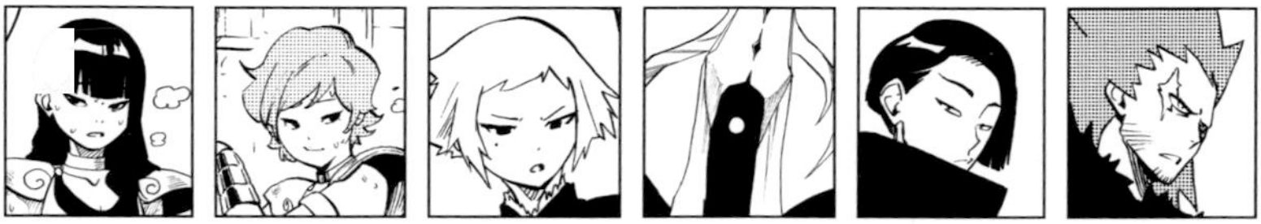

Dart Dragunov | Piodon | Adriel | Ullmina | Vérone | Sargon

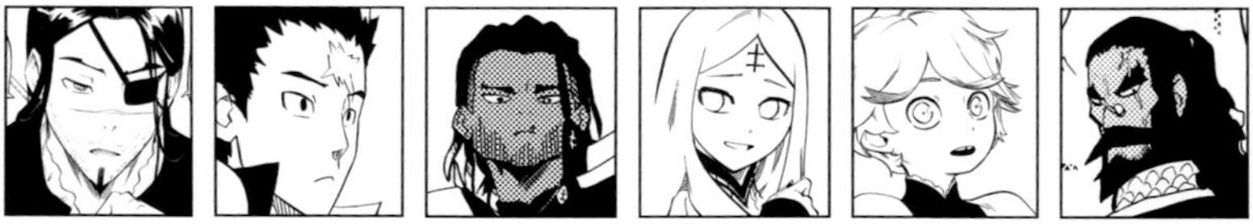

Ininna | Rini | Coclico Raïdon | Korkerik Kron | Yenne Lua | Enga Lua

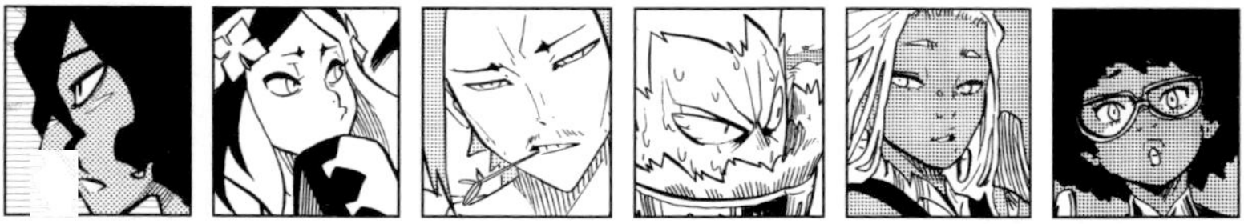

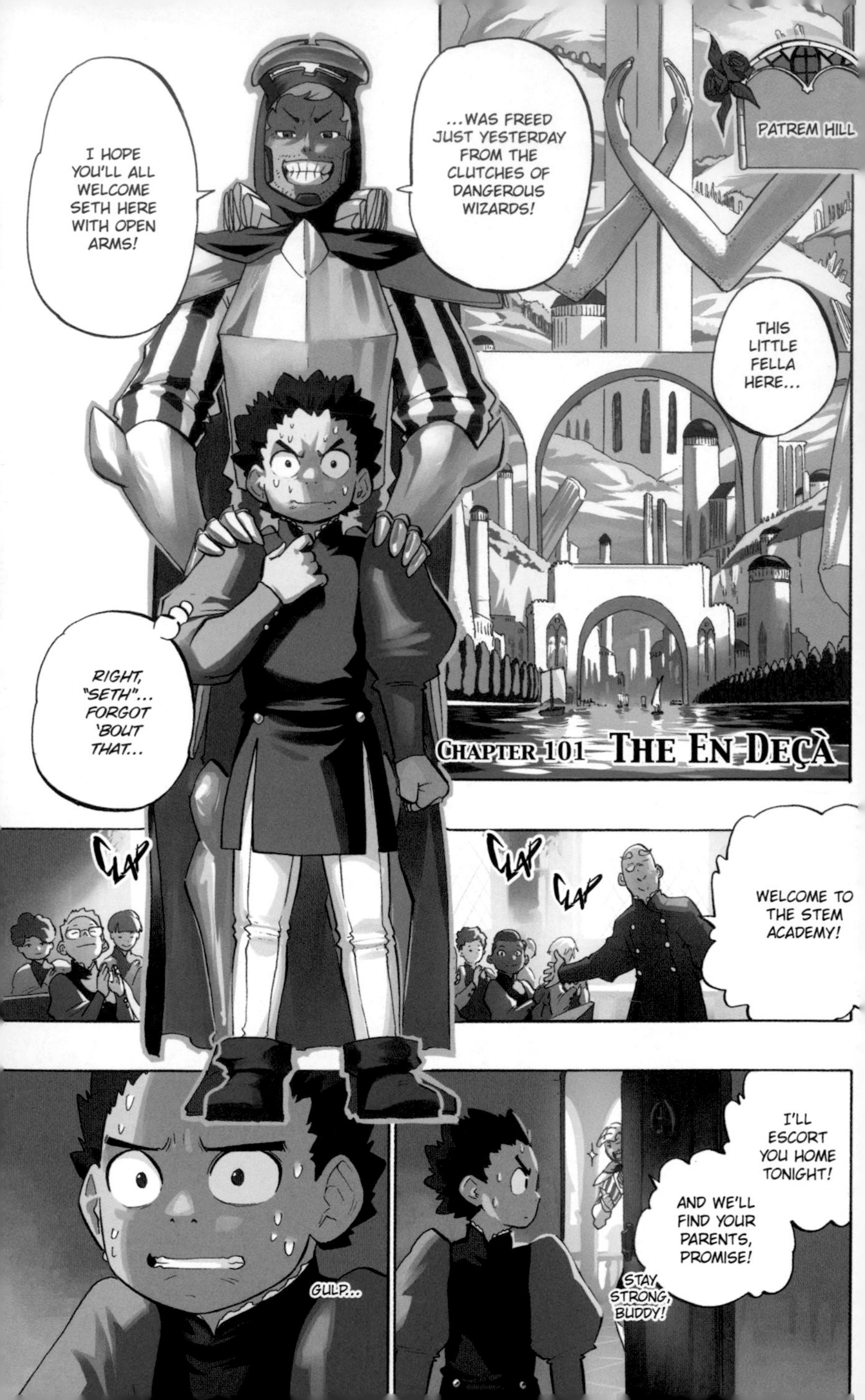
PATREM HILL
THIS LITTLE FELLA HERE...
...WAS FREED JUST YESTERDAY FROM THE CLUTCHES OF DANGEROUS WIZARDS!
I HOPE YOU'LL ALL WELCOME SETH HERE WITH OPEN ARMS!
RIGHT, "SETH"... FORGOT 'BOUT THAT...
CHAPTER 101 THE EN DEÇÀ
WELCOME TO THE STEM ACADEMY!
CLAP
CLAP
CLAP
I'LL ESCORT YOU HOME TONIGHT!
AND WE'LL FIND YOUR PARENTS, PROMISE!
STAY STRONG, BUDDY!
GULP...

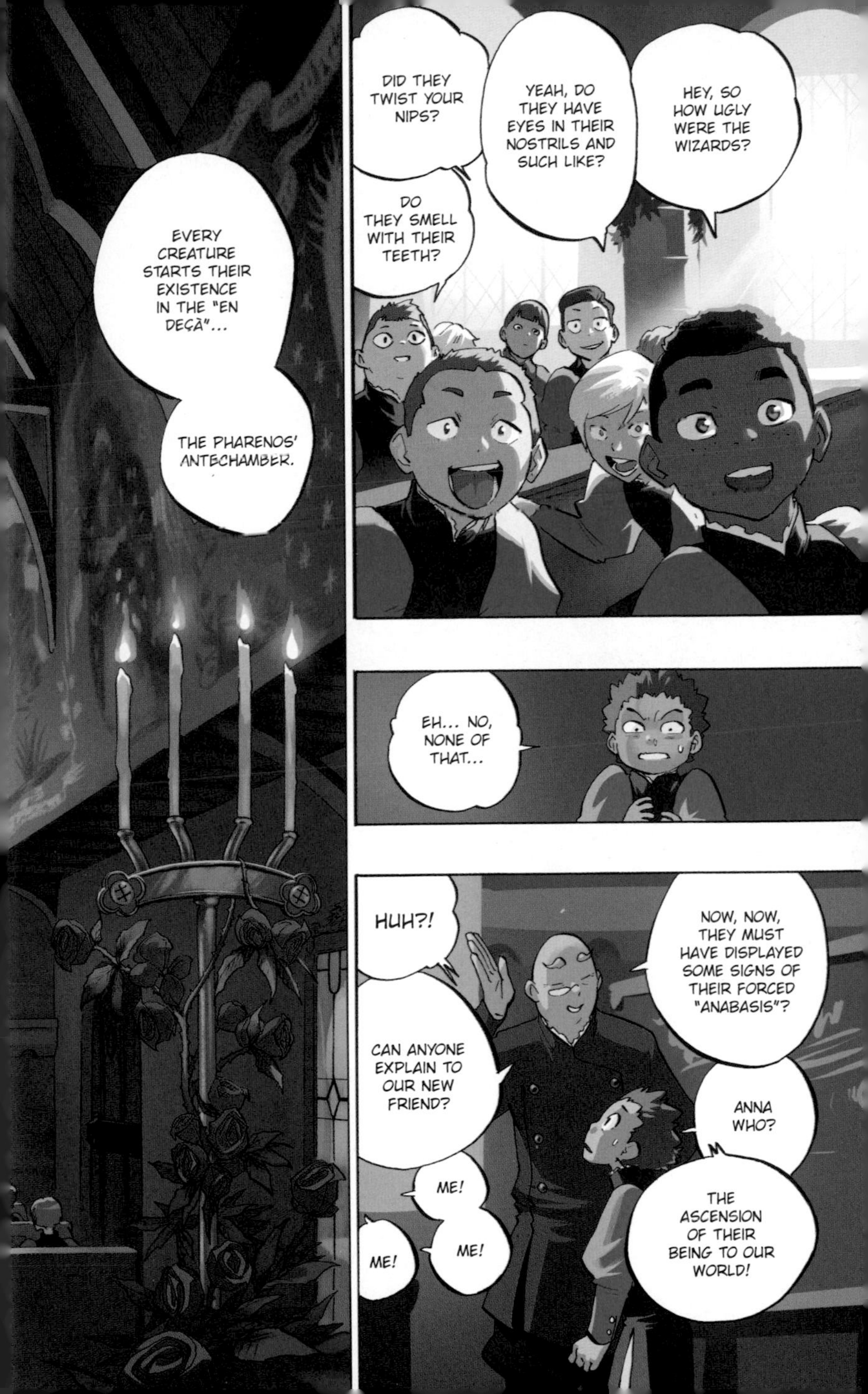
HEY, SO HOW UGLY WERE THE WIZARDS?
YEAH, DO THEY HAVE EYES IN THEIR NOSTRILS AND SUCH LIKE?
DID THEY TWIST YOUR NIPS?
DO THEY SMELL WITH THEIR TEETH?
EH... NO, NONE OF THAT...
NOW, NOW, THEY MUST HAVE DISPLAYED SOME SIGNS OF THEIR FORCED "ANABASIS"?
HUH?!
CAN ANYONE EXPLAIN TO OUR NEW FRIEND?
ANNA WHO?
ME!
ME!
ME!
THE ASCENSION OF THEIR BEING TO OUR WORLD!
EVERY CREATURE STARTS THEIR EXISTENCE IN THE "EN DEÇÀ"...
THE PHARENOS' ANTECHAMBER.

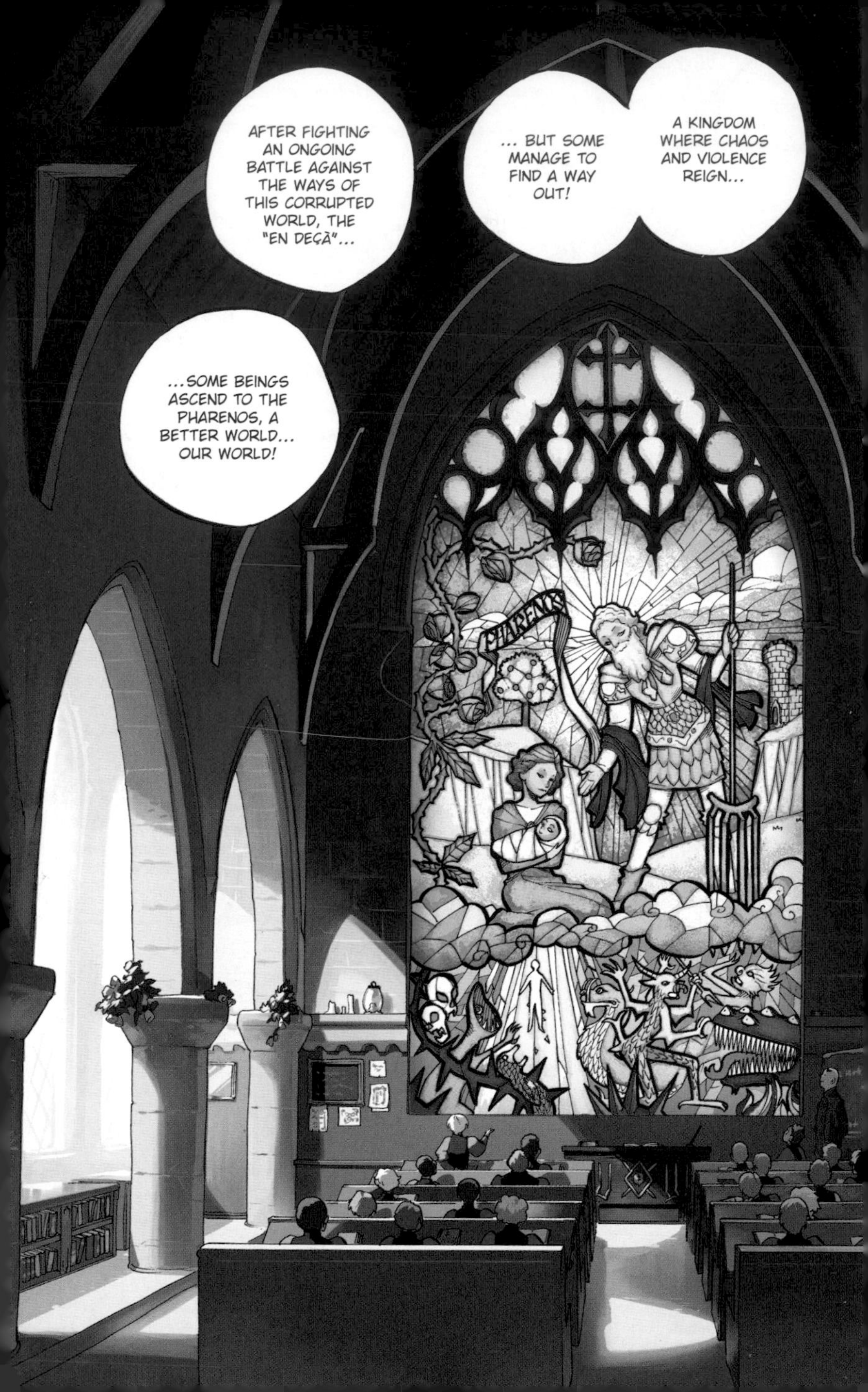
A KINGDOM WHERE CHAOS AND VIOLENCE REIGN...
... BUT SOME MANAGE TO FIND A WAY OUT!
AFTER FIGHTING AN ONGOING BATTLE AGAINST THE WAYS OF THIS CORRUPTED WORLD, THE "EN DEÇÀ"...
...SOME BEINGS ASCEND TO THE PHARENOS, A BETTER WORLD... OUR WORLD!
PHARENOS

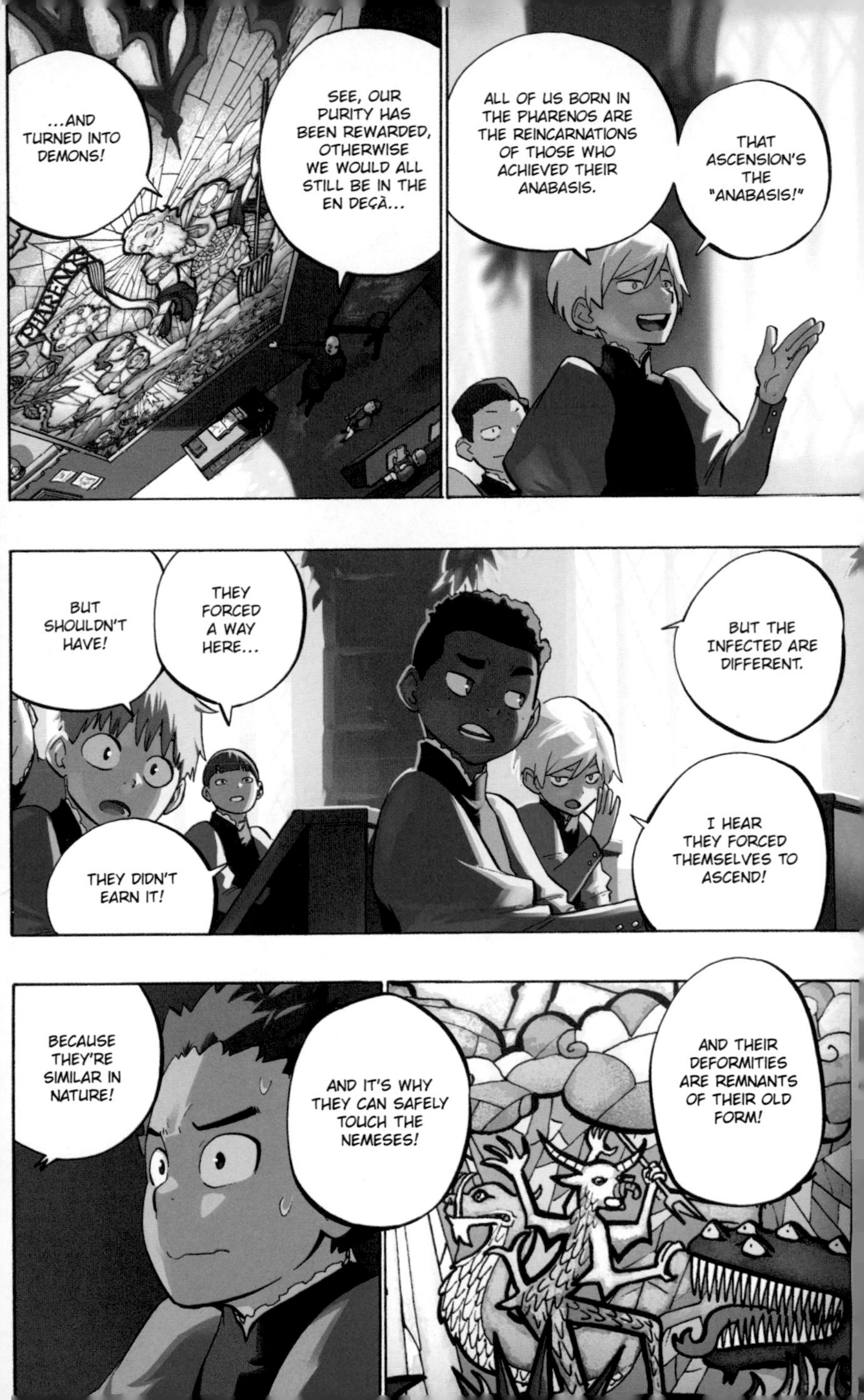
THAT ASCENSION'S THE "ANABASIS!"
ALL OF US BORN IN THE PHARENOS ARE THE REINCARNATIONS OF THOSE WHO ACHIEVED THEIR ANABASIS.
SEE, OUR PURITY HAS BEEN REWARDED, OTHERWISE WE WOULD ALL STILL BE IN THE EN DEÇÀ...
...AND TURNED INTO DEMONS!
BUT THE INFECTED ARE DIFFERENT.
I HEAR THEY FORCED THEMSELVES TO ASCEND!
THEY FORCED A WAY HERE...
BUT SHOULDN'T HAVE!
THEY DIDN'T EARN IT!
AND THEIR DEFORMITIES ARE REMNANTS OF THEIR OLD FORM!
AND IT'S WHY THEY CAN SAFELY TOUCH THE NEMESES!
BECAUSE THEY'RE SIMILAR IN NATURE!

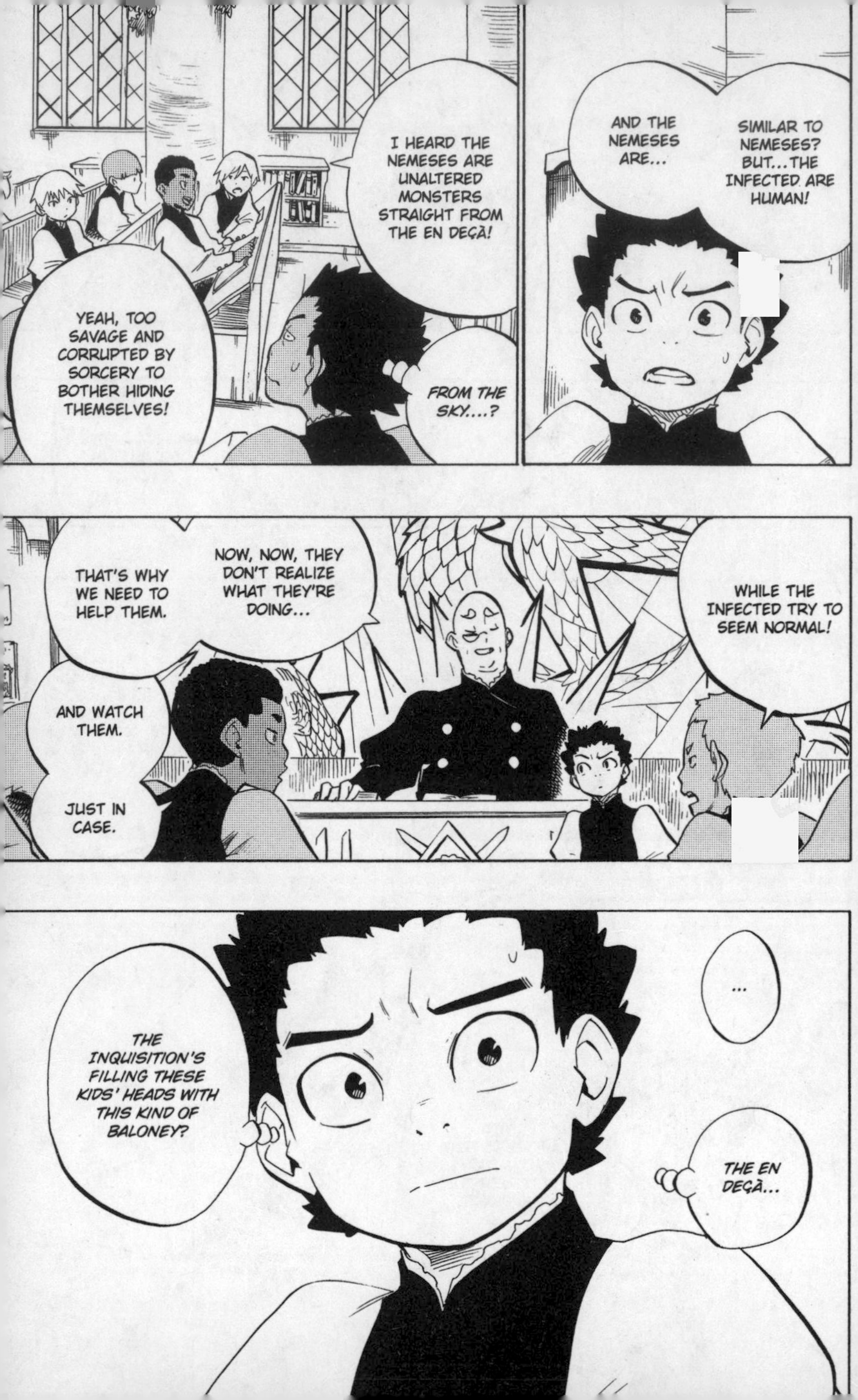
SIMILAR TO NEMESES? BUT...THE INFECTED ARE HUMAN!
AND THE NEMESES ARE...
I HEARD THE NEMESES ARE UNALTERED MONSTERS STRAIGHT FROM THE EN DEGÃ!
FROM THE SKY....?
YEAH, TOO SAVAGE AND CORRUPTED BY SORCERY TO BOTHER HIDING THEMSELVES!
WHILE THE INFECTED TRY TO SEEM NORMAL!
NOW, NOW, THEY DON'T REALIZE WHAT THEY'RE DOING...
THAT'S WHY WE NEED TO HELP THEM.
AND WATCH THEM.
JUST IN CASE.
...
THE EN DEGÃ...
THE INQUISITION'S FILLING THESE KIDS' HEADS WITH THIS KIND OF BALONEY?

CERTAIN POINTS ARE STILL BEING DEBATED!
AND IT IS UP TO **YOU**, FUTURE INQUISITORS, TO JOIN OUR LONG-STANDING QUEST FOR THE TRUTH!
ARCHEOLOGICAL EXCAVATIONS, TEACHER.
?
WHEN I'M MARSHALL INQUISITOR, I WILL MAKE SURE TO ACCELERATE OUR QUEST FOR TRUTH.
WITH ARCHEOLOGICAL EXCAVATIONS ALL OVER THE PHARENOS.
TH... THE THAUMA-TURGE KID?!
HAVE WE MET?
AAAAH !!!

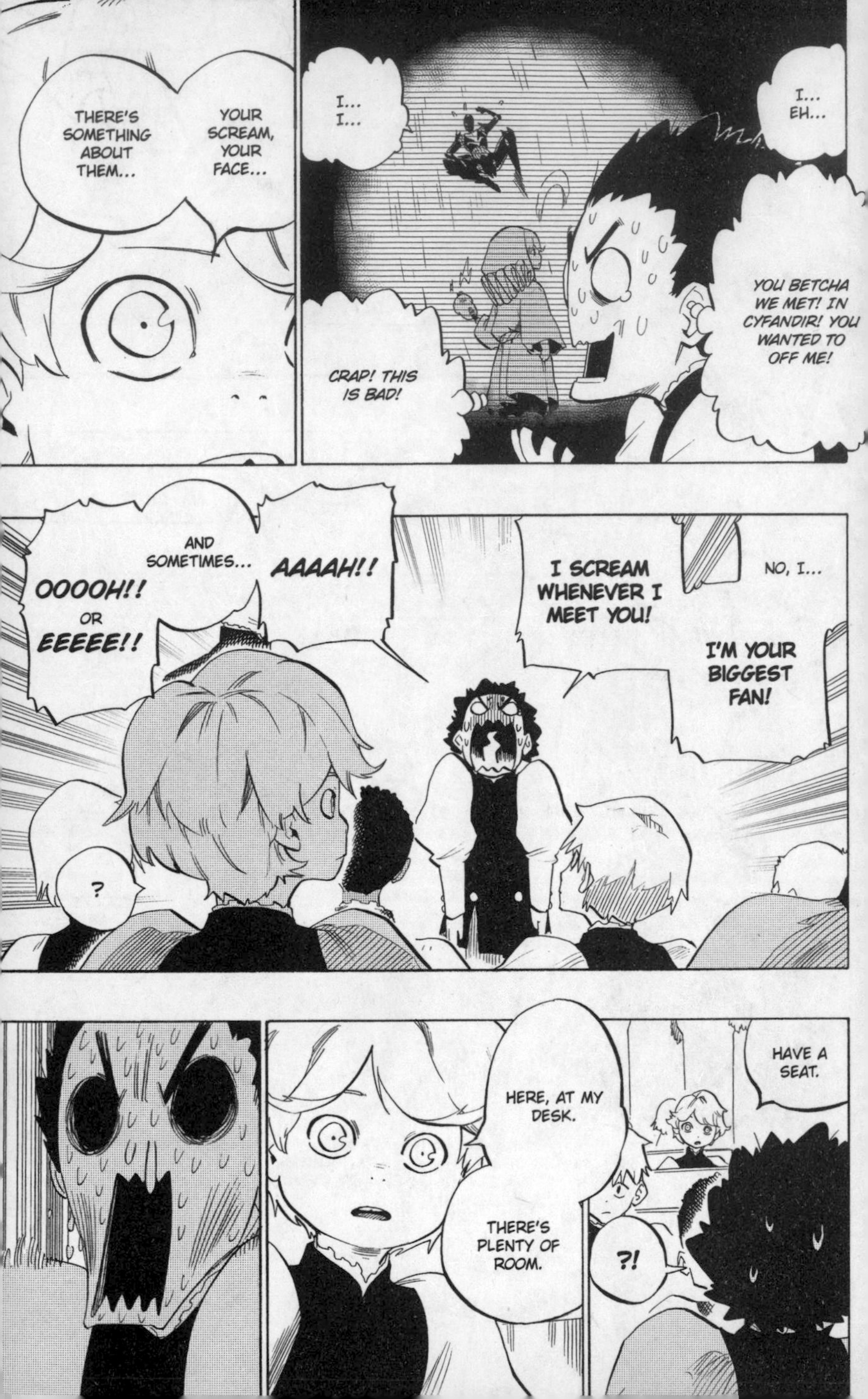

I... EH...
YOU BETCHA WE MET! IN CYFANDIR! YOU WANTED TO OFF ME!
I... I...
CRAP! THIS IS BAD!
YOUR SCREAM, YOUR FACE...
THERE'S SOMETHING ABOUT THEM...
NO, I...
I'M YOUR BIGGEST FAN!
I SCREAM WHENEVER I MEET YOU!
AAAAH!!
AND SOMETIMES...
OOOOH!! OR EEEEE!!
?
HAVE A SEAT.
?!
HERE, AT MY DESK.
THERE'S PLENTY OF ROOM.

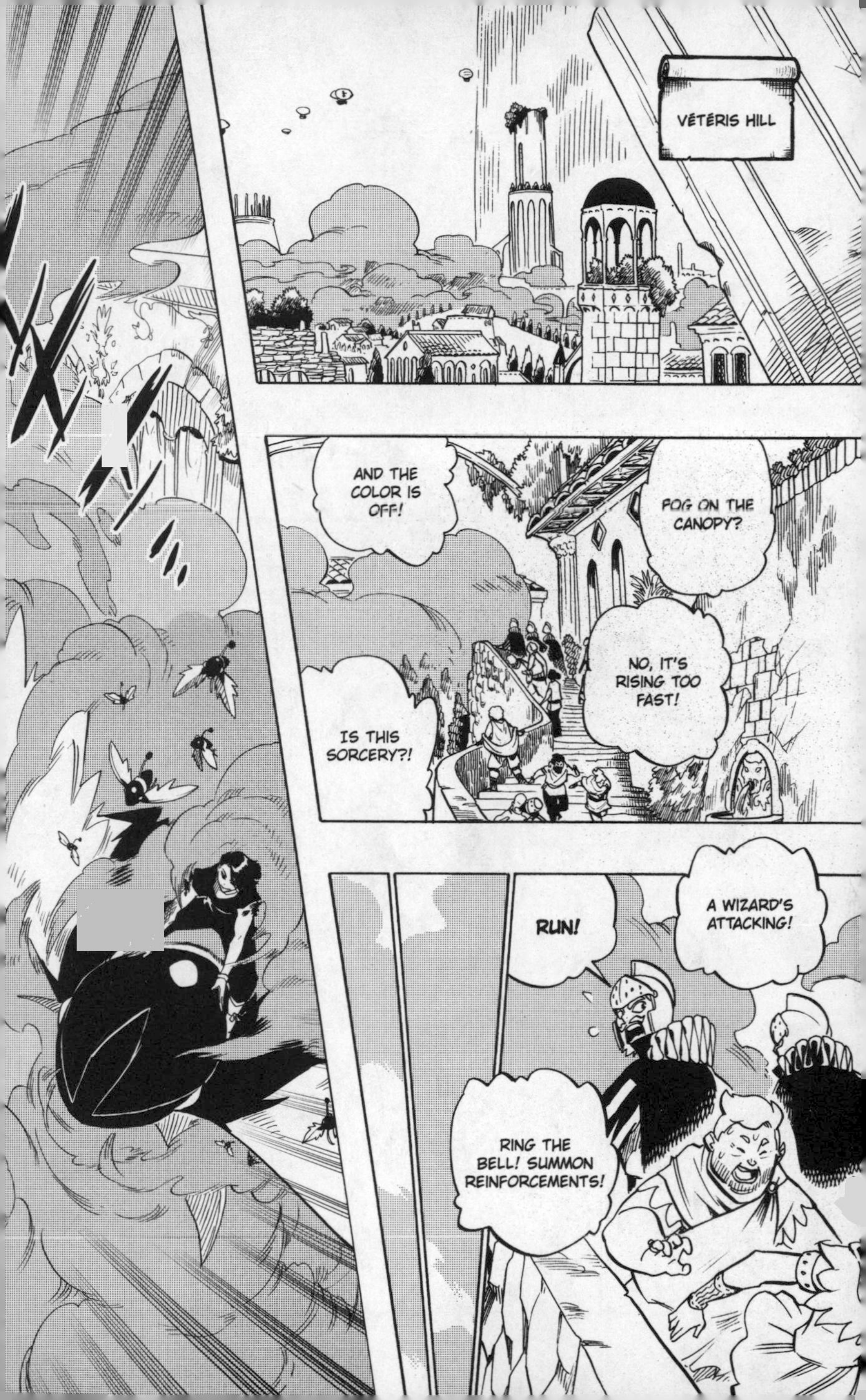
VÉTERIS HILL
FOG ON THE CANOPY?
AND THE COLOR IS OFF!
NO, IT'S RISING TOO FAST!
IS THIS SORCERY?!
A WIZARD'S ATTACKING!
RUN!
RING THE BELL! SUMMON REINFORCEMENTS!

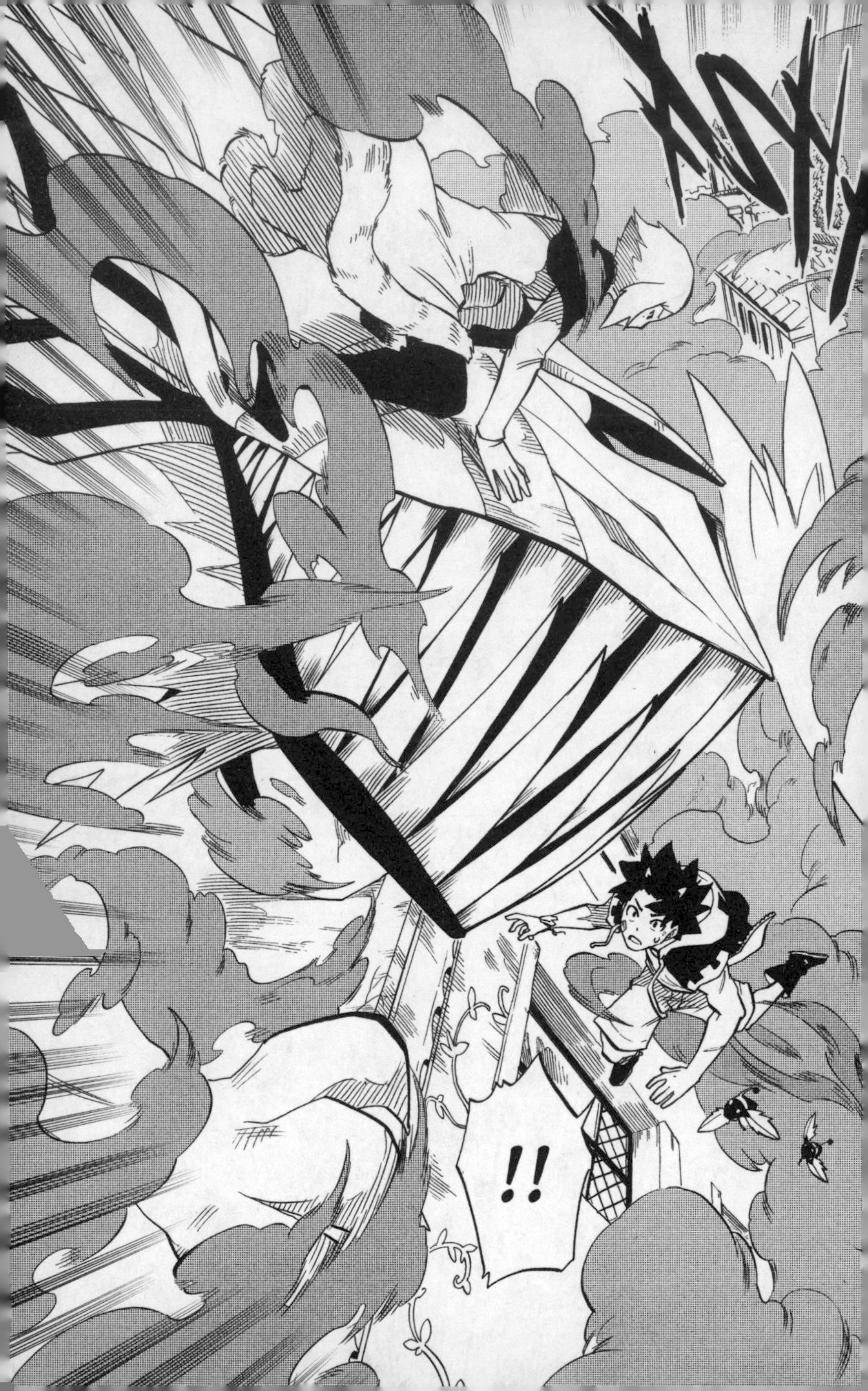
!!

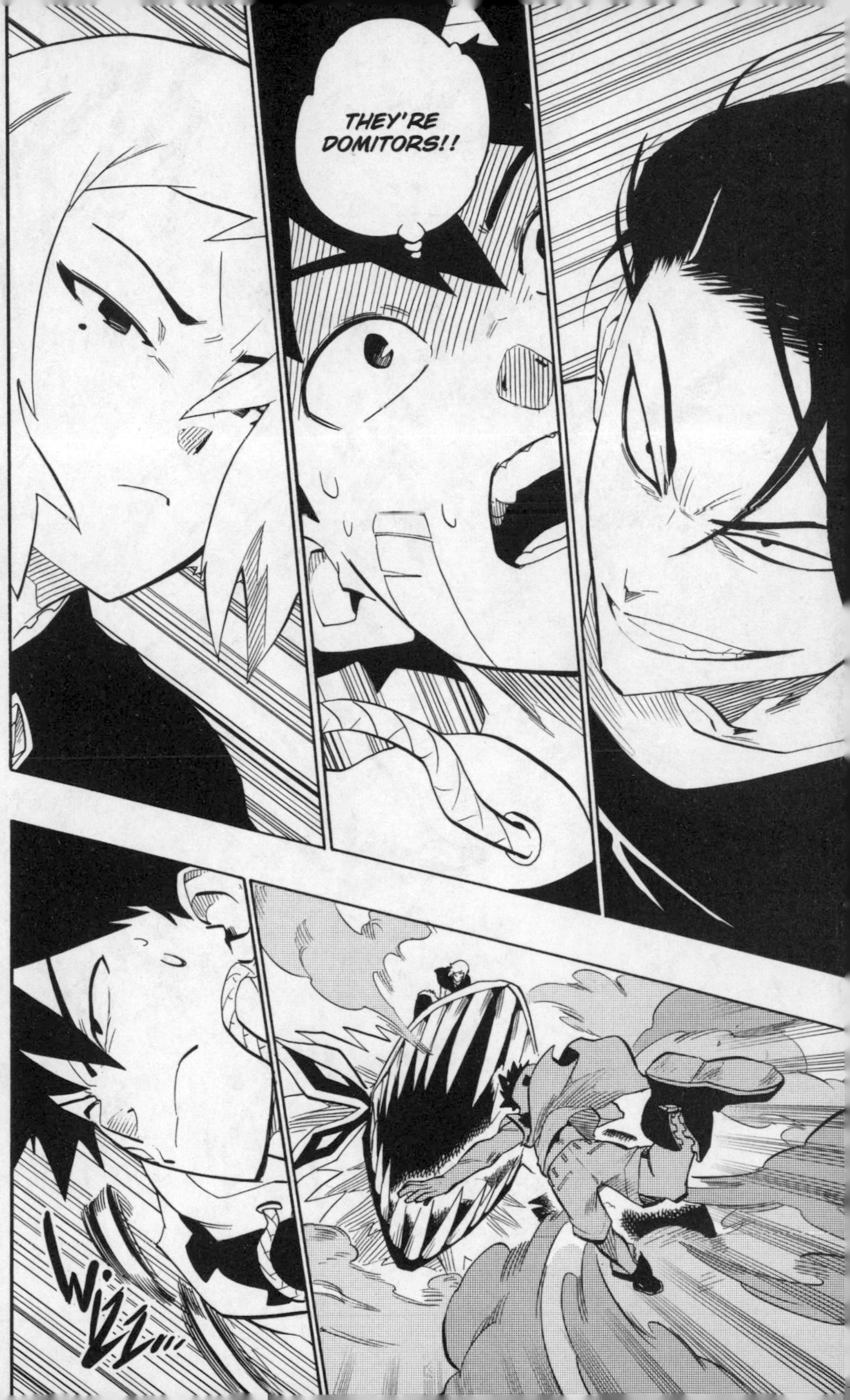
THEY'RE DOMITORS!!
WIZZZ...

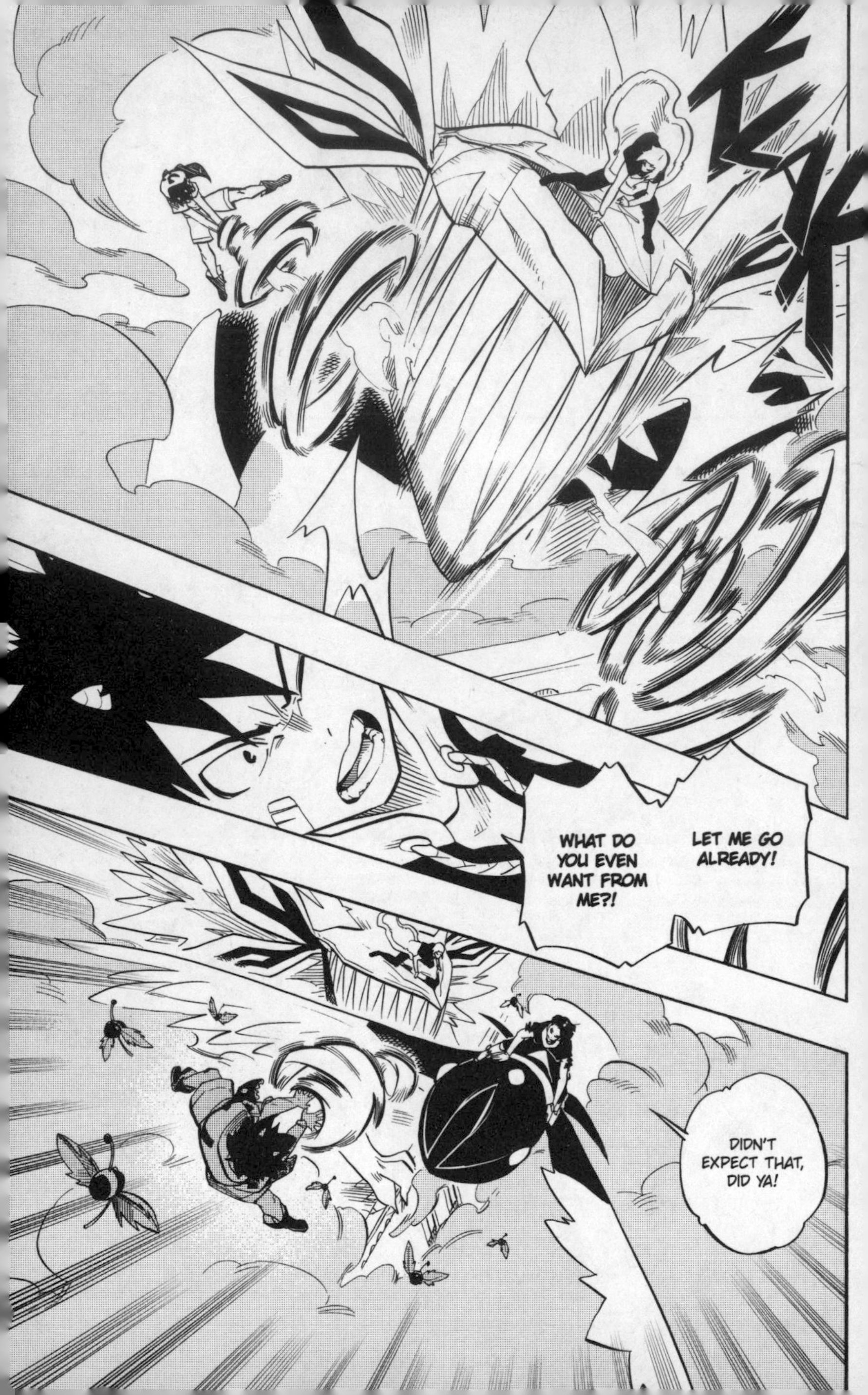
LET ME GO ALREADY!
WHAT DO YOU EVEN WANT FROM ME?!
DIDN'T EXPECT THAT, DID YA!

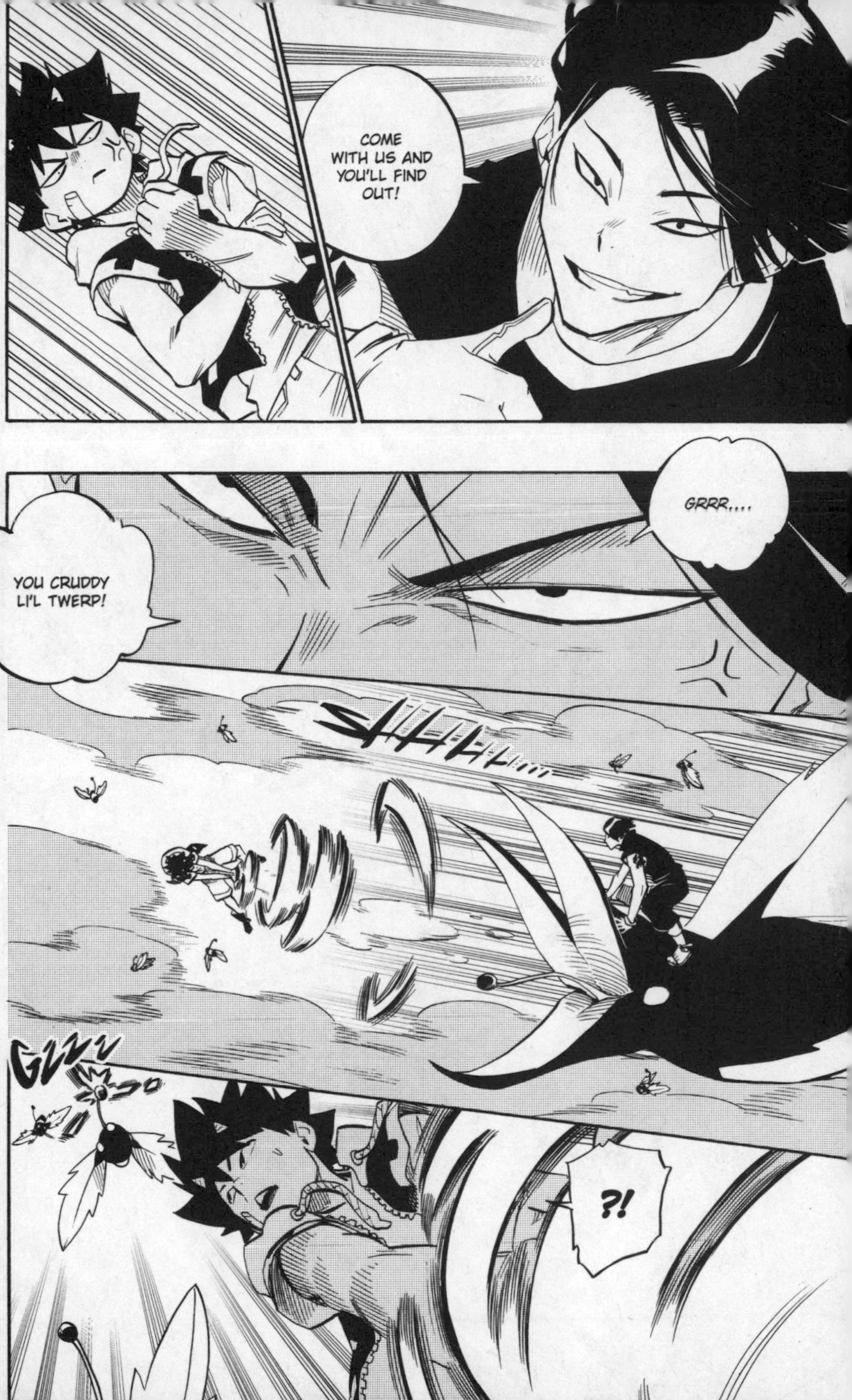
COME WITH US AND YOU'LL FIND OUT!
GRRR....
YOU CRUDDY LI'L TWERP!
?!

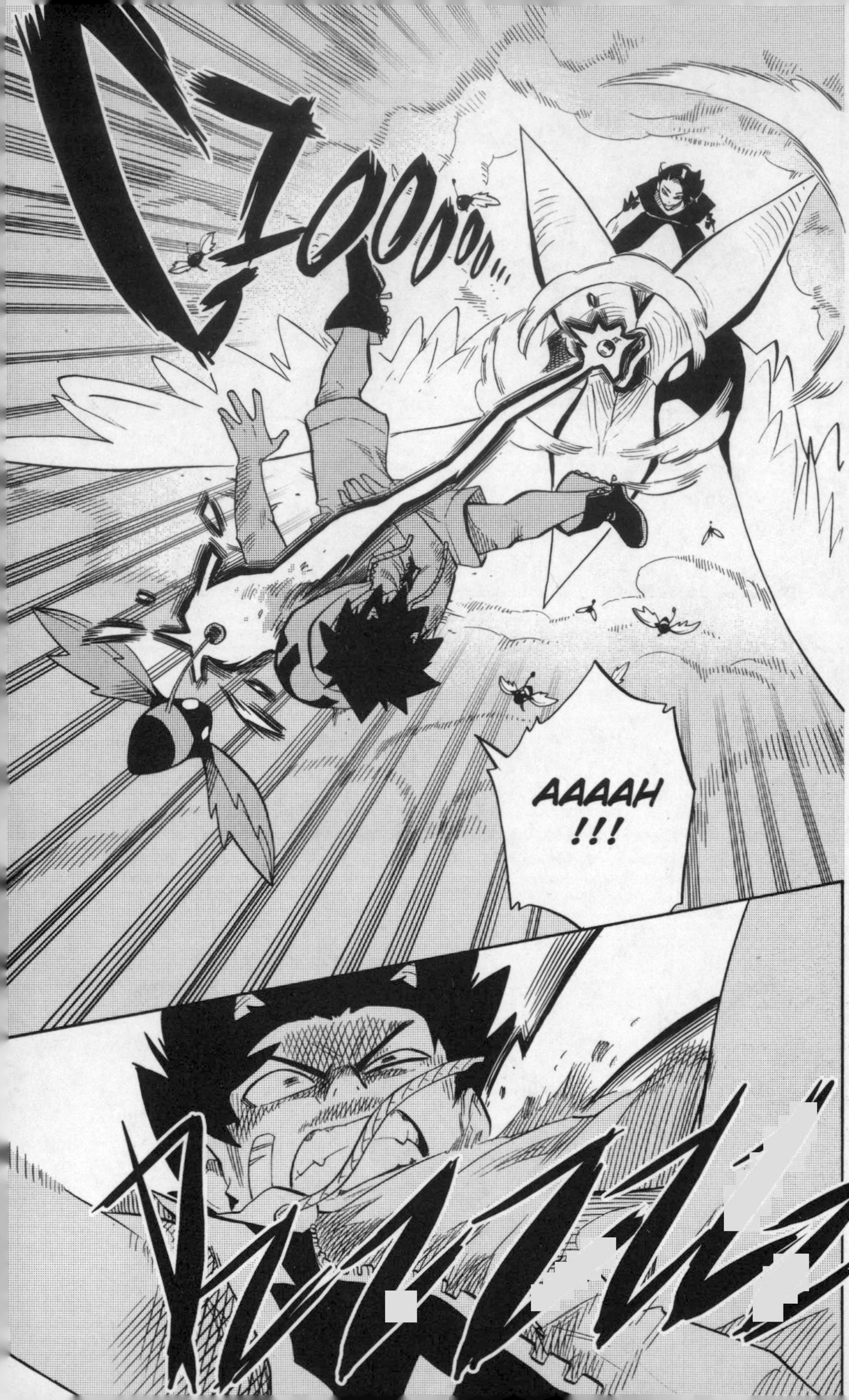
AAAAH !!!

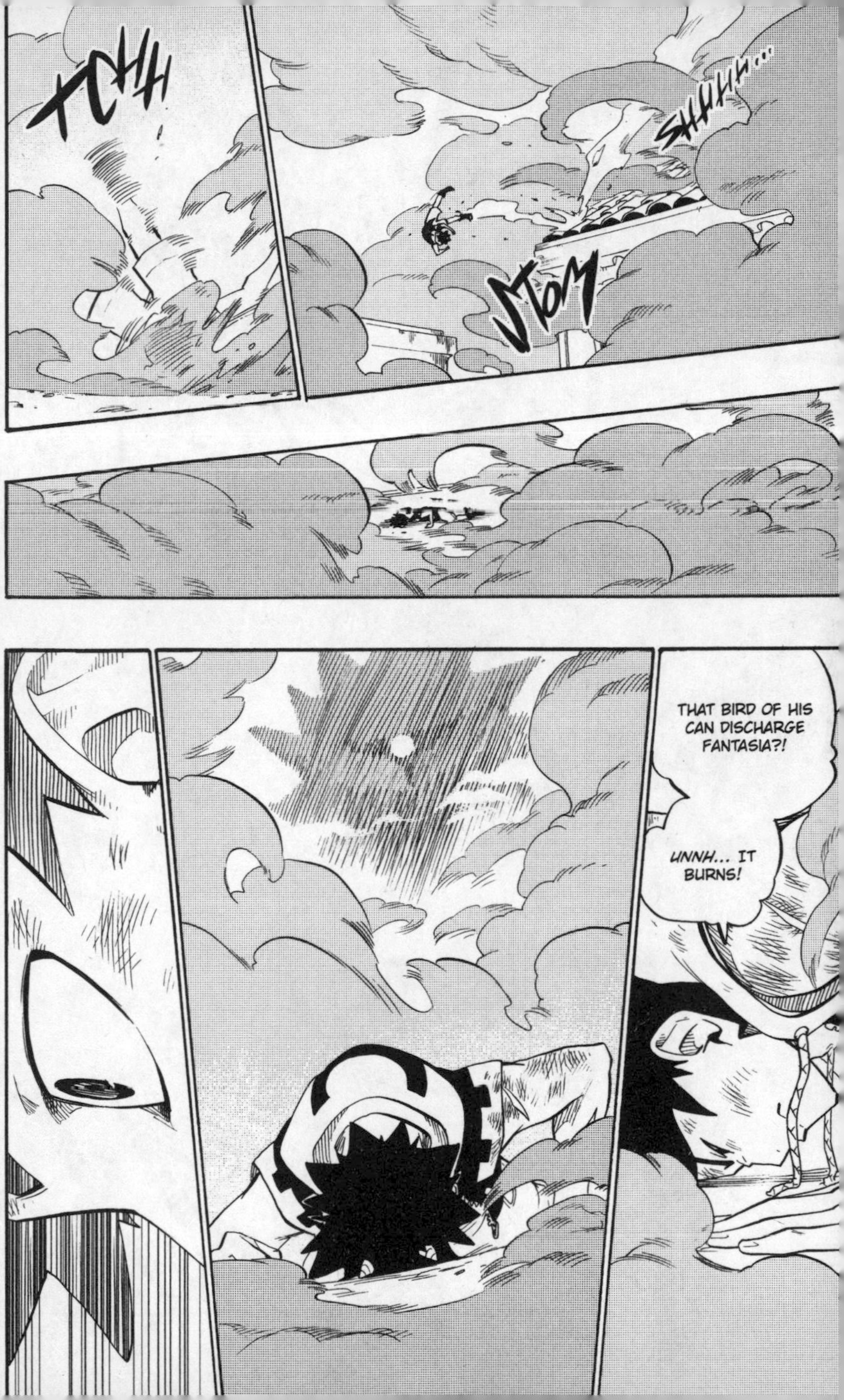
SHHHH...
STOM
TCHH
THAT BIRD OF HIS CAN DISCHARGE FANTASIA?!
UNNH... IT BURNS!

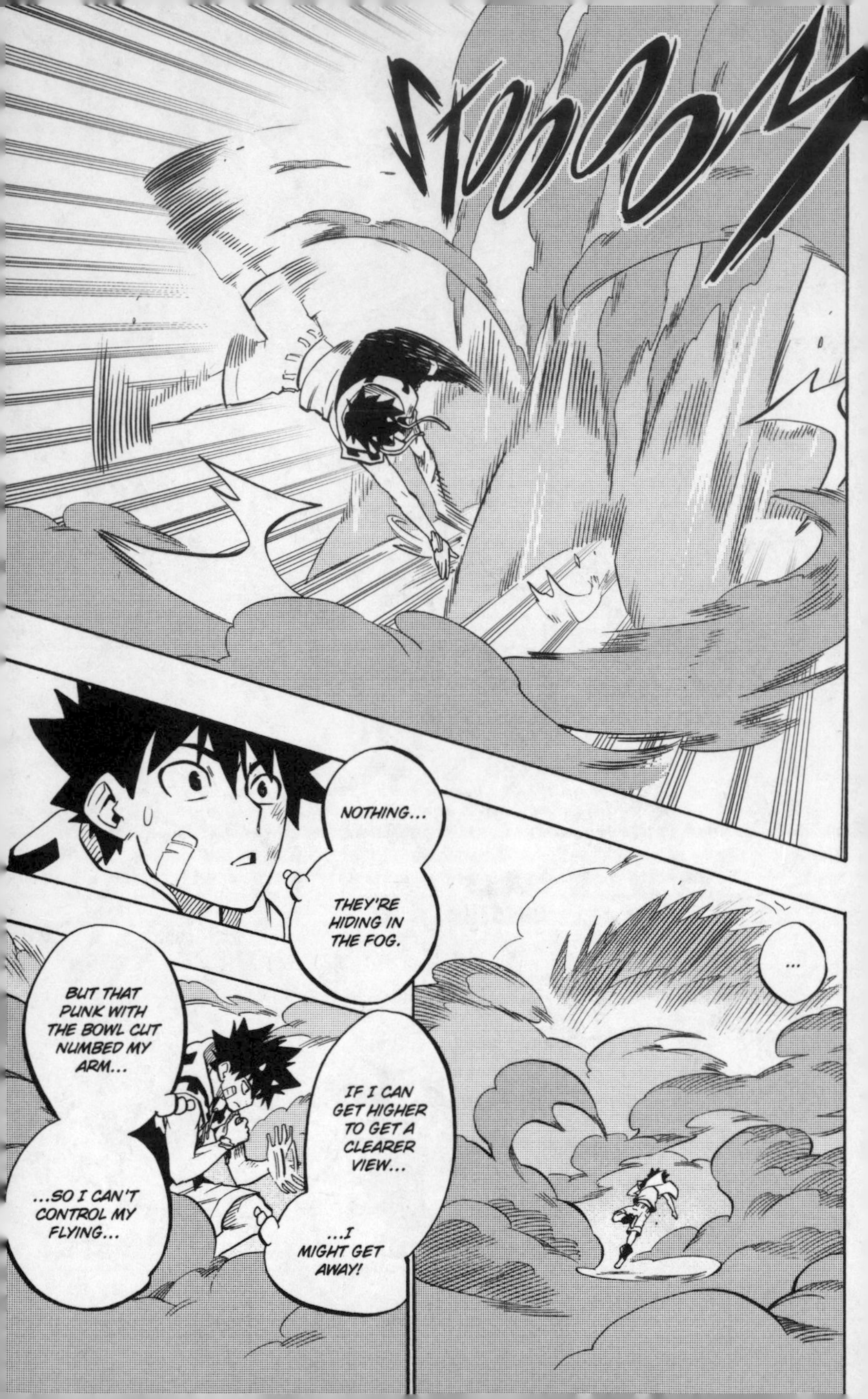
STOOOOM
NOTHING...
THEY'RE HIDING IN THE FOG.
...
BUT THAT PUNK WITH THE BOWL CUT NUMBED MY ARM...
...SO I CAN'T CONTROL MY FLYING...
IF I CAN GET HIGHER TO GET A CLEARER VIEW...
...I MIGHT GET AWAY!

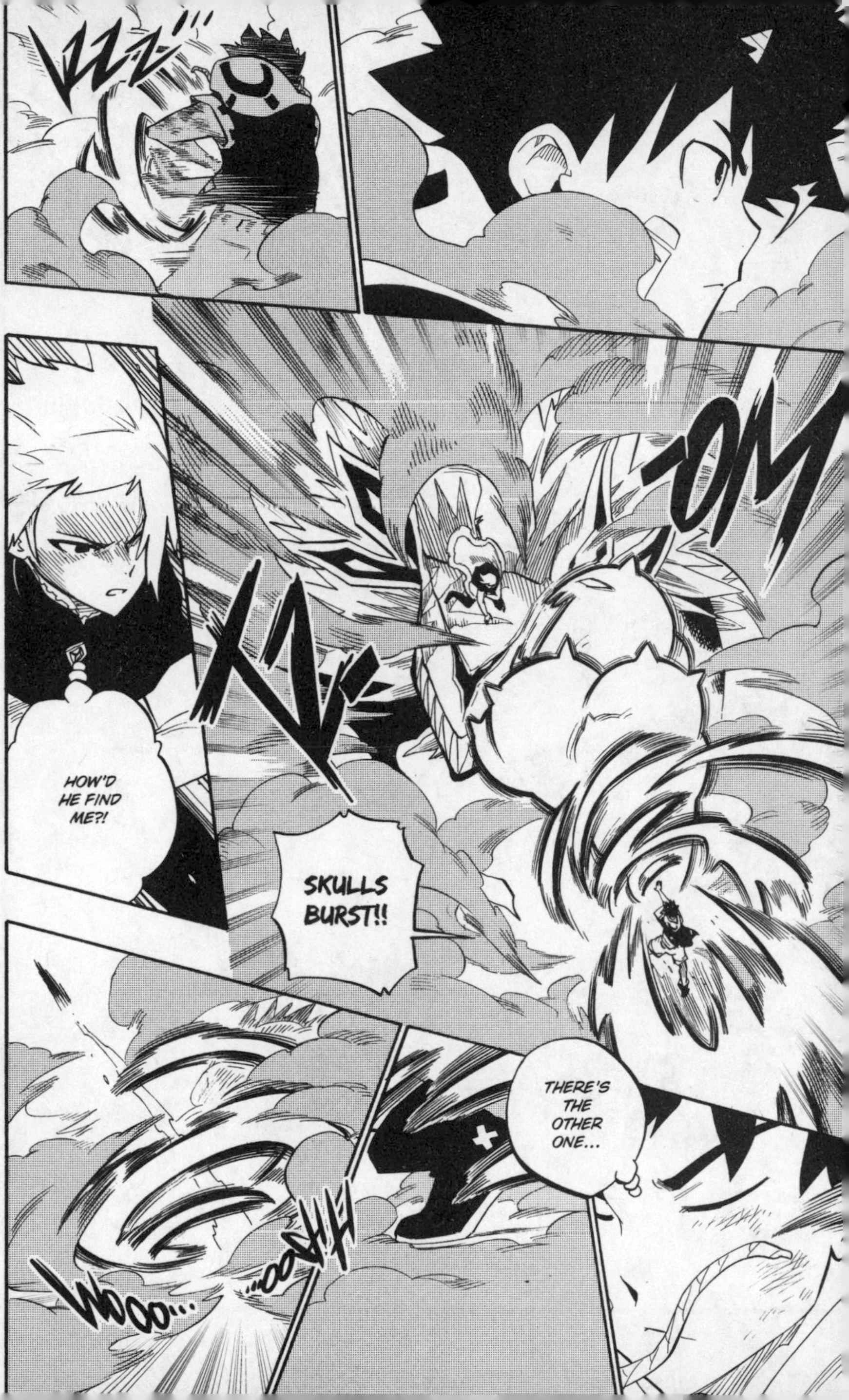
VZZZ
DOOM
SKULLS BURST!!
XAN
HOW'D HE FIND ME?!
THERE'S THE OTHER ONE...
WOOO......OOOH!!

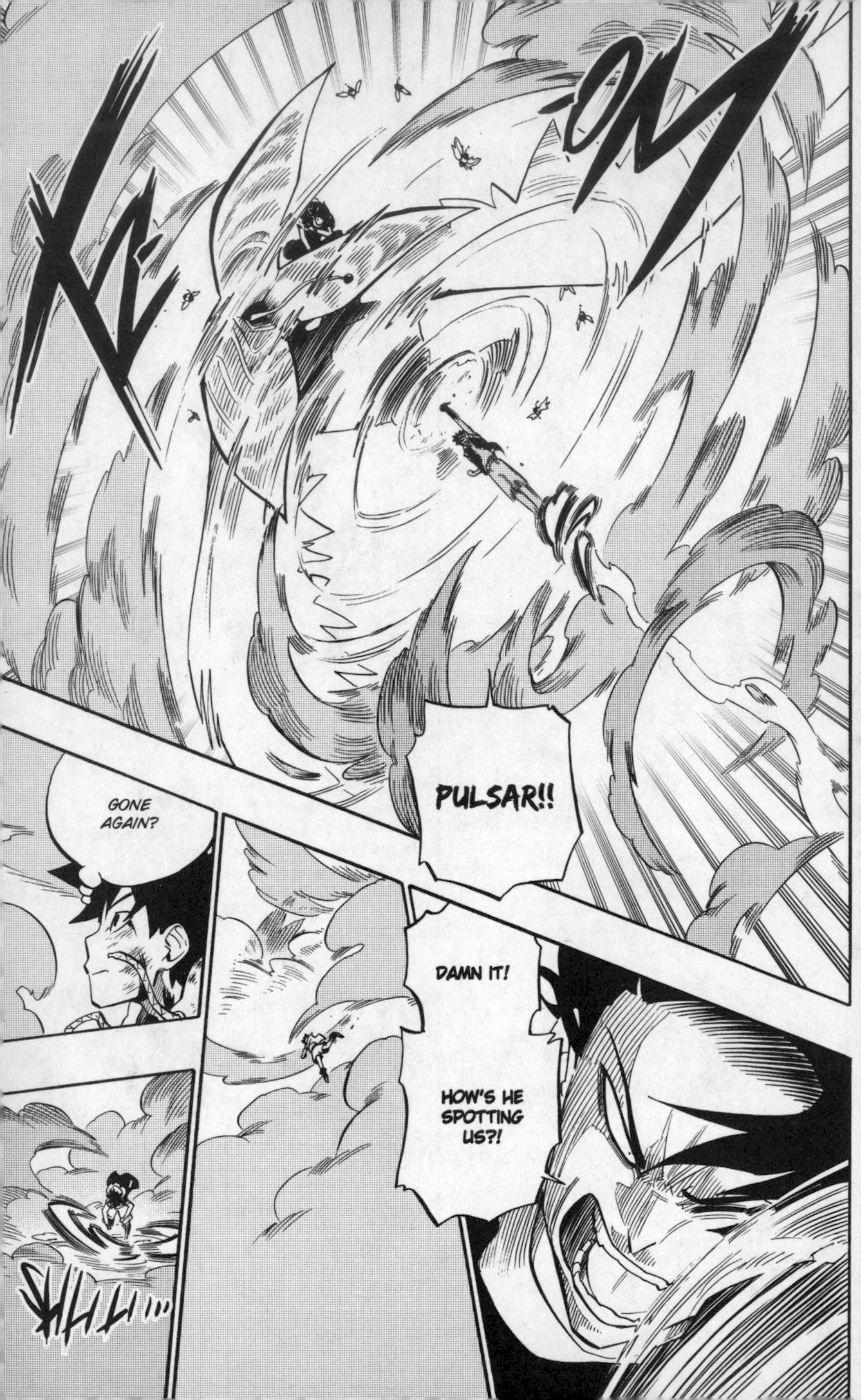
PULSAR!!
DAMN IT!
HOW'S HE SPOTTING US?!
GONE AGAIN?

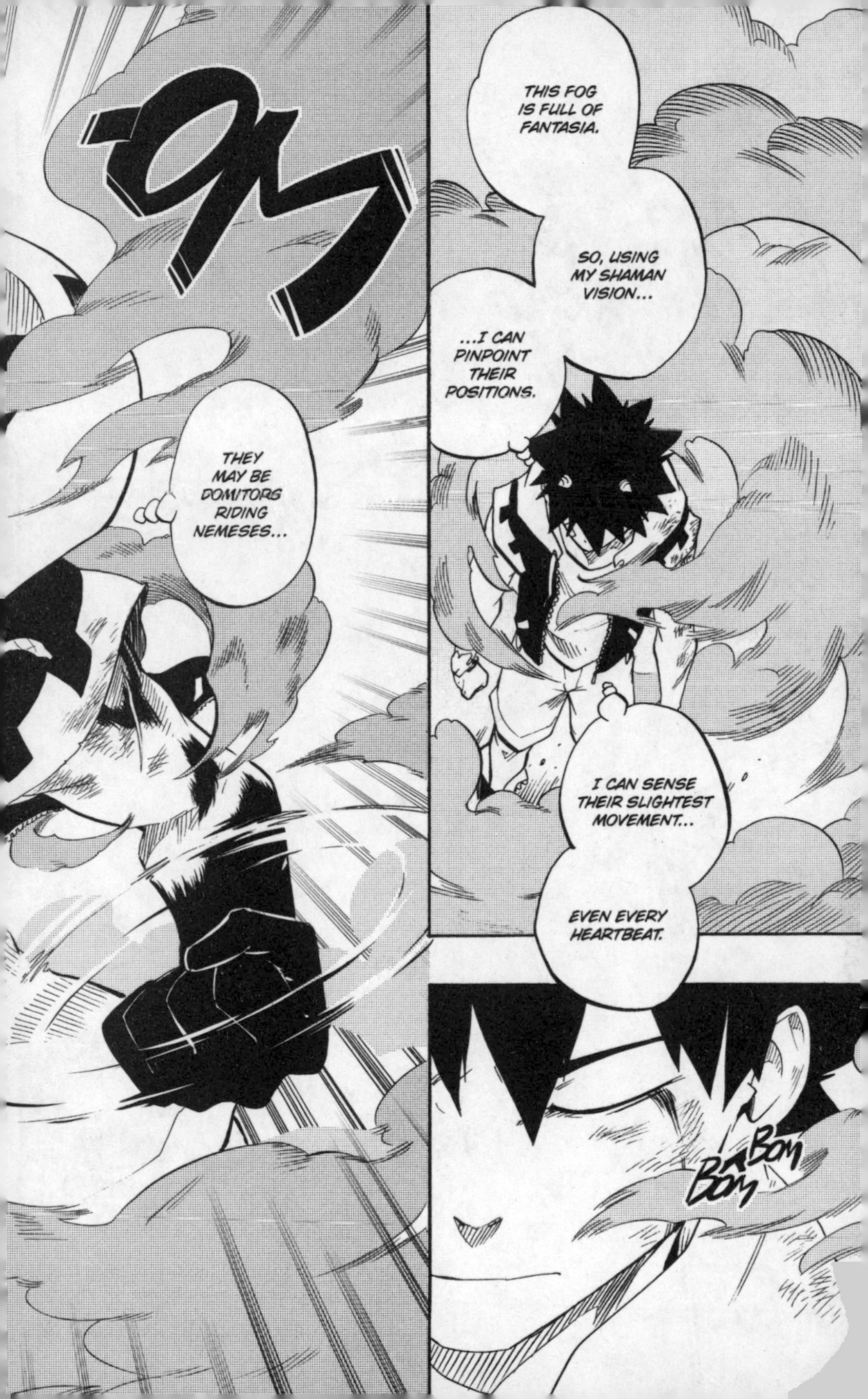
THIS FOG IS FULL OF FANTASIA.
SO, USING MY SHAMAN VISION...
...I CAN PINPOINT THEIR POSITIONS.
I CAN SENSE THEIR SLIGHTEST MOVEMENT...
EVEN EVERY HEARTBEAT.
BOM BOM
THEY MAY BE DOMITORS RIDING NEMESES...

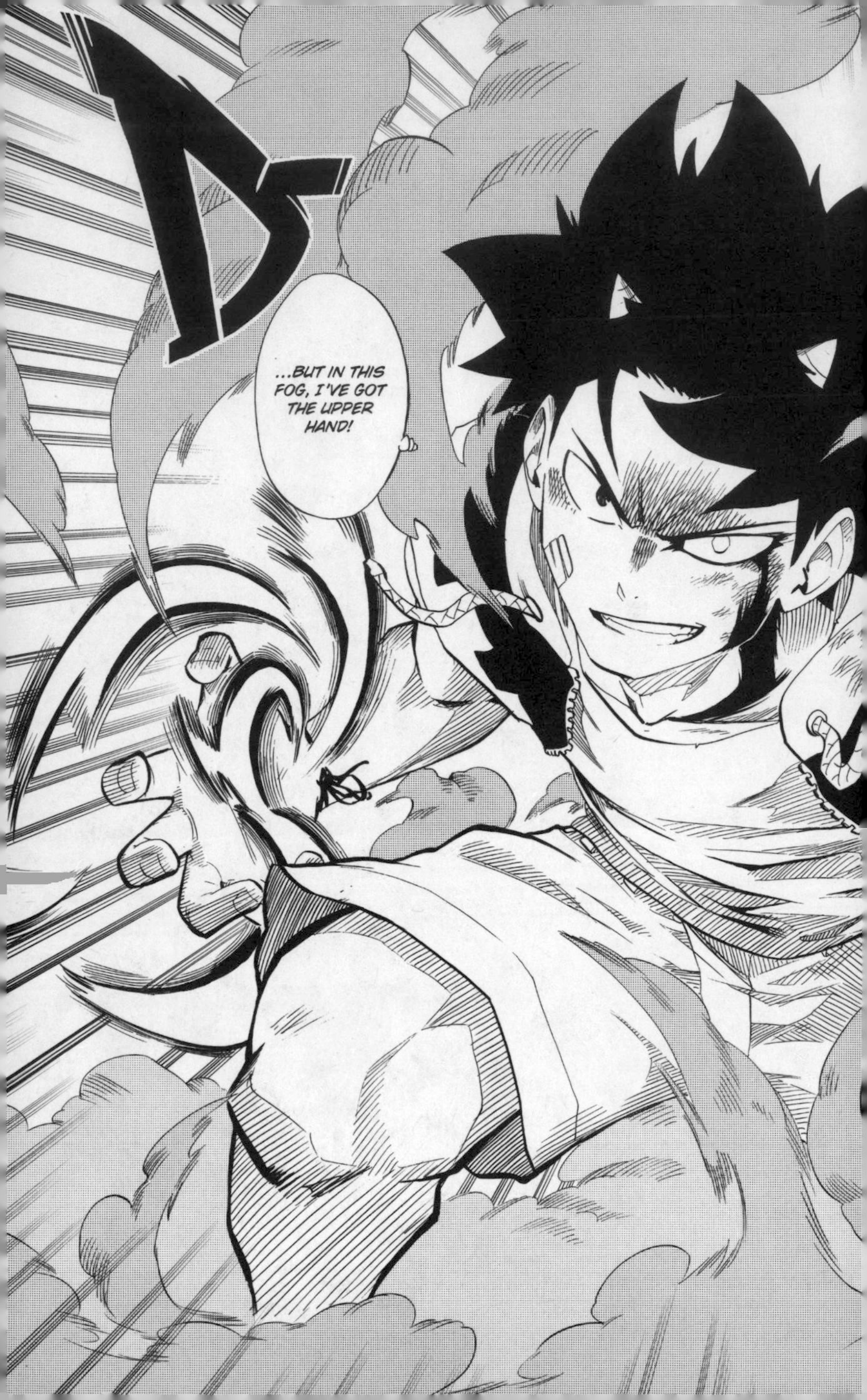
...BUT IN THIS FOG, I'VE GOT THE UPPER HAND!

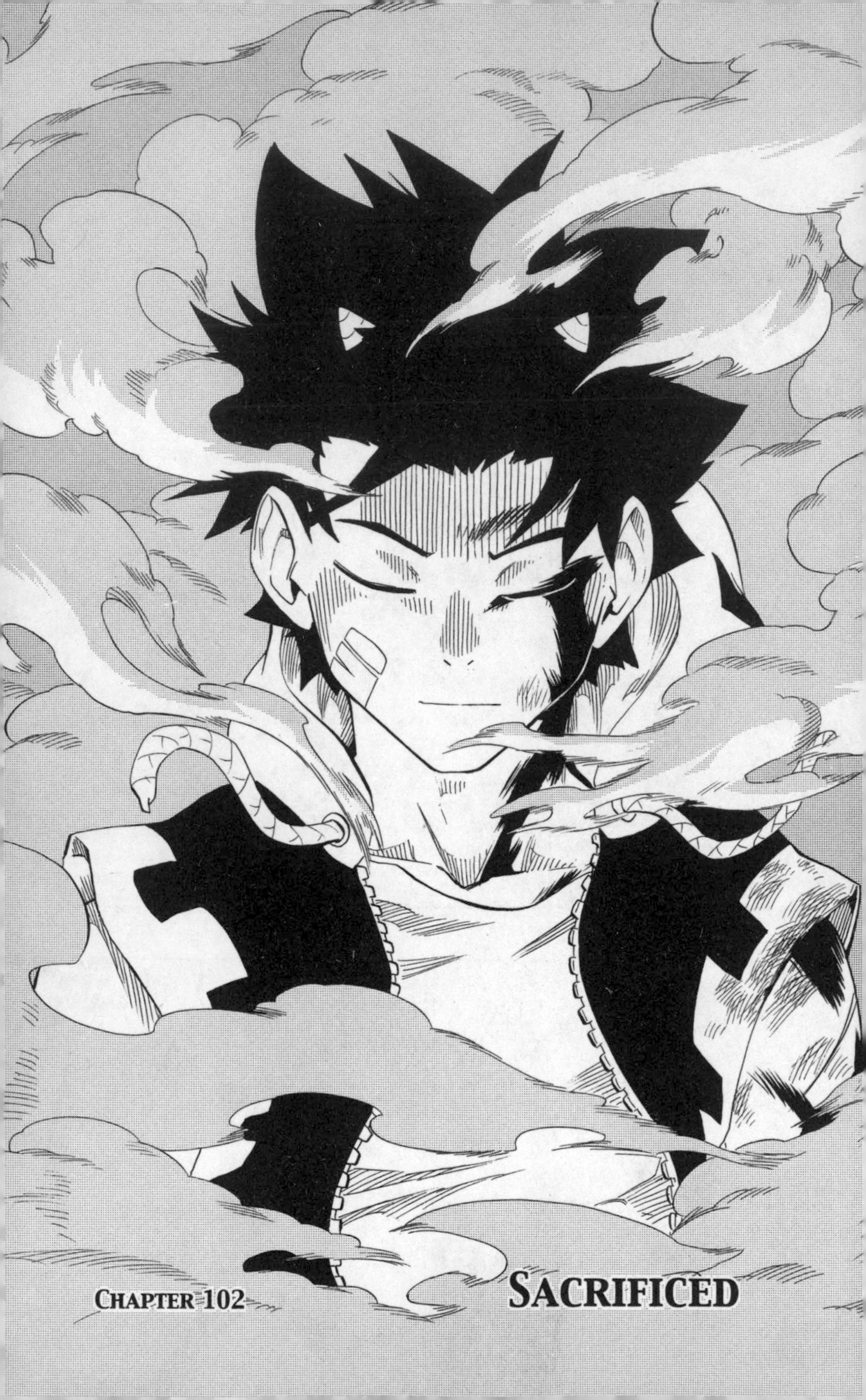
CHAPTER 102
SACRIFICED

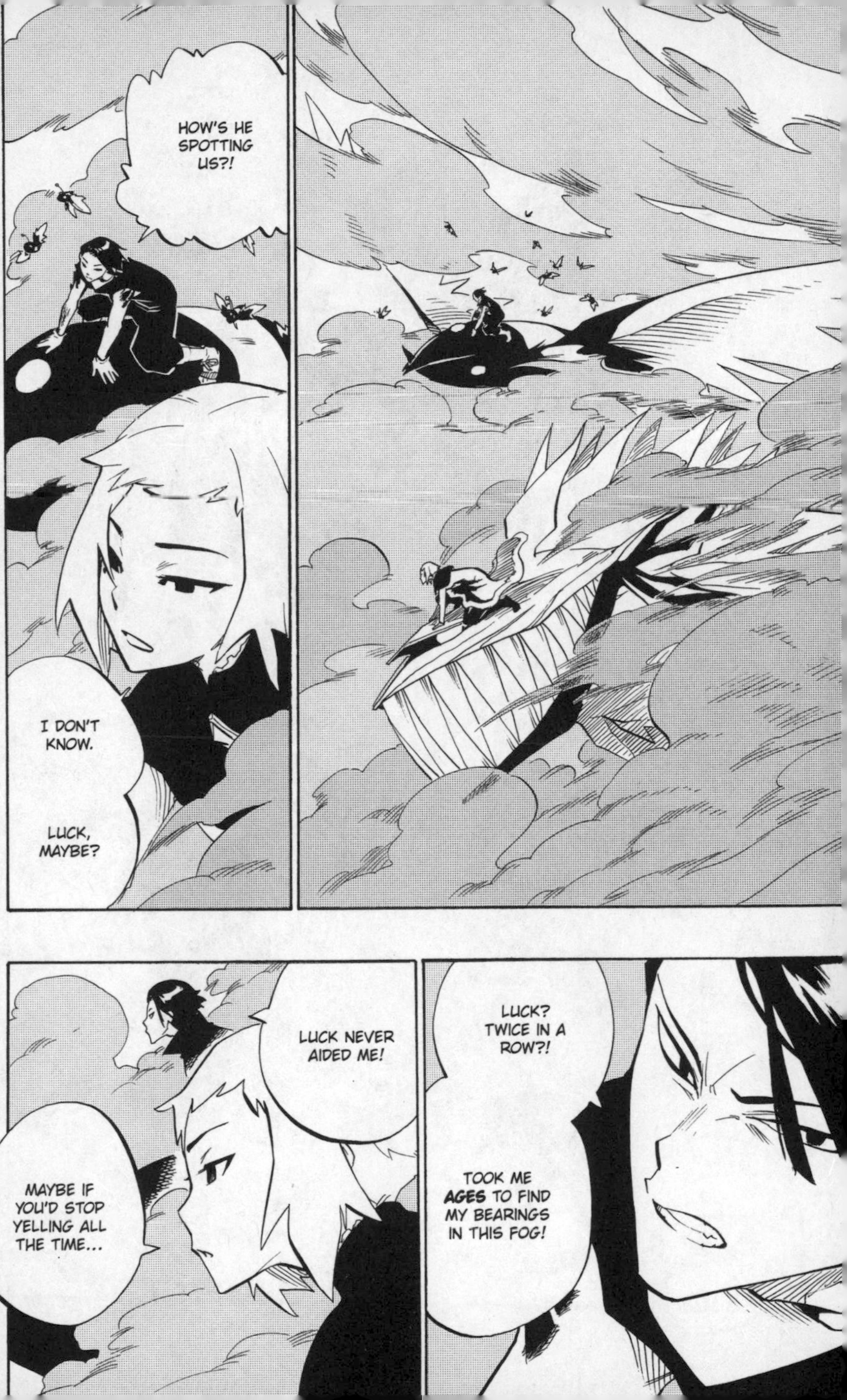
HOW'S HE SPOTTING US?!
I DON'T KNOW.
LUCK, MAYBE?
LUCK? TWICE IN A ROW?!
TOOK ME **AGES** TO FIND MY BEARINGS IN THIS FOG!
LUCK NEVER AIDED ME!
MAYBE IF YOU'D STOP YELLING ALL THE TIME...

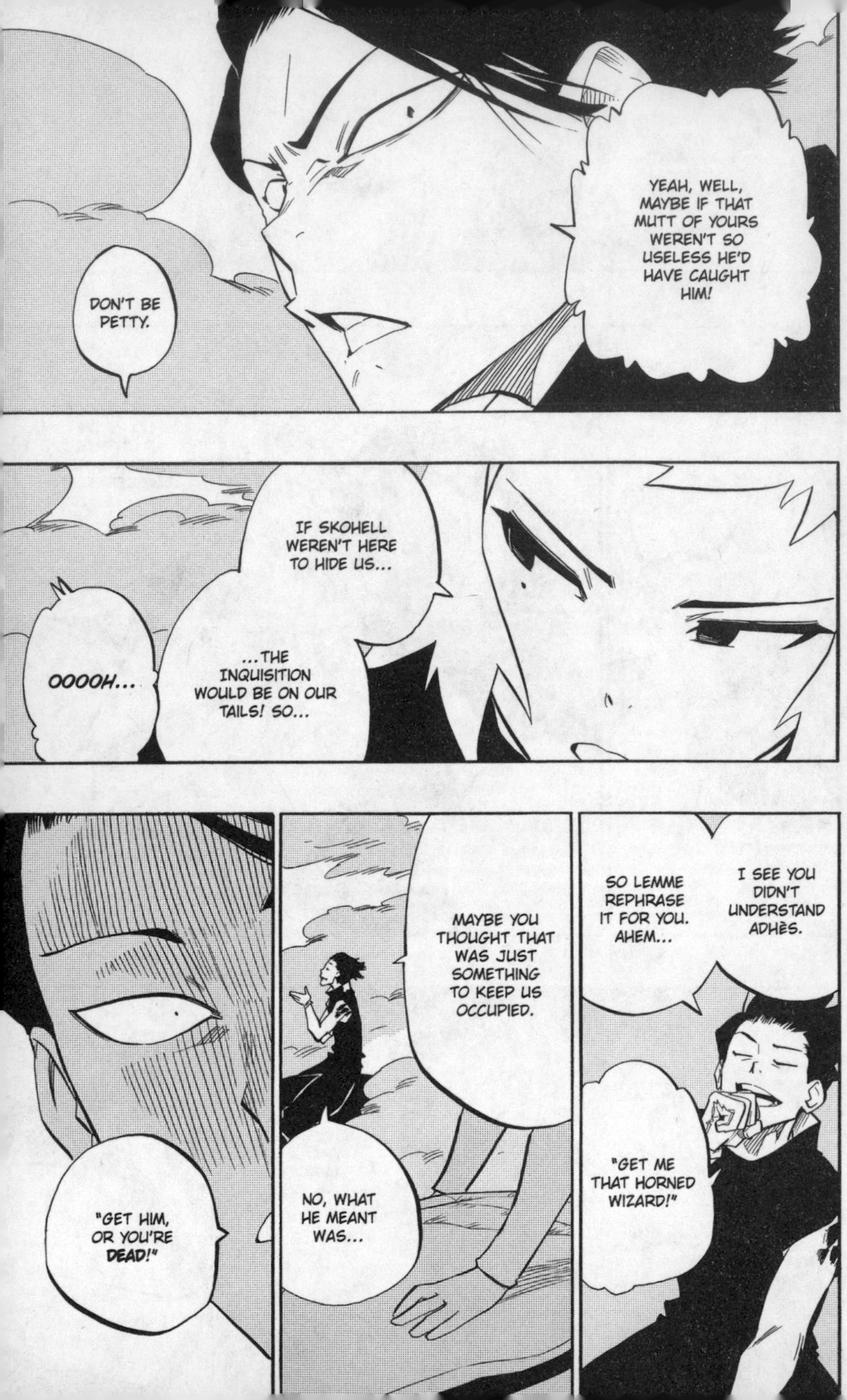
YEAH, WELL, MAYBE IF THAT MUTT OF YOURS WEREN'T SO USELESS HE'D HAVE CAUGHT HIM!
DON'T BE PETTY.
IF SKOHELL WEREN'T HERE TO HIDE US...
...THE INQUISITION WOULD BE ON OUR TAILS! SO...
OOOOH...
I SEE YOU DIDN'T UNDERSTAND ADHÈS.
SO LEMME REPHRASE IT FOR YOU. AHEM...
"GET ME THAT HORNED WIZARD!"
MAYBE YOU THOUGHT THAT WAS JUST SOMETHING TO KEEP US OCCUPIED.
NO, WHAT HE MEANT WAS...
"GET HIM, OR YOU'RE **DEAD!**"

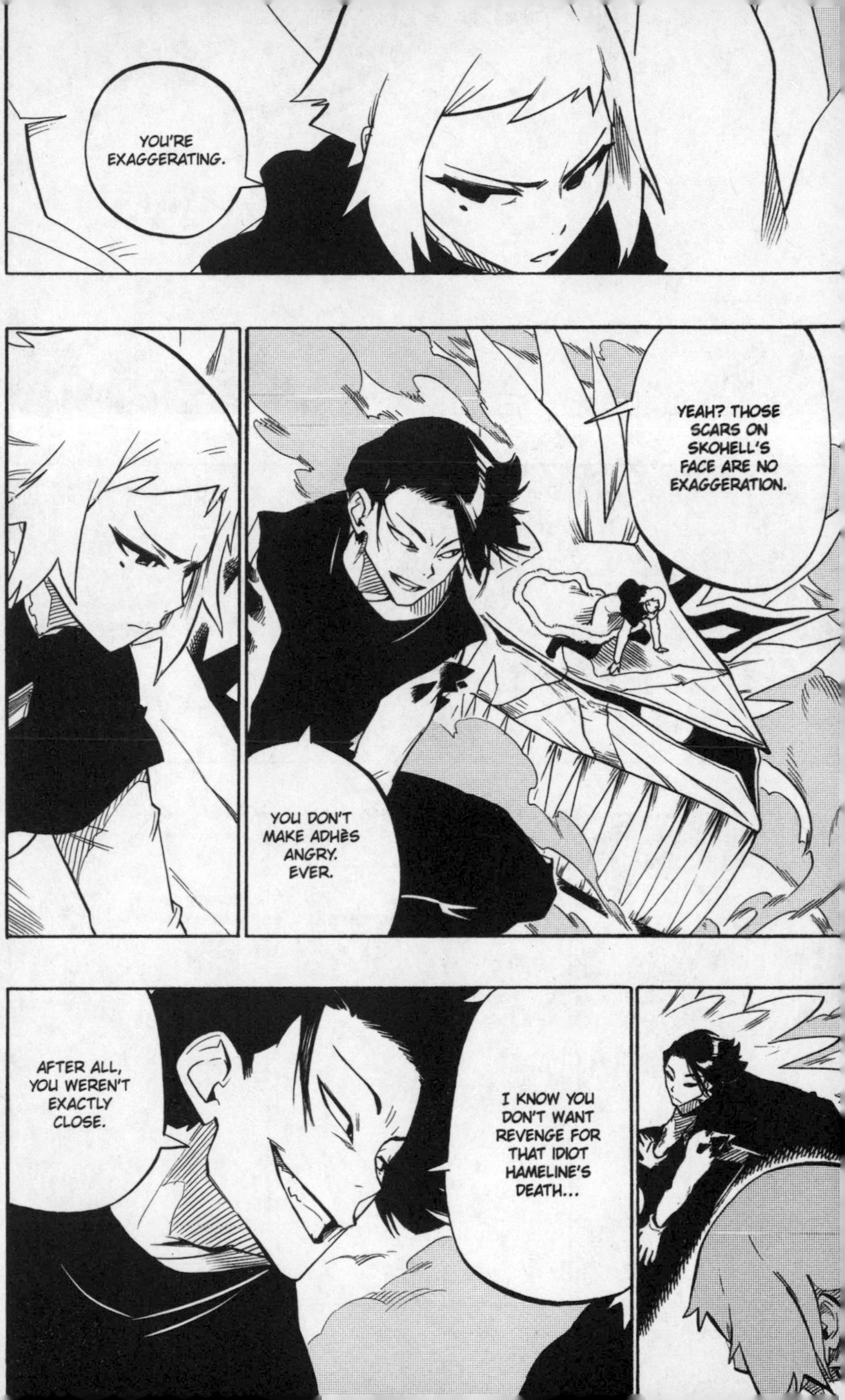
YOU'RE EXAGGERATING.
YEAH? THOSE SCARS ON SKOHELL'S FACE ARE NO EXAGGERATION.
YOU DON'T MAKE ADHÈS ANGRY. EVER.
I KNOW YOU DON'T WANT REVENGE FOR THAT IDIOT HAMELINE'S DEATH...
AFTER ALL, YOU WEREN'T EXACTLY CLOSE.

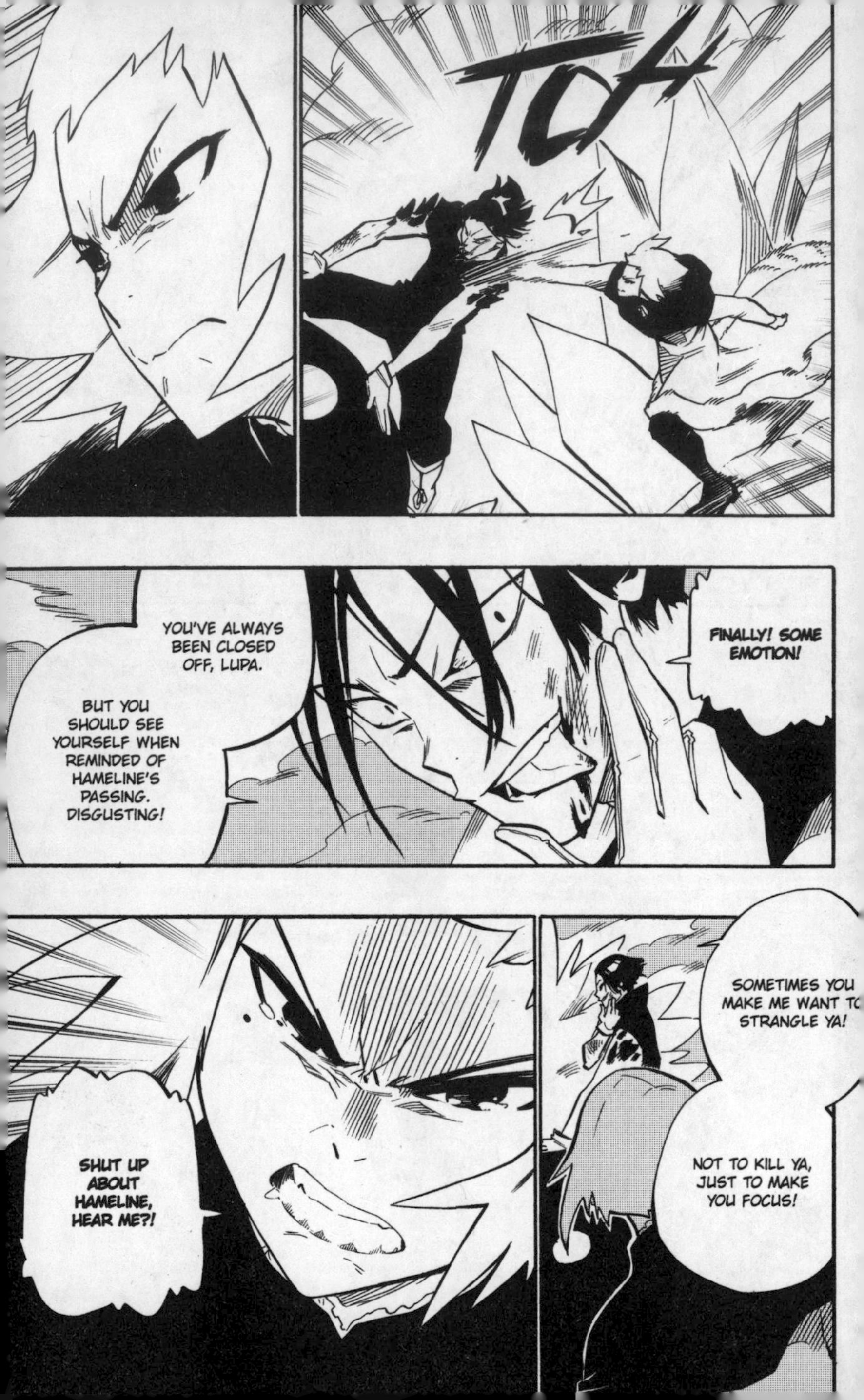
TCH
FINALLY! SOME EMOTION!
YOU'VE ALWAYS BEEN CLOSED OFF, LUPA.
BUT YOU SHOULD SEE YOURSELF WHEN REMINDED OF HAMELINE'S PASSING. DISGUSTING!
SOMETIMES YOU MAKE ME WANT TO STRANGLE YA!
NOT TO KILL YA, JUST TO MAKE YOU FOCUS!
SHUT UP ABOUT HAMELINE, HEAR ME?!

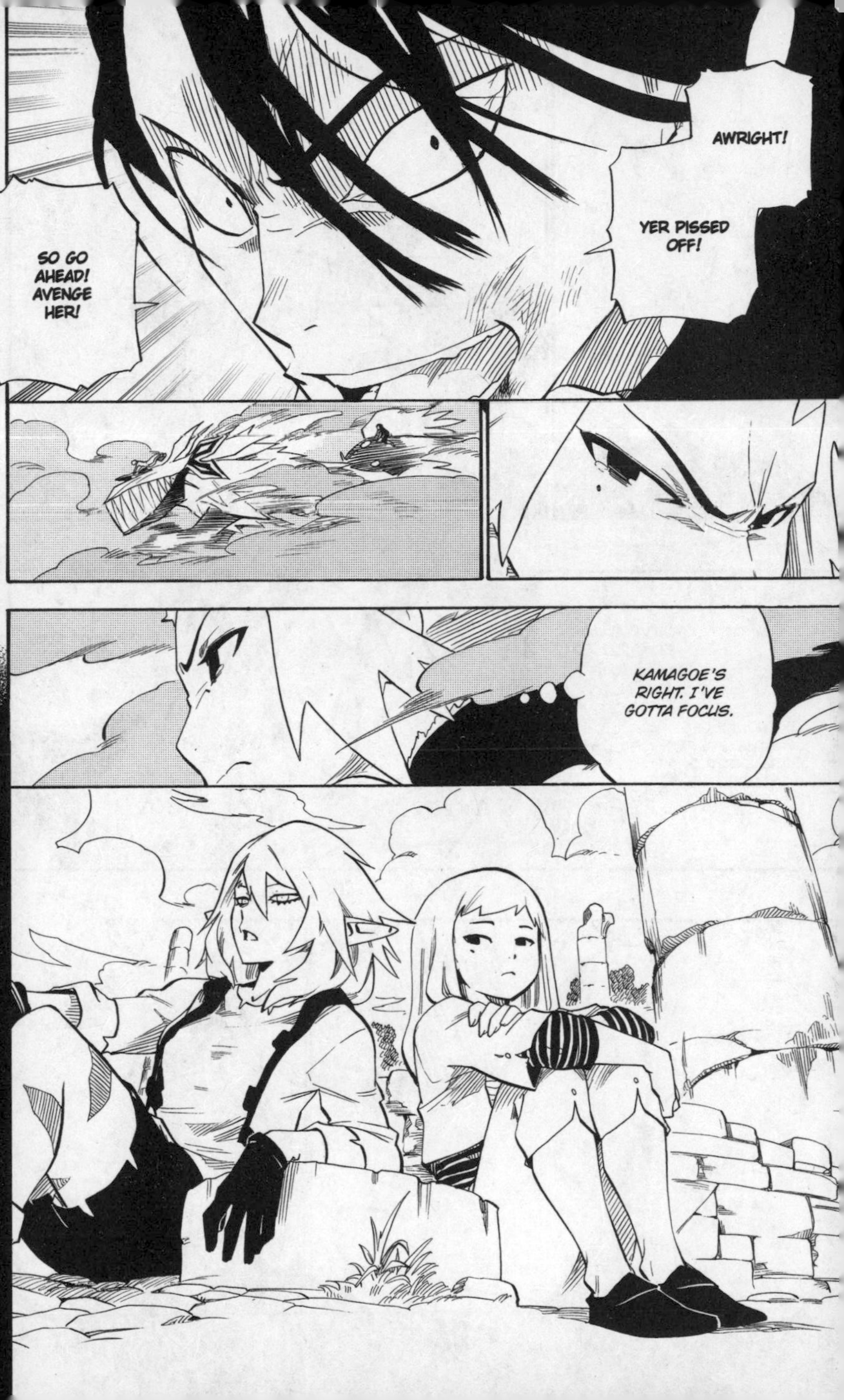
AWRIGHT!
YER PISSED OFF!
SO GO AHEAD! AVENGE HER!
KAMAGOE'S RIGHT. I'VE GOTTA FOCUS.

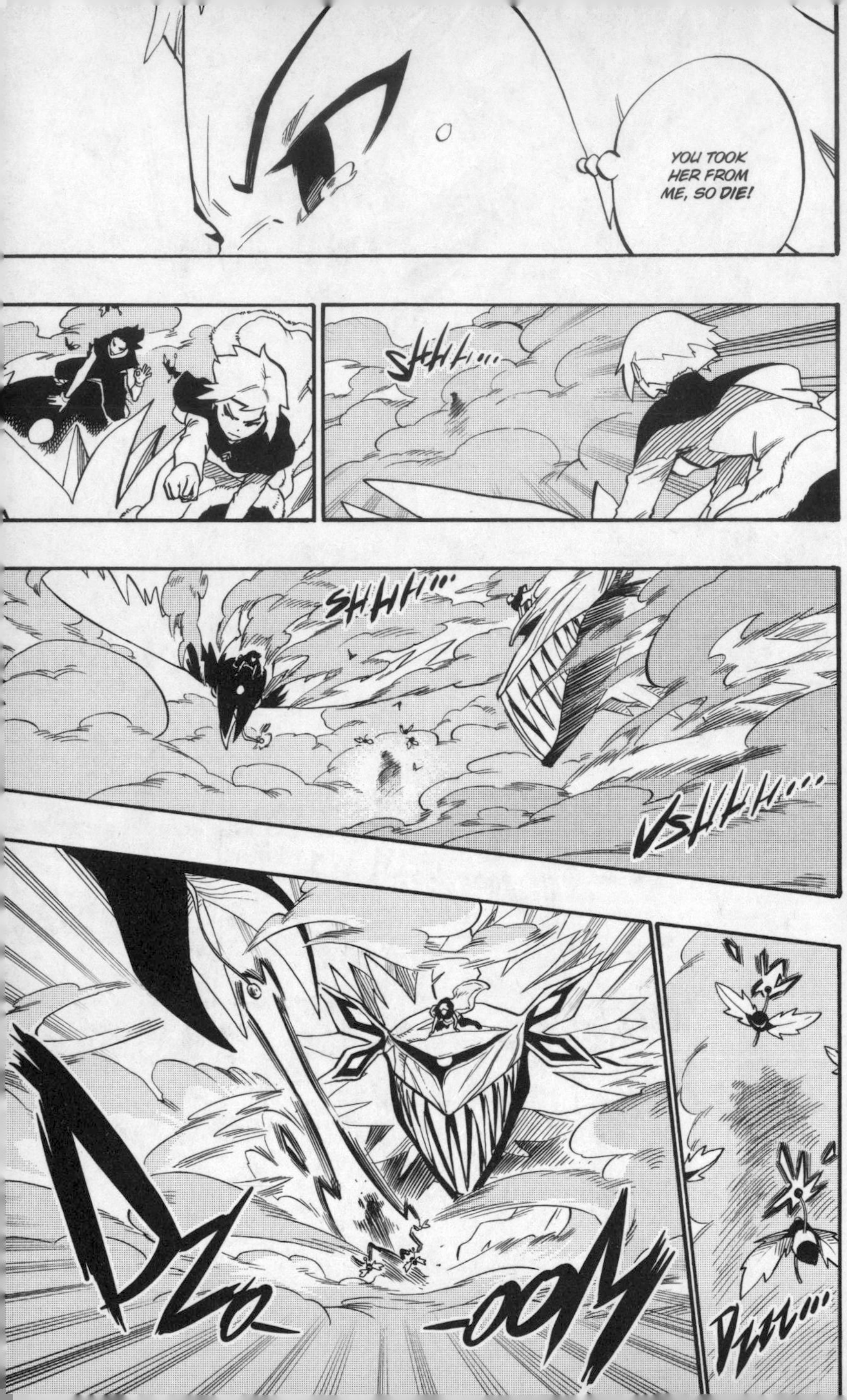
YOU TOOK HER FROM ME, SO DIE!
SHHH...
SHHH...
VSHHH...
DZZZ...
DZZO-OOM

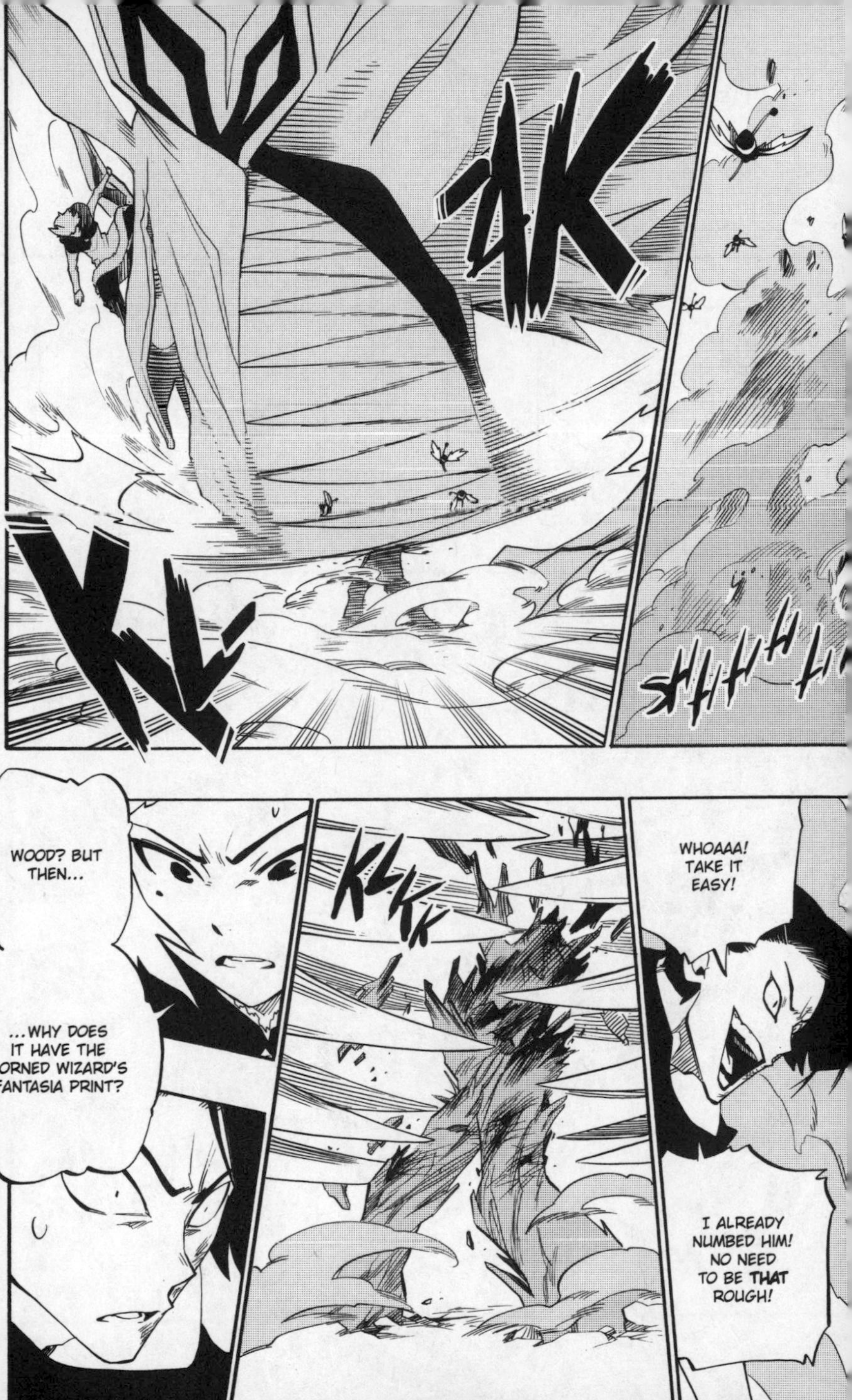
WHOAAA! TAKE IT EASY!
I ALREADY NUMBED HIM! NO NEED TO BE THAT ROUGH!
WOOD? BUT THEN...
...WHY DOES IT HAVE THE HORNED WIZARD'S FANTASIA PRINT?

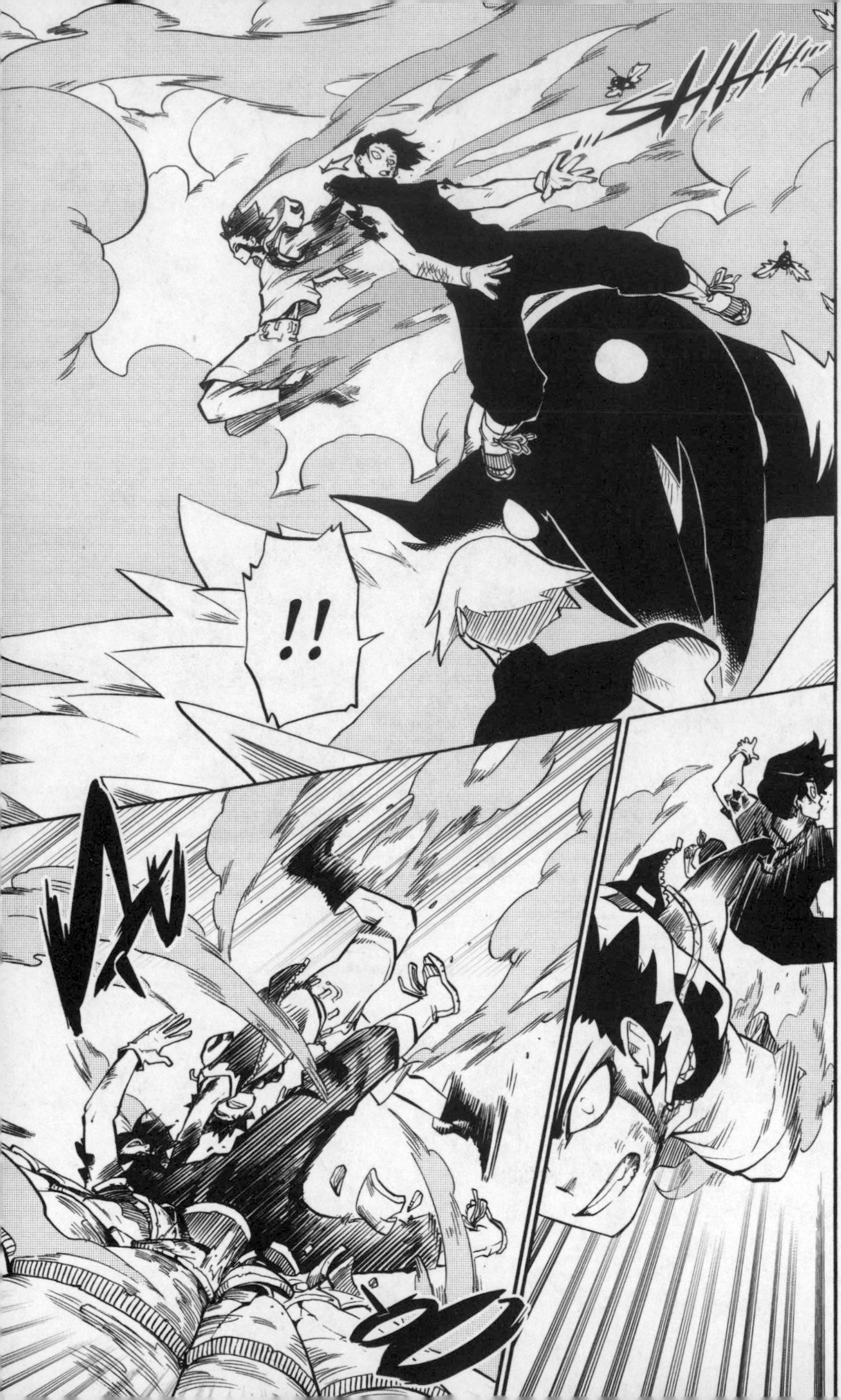
SHHHH
!!

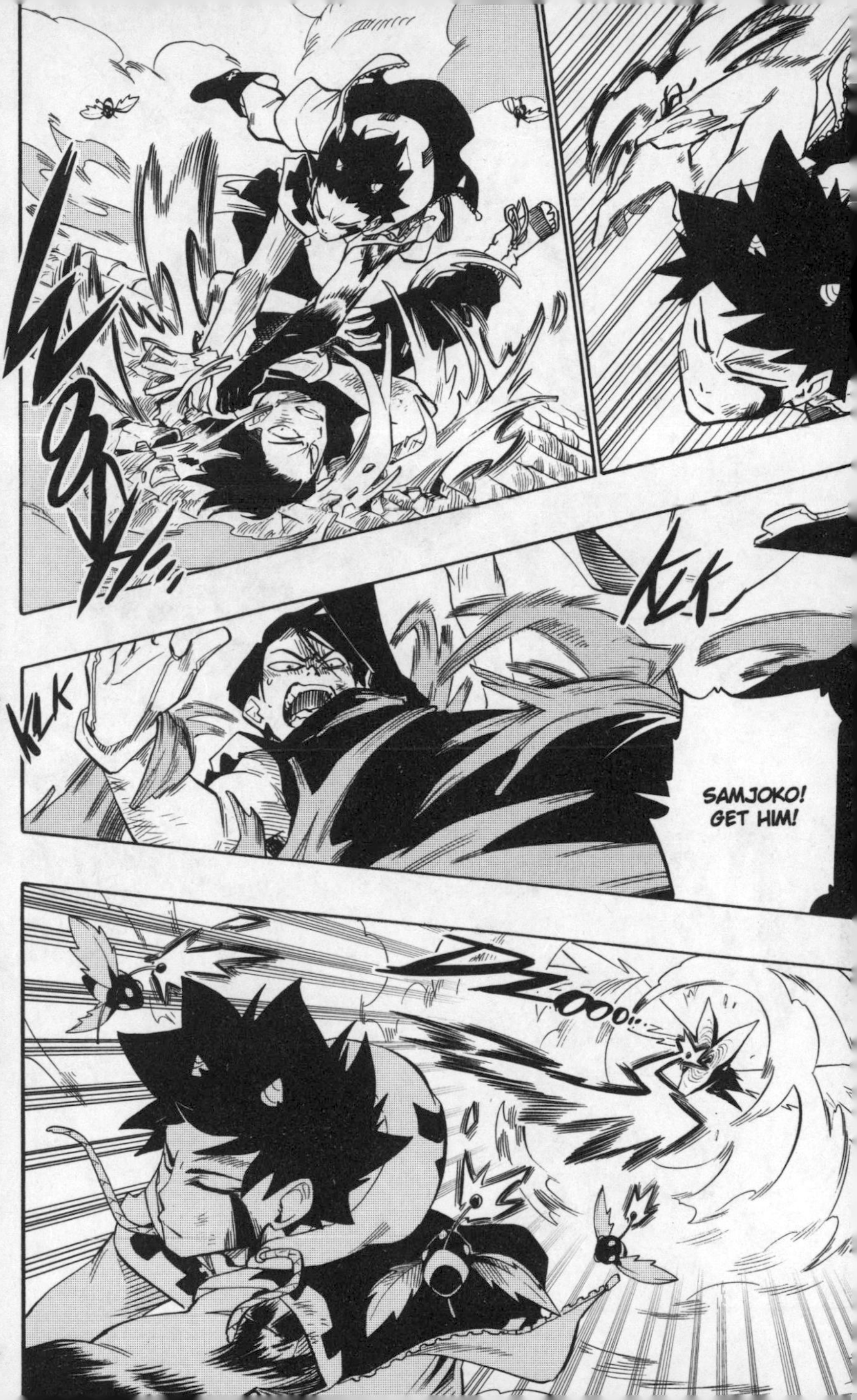
KLK
SAMJOKO!
GET HIM!
KLK

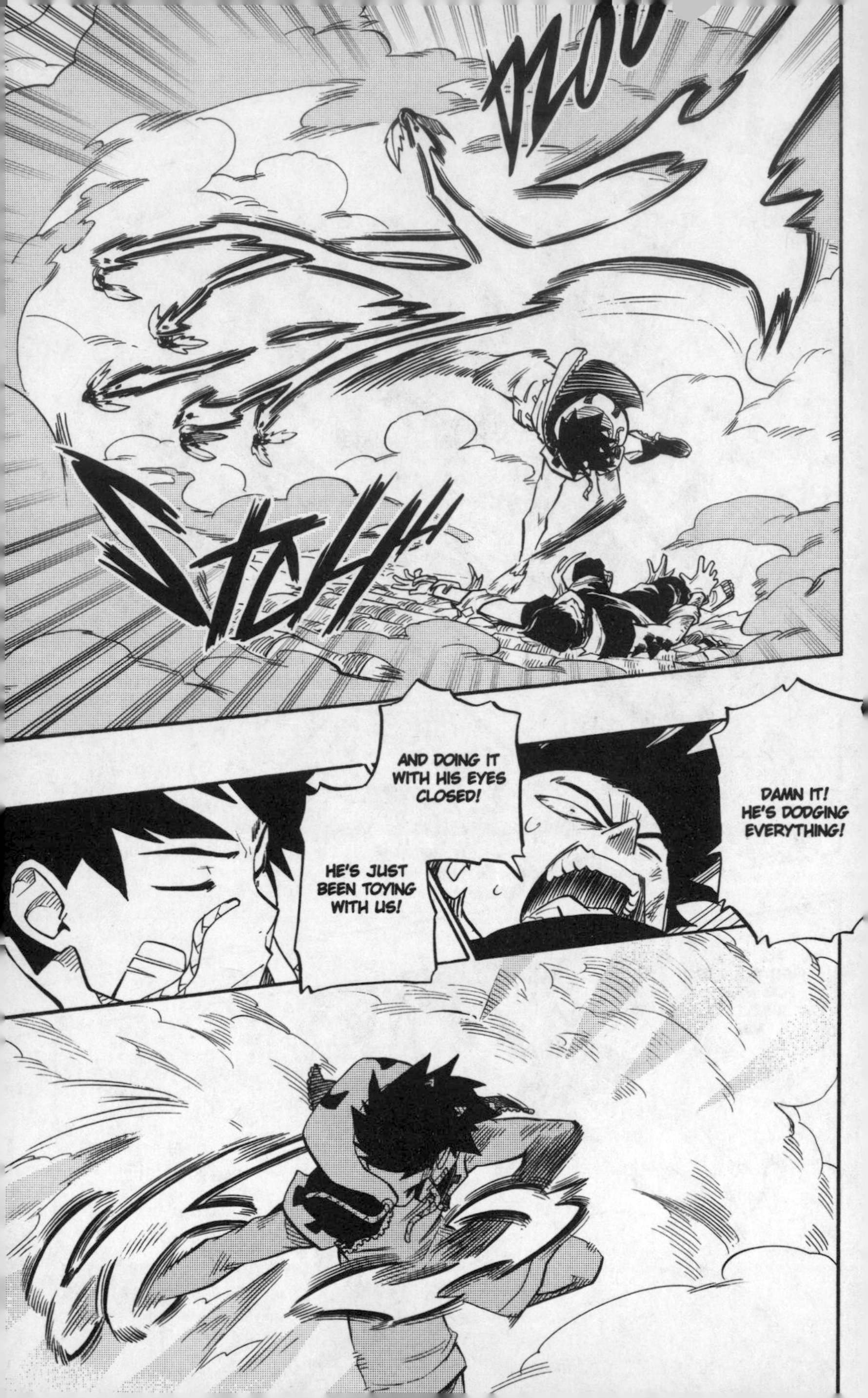
DAMN IT! HE'S DODGING EVERYTHING!
HE'S JUST BEEN TOYING WITH US!
AND DOING IT WITH HIS EYES CLOSED!

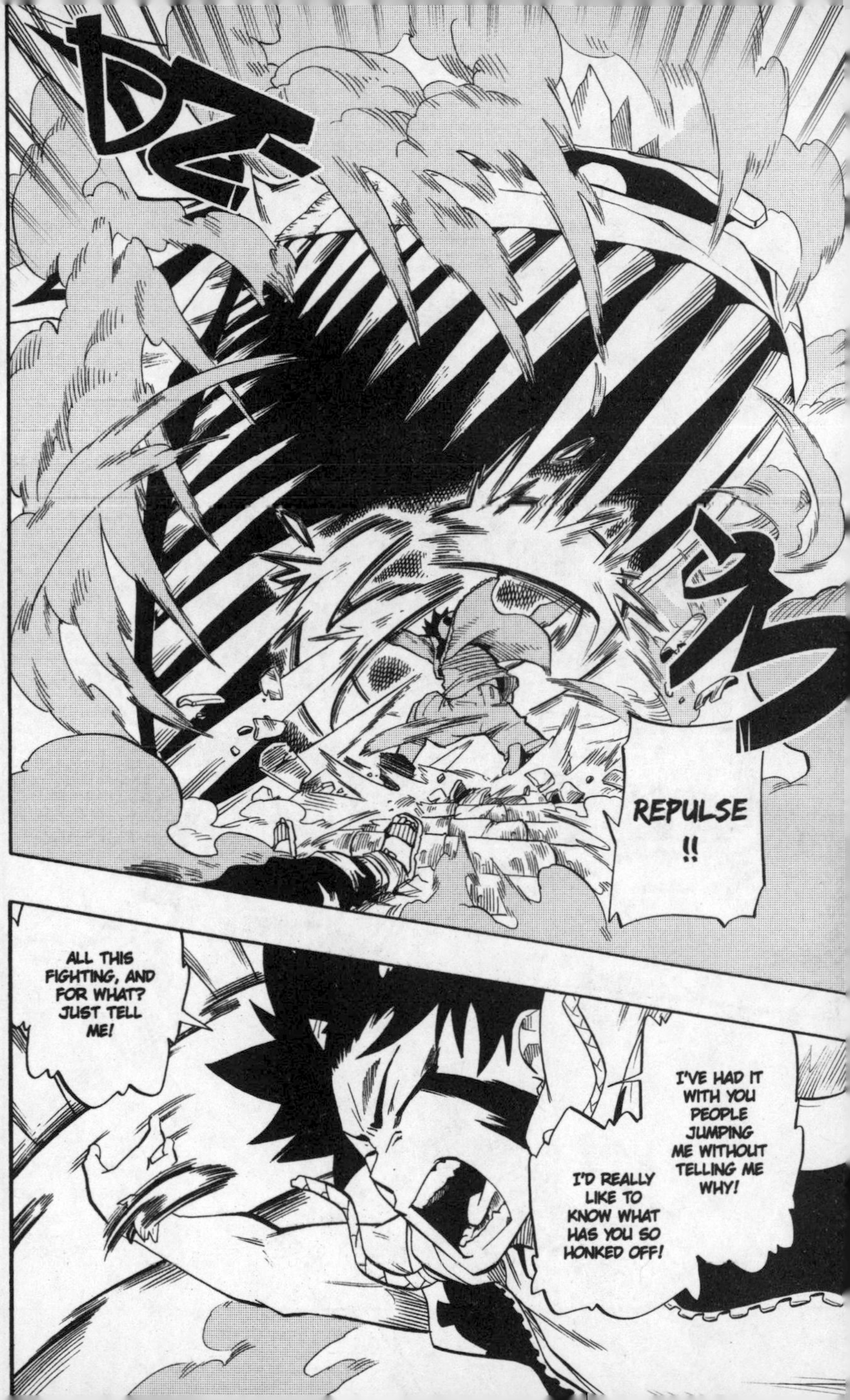
REPULSE !!
I'VE HAD IT WITH YOU PEOPLE JUMPING ME WITHOUT TELLING ME WHY!
I'D REALLY LIKE TO KNOW WHAT HAS YOU SO HONKED OFF!
ALL THIS FIGHTING, AND FOR WHAT? JUST TELL ME!

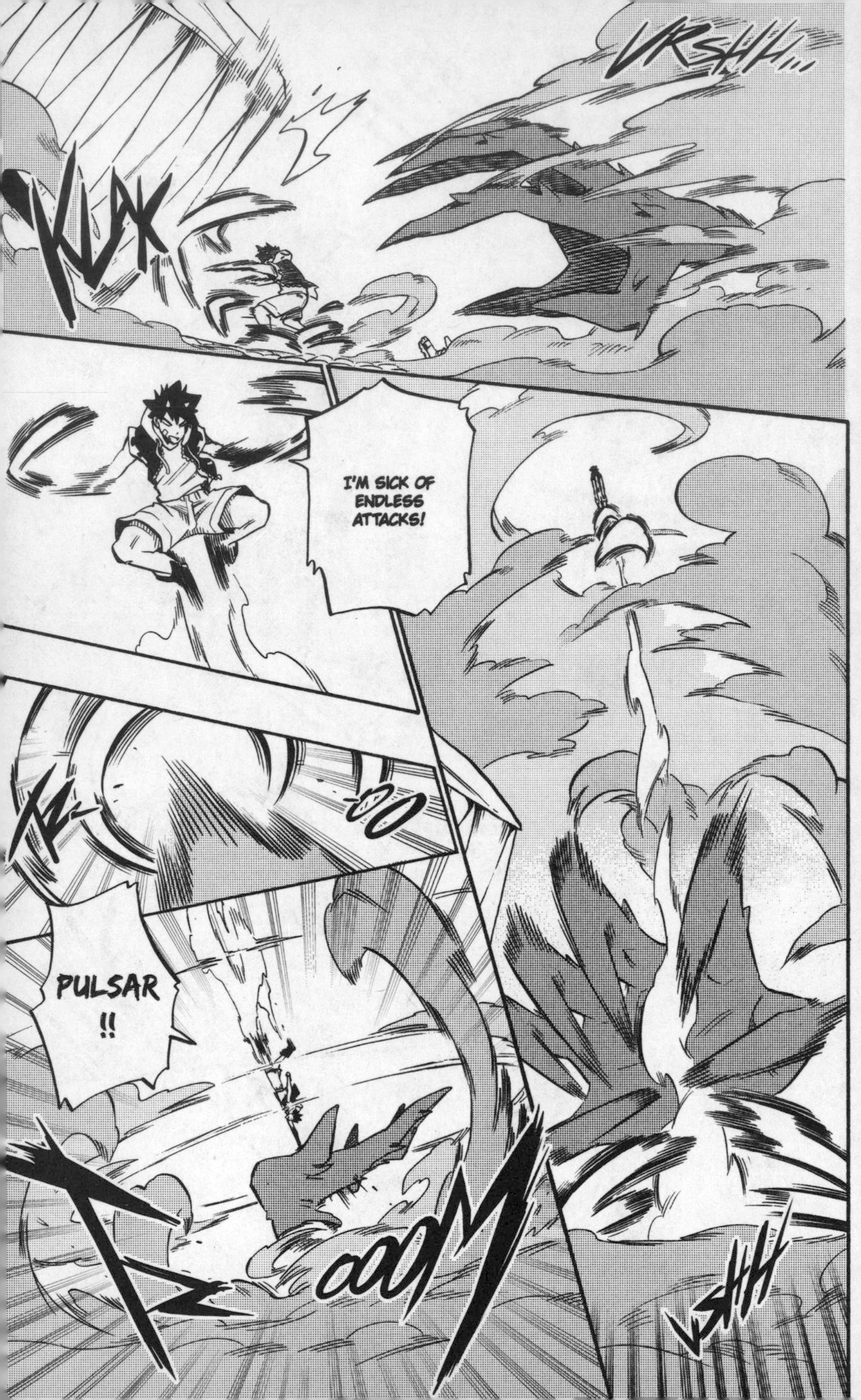
VRSHH...
KLAK
I'M SICK OF ENDLESS ATTACKS!
PULSAR !!

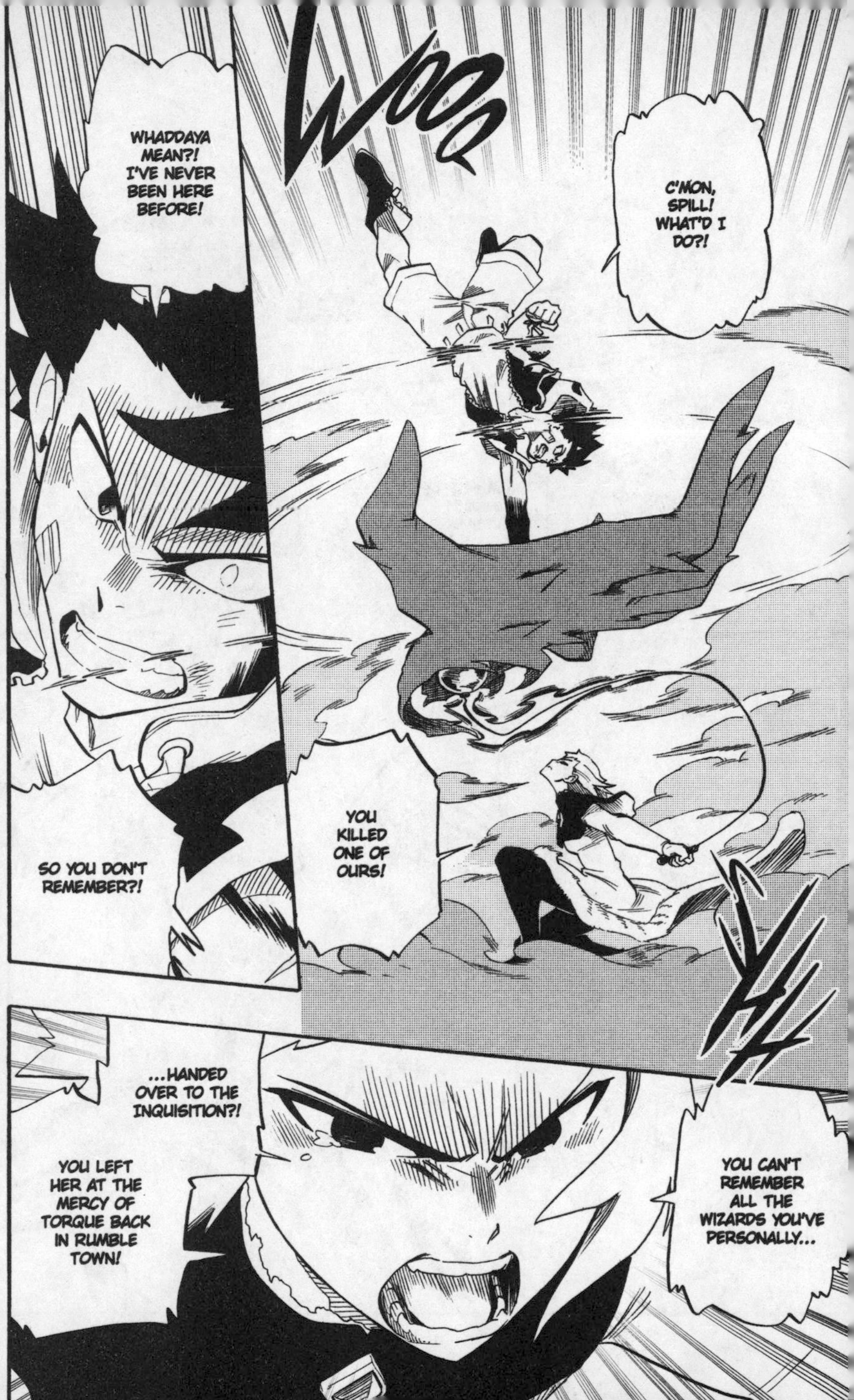
C'MON, SPILL! WHAT'D I DO?!
WOOO
YOU KILLED ONE OF OURS!
SHH
WHADDAYA MEAN?! I'VE NEVER BEEN HERE BEFORE!
SO YOU DON'T REMEMBER?!
YOU CAN'T REMEMBER ALL THE WIZARDS YOU'VE PERSONALLY...
...HANDED OVER TO THE INQUISITION?!
YOU LEFT HER AT THE MERCY OF TORQUE BACK IN RUMBLE TOWN!

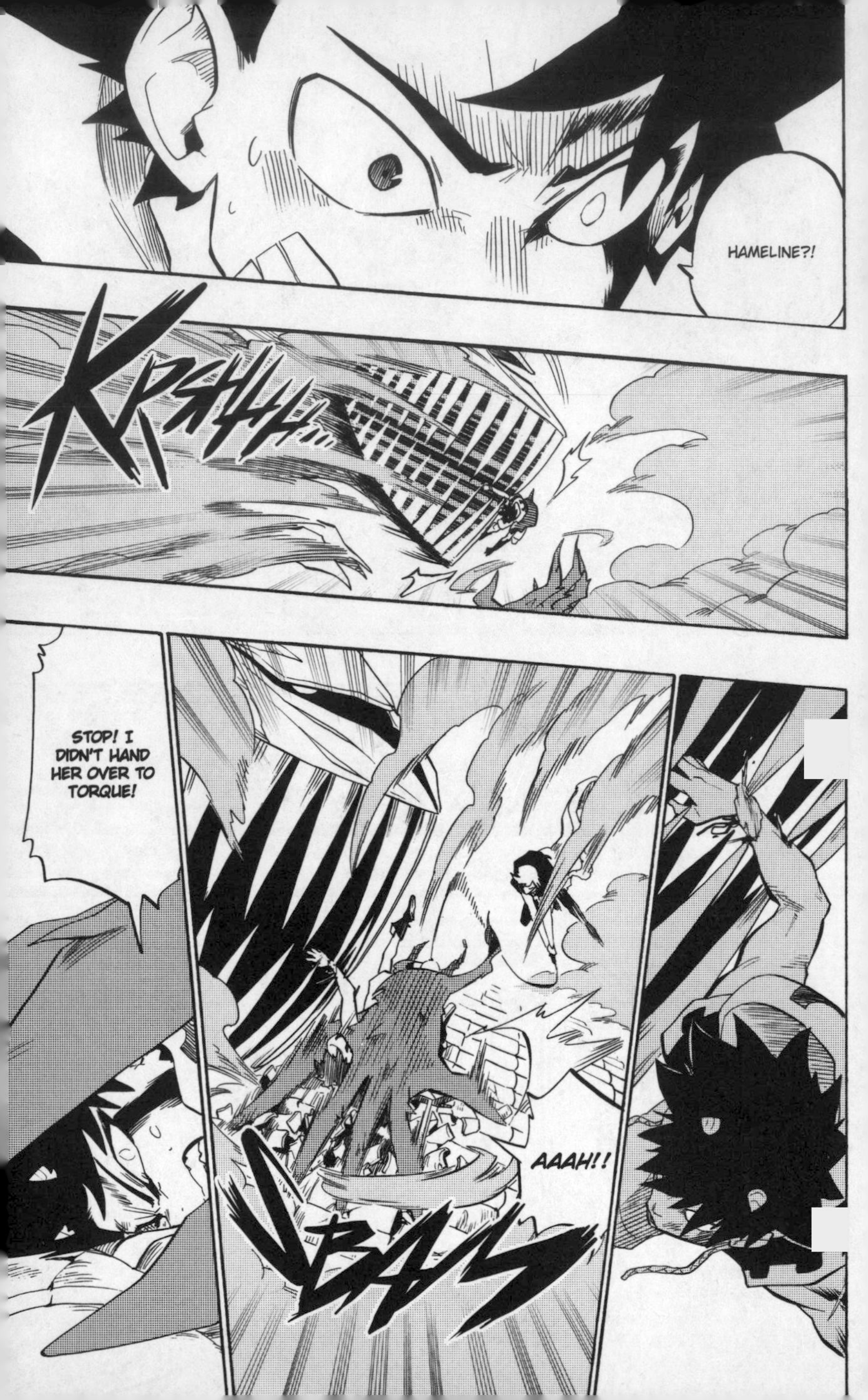
HAMELINE?!
AAAH!!
STOP! I DIDN'T HAND HER OVER TO TORQUE!

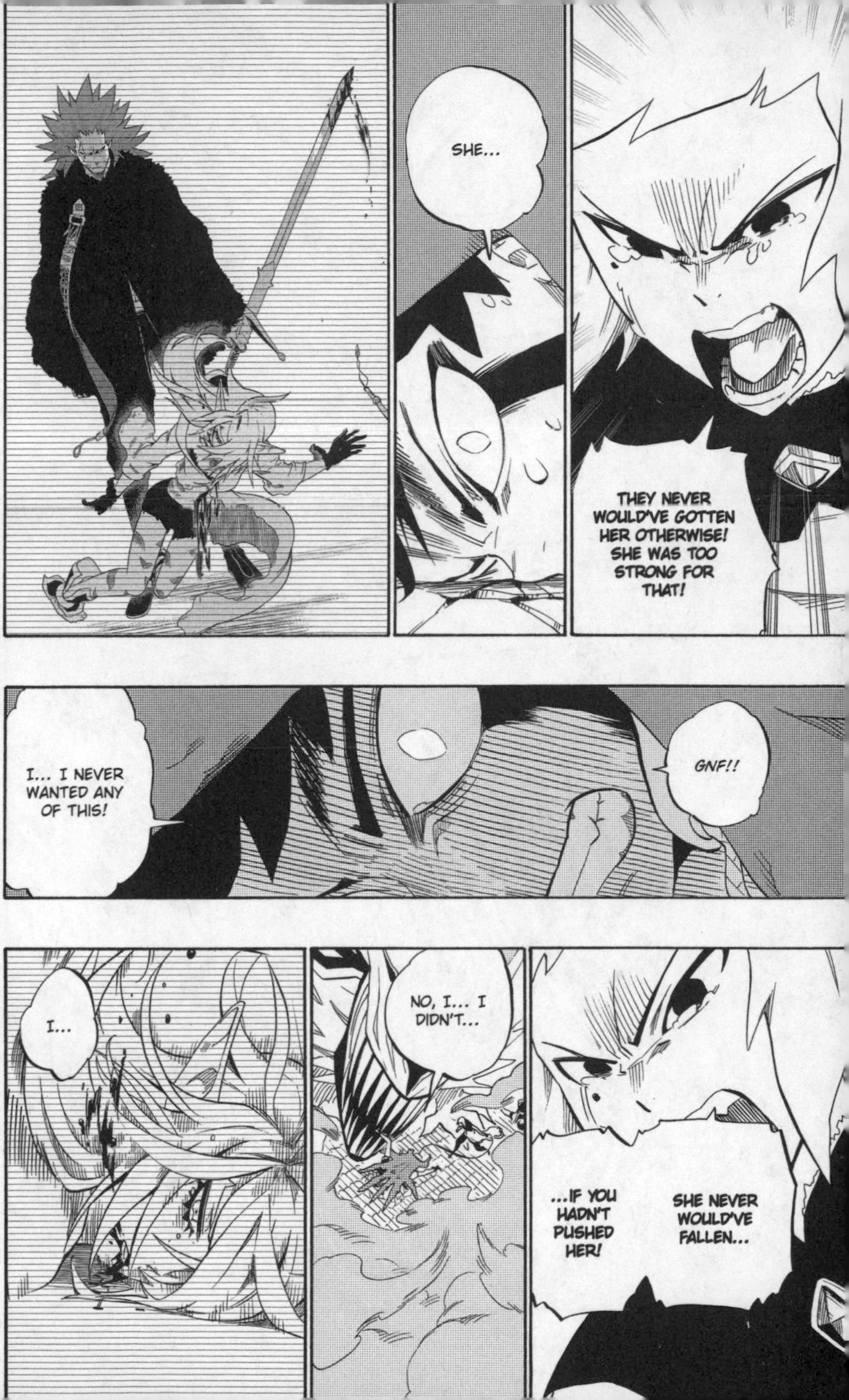
THEY NEVER WOULD'VE GOTTEN HER OTHERWISE! SHE WAS TOO STRONG FOR THAT!
SHE...
GNF!!
I... I NEVER WANTED ANY OF THIS!
SHE NEVER WOULD'VE FALLEN...
...IF YOU HADN'T PUSHED HER!
NO, I... I DIDN'T...
I...

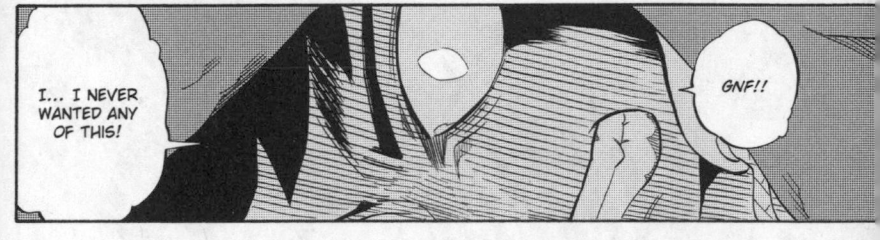

SHE SHOULDN'T HAVE DIED!
SHE'S DEAD BECAUSE OF YOU!
I...
I...
YOU KILLED HER!!!

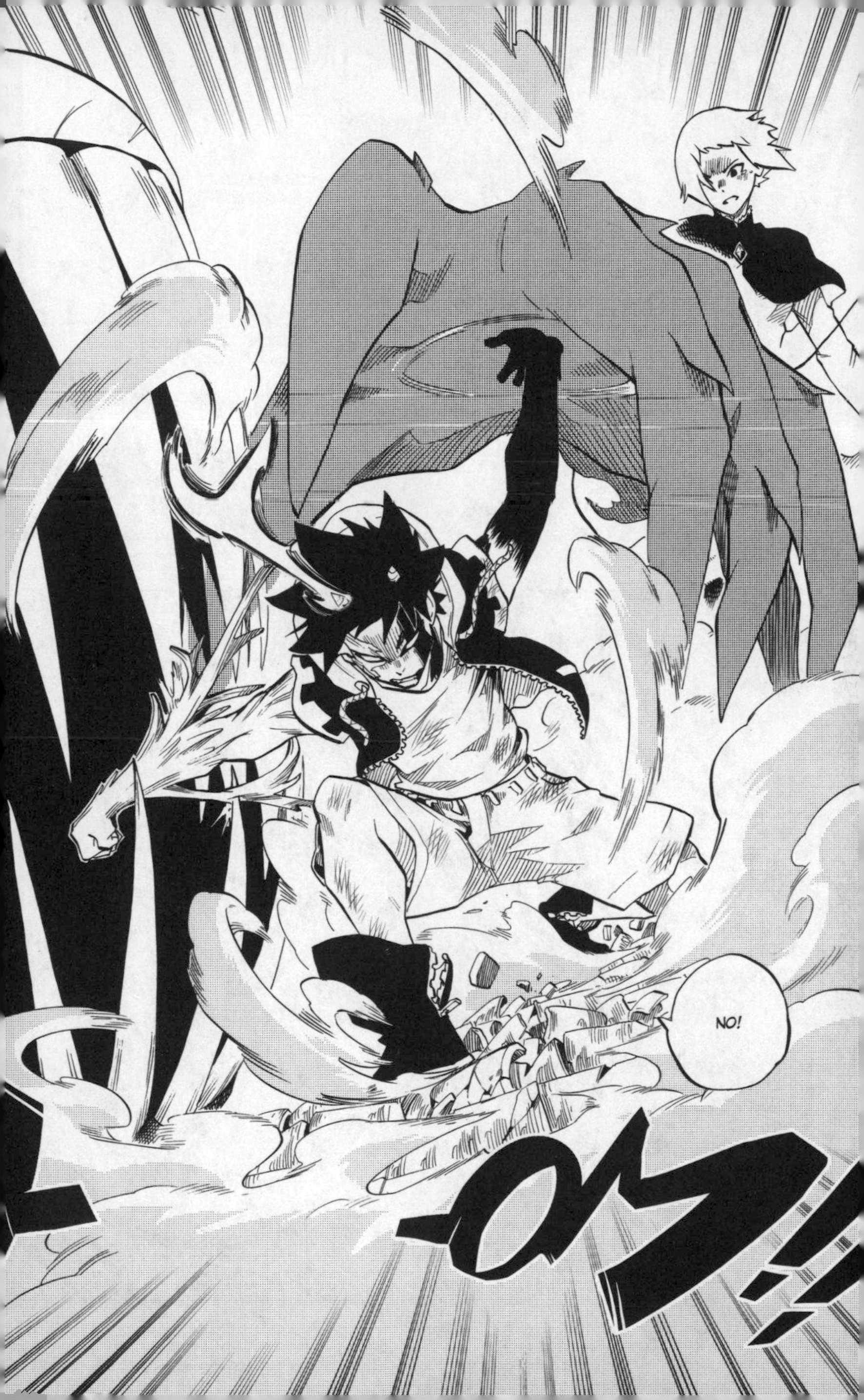
NO!

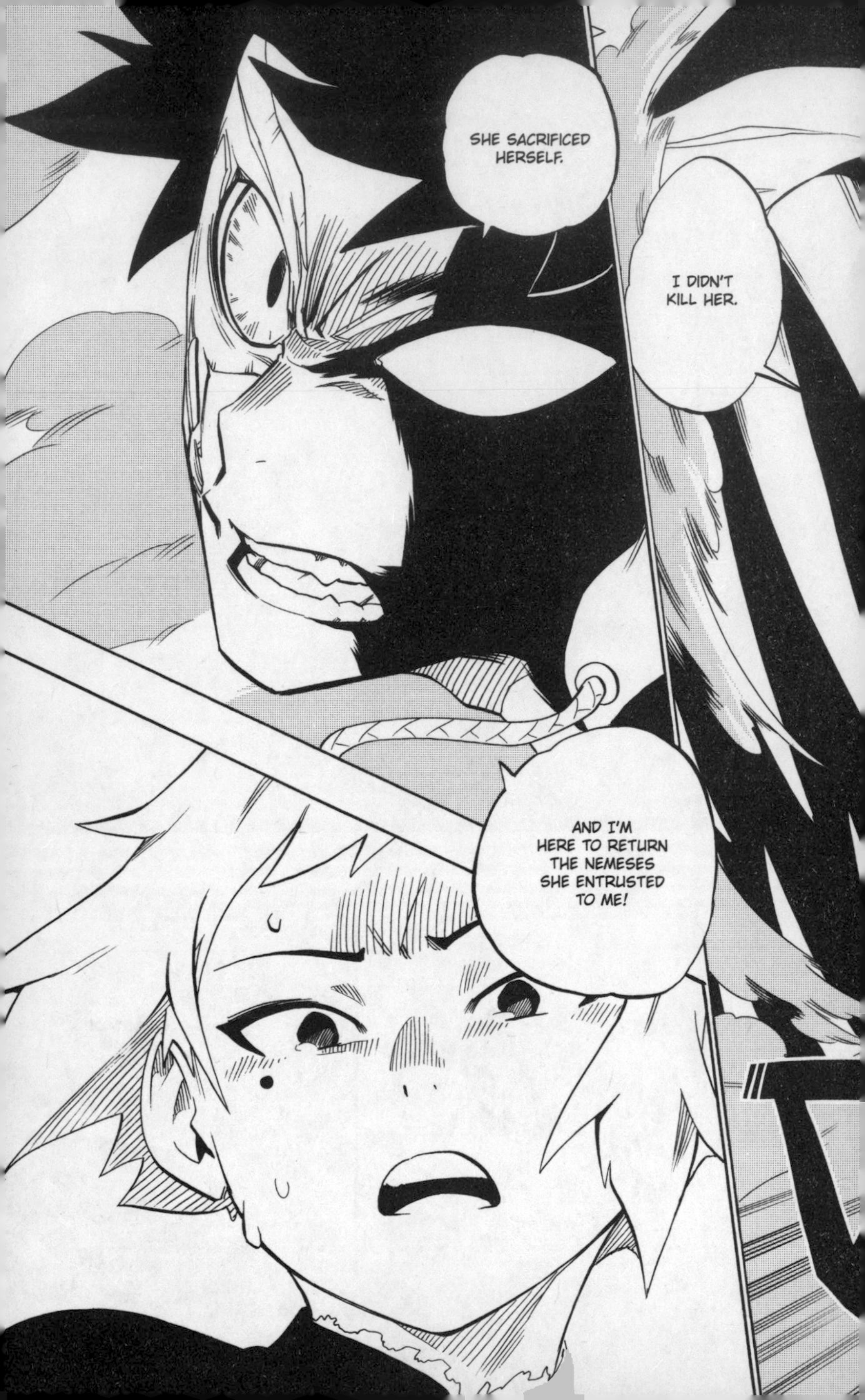
I DIDN'T KILL HER.
SHE SACRIFICED HERSELF.
AND I'M HERE TO RETURN THE NEMESES SHE ENTRUSTED TO ME!

SAMJOKO! GET ME LOOSE!
KRRR

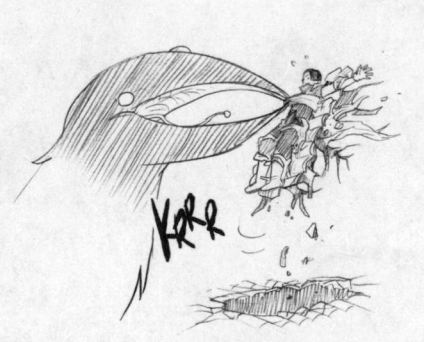

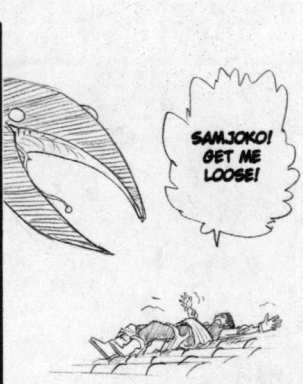

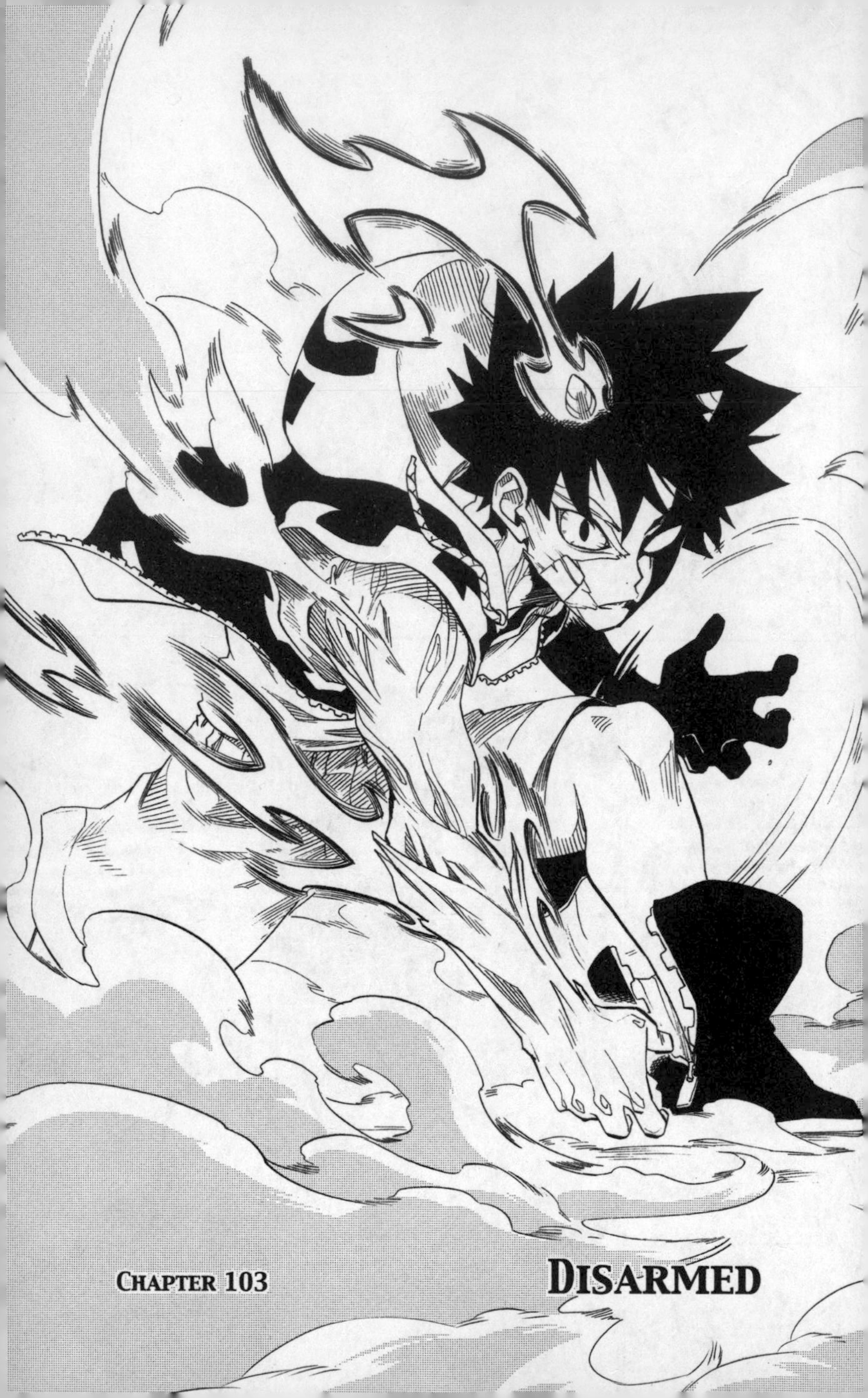

Chapter 103

Disarmed

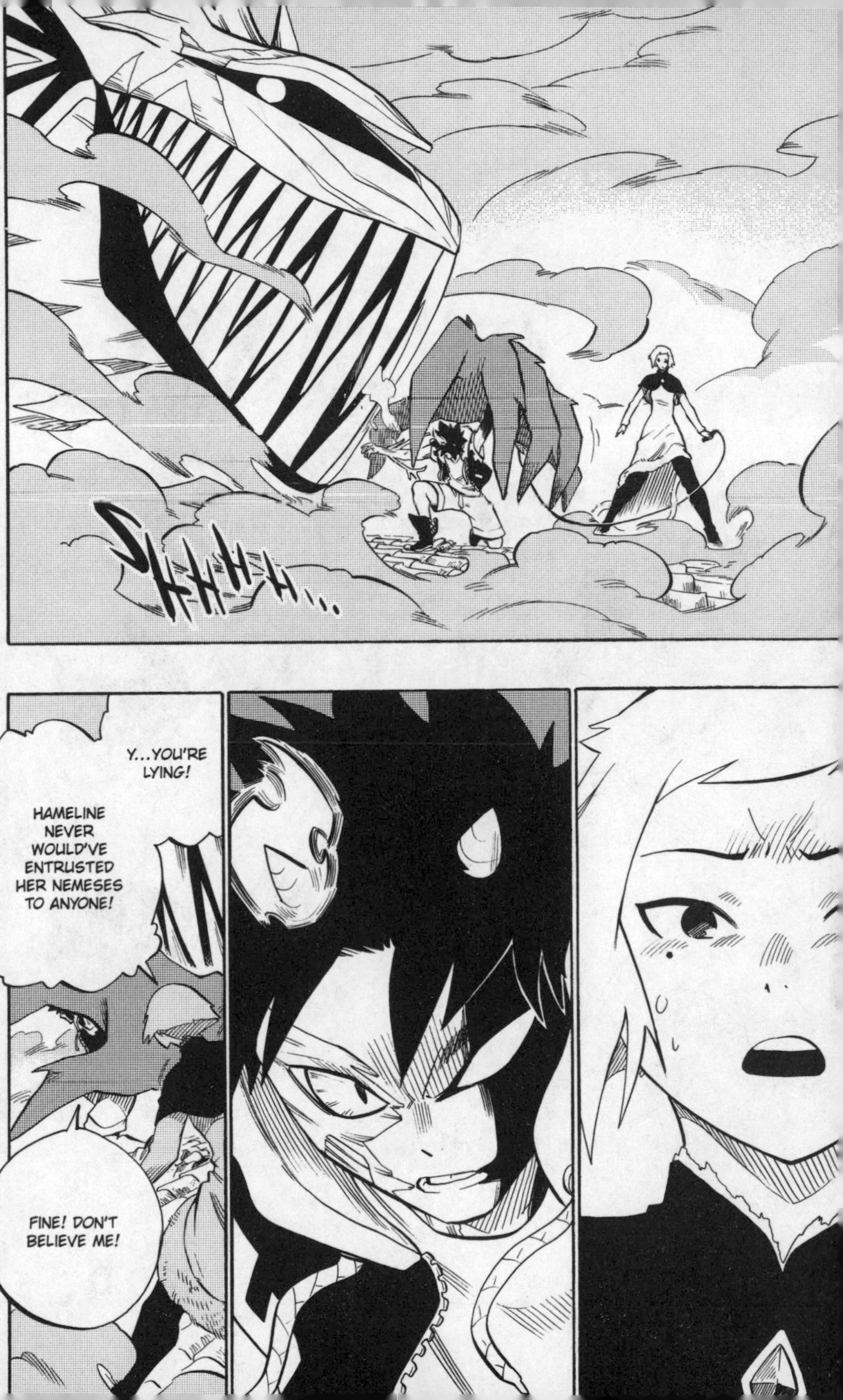
SHHHH...
Y...YOU'RE LYING!
HAMELINE NEVER WOULD'VE ENTRUSTED HER NEMESES TO ANYONE!
FINE! DON'T BELIEVE ME!

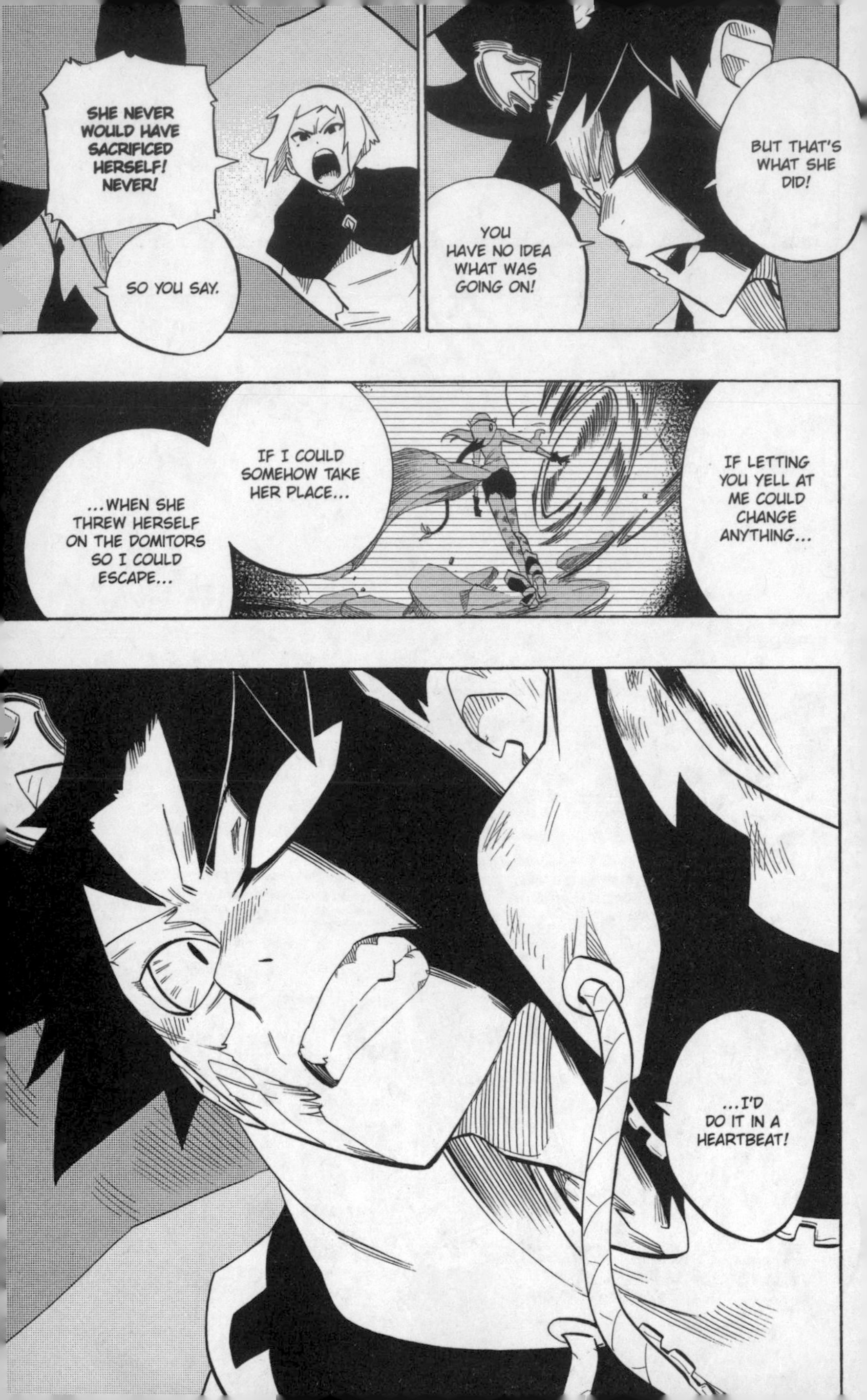
BUT THAT'S WHAT SHE DID!
YOU HAVE NO IDEA WHAT WAS GOING ON!
SHE NEVER WOULD HAVE SACRIFICED HERSELF! NEVER!
SO YOU SAY.
IF LETTING YOU YELL AT ME COULD CHANGE ANYTHING...
IF I COULD SOMEHOW TAKE HER PLACE...
...WHEN SHE THREW HERSELF ON THE DOMITORS SO I COULD ESCAPE...
...I'D DO IT IN A HEARTBEAT!

NO...
SHE...
SHE COULDN'T HAVE GIVEN HER LIFE FOR YOU.
YOU! A STRANGER?!
YOU'RE LYING! AAAH!!!

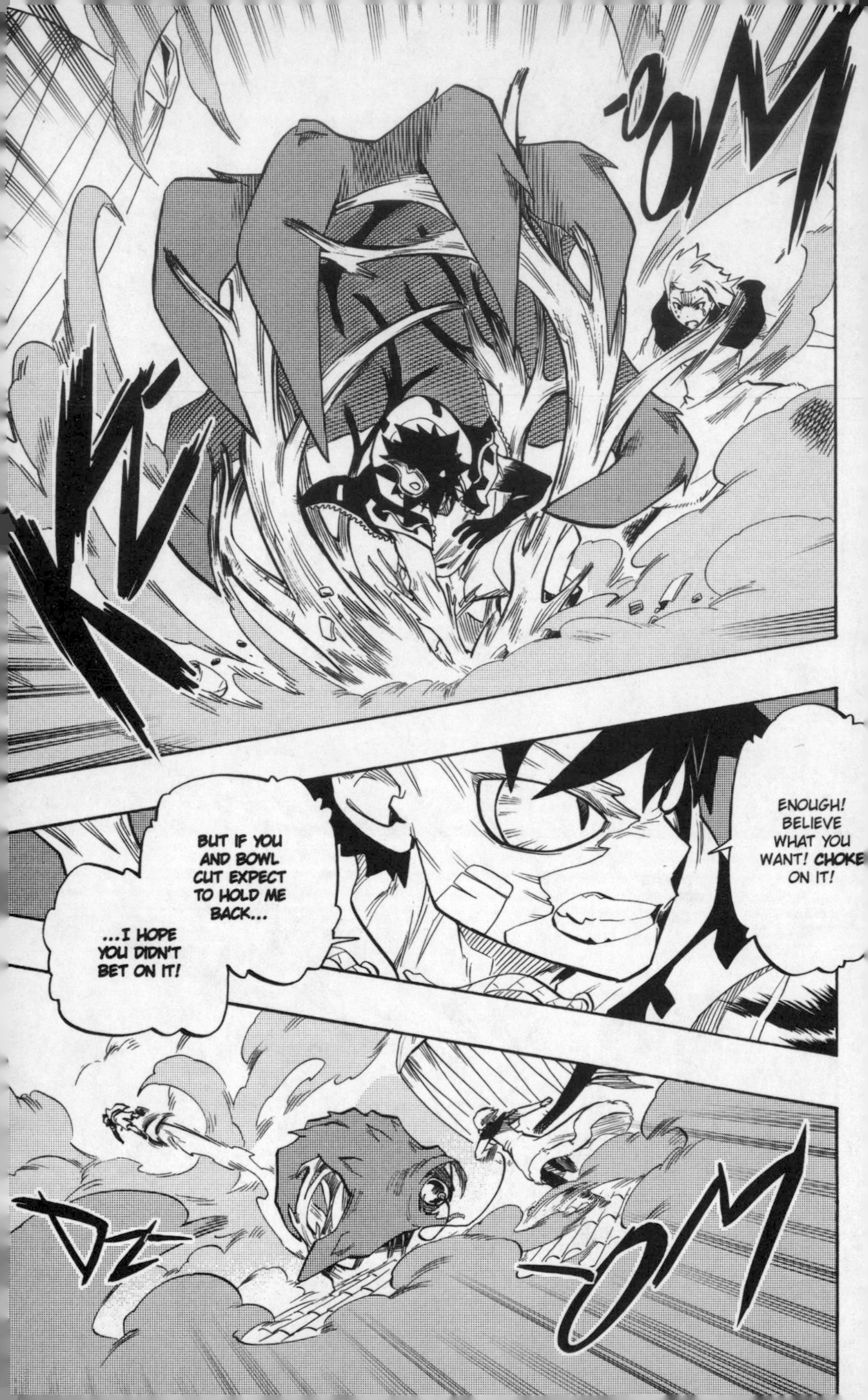
ENOUGH! BELIEVE WHAT YOU WANT! **CHOKE** ON IT!
BUT IF YOU AND BOWL CUT EXPECT TO HOLD ME BACK...
...I HOPE YOU DIDN'T BET ON IT!

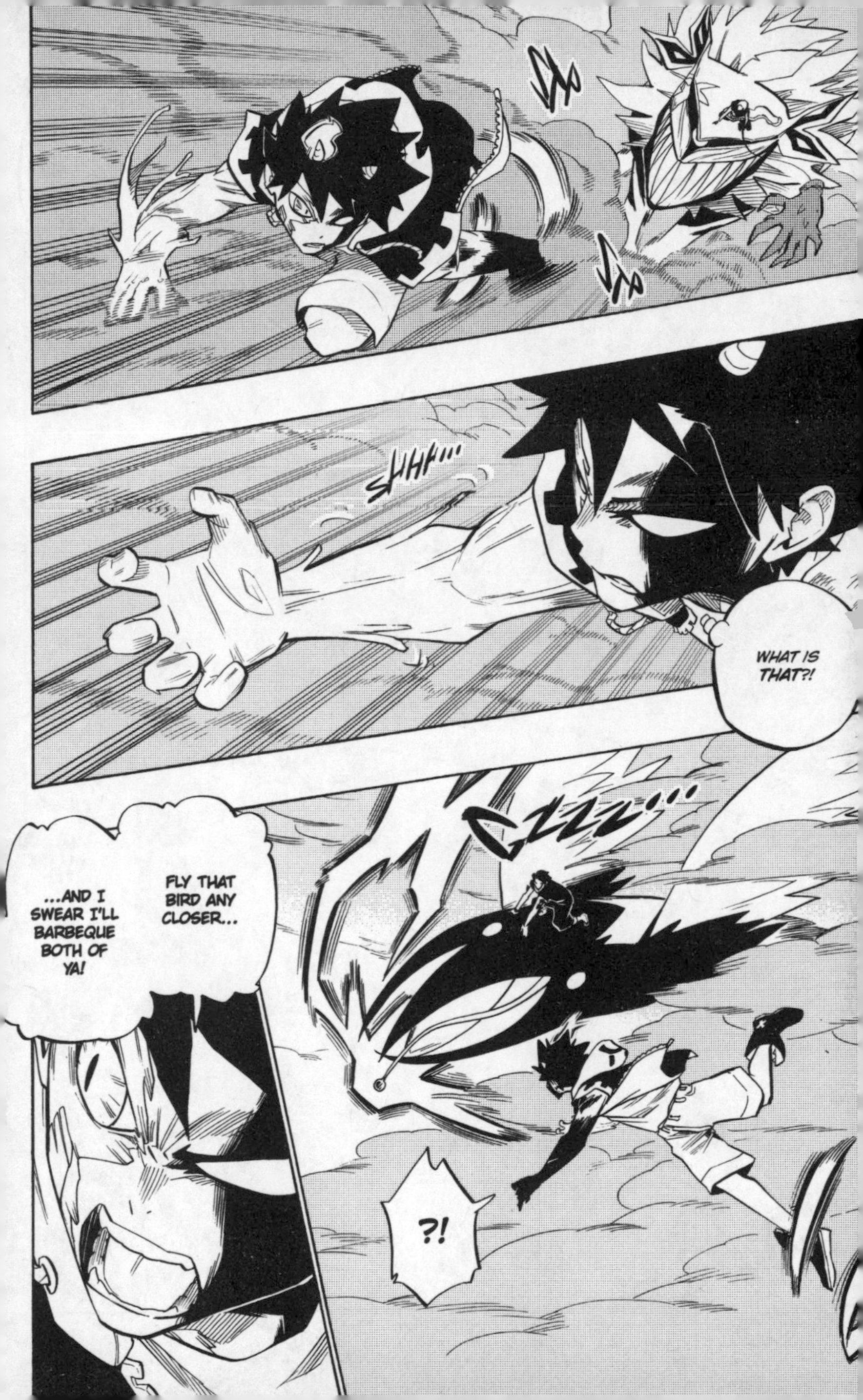
WHAT IS THAT?!
?!
FLY THAT BIRD ANY CLOSER...
...AND I SWEAR I'LL BARBEQUE BOTH OF YA!

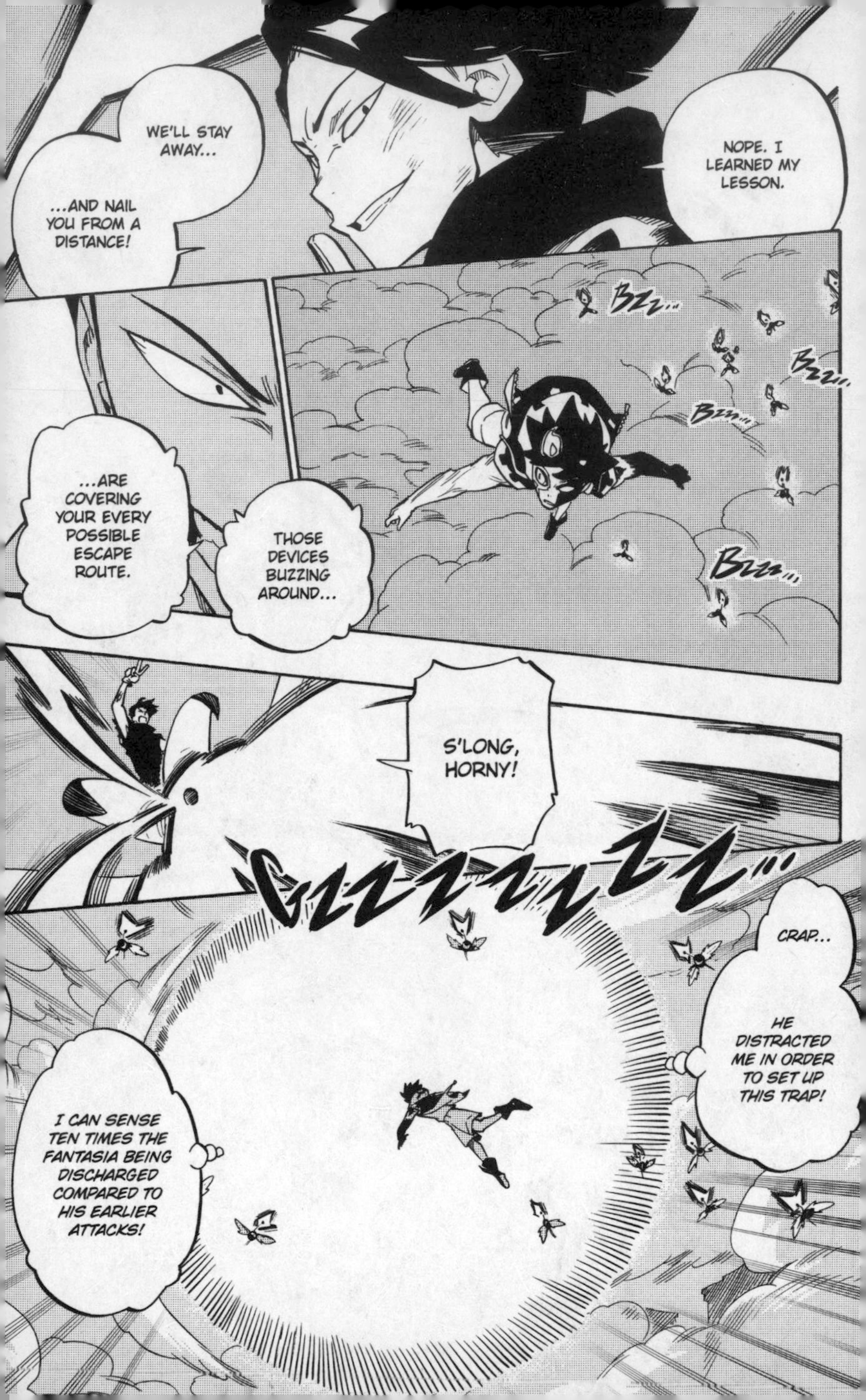
NOPE. I LEARNED MY LESSON.
WE'LL STAY AWAY...
...AND NAIL YOU FROM A DISTANCE!
Bzz...
Bzz...
Bzz...
Bzz...
THOSE DEVICES BUZZING AROUND...
...ARE COVERING YOUR EVERY POSSIBLE ESCAPE ROUTE.
S'LONG, HORNY!
GZZZZZZZZZ!!
CRAP...
HE DISTRACTED ME IN ORDER TO SET UP THIS TRAP!
I CAN SENSE TEN TIMES THE FANTASIA BEING DISCHARGED COMPARED TO HIS EARLIER ATTACKS!

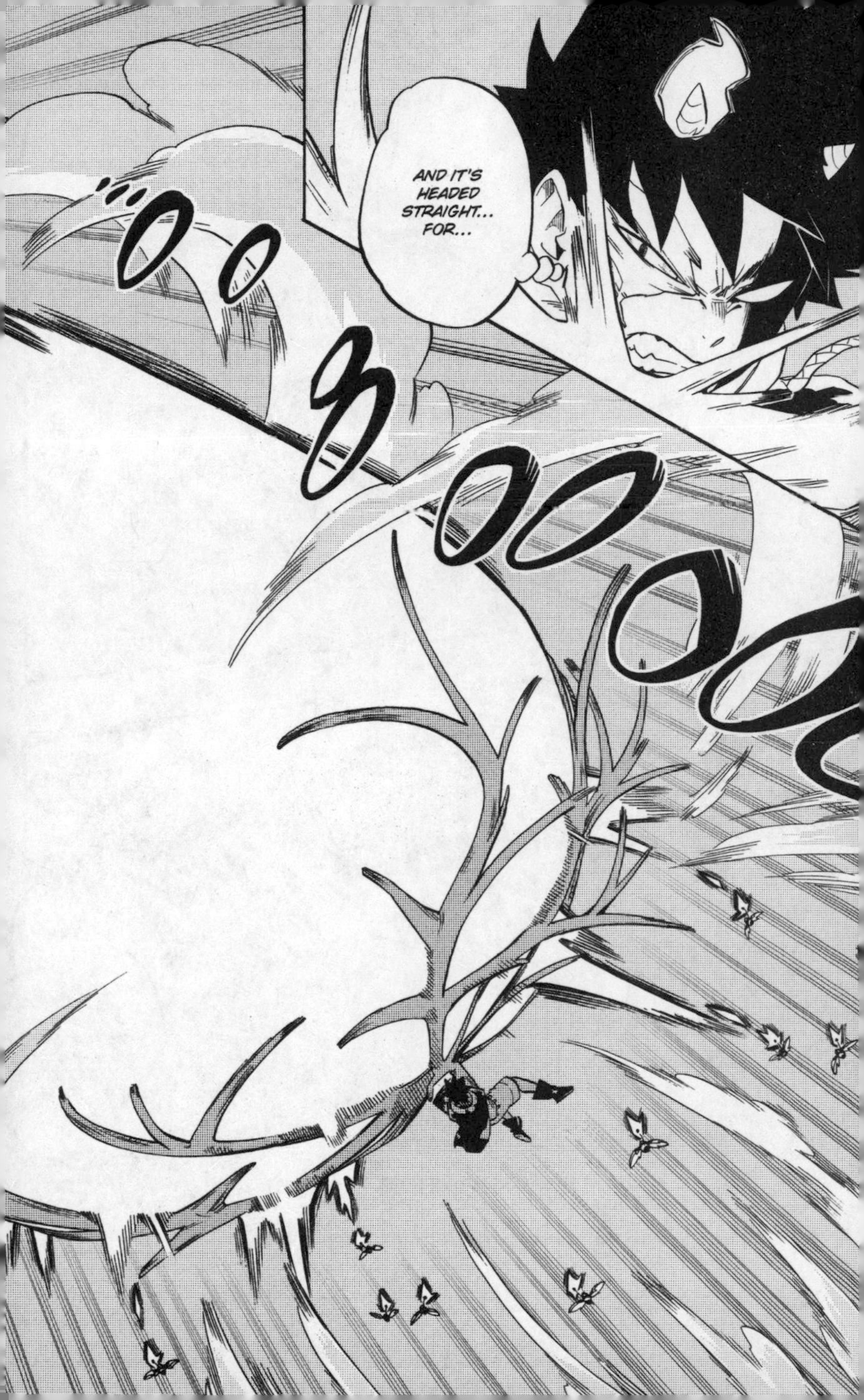
AND IT'S HEADED STRAIGHT... FOR...
DOOOOOOO

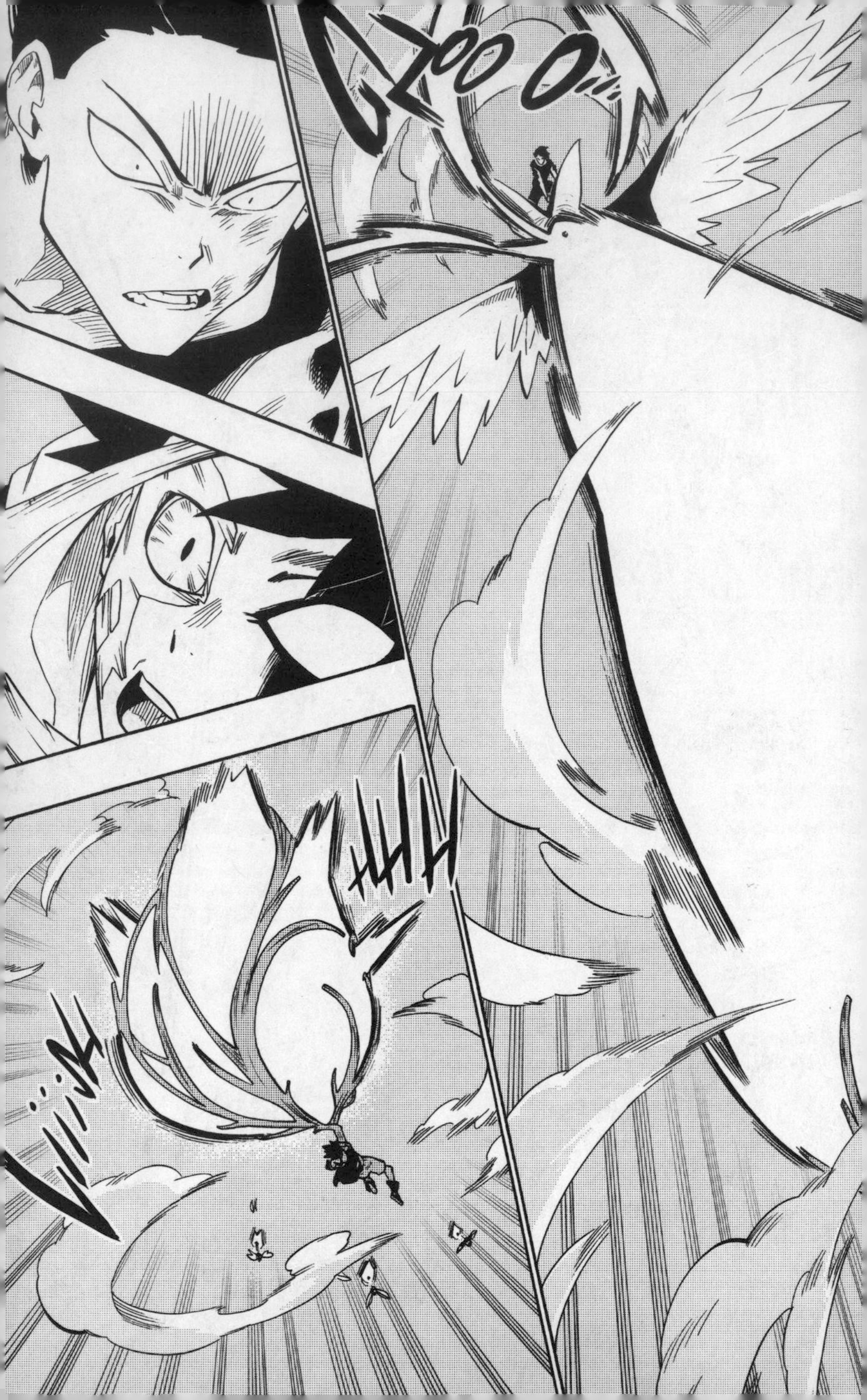
GZOOO...

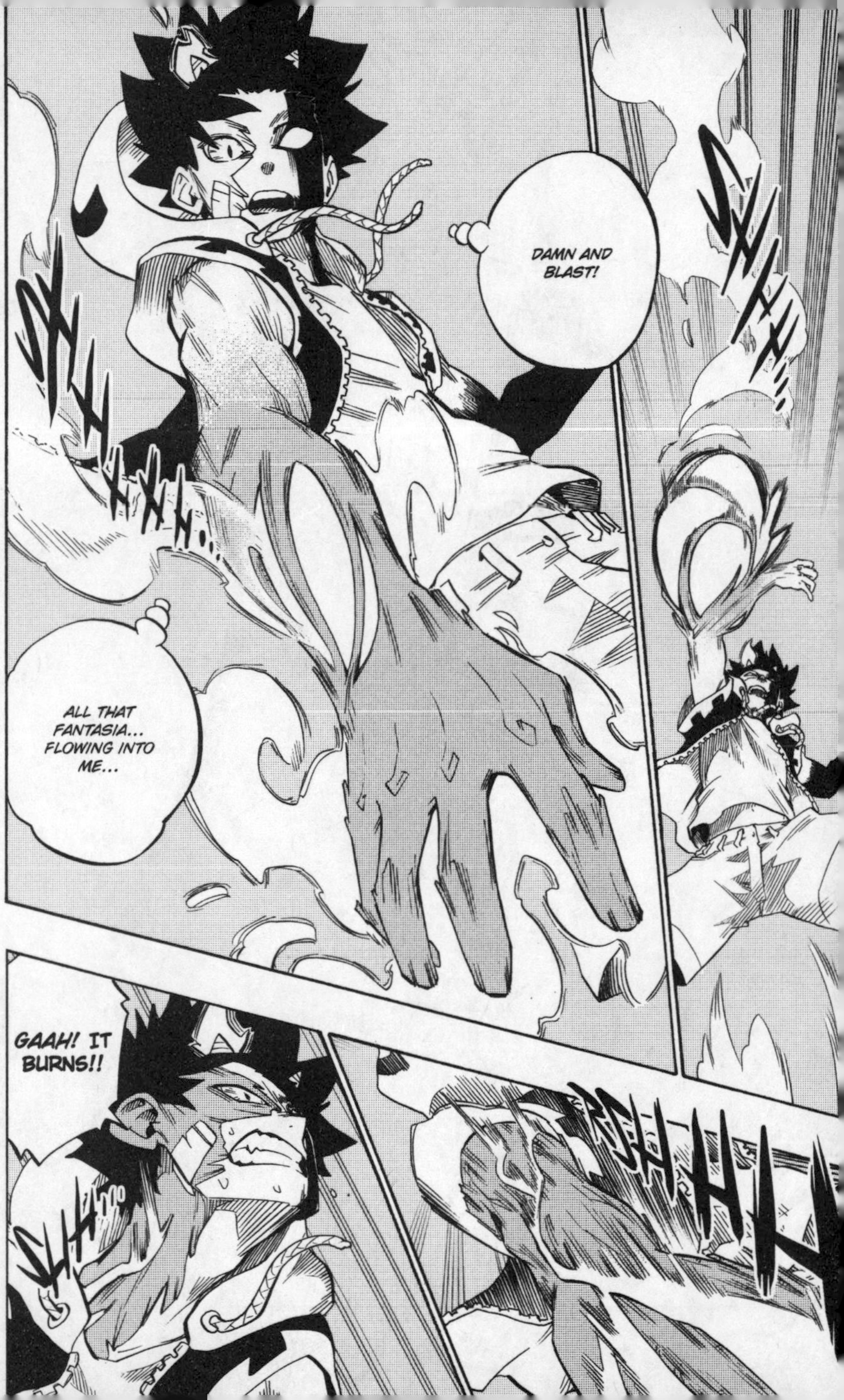
DAMN AND BLAST!
ALL THAT FANTASIA... FLOWING INTO ME...
GAAH! IT BURNS!!

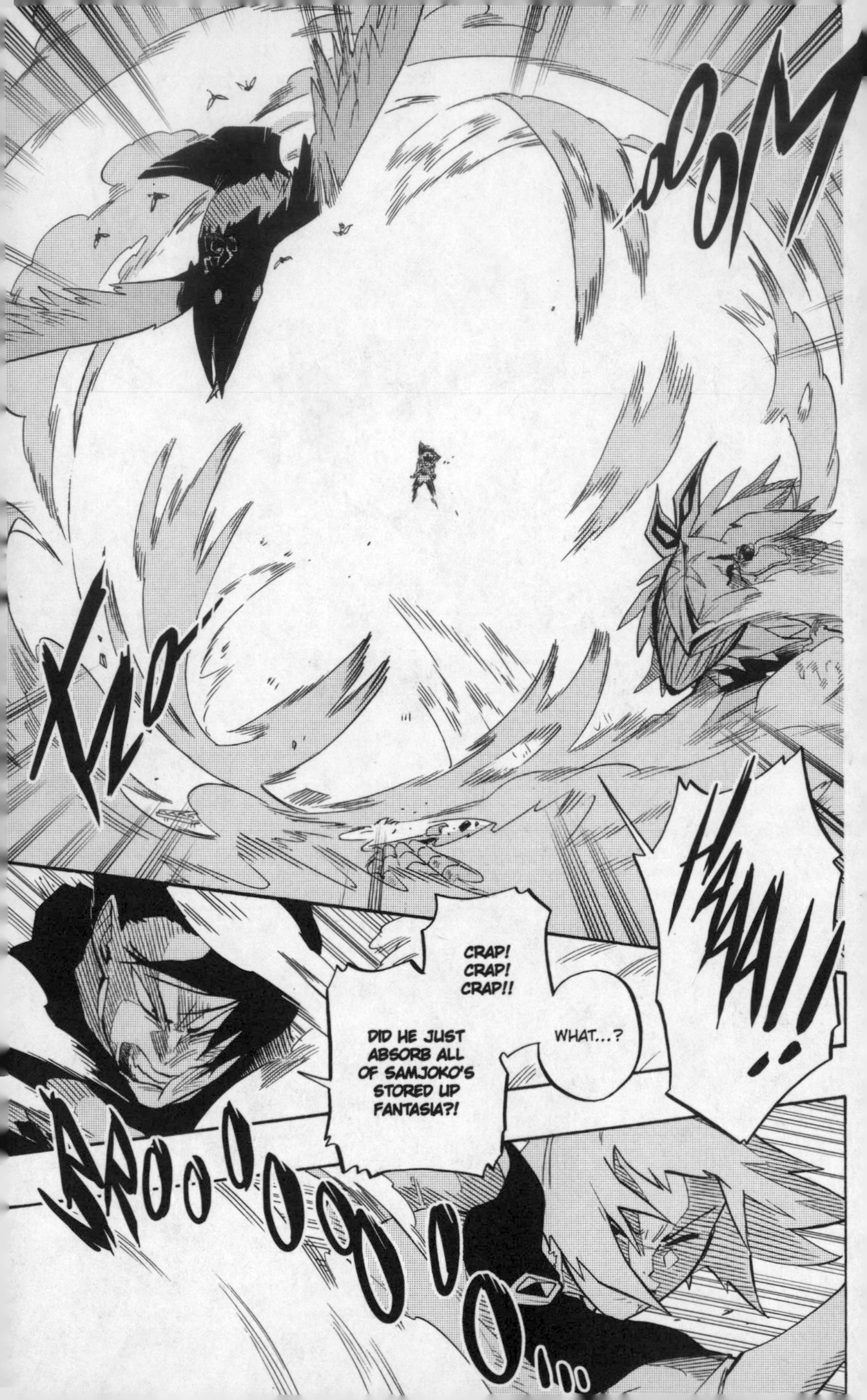
WHAT...?
CRAP! CRAP! CRAP!!
DID HE JUST ABSORB ALL OF SAMJOKO'S STORED UP FANTASIA?!

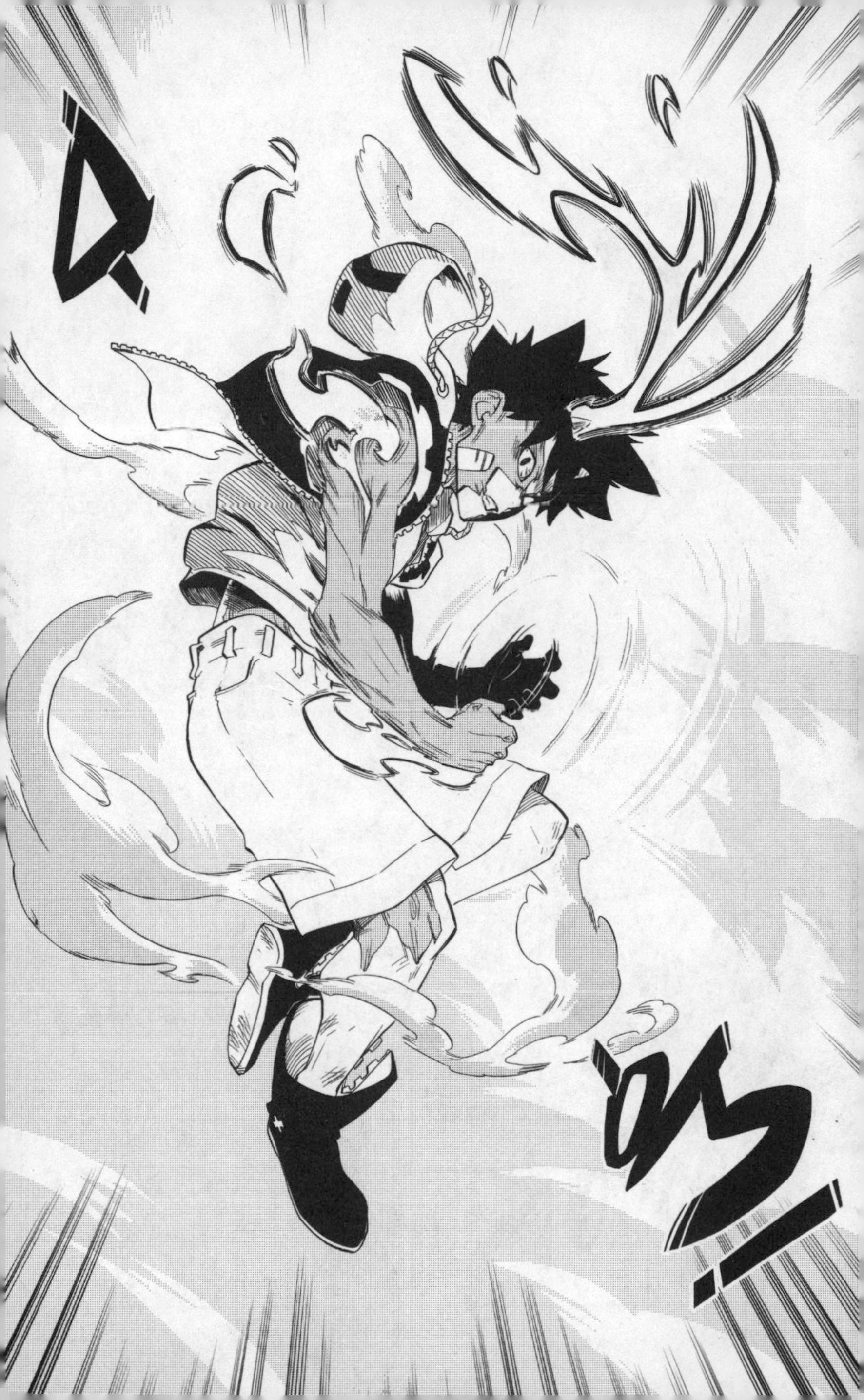

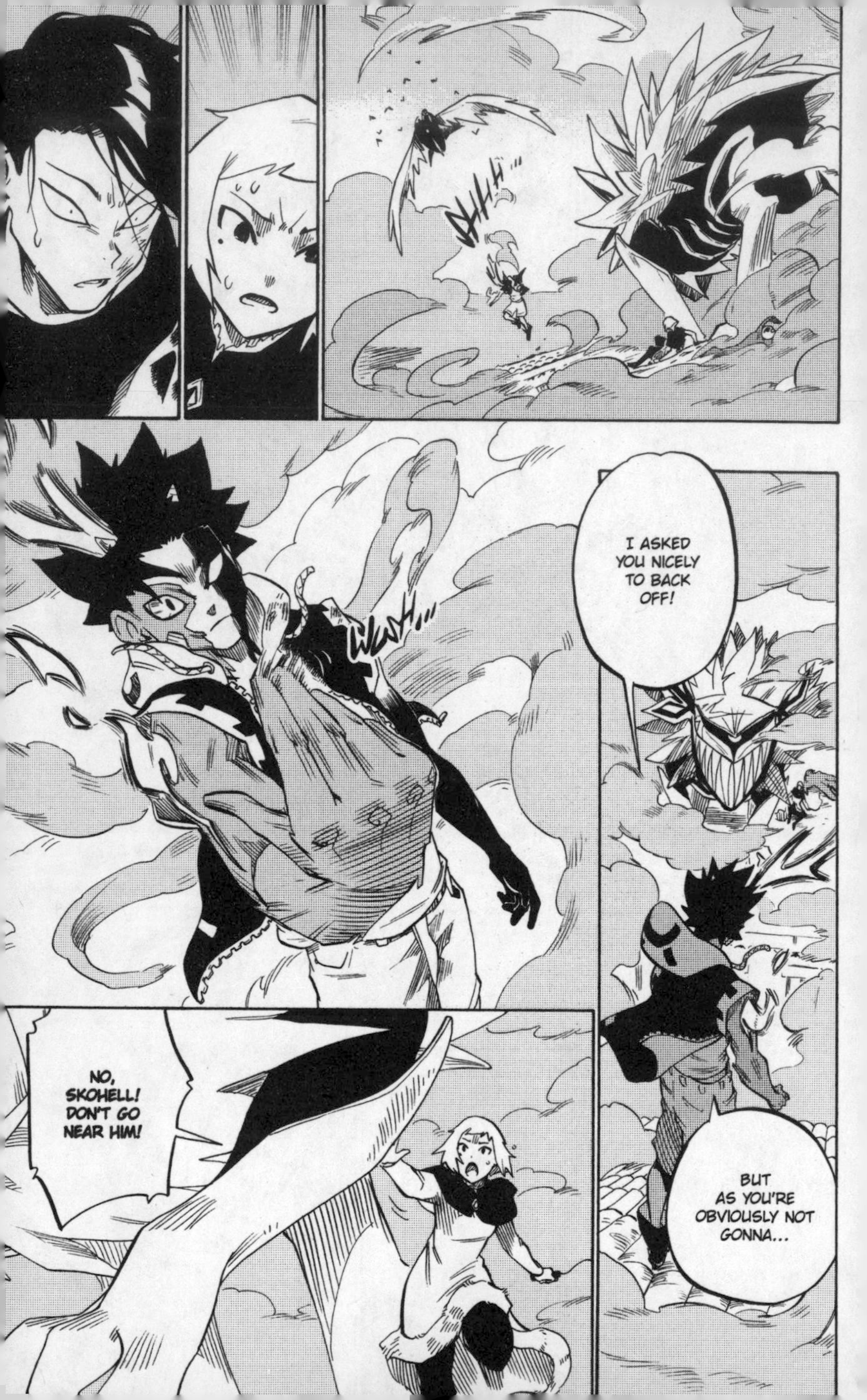
I ASKED YOU NICELY TO BACK OFF!
BUT AS YOU'RE OBVIOUSLY NOT GONNA...
NO, SKOHELL! DON'T GO NEAR HIM!

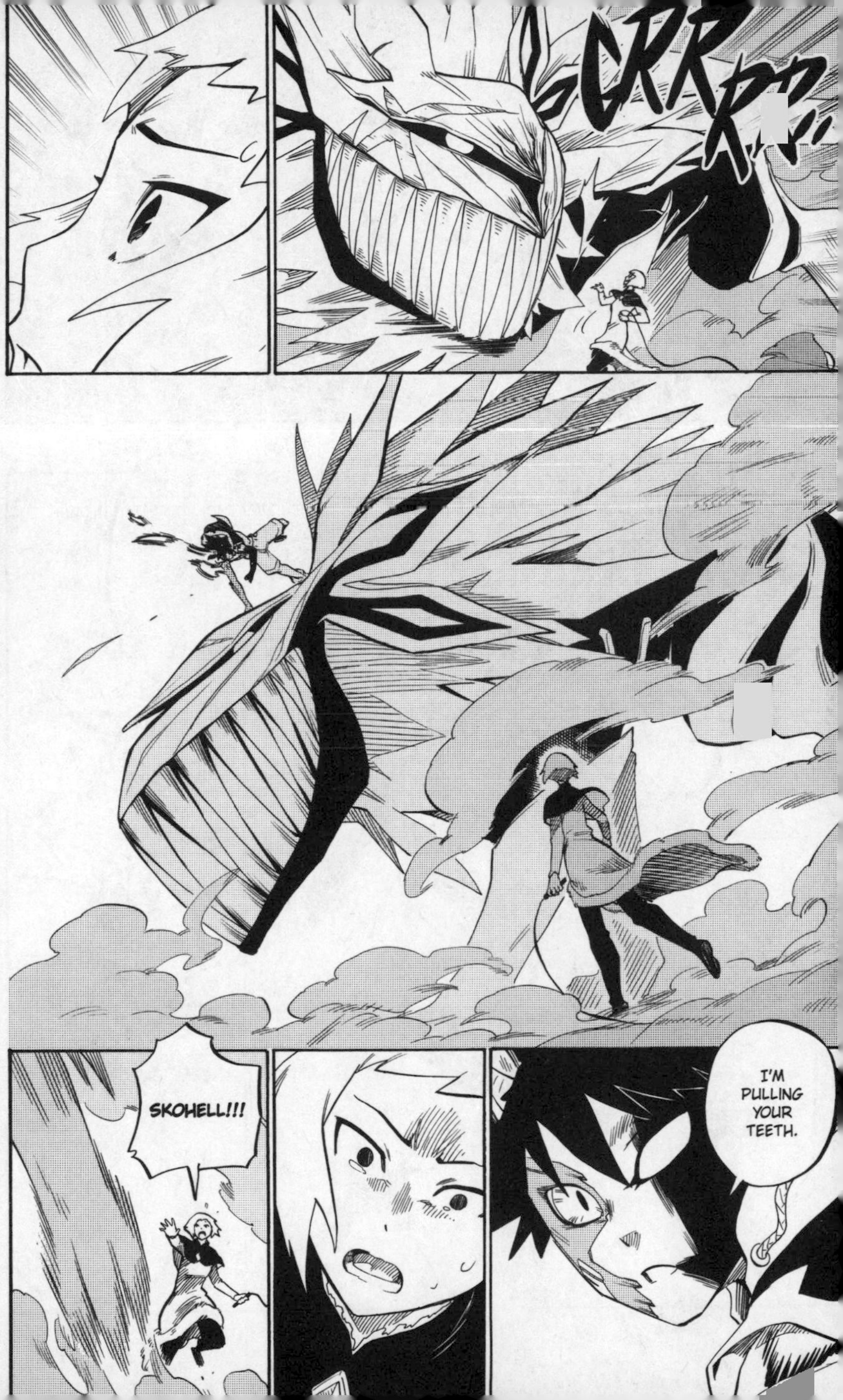
SCRRRR
I'M PULLING YOUR TEETH.
SKOHELL!!!

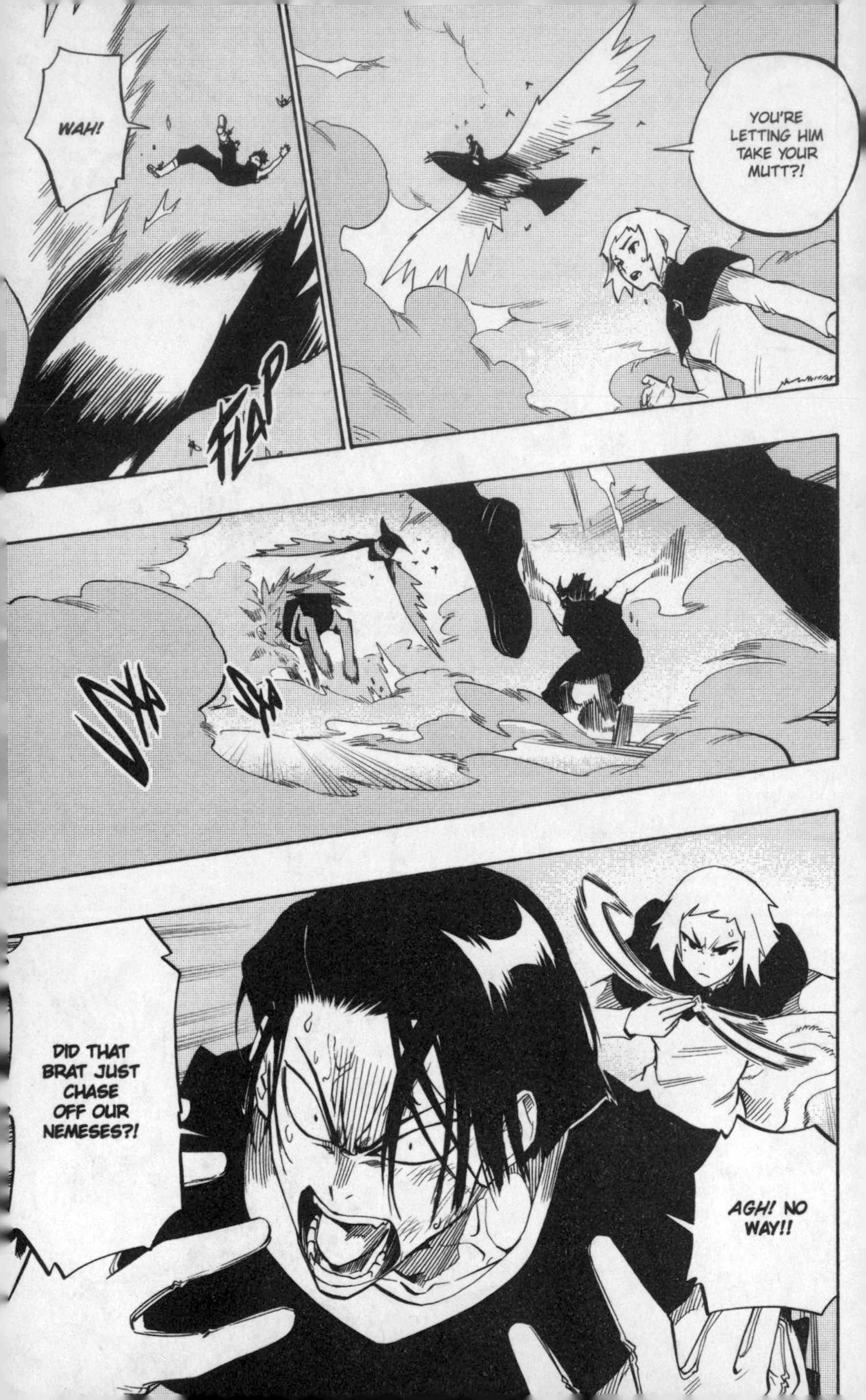
YOU'RE LETTING HIM TAKE YOUR MUTT?!
WAH!
FLAP
DID THAT BRAT JUST CHASE OFF OUR NEMESES?!
AGH! NO WAY!!

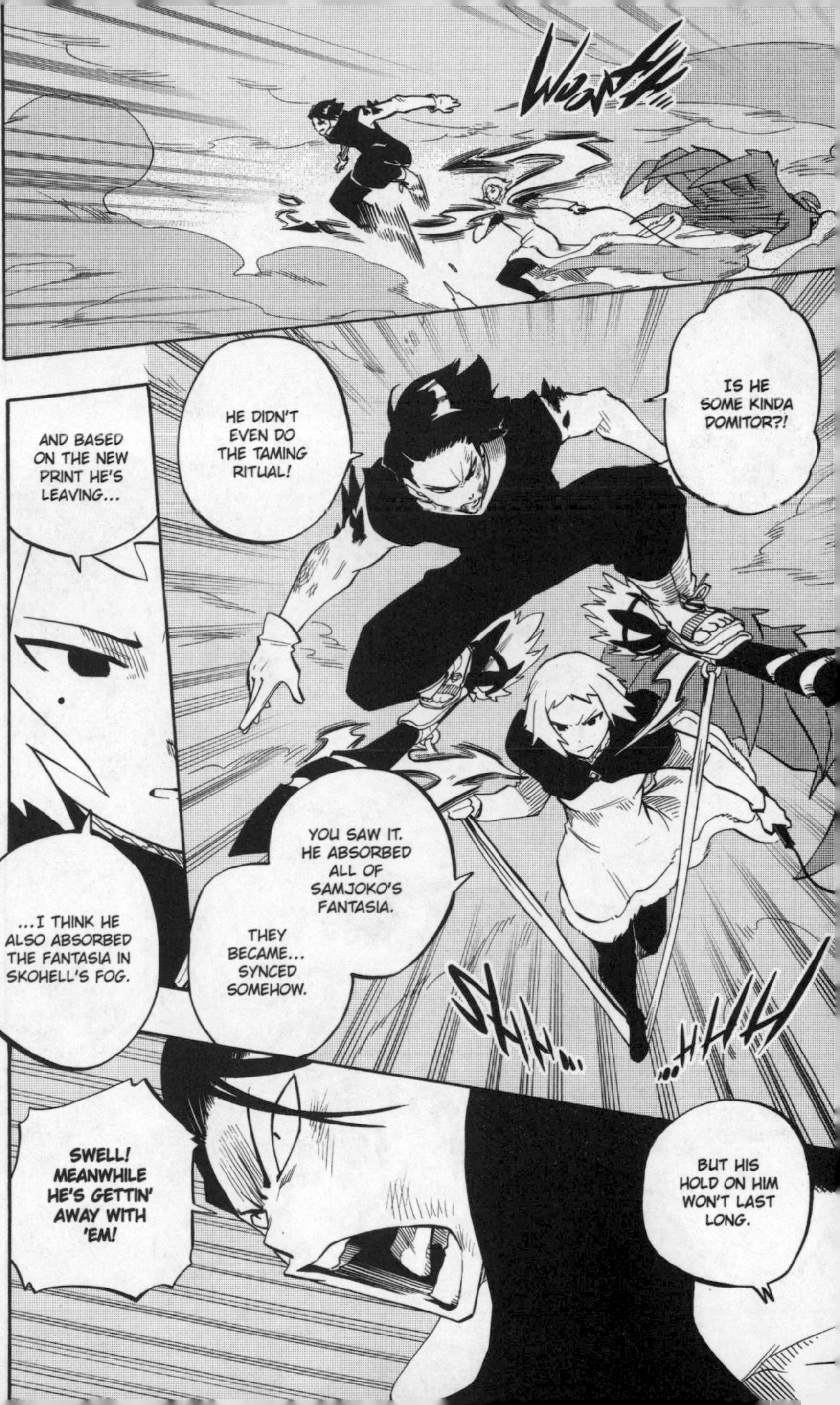
IS HE SOME KINDA DOMITOR?!
HE DIDN'T EVEN DO THE TAMING RITUAL!
YOU SAW IT. HE ABSORBED ALL OF SAMJOKO'S FANTASIA.
THEY BECAME... SYNCED SOMEHOW.
AND BASED ON THE NEW PRINT HE'S LEAVING...
...I THINK HE ALSO ABSORBED THE FANTASIA IN SKOHELL'S FOG.
BUT HIS HOLD ON HIM WON'T LAST LONG.
SWELL! MEANWHILE HE'S GETTIN' AWAY WITH 'EM!

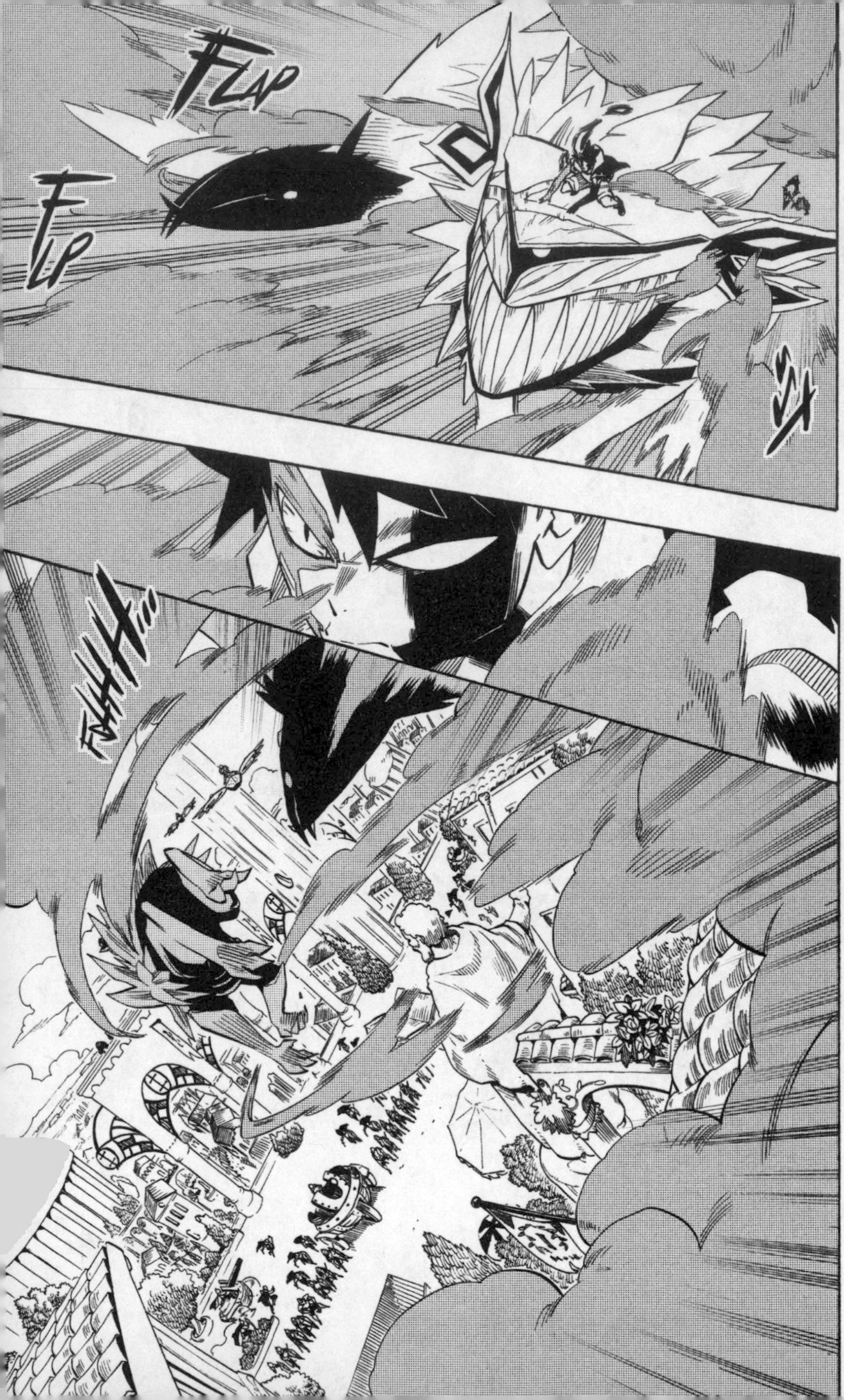
FLAP
FLAP
SSH
FWHHH!!!

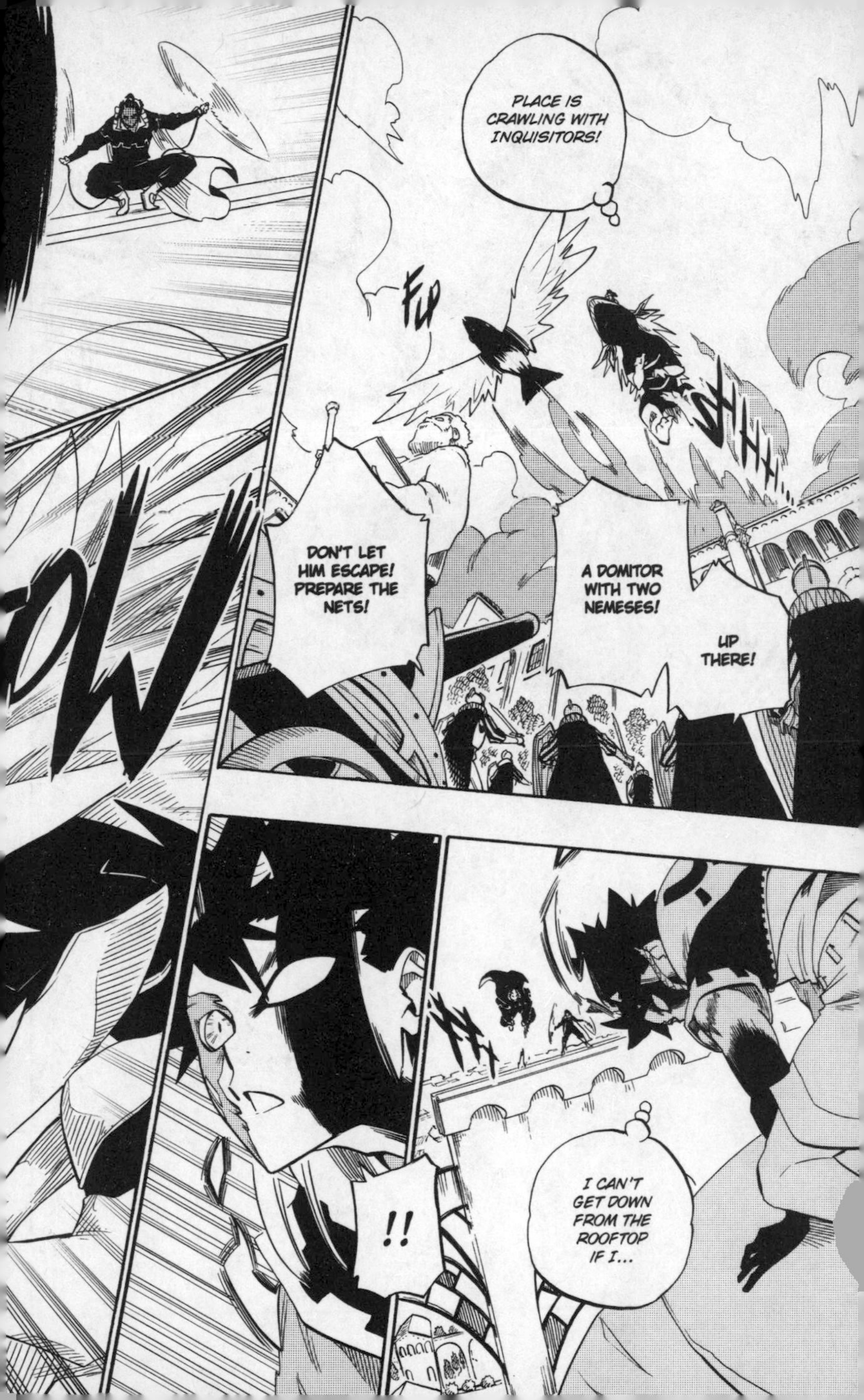
PLACE IS CRAWLING WITH INQUISITORS!
UP THERE!
A DOMITOR WITH TWO NEMESES!
DON'T LET HIM ESCAPE! PREPARE THE NETS!
I CAN'T GET DOWN FROM THE ROOFTOP IF I...
!!

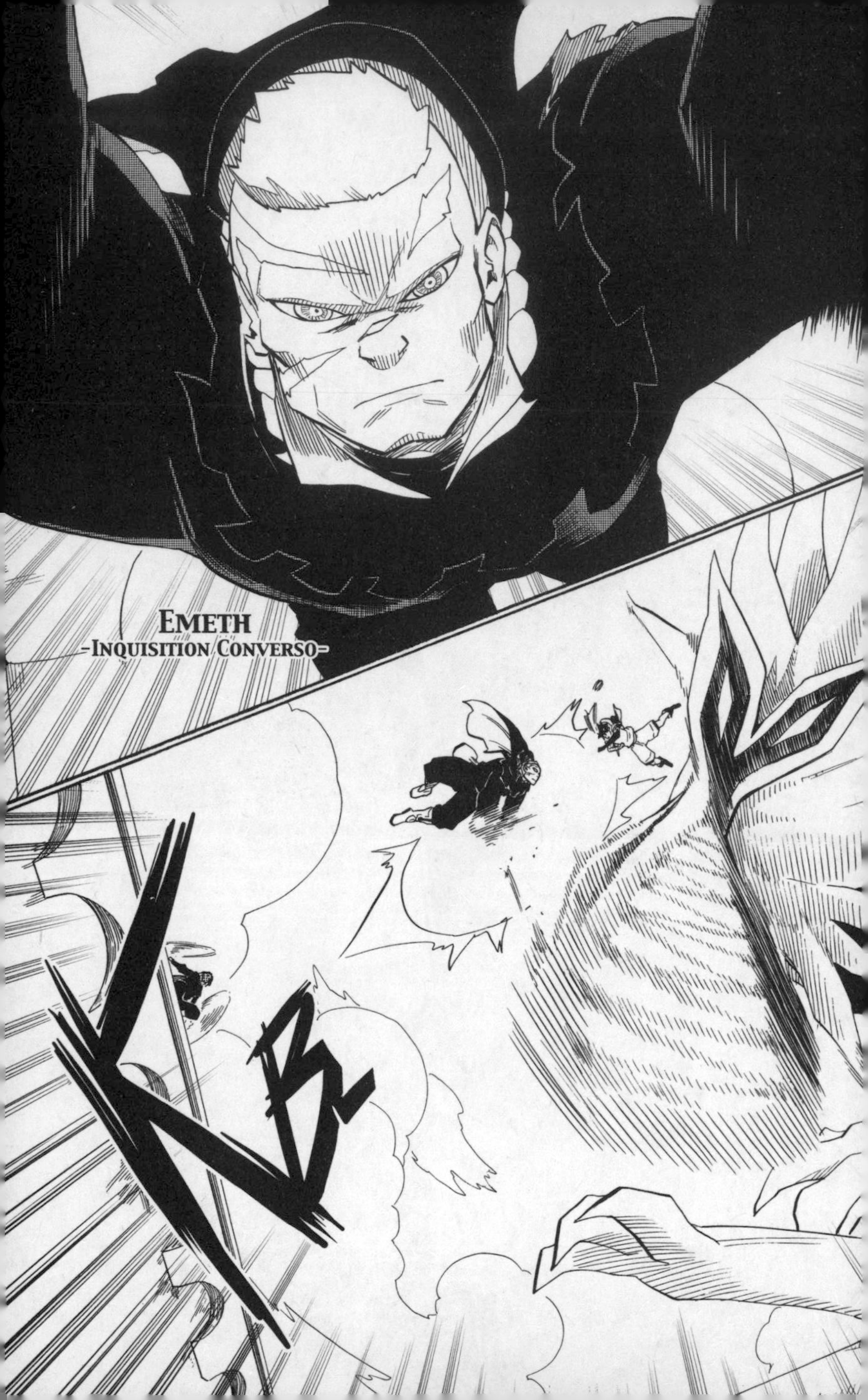
EMETH
-INQUISITION CONVERSO-

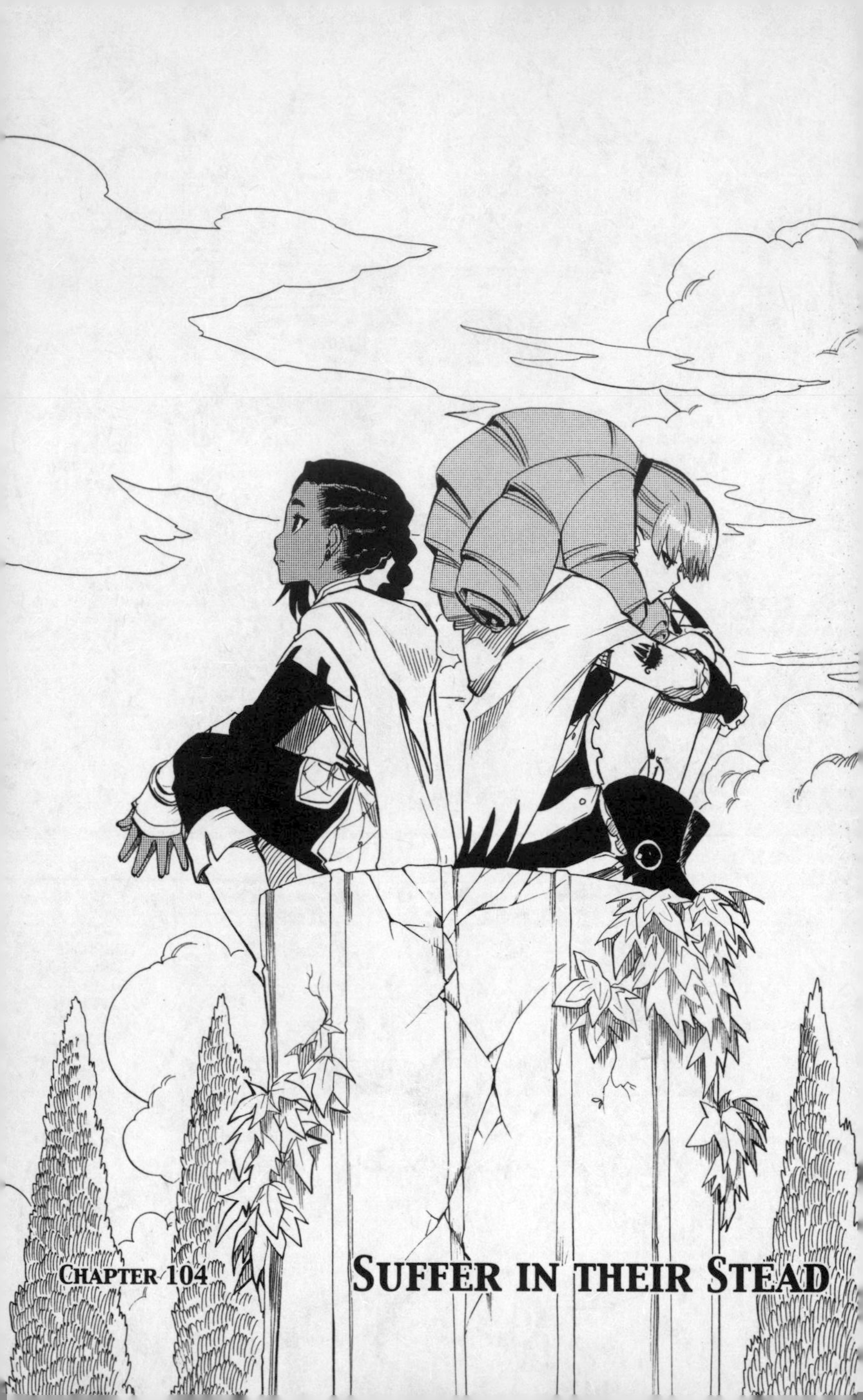

Chapter 104 Suffer in their Stead

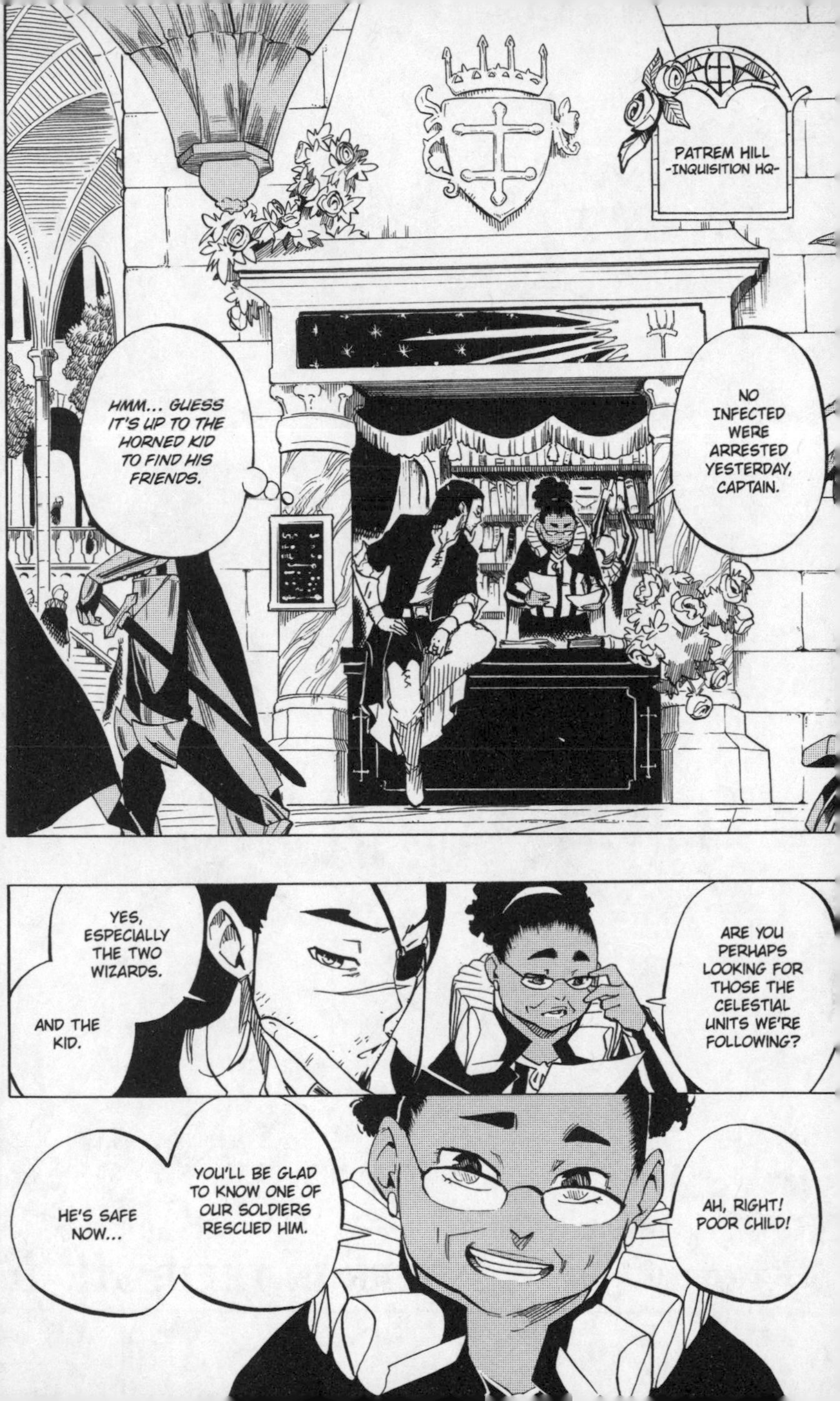
PATREM HILL
-INQUISITION HQ-
NO INFECTED WERE ARRESTED YESTERDAY, CAPTAIN.
HMM... GUESS IT'S UP TO THE HORNED KID TO FIND HIS FRIENDS.
ARE YOU PERHAPS LOOKING FOR THOSE THE CELESTIAL UNITS WE'RE FOLLOWING?
YES, ESPECIALLY THE TWO WIZARDS.
AND THE KID.
AH, RIGHT! POOR CHILD!
YOU'LL BE GLAD TO KNOW ONE OF OUR SOLDIERS RESCUED HIM.
HE'S SAFE NOW...

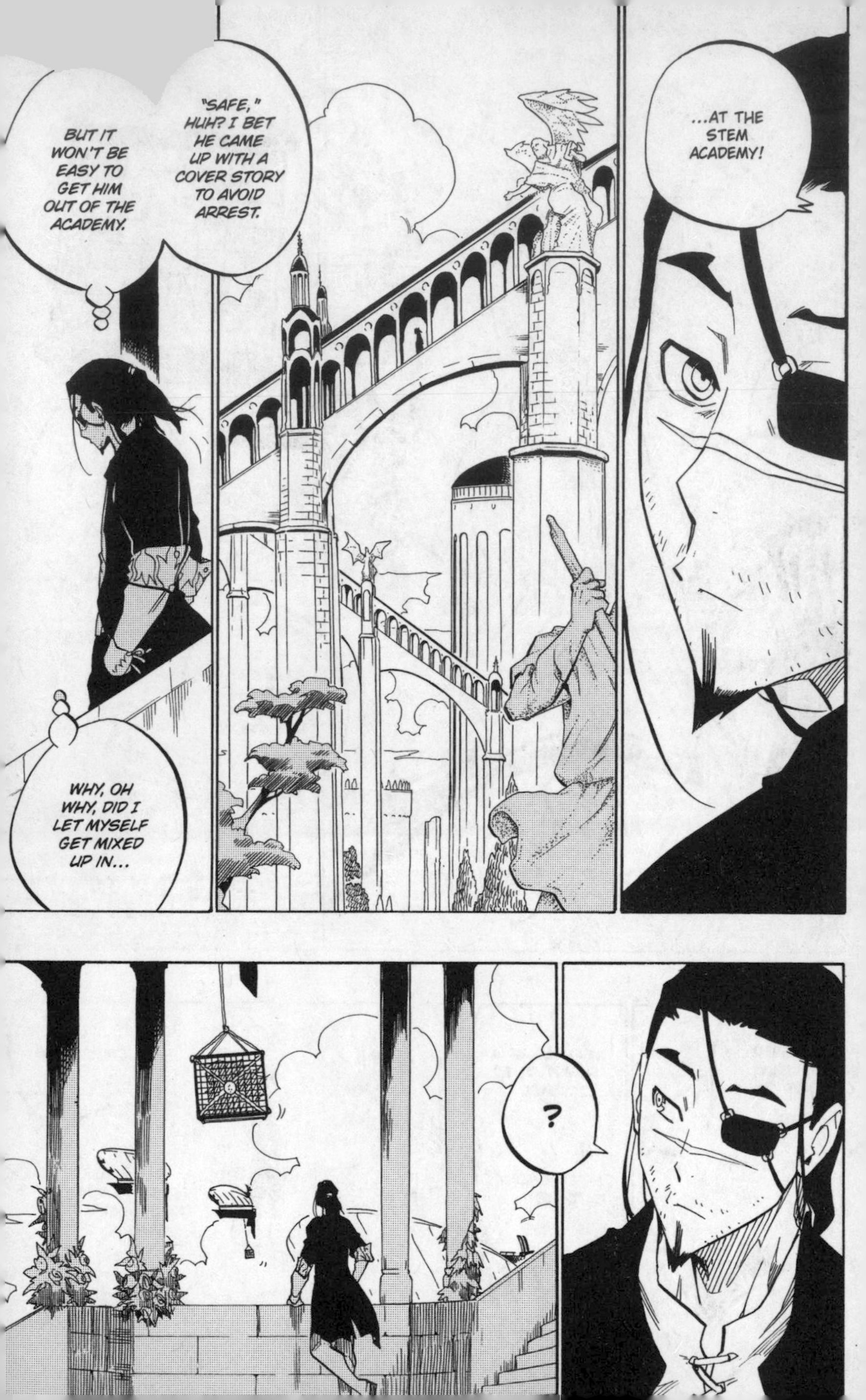
"SAFE," HUH? I BET HE CAME UP WITH A COVER STORY TO AVOID ARREST.
BUT IT WON'T BE EASY TO GET HIM OUT OF THE ACADEMY.
WHY, OH WHY, DID I LET MYSELF GET MIXED UP IN...
...AT THE STEM ACADEMY!
?

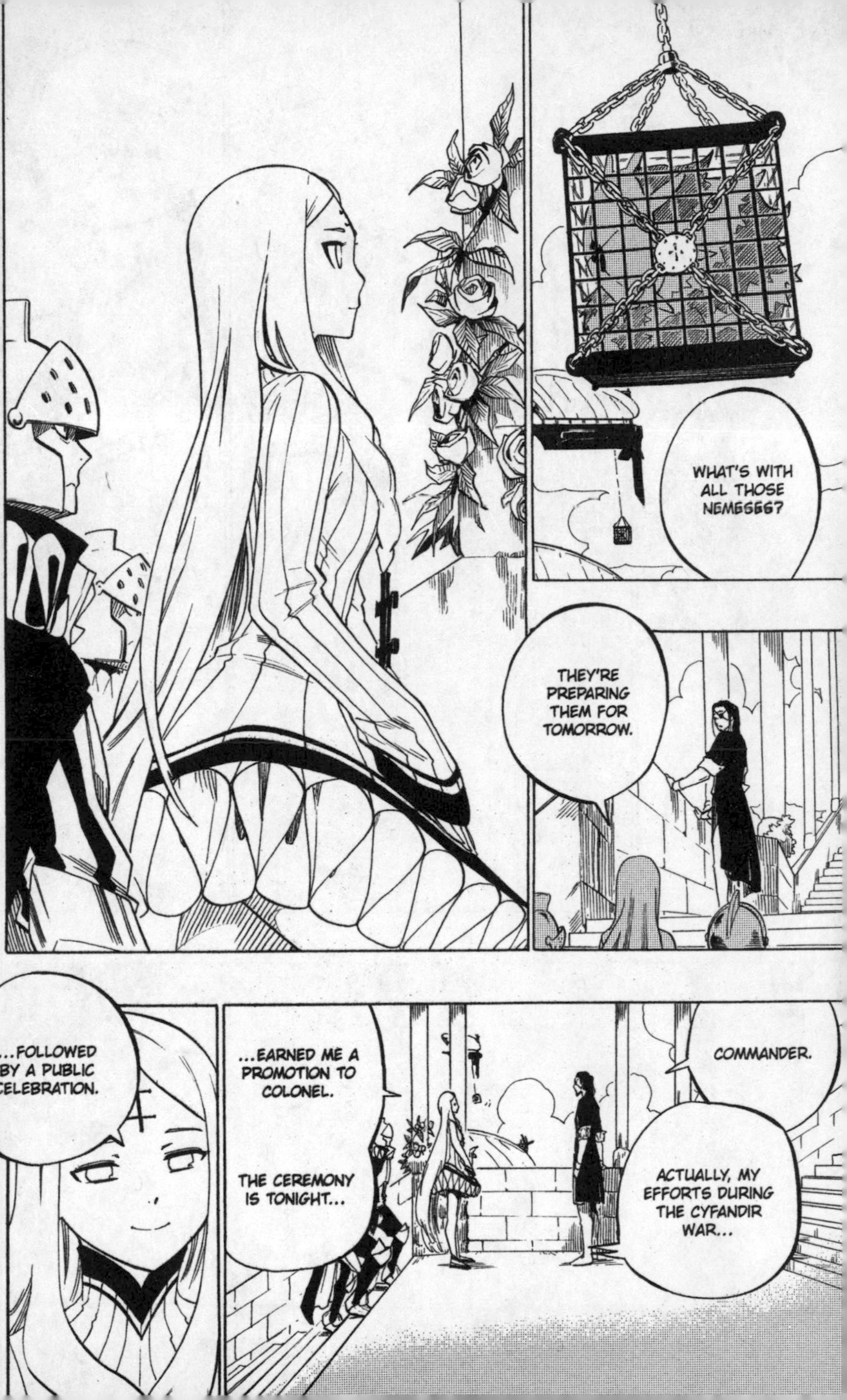
WHAT'S WITH ALL THOSE NEMESES?
THEY'RE PREPARING THEM FOR TOMORROW.
COMMANDER.
ACTUALLY, MY EFFORTS DURING THE CYFANDIR WAR...
...EARNED ME A PROMOTION TO COLONEL.
THE CEREMONY IS TONIGHT...
...FOLLOWED BY A PUBLIC CELEBRATION.

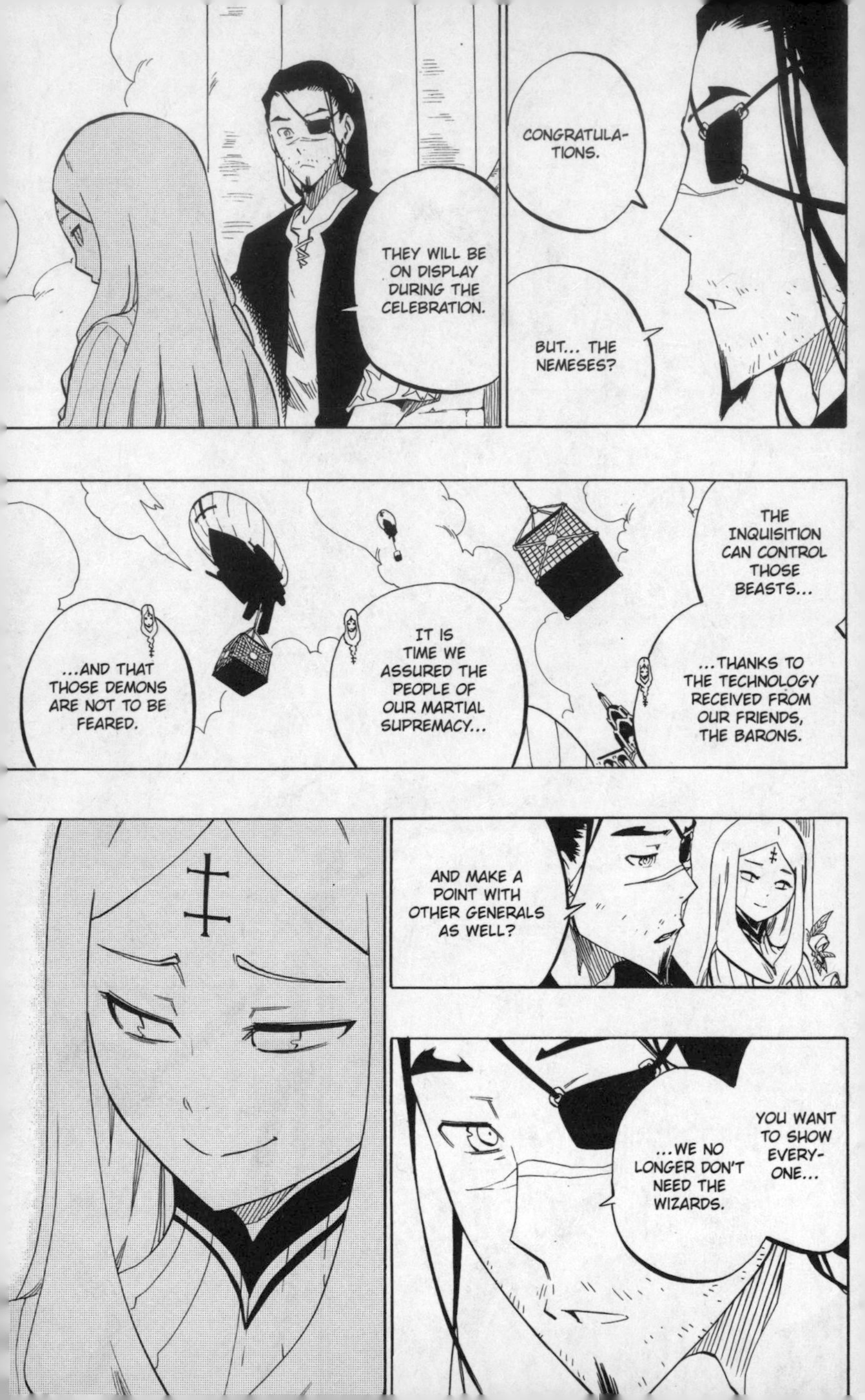
CONGRATULATIONS.
BUT... THE NEMESES?
THEY WILL BE ON DISPLAY DURING THE CELEBRATION.
THE INQUISITION CAN CONTROL THOSE BEASTS...
...THANKS TO THE TECHNOLOGY RECEIVED FROM OUR FRIENDS, THE BARONS.
IT IS TIME WE ASSURED THE PEOPLE OF OUR MARTIAL SUPREMACY...
...AND THAT THOSE DEMONS ARE NOT TO BE FEARED.
AND MAKE A POINT WITH OTHER GENERALS AS WELL?
YOU WANT TO SHOW EVERYONE...
...WE NO LONGER DON'T NEED THE WIZARDS.

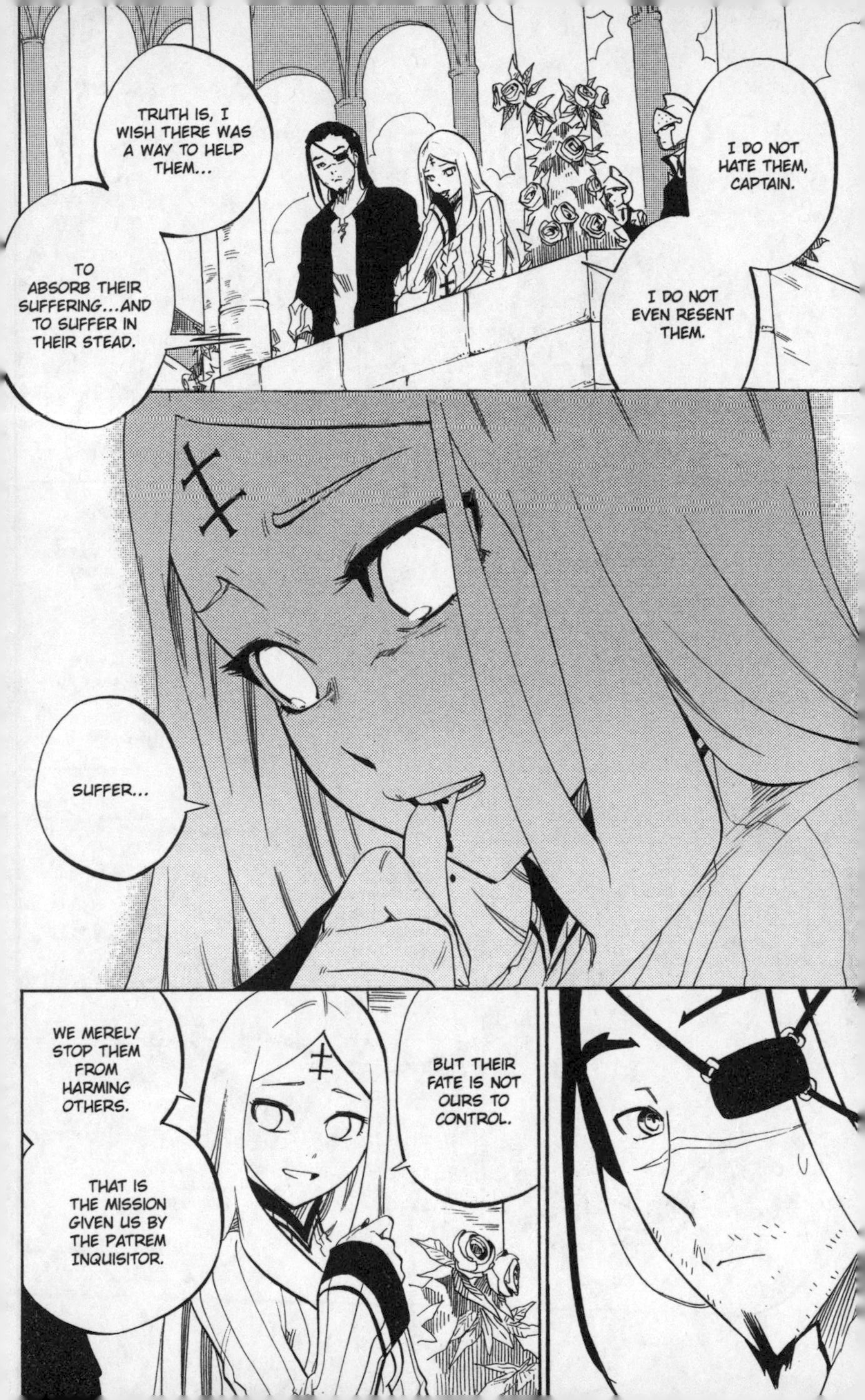
I DO NOT HATE THEM, CAPTAIN.
I DO NOT EVEN RESENT THEM.
TRUTH IS, I WISH THERE WAS A WAY TO HELP THEM...
TO ABSORB THEIR SUFFERING...AND TO SUFFER IN THEIR STEAD.
SUFFER...
BUT THEIR FATE IS NOT OURS TO CONTROL.
WE MERELY STOP THEM FROM HARMING OTHERS.
THAT IS THE MISSION GIVEN US BY THE PATREM INQUISITOR.

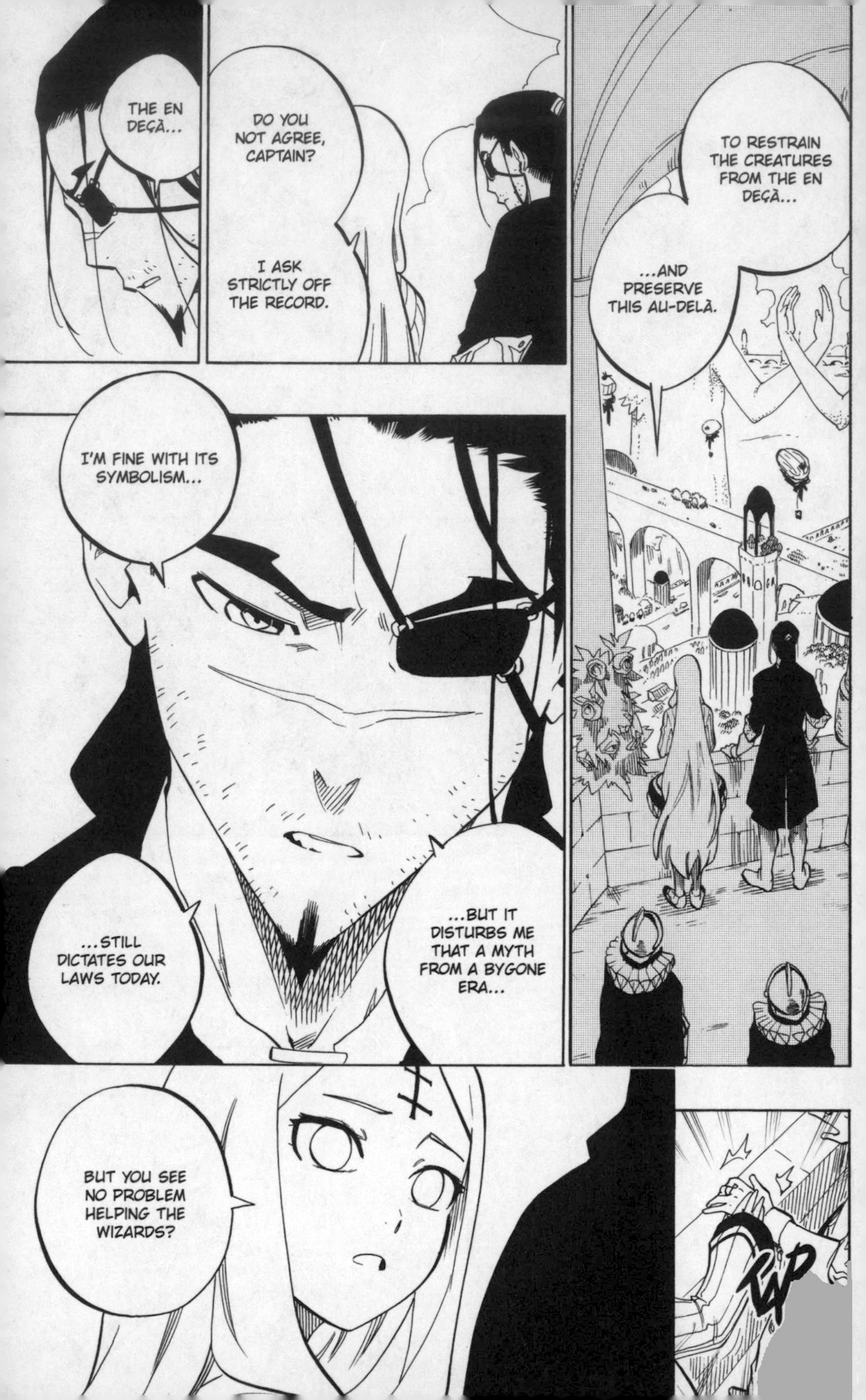
TO RESTRAIN THE CREATURES FROM THE EN DEÇÀ...
...AND PRESERVE THIS AU-DELÀ.
DO YOU NOT AGREE, CAPTAIN?
I ASK STRICTLY OFF THE RECORD.
THE EN DEÇÀ...
I'M FINE WITH ITS SYMBOLISM...
...BUT IT DISTURBS ME THAT A MYTH FROM A BYGONE ERA...
...STILL DICTATES OUR LAWS TODAY.
BUT YOU SEE NO PROBLEM HELPING THE WIZARDS?

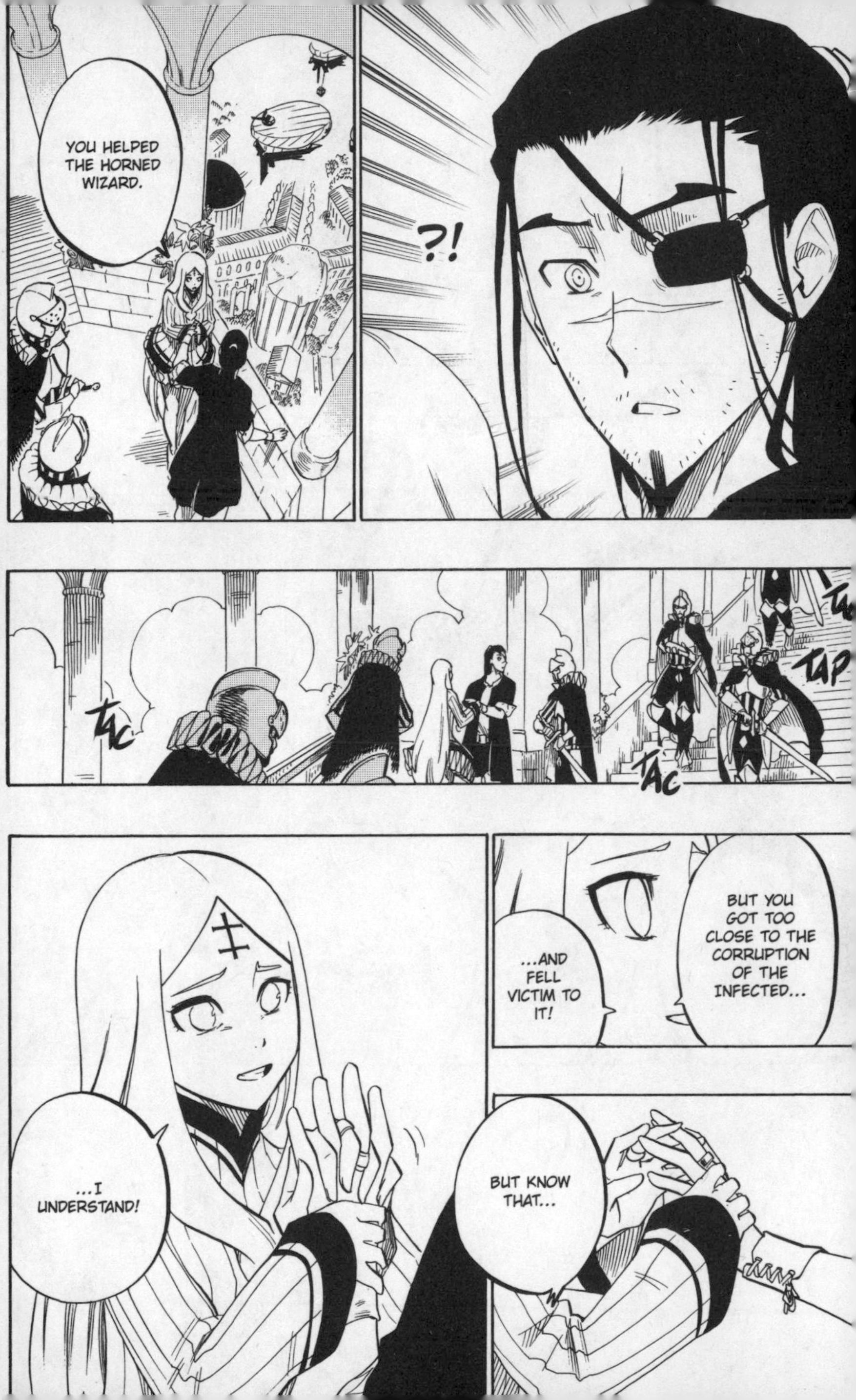
?!
YOU HELPED THE HORNED WIZARD.
TAP
TAC
TAC
BUT YOU GOT TOO CLOSE TO THE CORRUPTION OF THE INFECTED...
...AND FELL VICTIM TO IT!
BUT KNOW THAT...
...I UNDERSTAND!

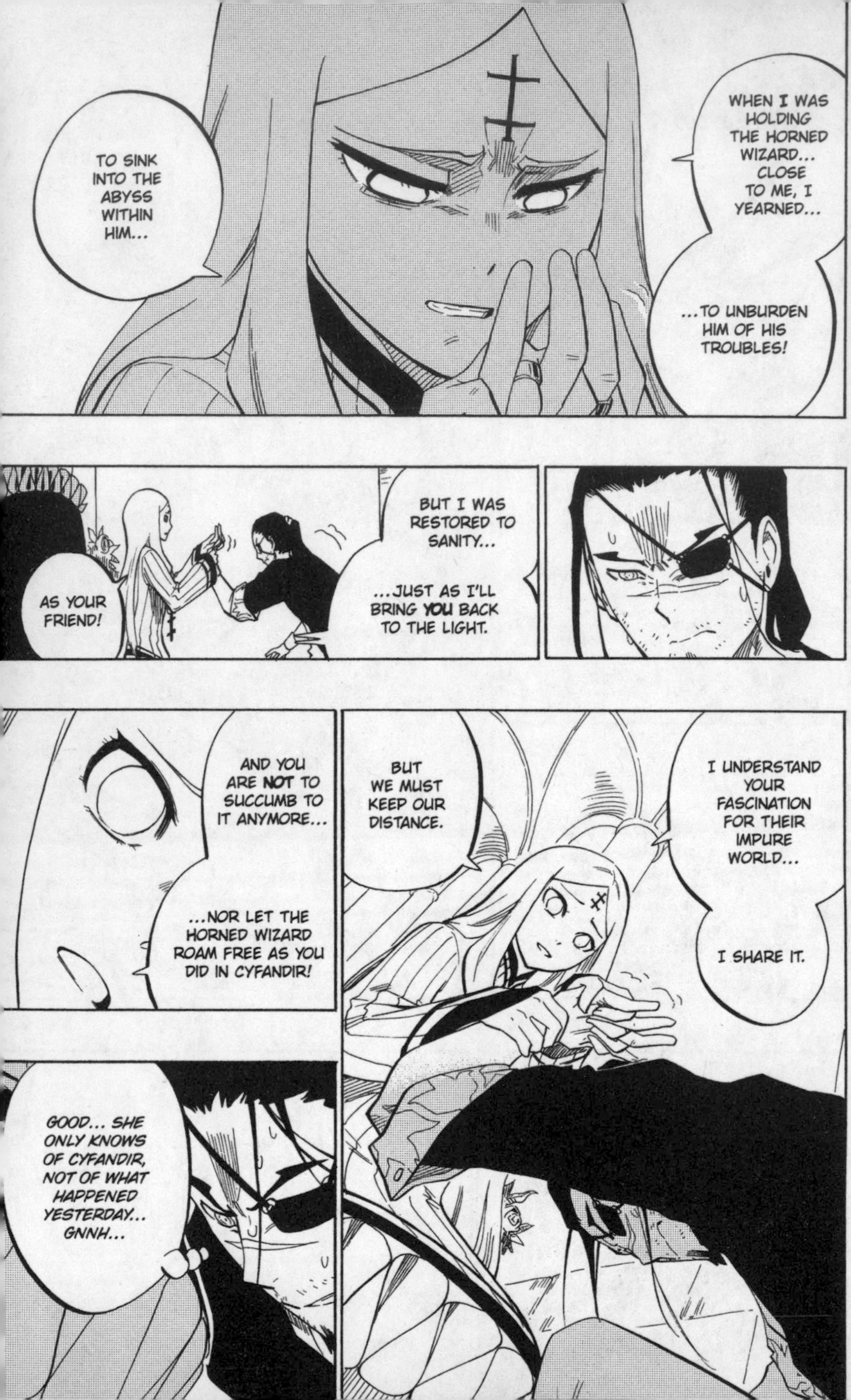
WHEN I WAS HOLDING THE HORNED WIZARD... CLOSE TO ME, I YEARNED...
...TO UNBURDEN HIM OF HIS TROUBLES!
TO SINK INTO THE ABYSS WITHIN HIM...
BUT I WAS RESTORED TO SANITY...
...JUST AS I'LL BRING **YOU** BACK TO THE LIGHT.
AS YOUR FRIEND!
I UNDERSTAND YOUR FASCINATION FOR THEIR IMPURE WORLD...
I SHARE IT.
BUT WE MUST KEEP OUR DISTANCE.
AND YOU ARE **NOT** TO SUCCUMB TO IT ANYMORE...
...NOR LET THE HORNED WIZARD ROAM FREE AS YOU DID IN CYFANDIR!
GOOD... SHE ONLY KNOWS OF CYFANDIR, NOT OF WHAT HAPPENED YESTERDAY... GNNH...

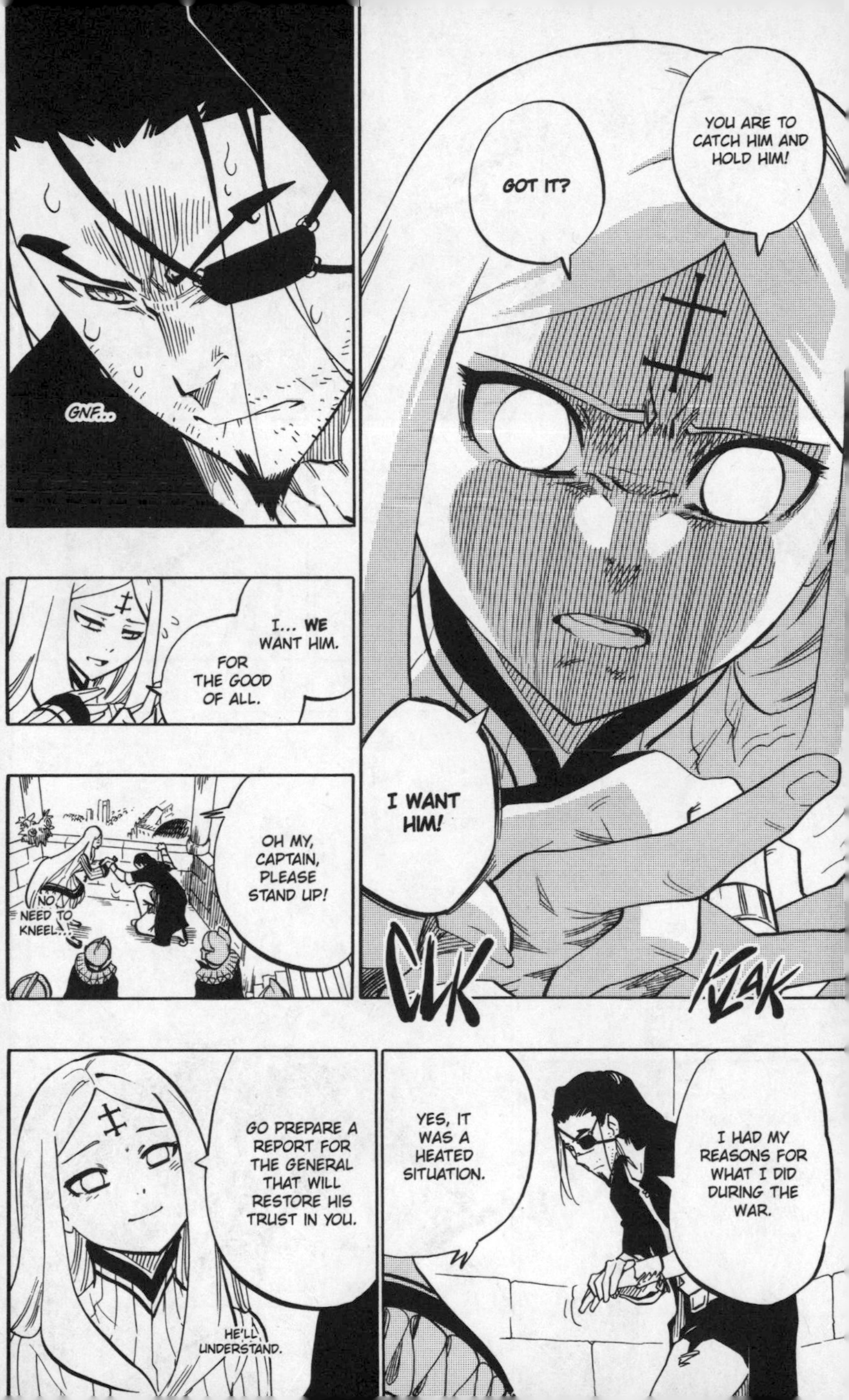
YOU ARE TO CATCH HIM AND HOLD HIM!
GOT IT?
I WANT HIM!
KLAK
CLK
GNF...
I... WE WANT HIM.
FOR THE GOOD OF ALL.
OH MY, CAPTAIN, PLEASE STAND UP!
NO NEED TO KNEEL...
I HAD MY REASONS FOR WHAT I DID DURING THE WAR.
YES, IT WAS A HEATED SITUATION.
GO PREPARE A REPORT FOR THE GENERAL THAT WILL RESTORE HIS TRUST IN YOU.
HE'LL UNDERSTAND.

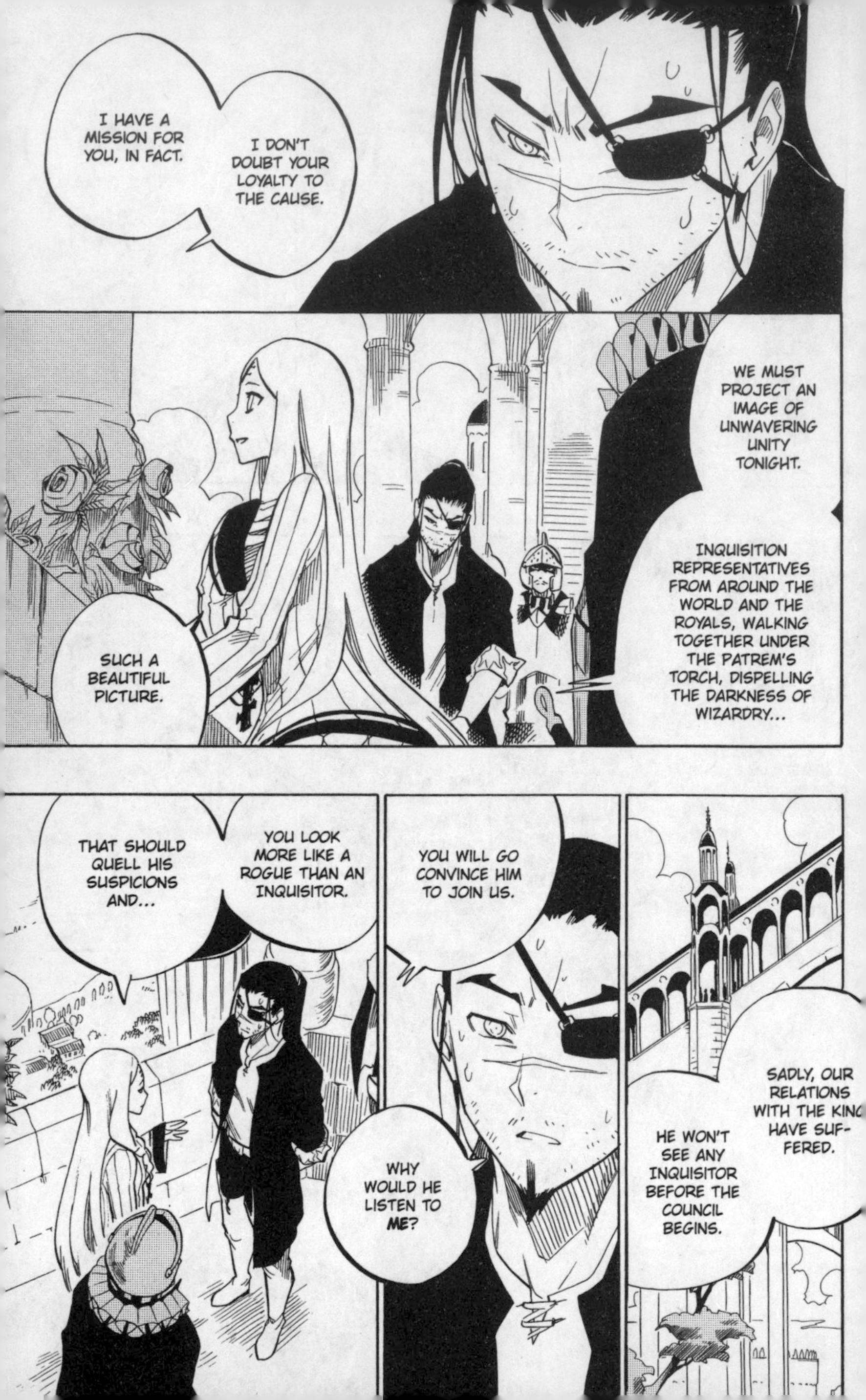
I DON'T DOUBT YOUR LOYALTY TO THE CAUSE.
I HAVE A MISSION FOR YOU, IN FACT.
WE MUST PROJECT AN IMAGE OF UNWAVERING UNITY TONIGHT.
INQUISITION REPRESENTATIVES FROM AROUND THE WORLD AND THE ROYALS, WALKING TOGETHER UNDER THE PATREM'S TORCH, DISPELLING THE DARKNESS OF WIZARDRY...
SUCH A BEAUTIFUL PICTURE.
SADLY, OUR RELATIONS WITH THE KING HAVE SUFFERED.
HE WON'T SEE ANY INQUISITOR BEFORE THE COUNCIL BEGINS.
YOU WILL GO CONVINCE HIM TO JOIN US.
WHY WOULD HE LISTEN TO *ME*?
YOU LOOK MORE LIKE A ROGUE THAN AN INQUISITOR.
THAT SHOULD QUELL HIS SUSPICIONS AND...

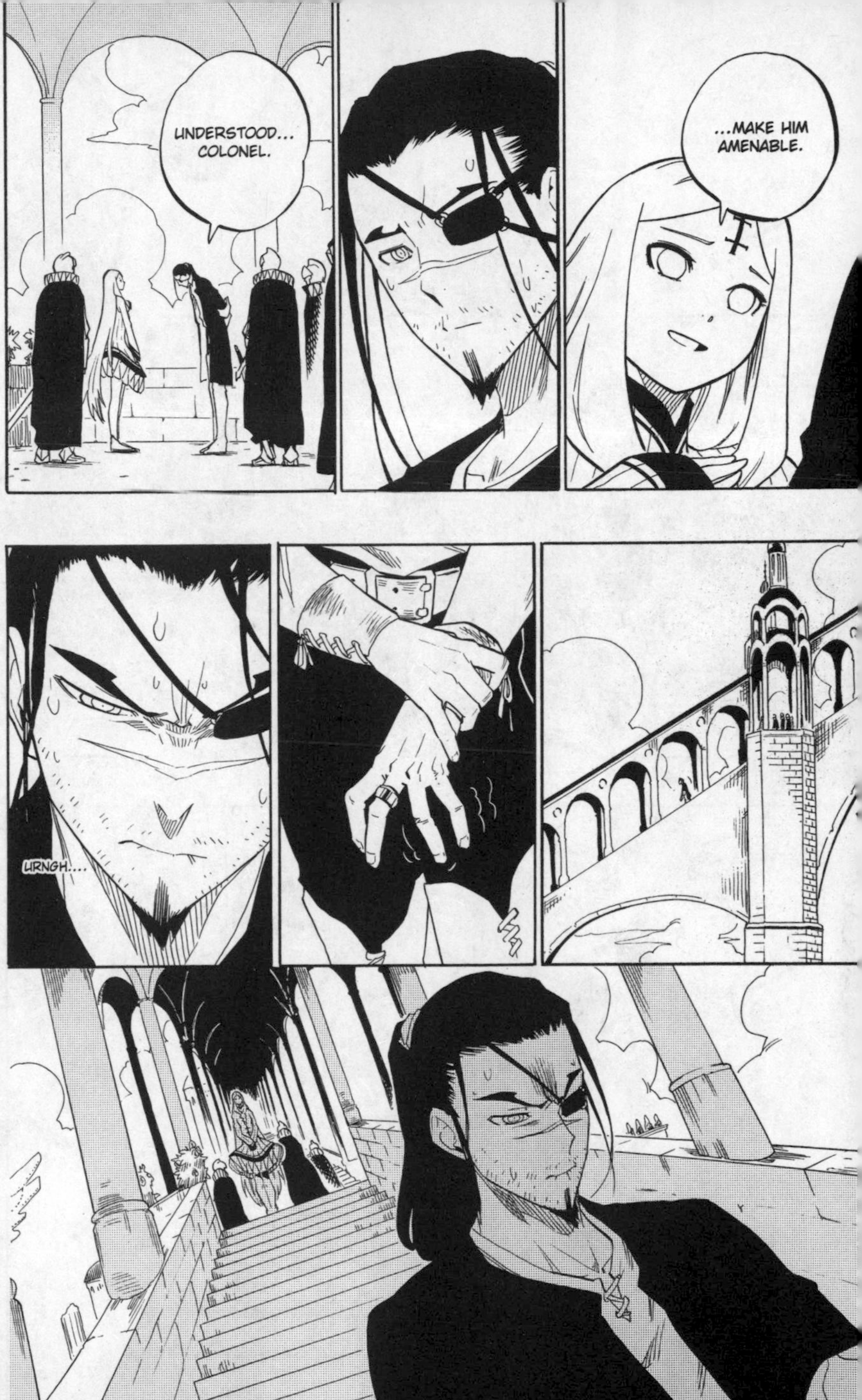
...MAKE HIM AMENABLE.
UNDERSTOOD... COLONEL.
URNGH....

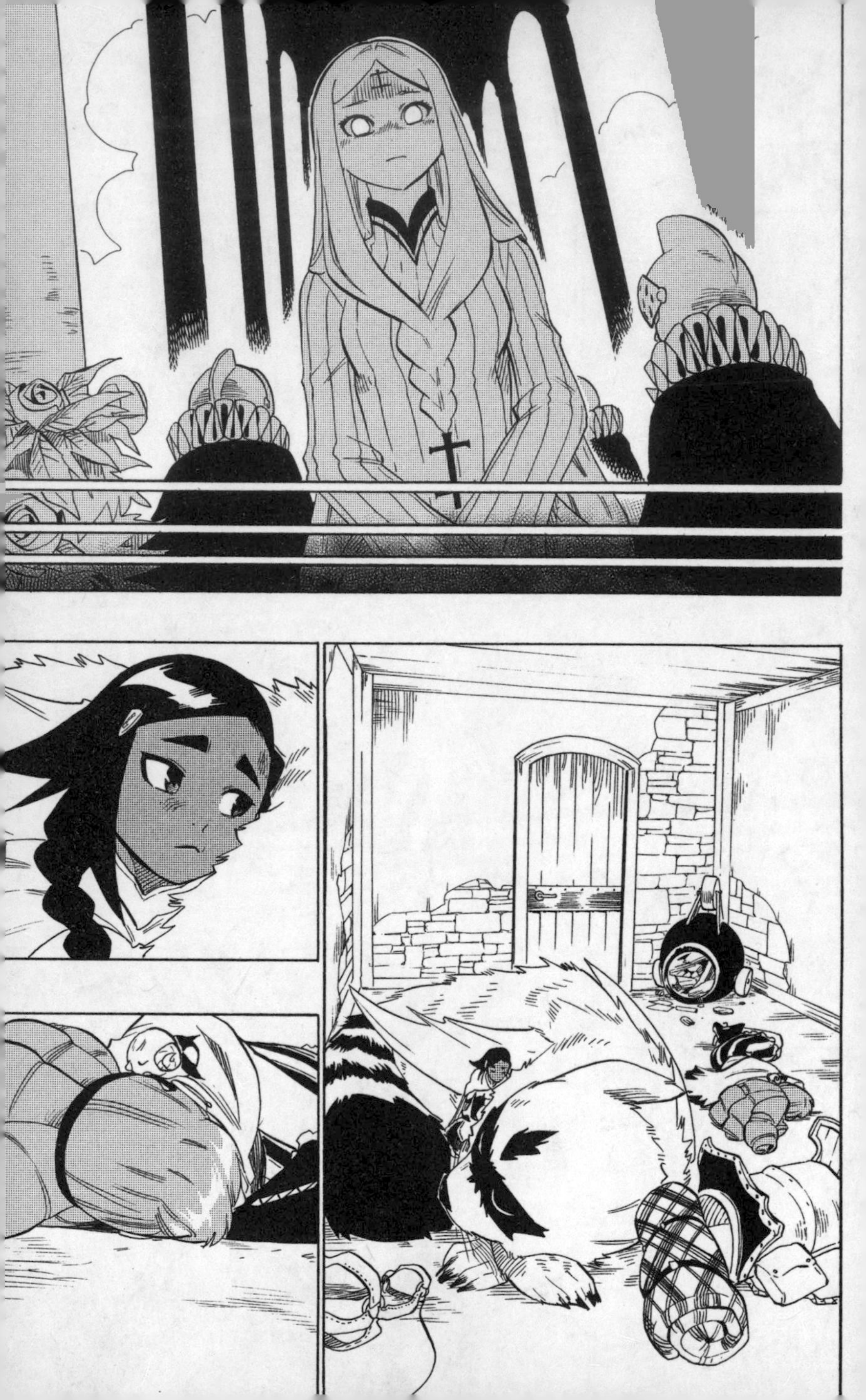

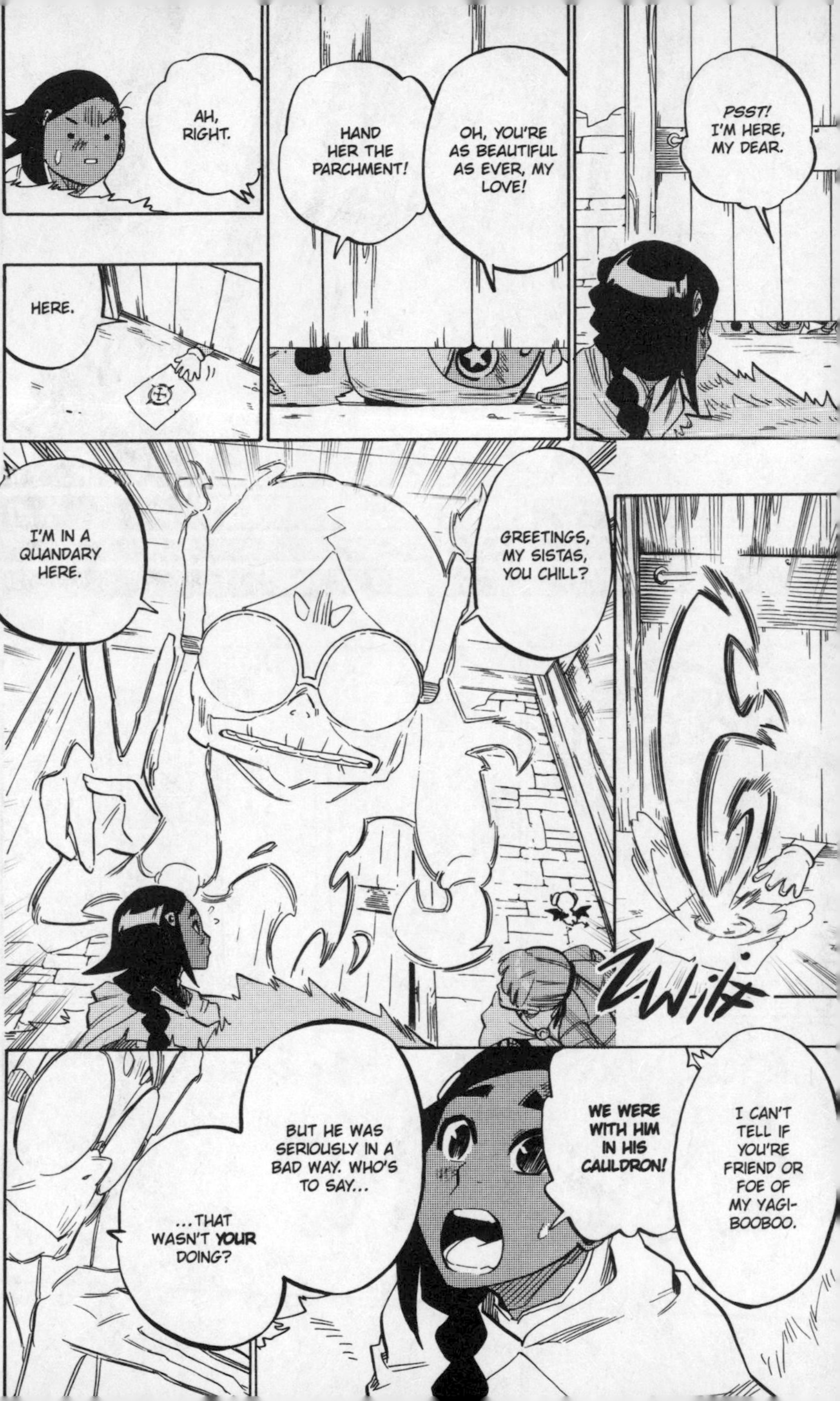
PSST! I'M HERE, MY DEAR.
OH, YOU'RE AS BEAUTIFUL AS EVER, MY LOVE!
HAND HER THE PARCHMENT!
AH, RIGHT.
HERE.
ZWIK
GREETINGS, MY SISTAS, YOU CHILL?
I'M IN A QUANDARY HERE.
I CAN'T TELL IF YOU'RE FRIEND OR FOE OF MY YAGI-BOOBOO.
WE WERE WITH HIM IN HIS CAULDRON!
BUT HE WAS SERIOUSLY IN A BAD WAY. WHO'S TO SAY...
...THAT WASN'T **YOUR** DOING?

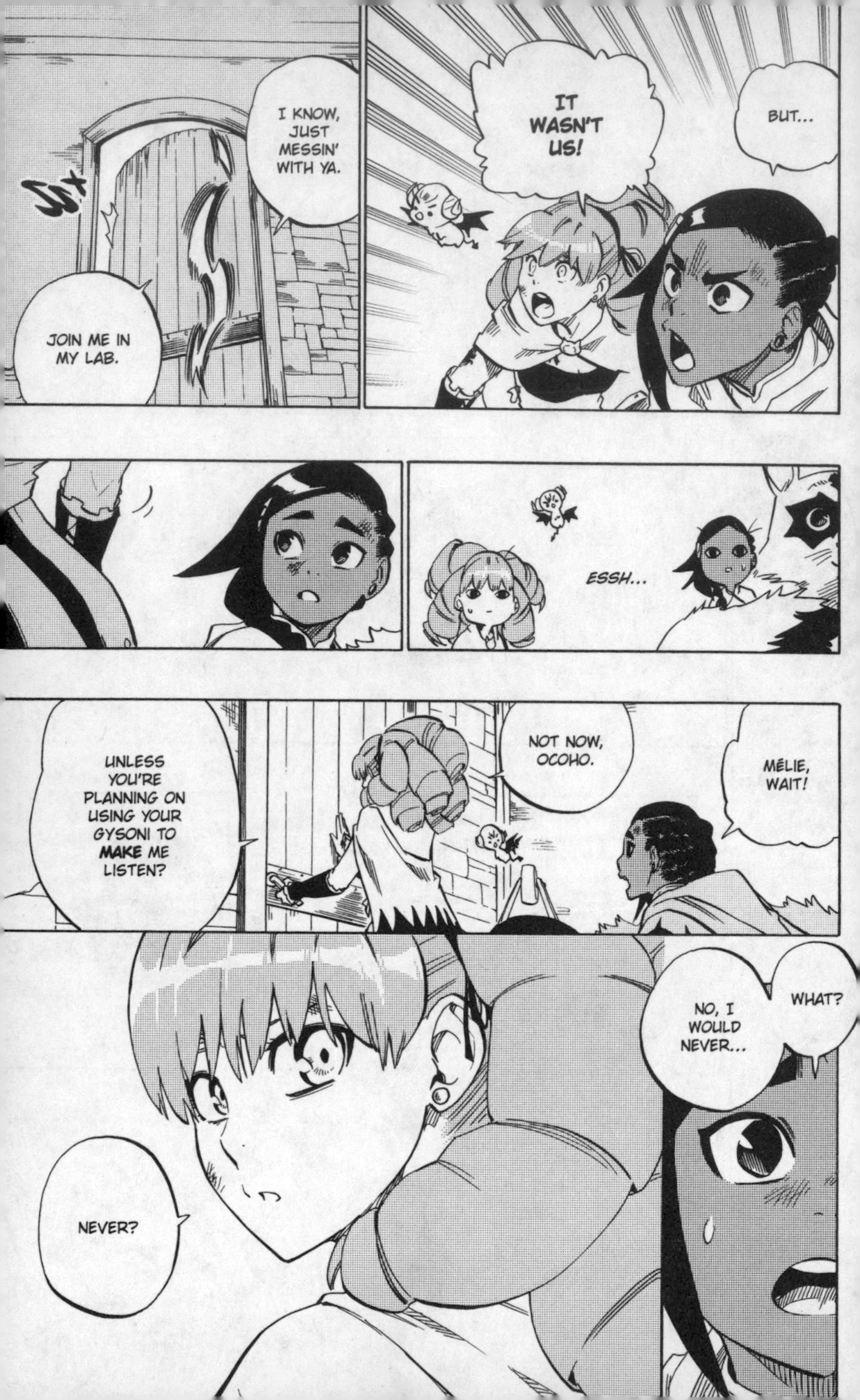
BUT...
IT WASN'T US!
I KNOW, JUST MESSIN' WITH YA.
JOIN ME IN MY LAB.
ESSH...
MÉLIE, WAIT!
NOT NOW, OCOHO.
UNLESS YOU'RE PLANNING ON USING YOUR GYSONI TO **MAKE** ME LISTEN?
WHAT?
NO, I WOULD NEVER...
NEVER?

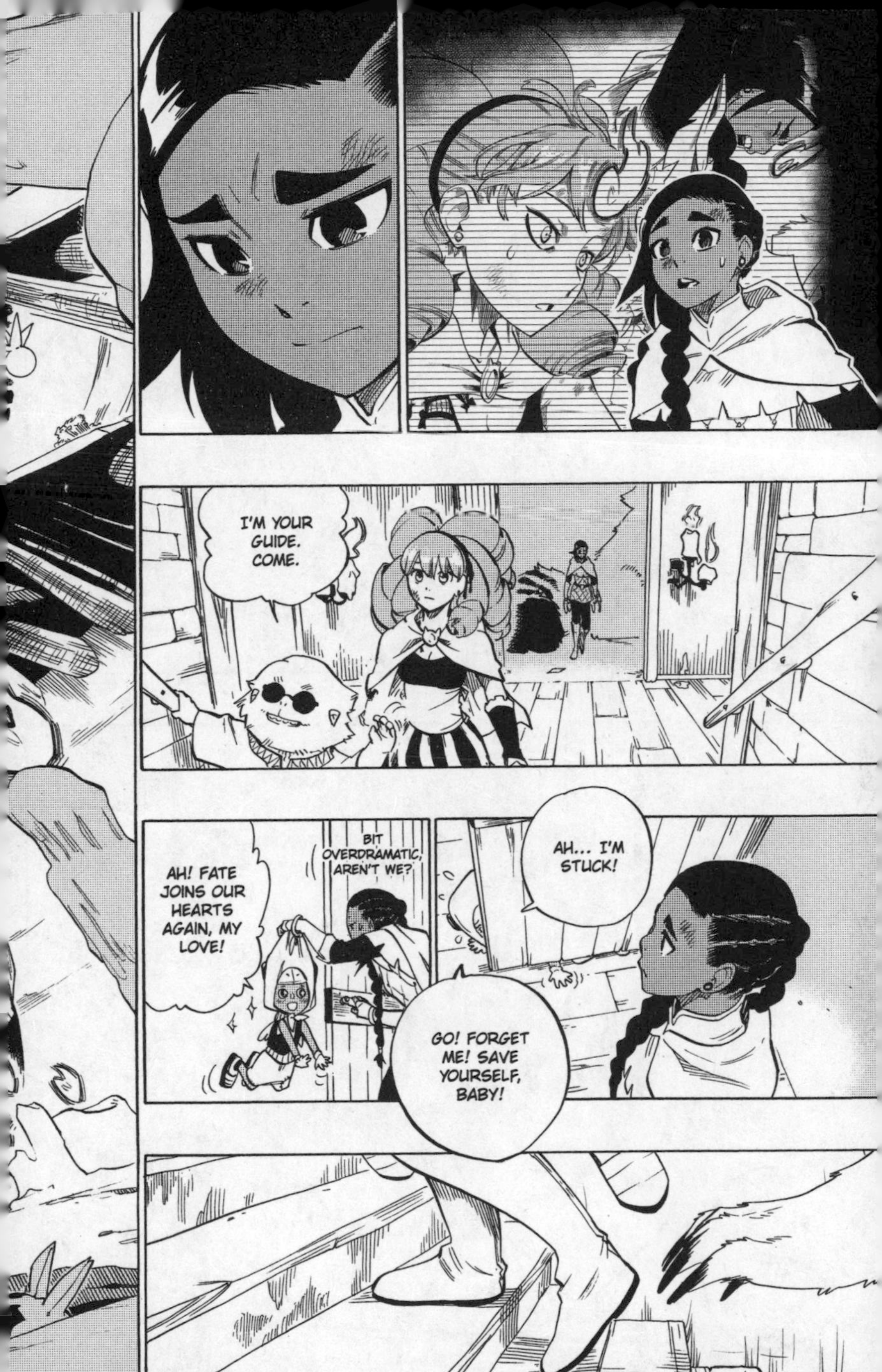
I'M YOUR GUIDE. COME.
AH... I'M STUCK!
GO! FORGET ME! SAVE YOURSELF, BABY!
BIT OVERDRAMATIC, AREN'T WE?
AH! FATE JOINS OUR HEARTS AGAIN, MY LOVE!

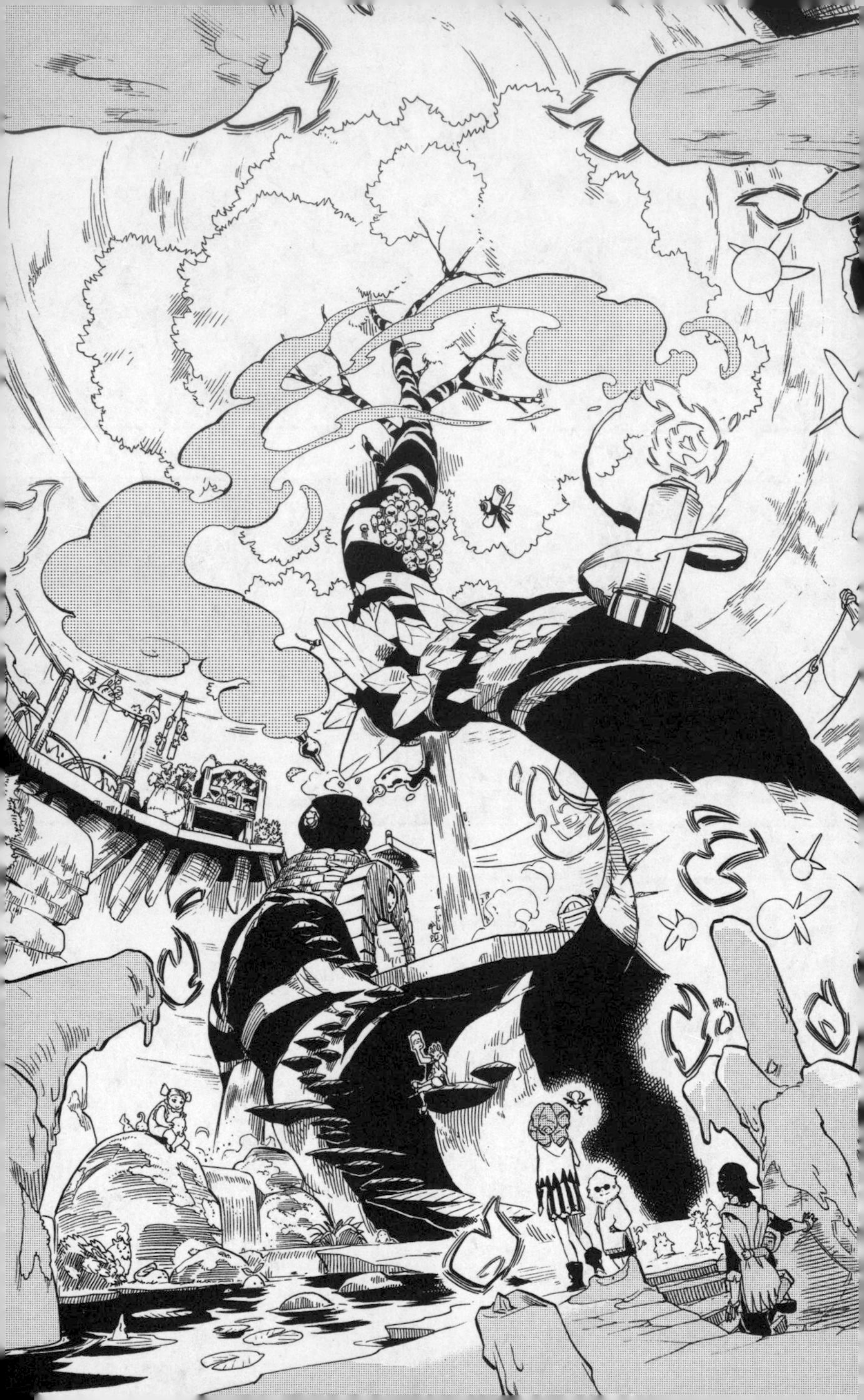

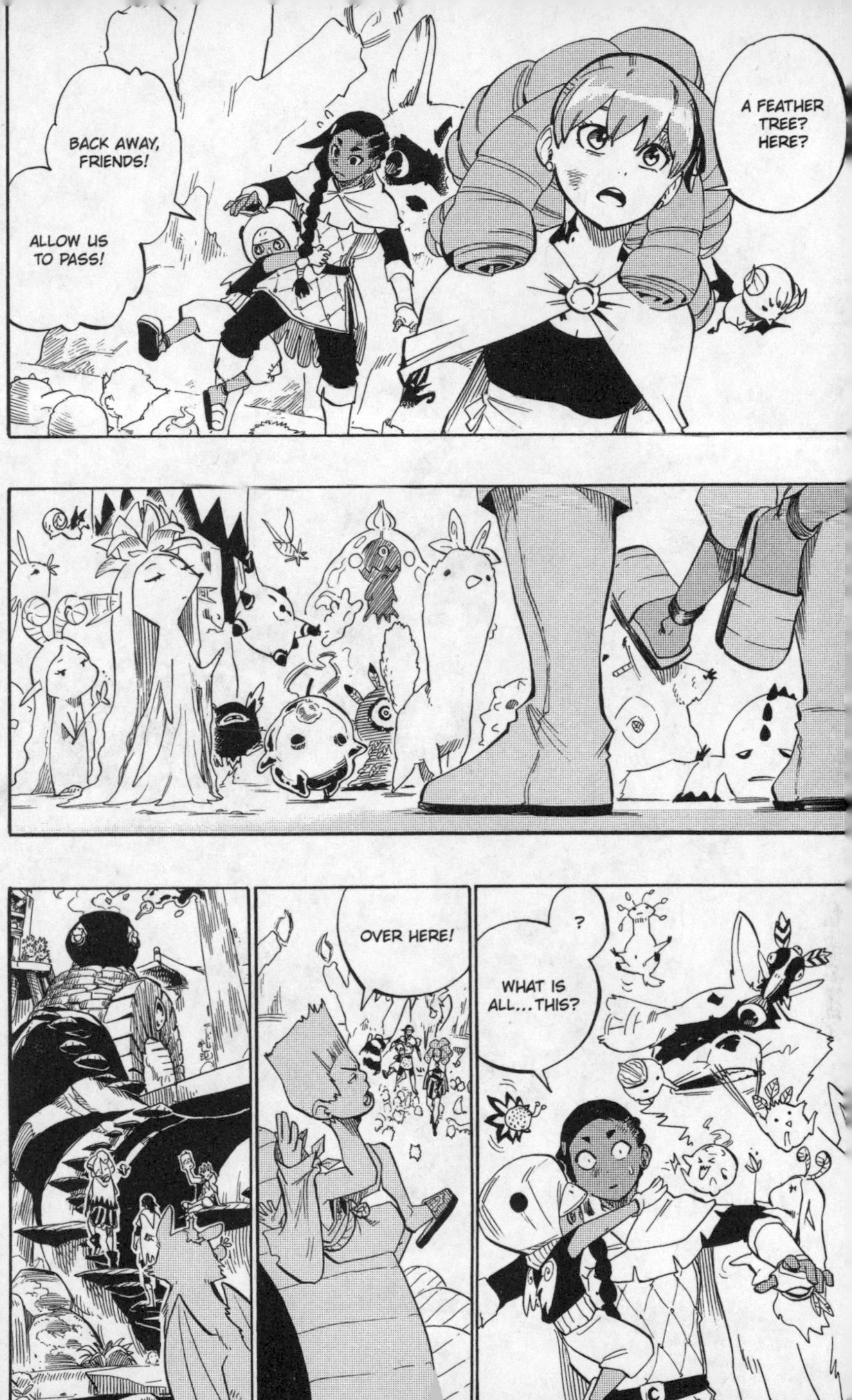
A FEATHER TREE? HERE?
BACK AWAY, FRIENDS!
ALLOW US TO PASS!
?
WHAT IS ALL...THIS?
OVER HERE!

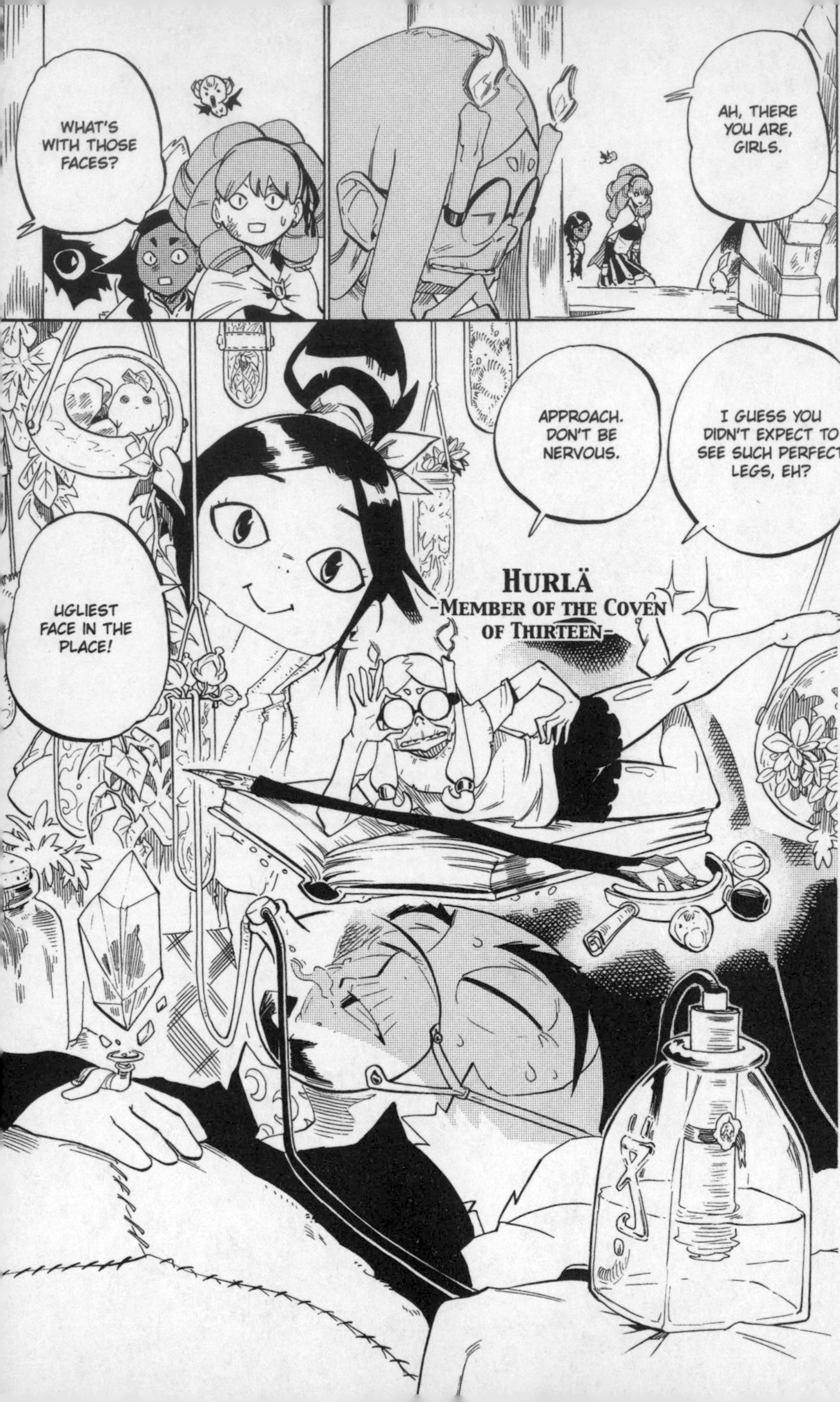
AH, THERE YOU ARE, GIRLS.
WHAT'S WITH THOSE FACES?
I GUESS YOU DIDN'T EXPECT TO SEE SUCH PERFECT LEGS, EH?
APPROACH. DON'T BE NERVOUS.
HURLÄ
-MEMBER OF THE COVEN OF THIRTEEN-
UGLIEST FACE IN THE PLACE!

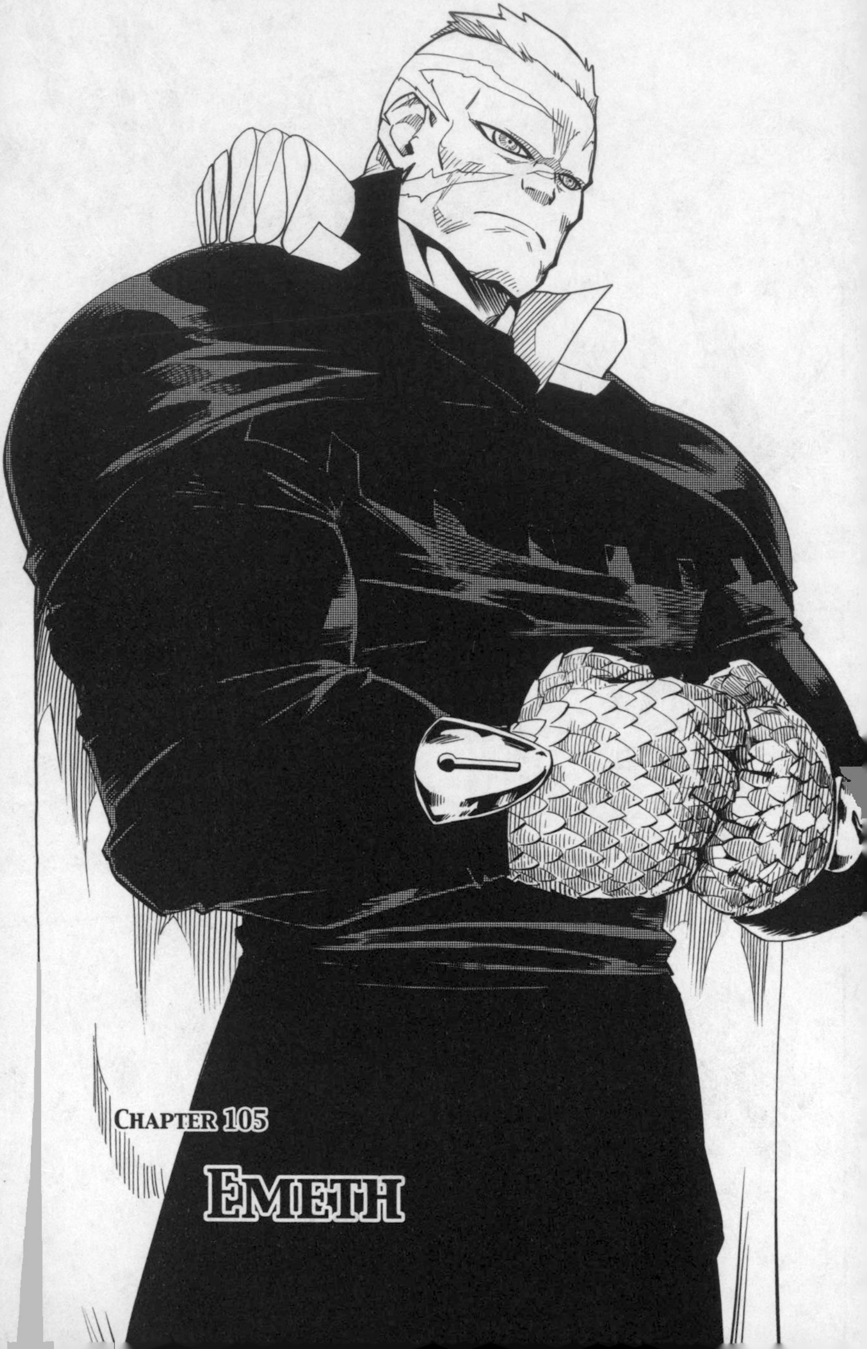
CHAPTER 105
EMETH

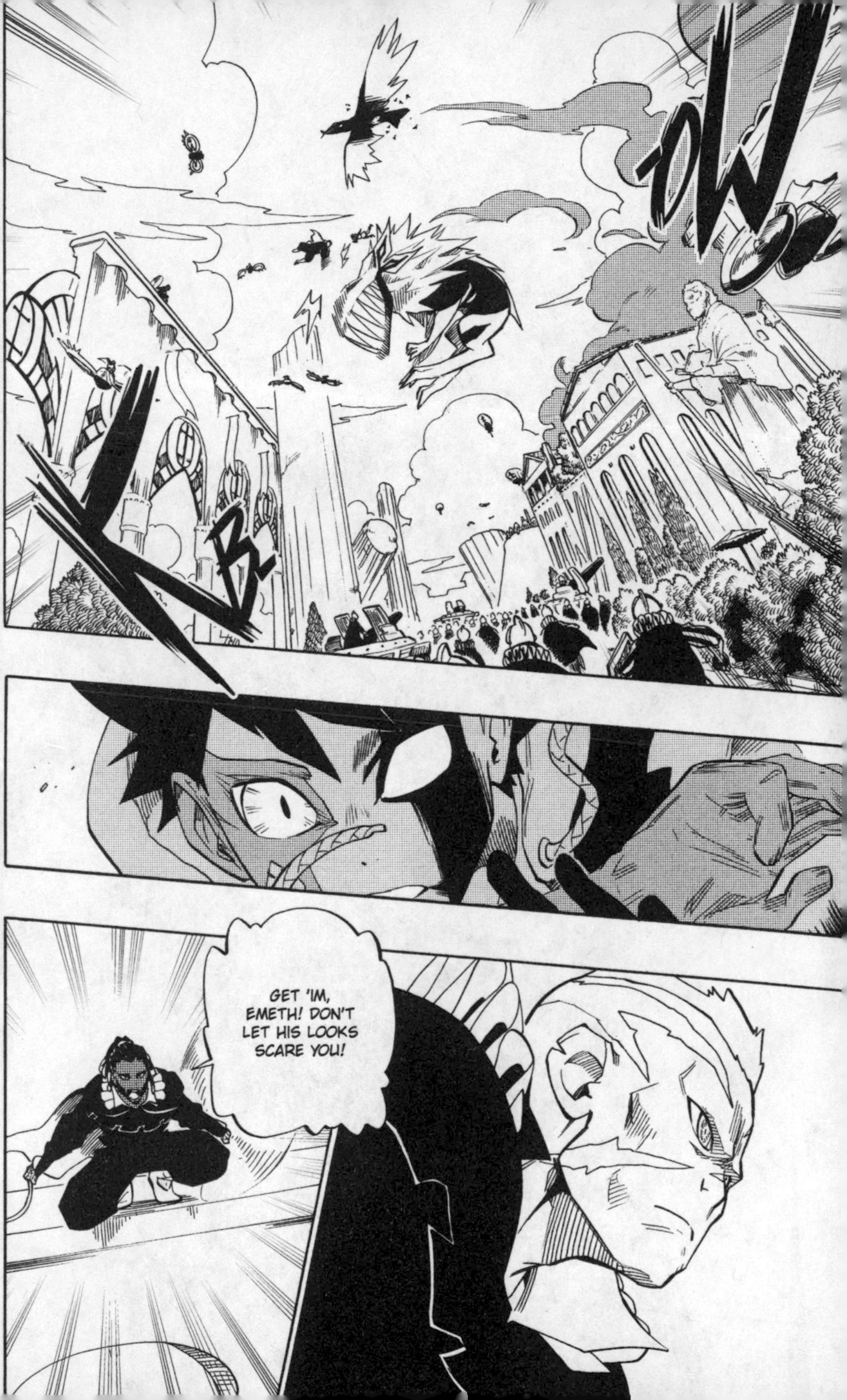
GET 'IM, EMETH! DON'T LET HIS LOOKS SCARE YOU!

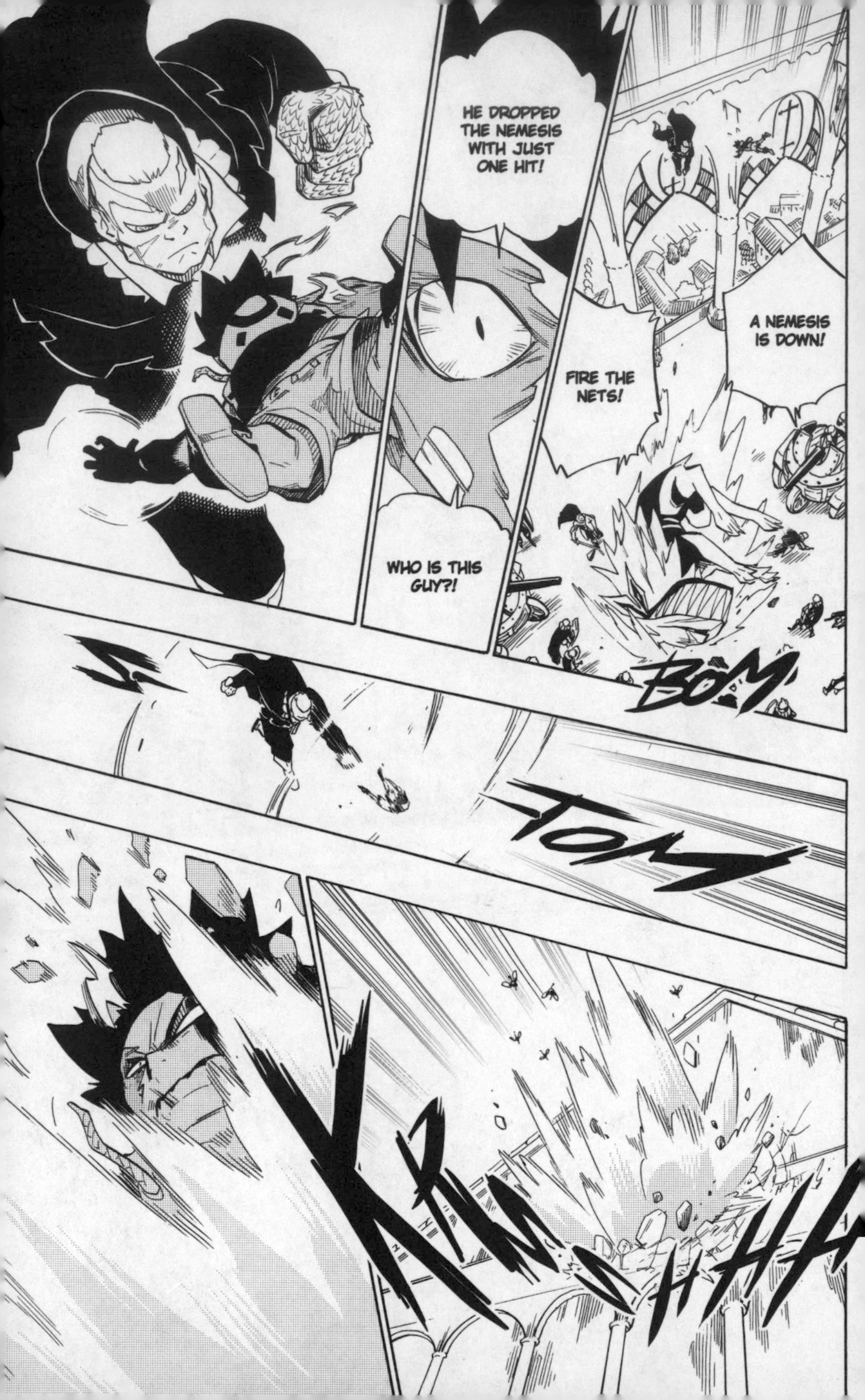
A NEMESIS IS DOWN!
FIRE THE NETS!
BOOM
HE DROPPED THE NEMESIS WITH JUST ONE HIT!
WHO IS THIS GUY?!
TOM

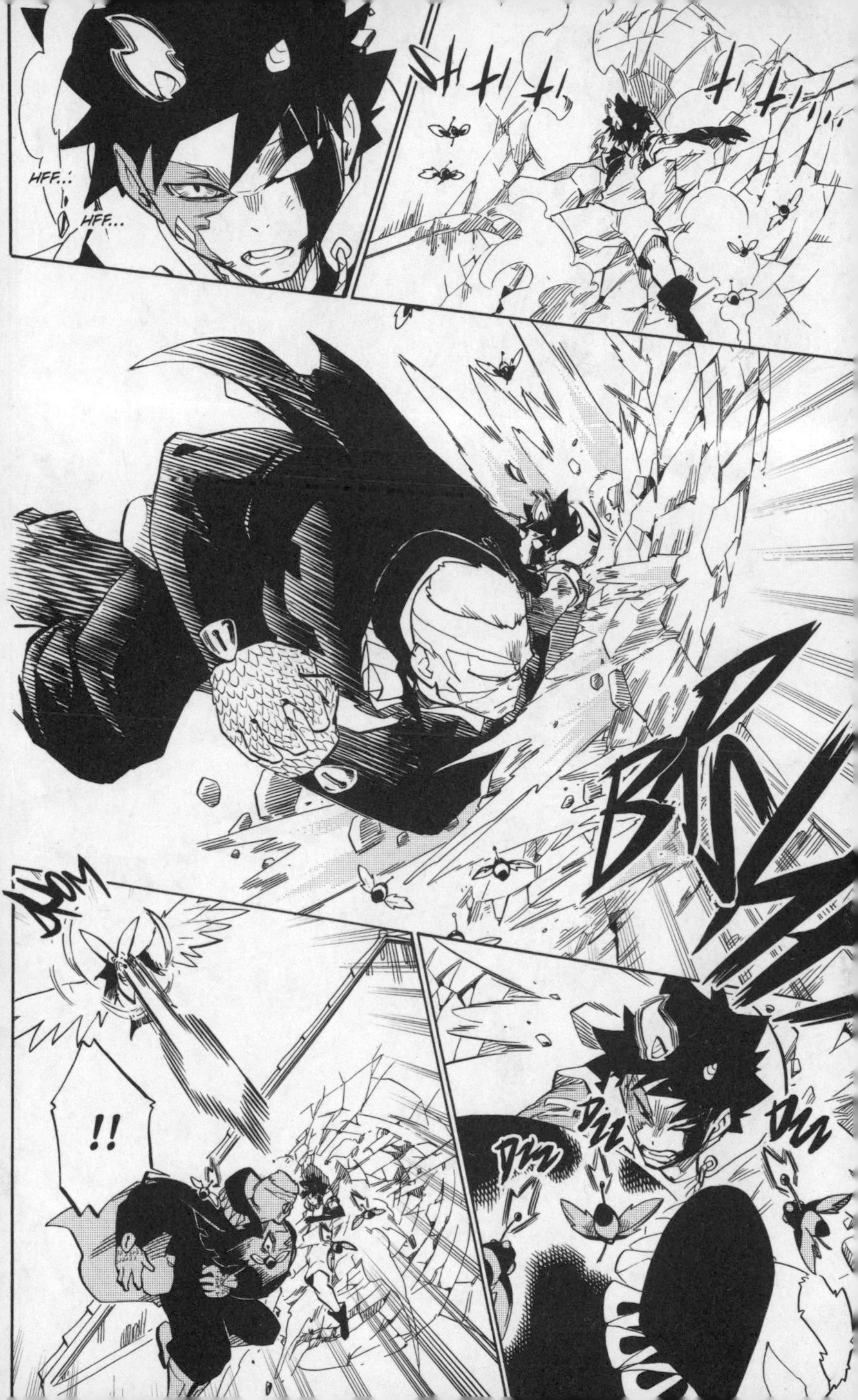
HFF...
HFF...
DZZ
DZZ
DZZ
!!

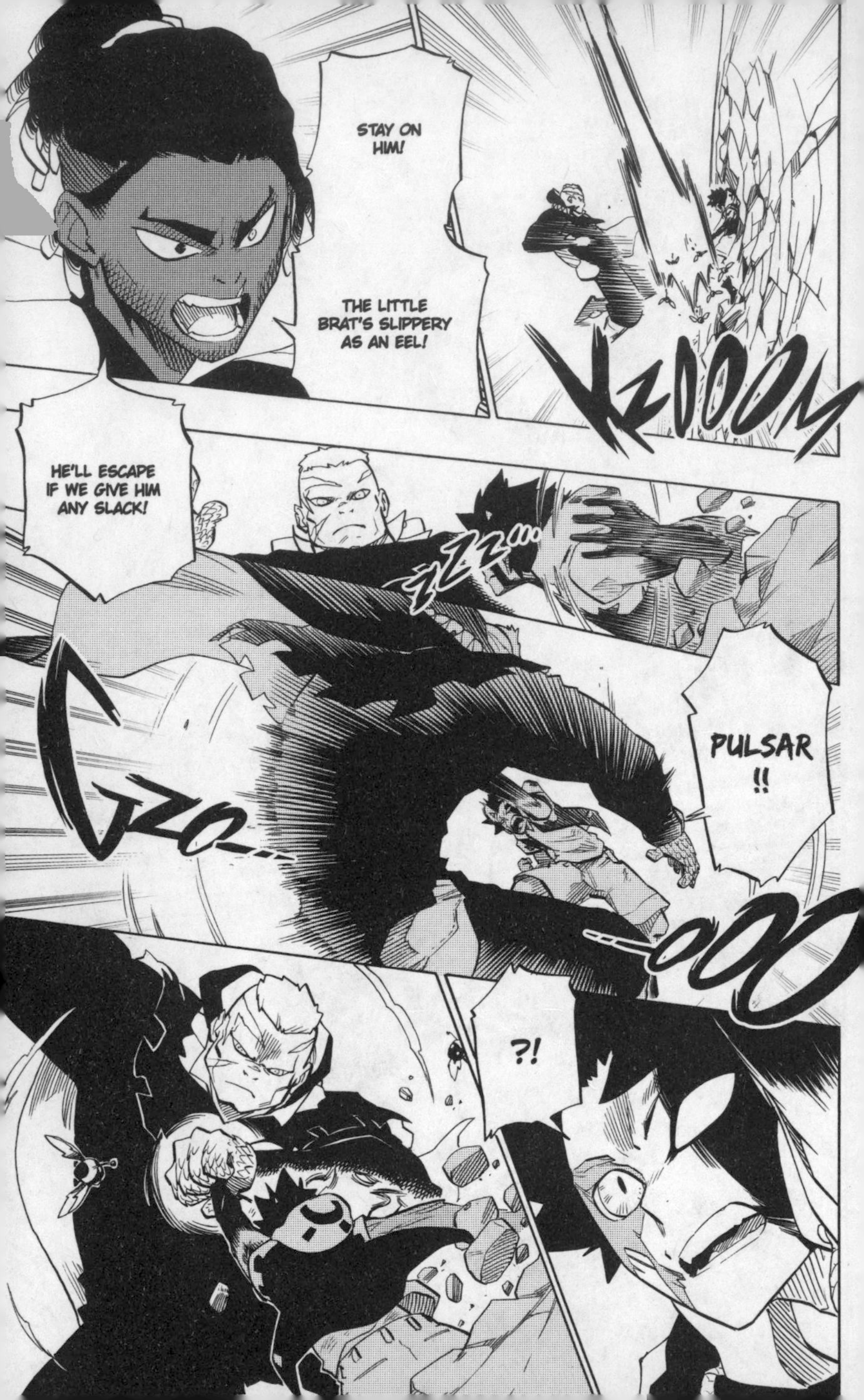
KZOOOM
STAY ON HIM!
THE LITTLE BRAT'S SLIPPERY AS AN EEL!
HE'LL ESCAPE IF WE GIVE HIM ANY SLACK!
ZZZ...
PULSAR !!
GZO...
OOO
?!

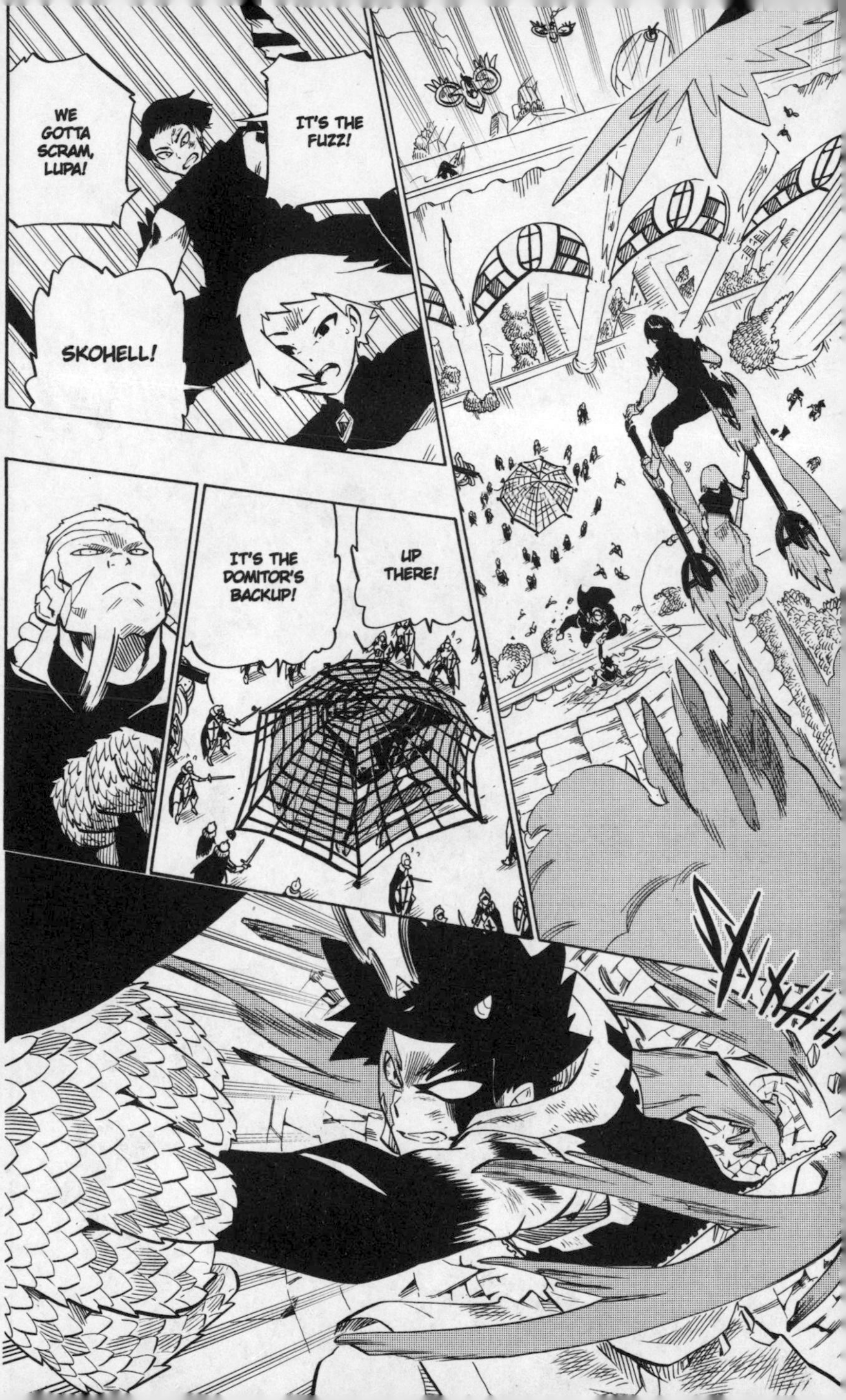
IT'S THE FUZZ!
WE GOTTA SCRAM, LUPA!
SKOHELL!
UP THERE!
IT'S THE DOMITOR'S BACKUP!

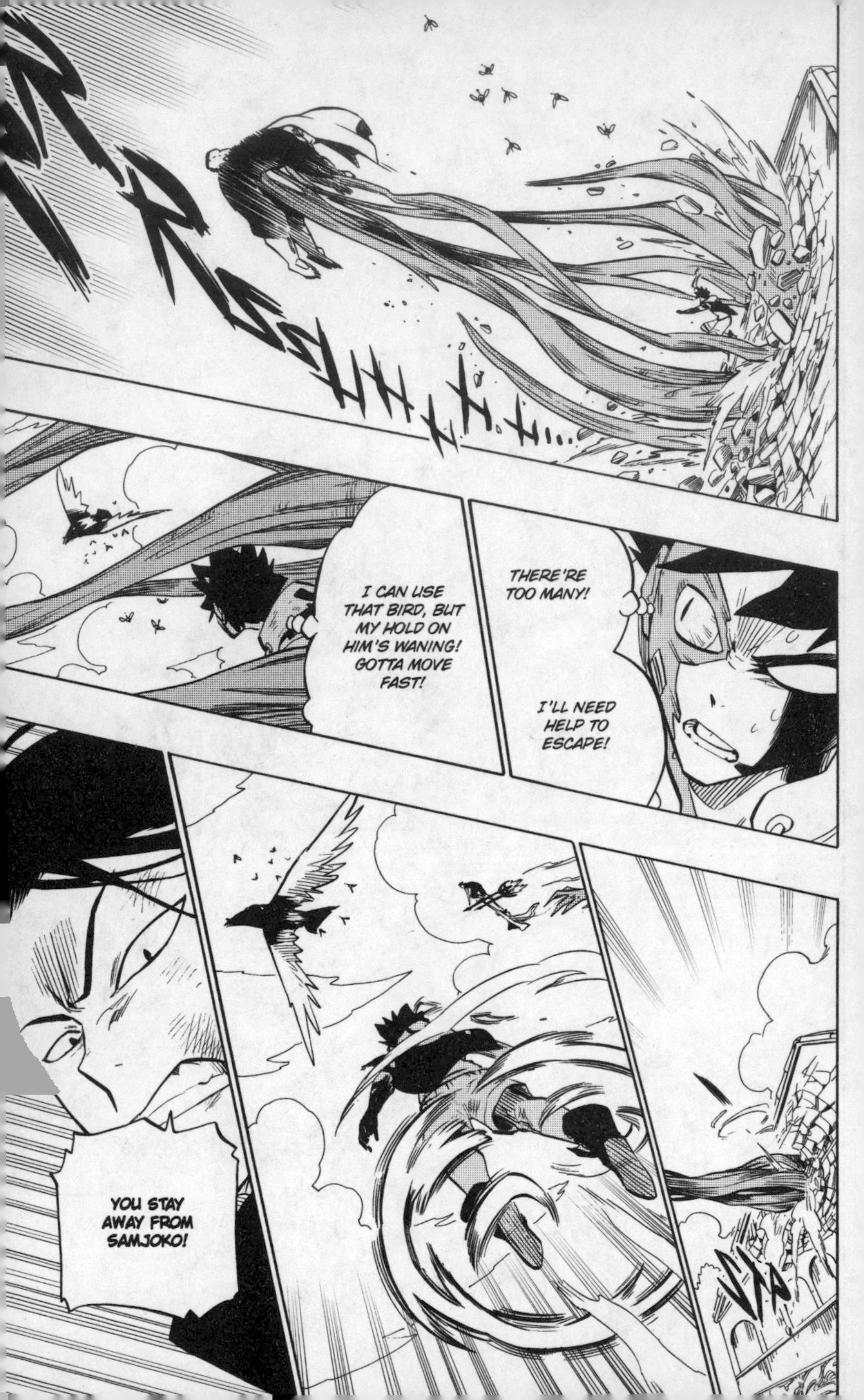
THERE'RE TOO MANY!
I'LL NEED HELP TO ESCAPE!
I CAN USE THAT BIRD, BUT MY HOLD ON HIM'S WANING! GOTTA MOVE FAST!
YOU STAY AWAY FROM SAMJOKO!

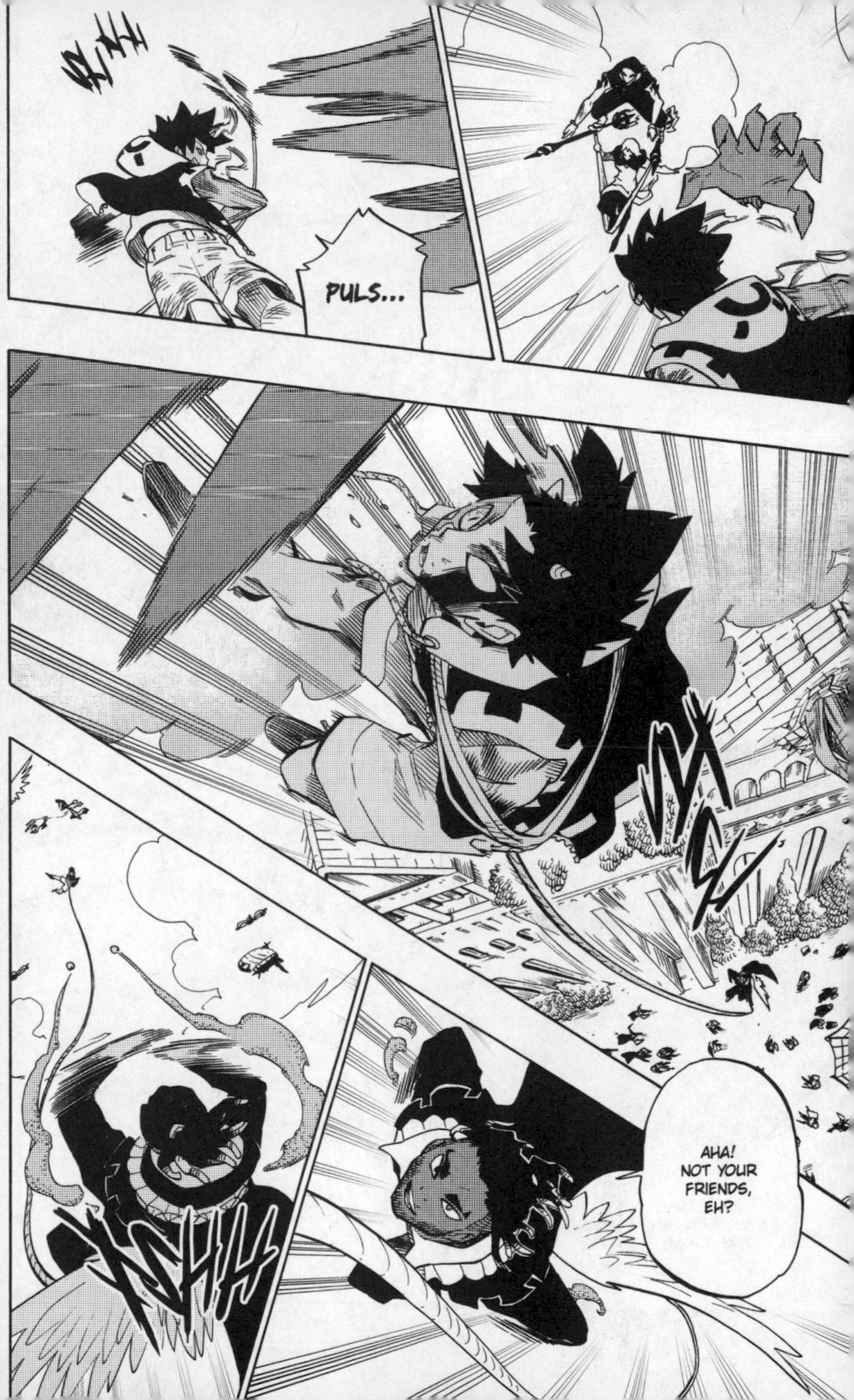
PULS...
AHA! NOT YOUR FRIENDS, EH?

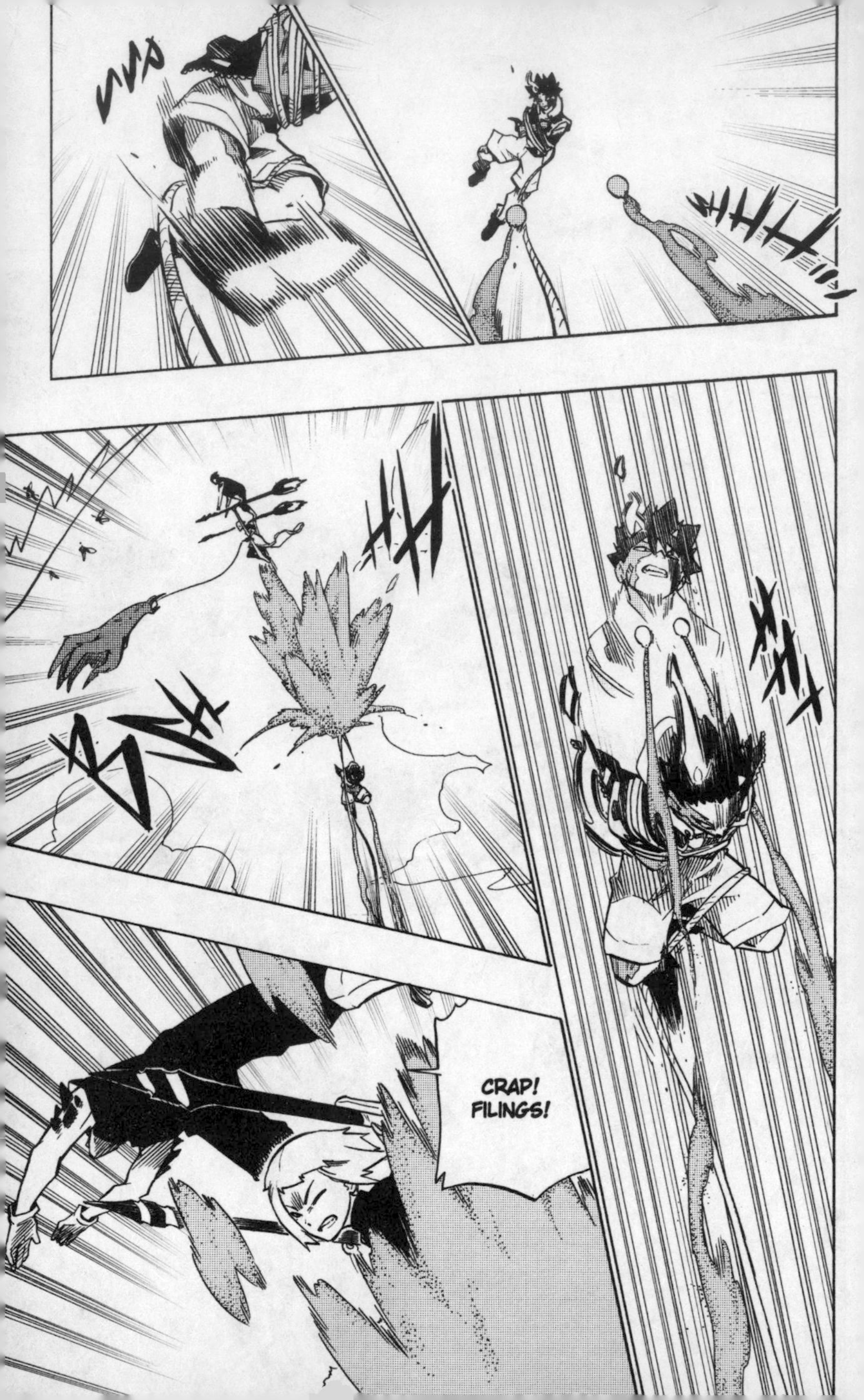
CRAP! FILINGS!

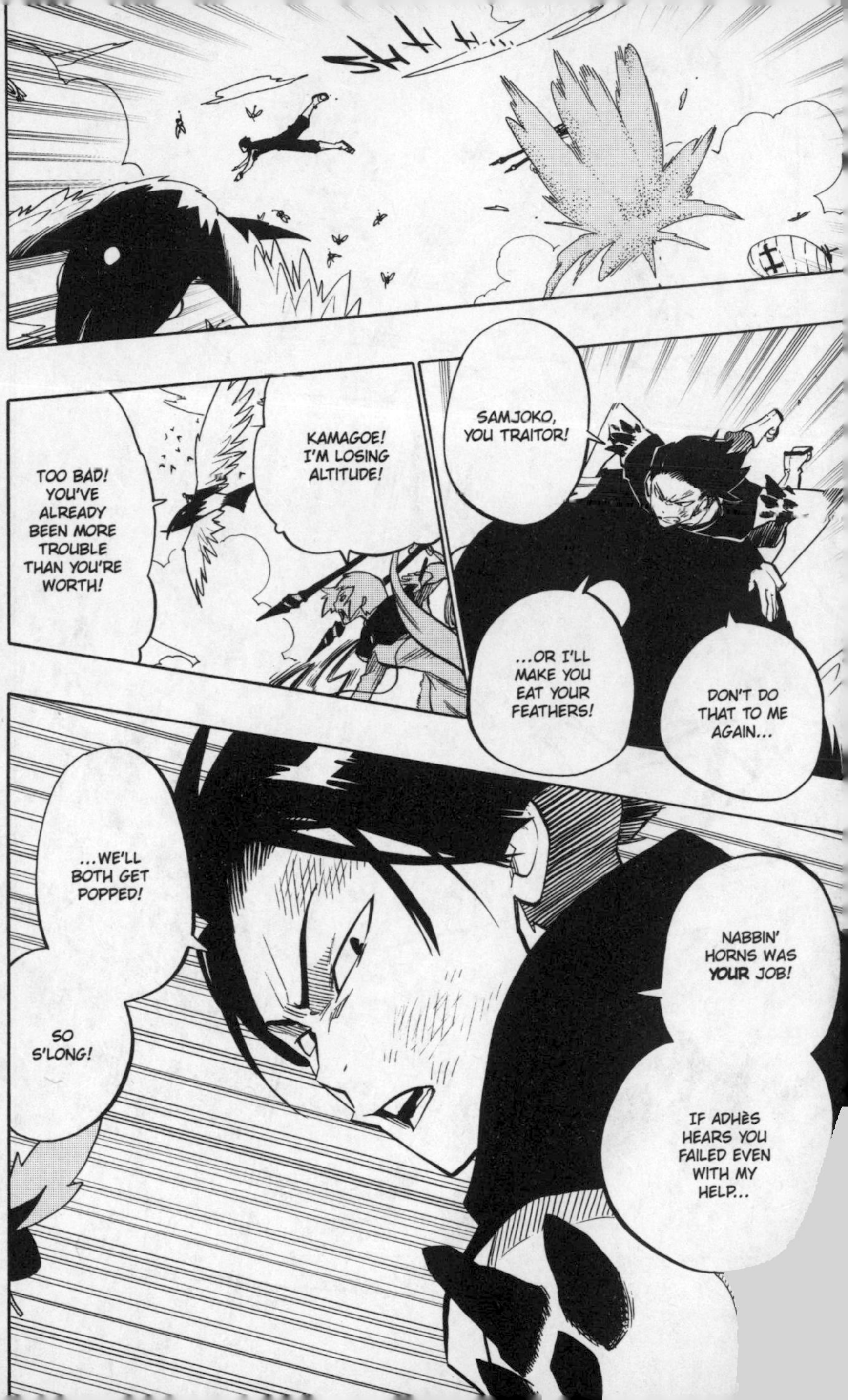
SAMJOKO, YOU TRAITOR!
DON'T DO THAT TO ME AGAIN...
...OR I'LL MAKE YOU EAT YOUR FEATHERS!
KAMAGOE! I'M LOSING ALTITUDE!
TOO BAD! YOU'VE ALREADY BEEN MORE TROUBLE THAN YOU'RE WORTH!
NABBIN' HORNS WAS **YOUR** JOB!
IF ADHÈS HEARS YOU FAILED EVEN WITH MY HELP...
...WE'LL BOTH GET POPPED!
SO S'LONG!

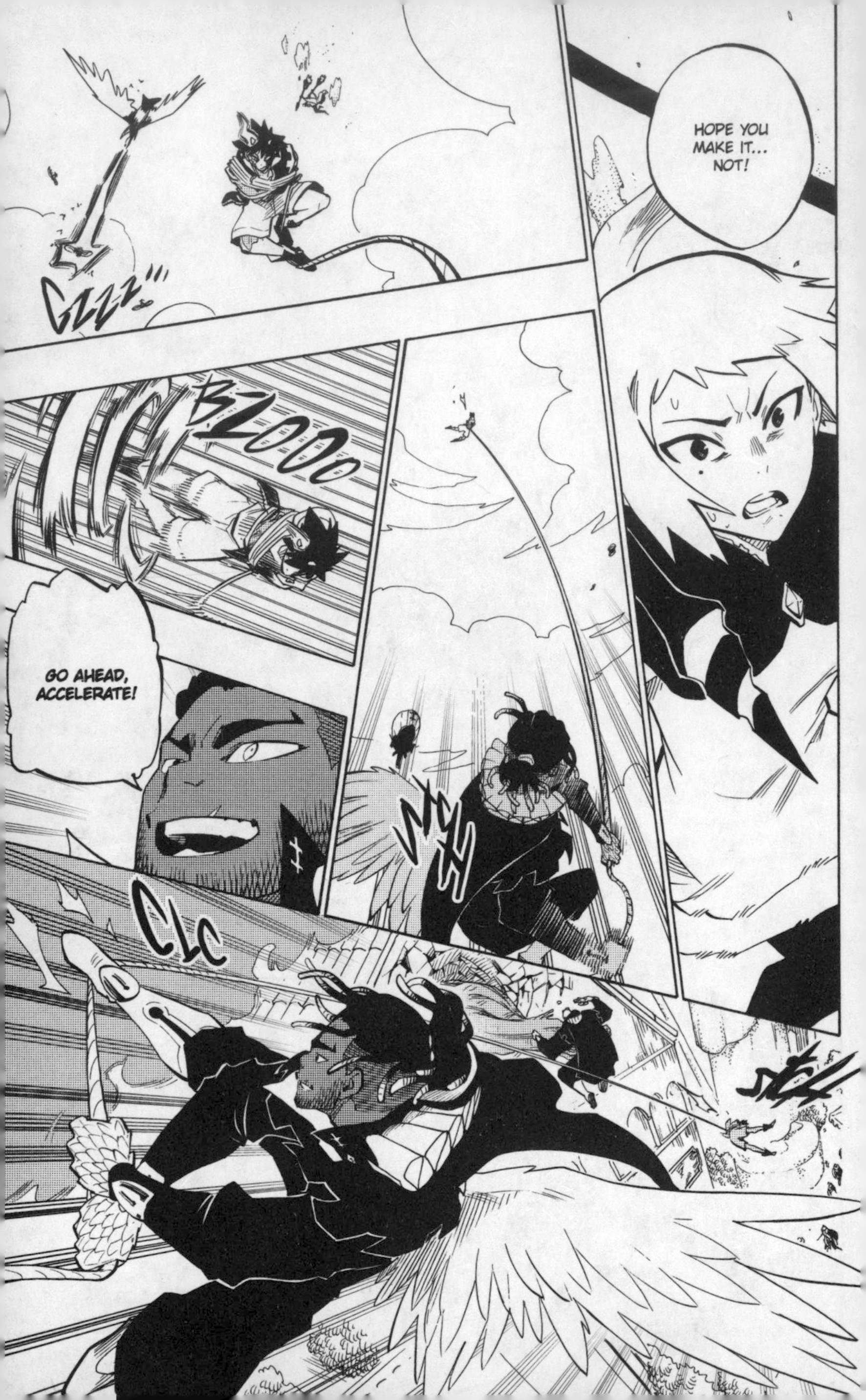

HOPE YOU MAKE IT... NOT!
GZZZZ
BZOOO
GO AHEAD, ACCELERATE!

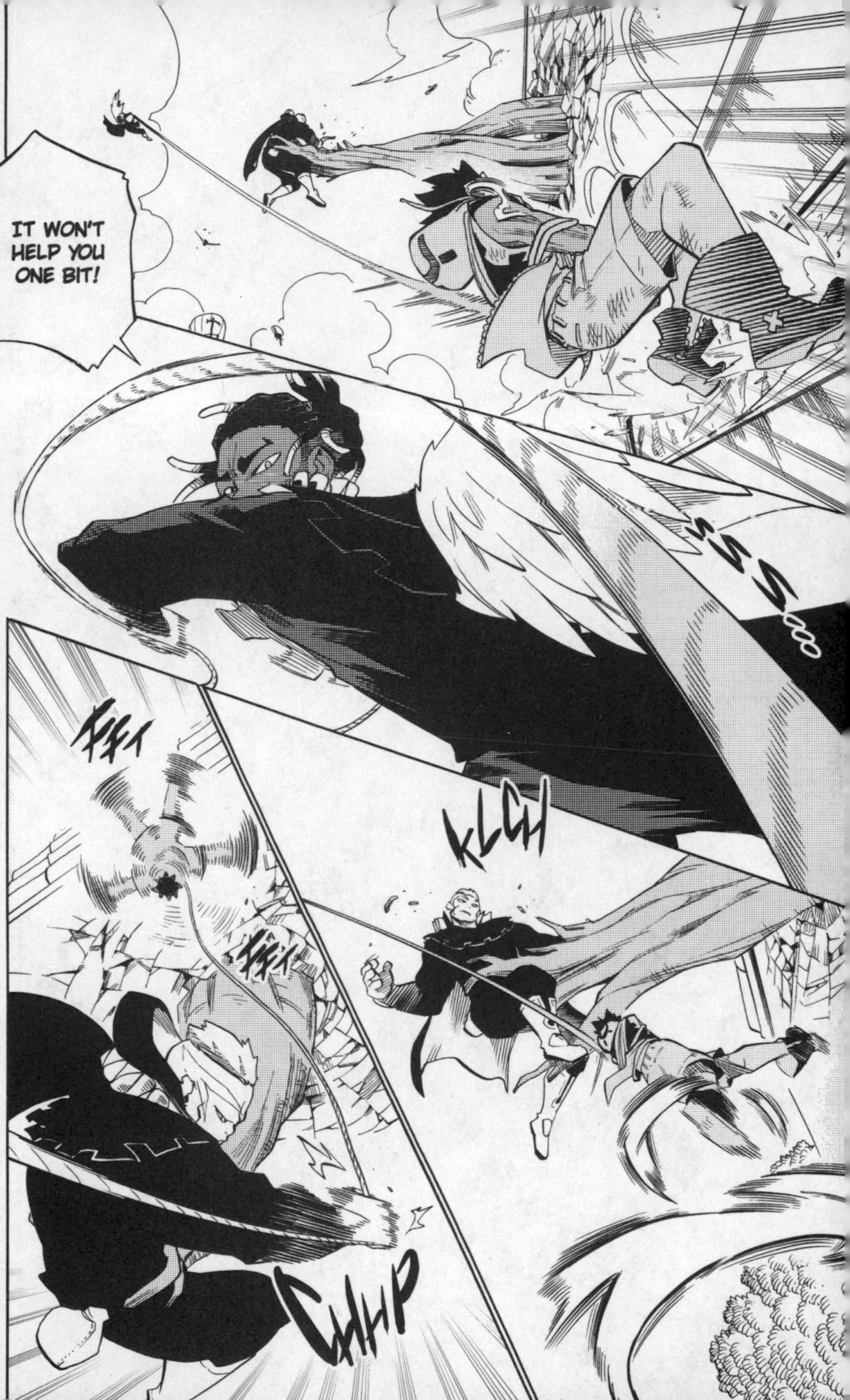
IT WON'T HELP YOU ONE BIT!
SSSooo
KLCH
CHHP

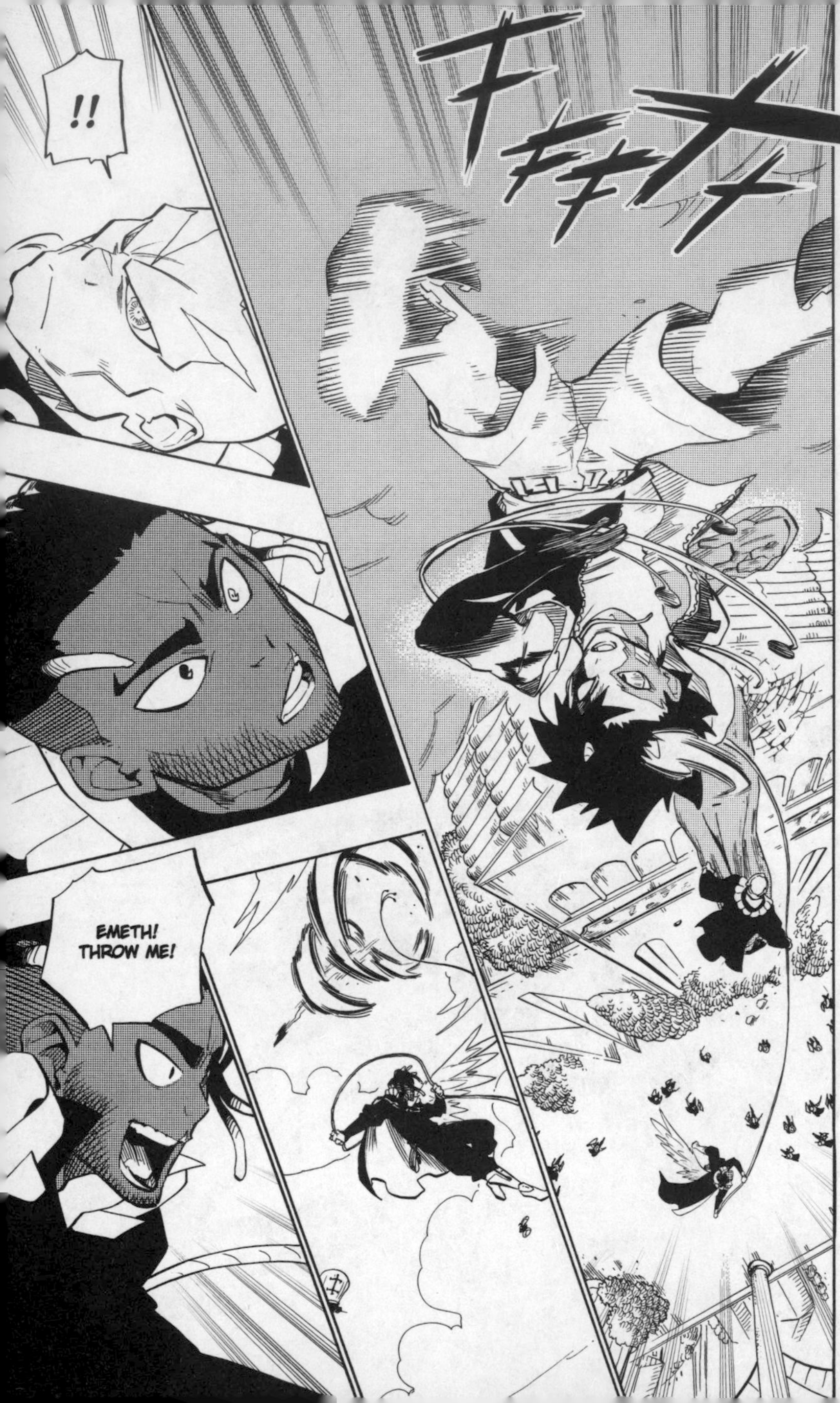
!!
EMETH! THROW ME!

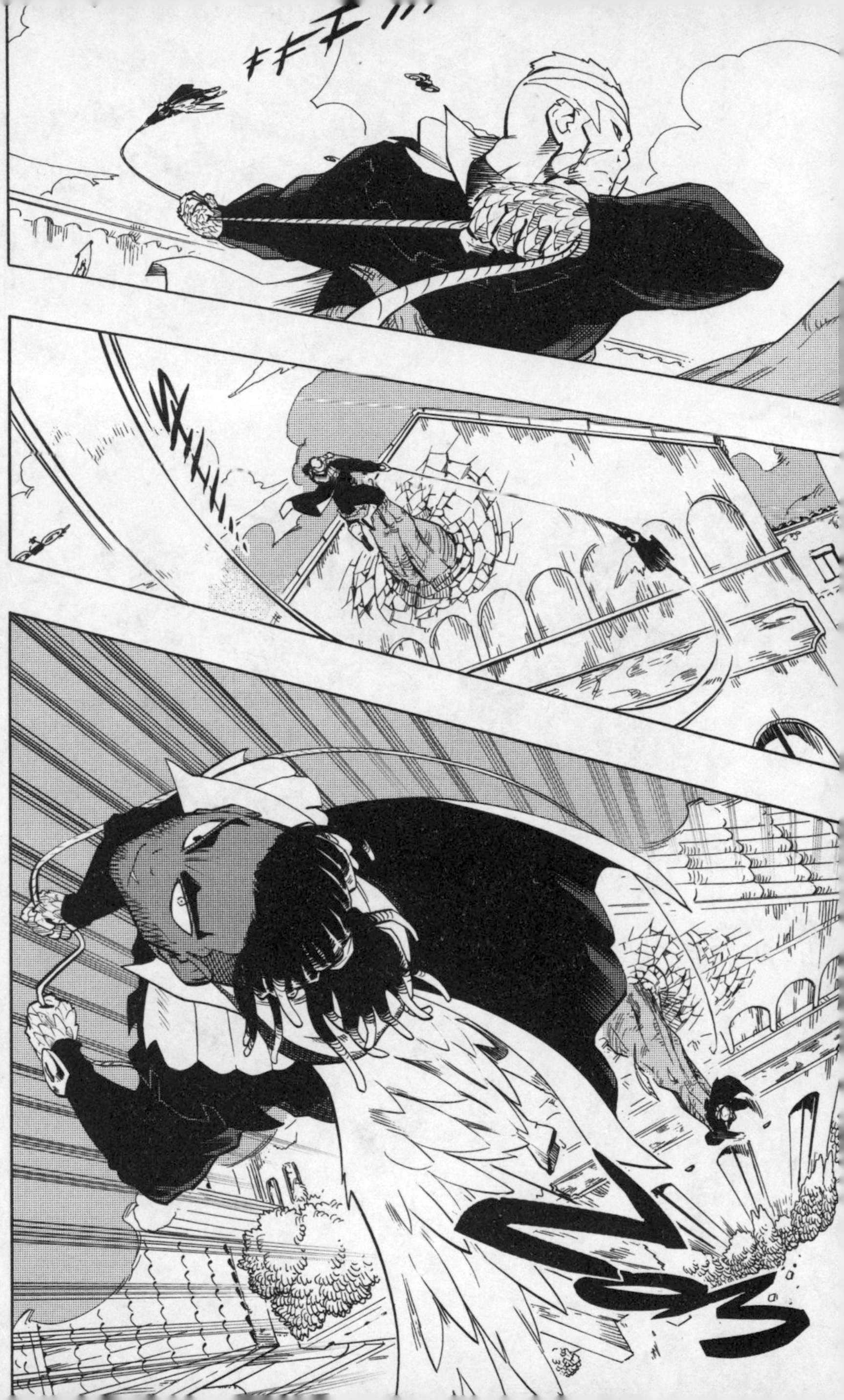
FFT!!
SHHH..!!

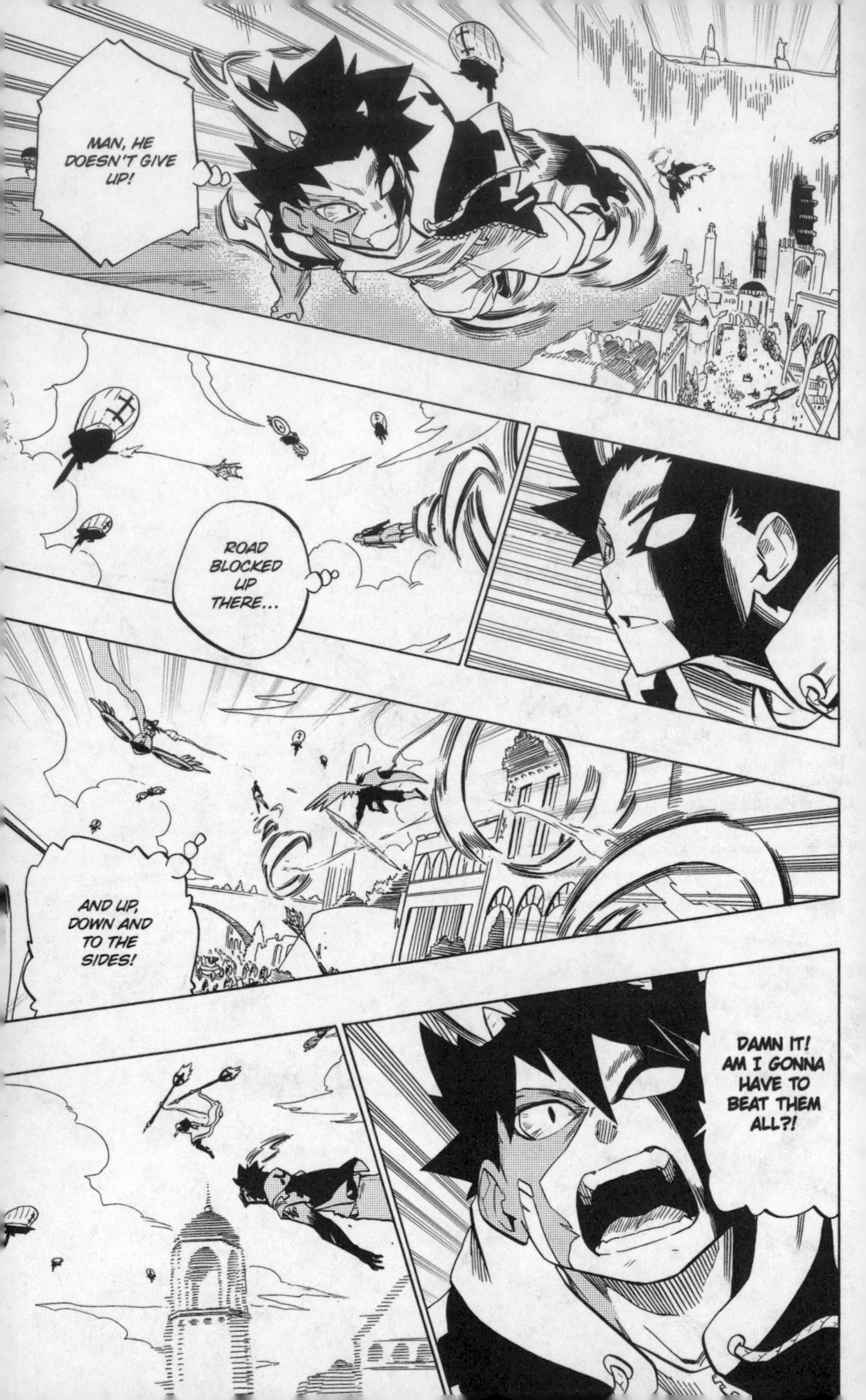
MAN, HE DOESN'T GIVE UP!
ROAD BLOCKED UP THERE...
AND UP, DOWN AND TO THE SIDES!
DAMN IT! AM I GONNA HAVE TO BEAT THEM ALL?!

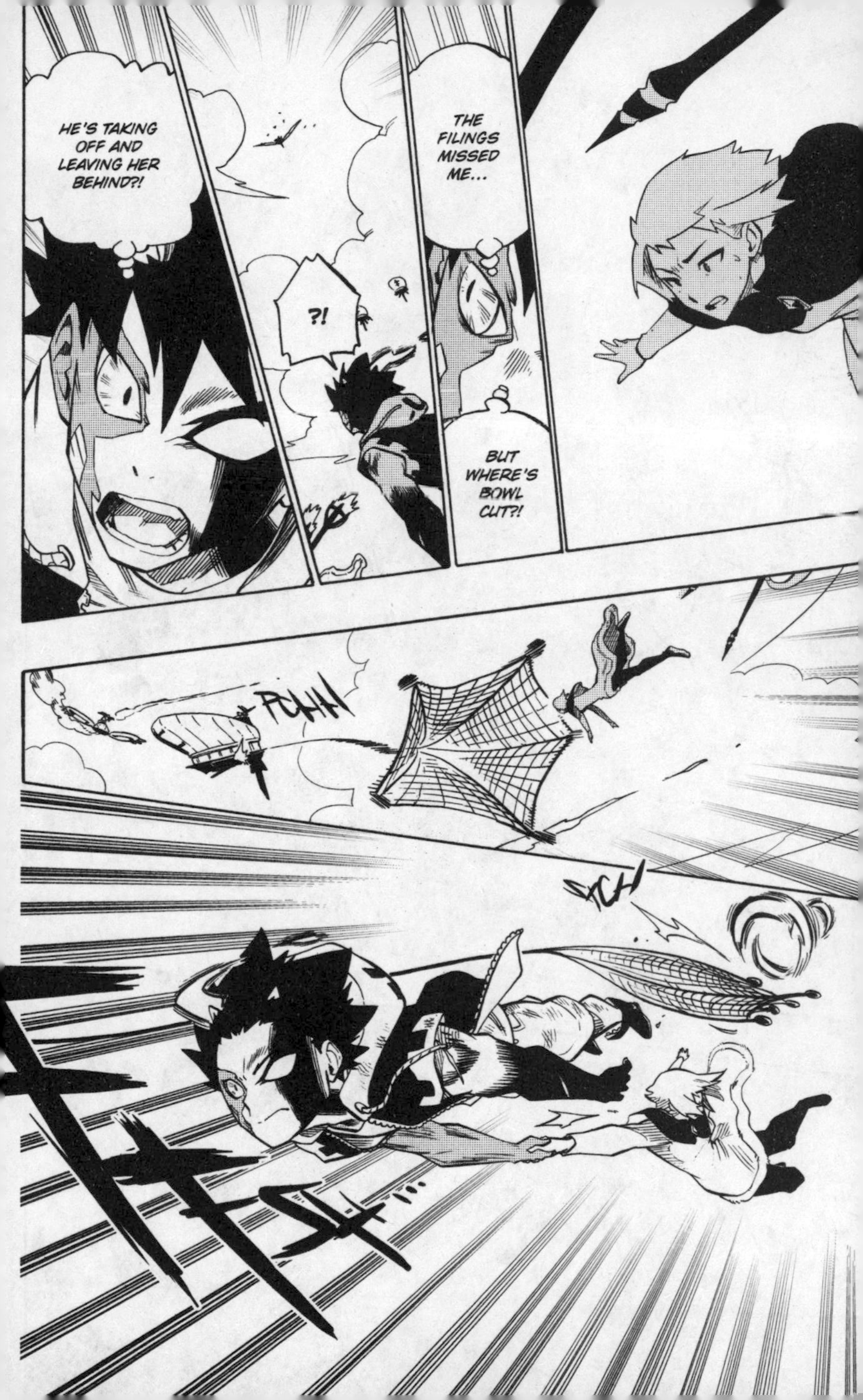
THE FILINGS MISSED ME...
BUT WHERE'S BOWL CUT?!
?!
HE'S TAKING OFF AND LEAVING HER BEHIND?!
FCHH
SKCH

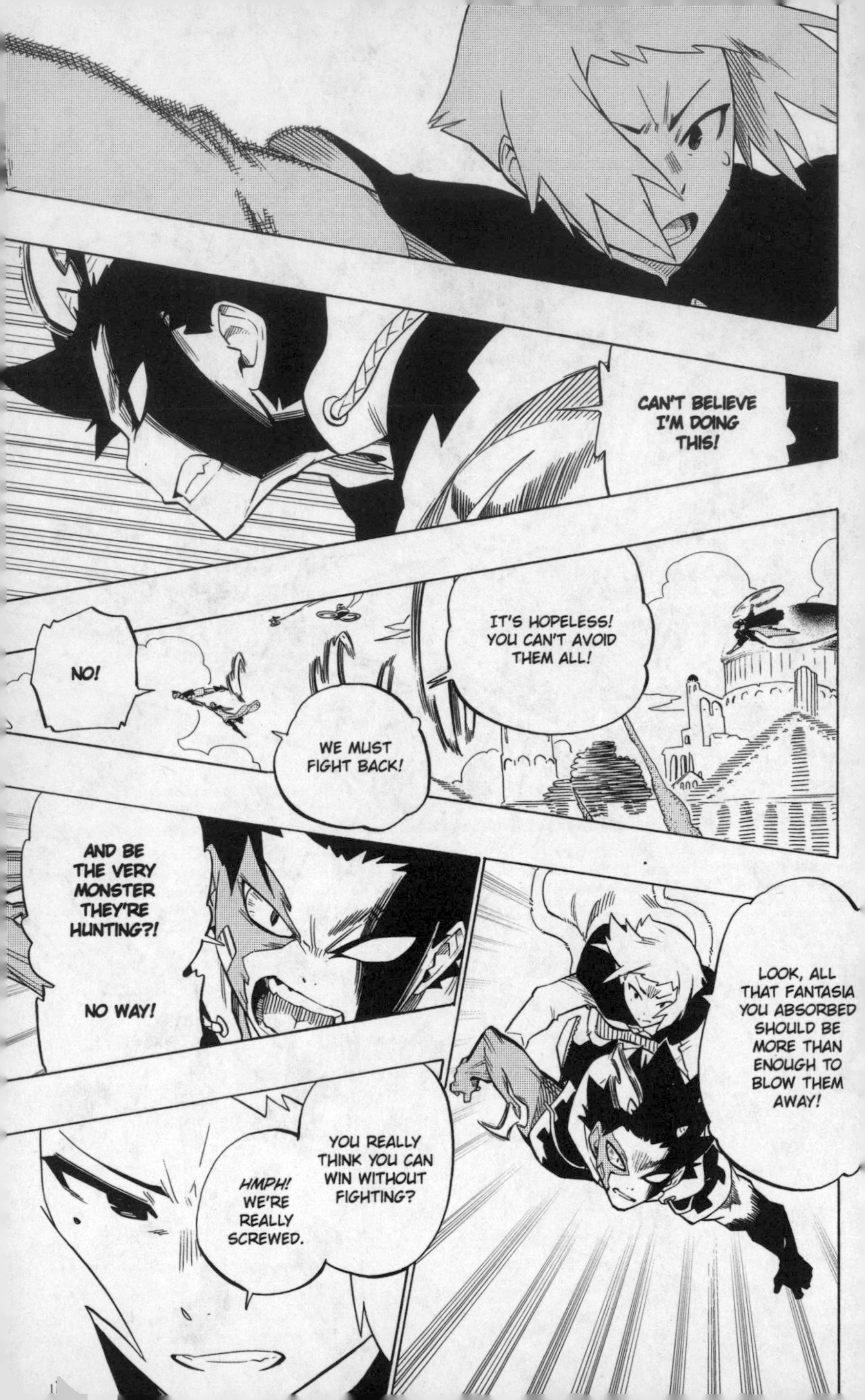
CAN'T BELIEVE I'M DOING THIS!
IT'S HOPELESS! YOU CAN'T AVOID THEM ALL!
WE MUST FIGHT BACK!
NO!
LOOK, ALL THAT FANTASIA YOU ABSORBED SHOULD BE MORE THAN ENOUGH TO BLOW THEM AWAY!
AND BE THE VERY MONSTER THEY'RE HUNTING?!
NO WAY!
YOU REALLY THINK YOU CAN WIN WITHOUT FIGHTING?
HMPH! WE'RE REALLY SCREWED.

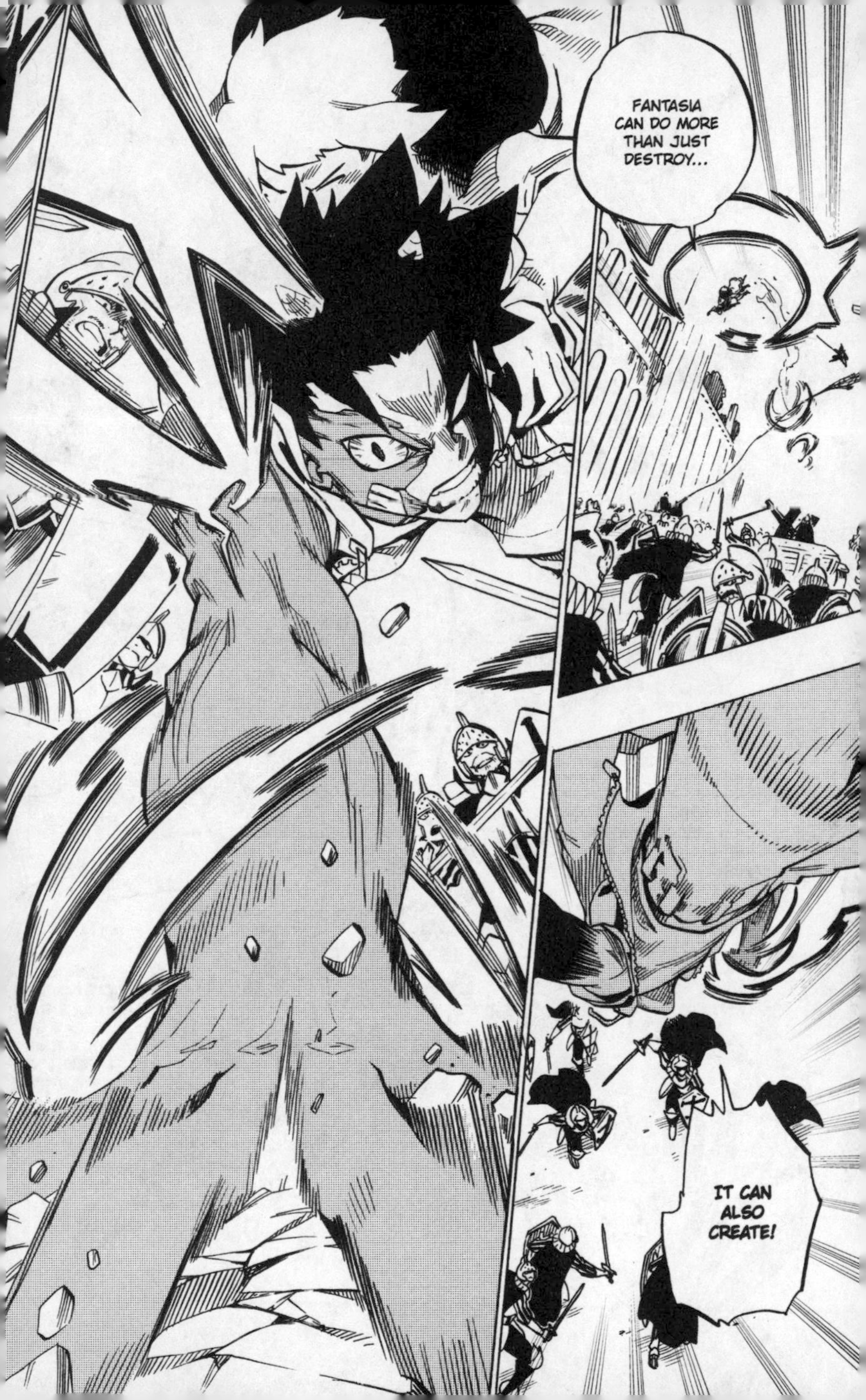
FANTASIA CAN DO MORE THAN JUST DESTROY...
IT CAN ALSO CREATE!

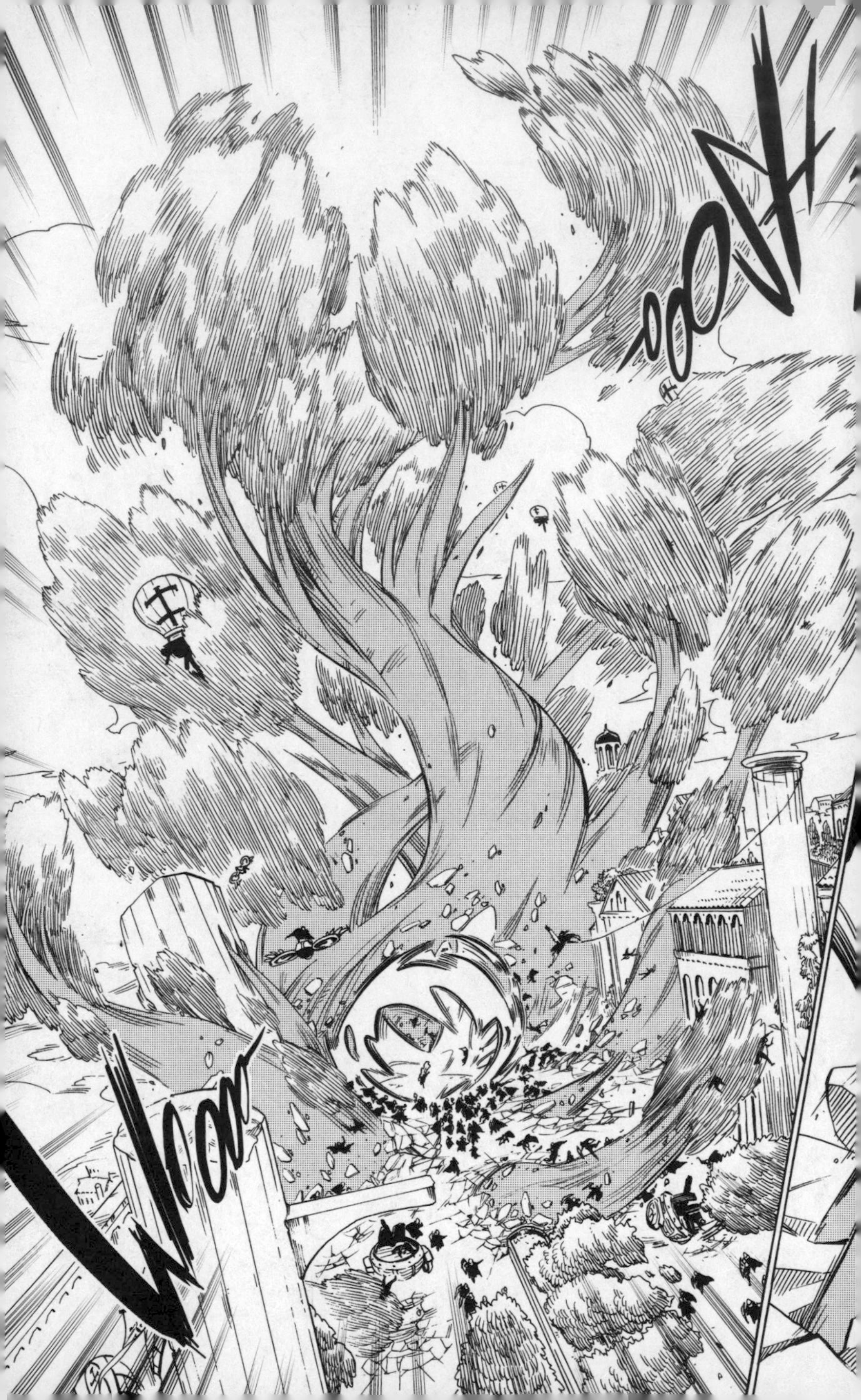

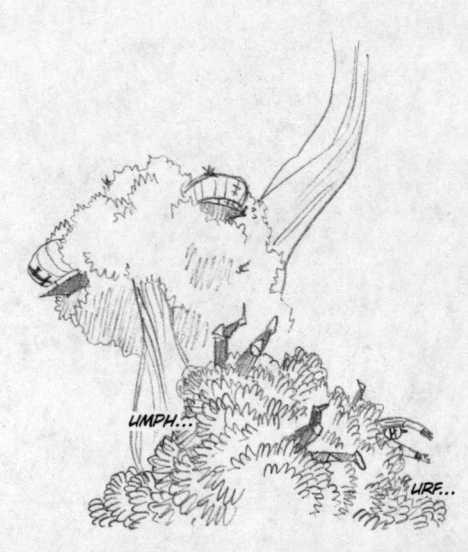

UMPH...

URF...

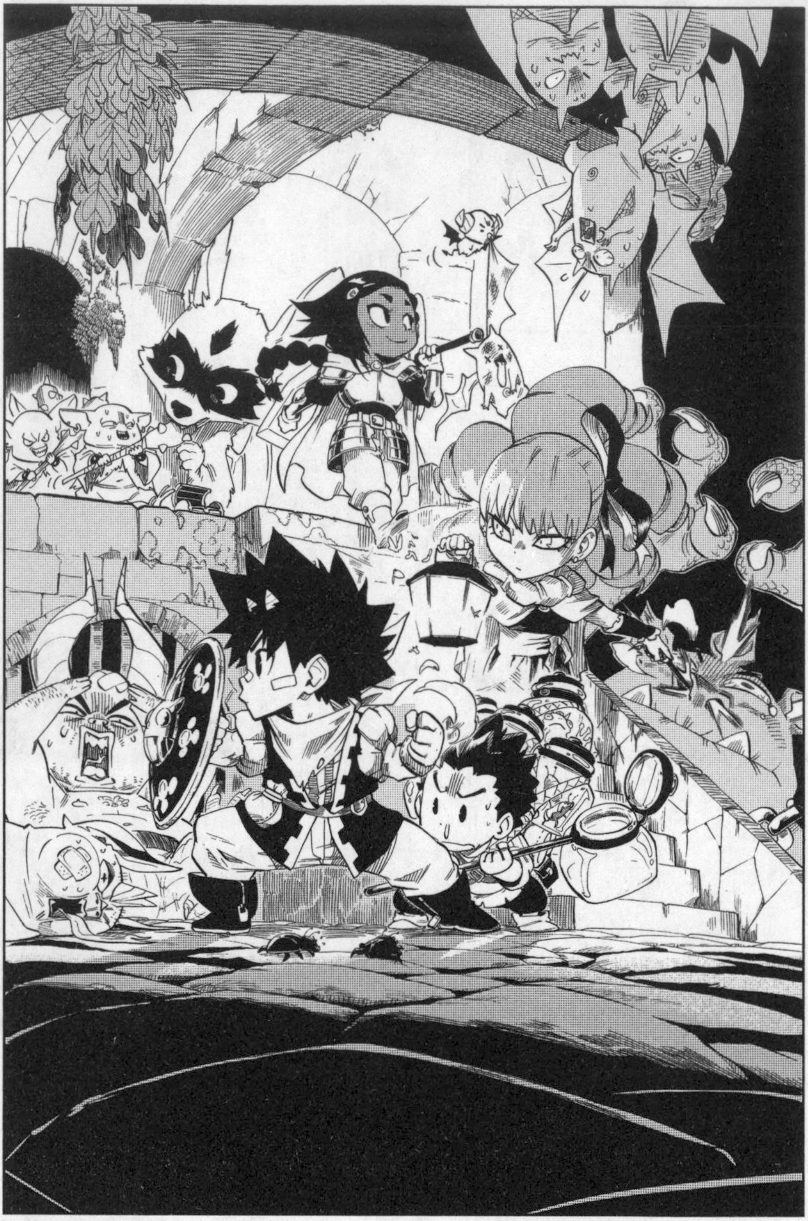

Chapter 106

Just Scared

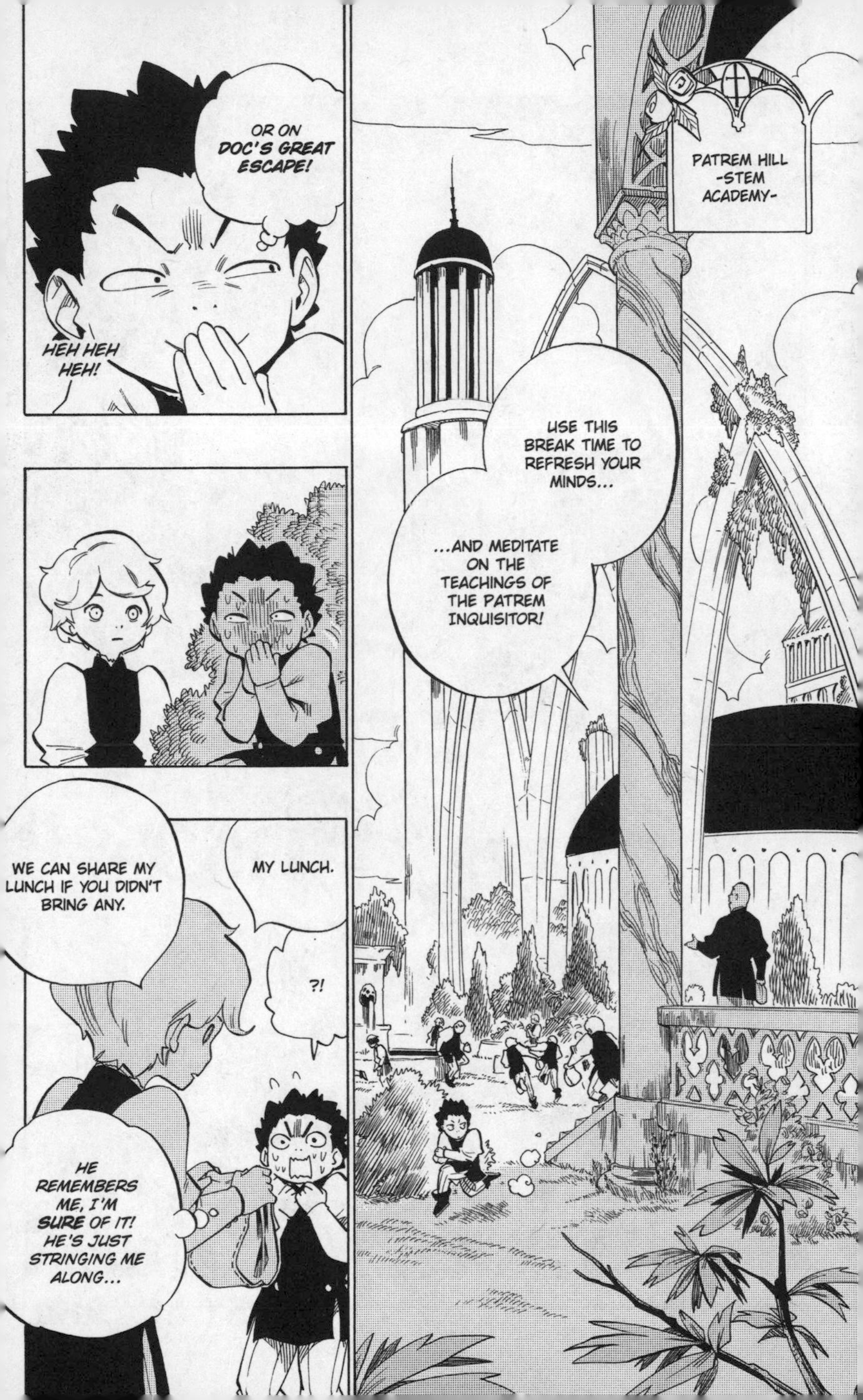
PATREM HILL
-STEM ACADEMY-
USE THIS BREAK TIME TO REFRESH YOUR MINDS...
...AND MEDITATE ON THE TEACHINGS OF THE PATREM INQUISITOR!
OR ON DOC'S GREAT ESCAPE!
HEH HEH HEH!
MY LUNCH.
WE CAN SHARE MY LUNCH IF YOU DIDN'T BRING ANY.
?!
HE REMEMBERS ME, I'M SURE OF IT! HE'S JUST STRINGING ME ALONG...

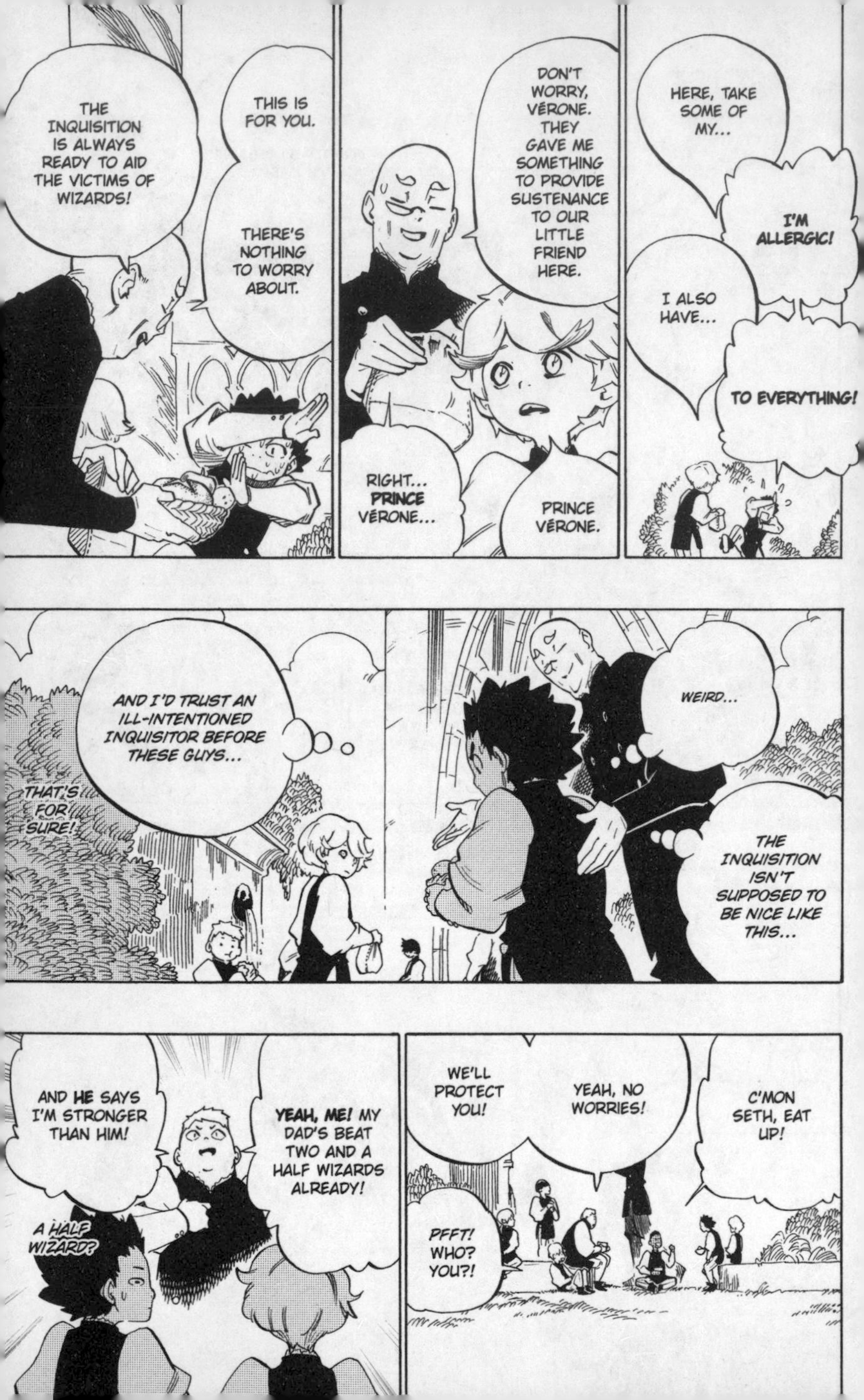
HERE, TAKE SOME OF MY...
I'M ALLERGIC!
I ALSO HAVE...
TO EVERYTHING!
DON'T WORRY, VÉRONE. THEY GAVE ME SOMETHING TO PROVIDE SUSTENANCE TO OUR LITTLE FRIEND HERE.
PRINCE VÉRONE.
RIGHT... PRINCE VÉRONE...
THIS IS FOR YOU.
THERE'S NOTHING TO WORRY ABOUT.
THE INQUISITION IS ALWAYS READY TO AID THE VICTIMS OF WIZARDS!
WEIRD...
THE INQUISITION ISN'T SUPPOSED TO BE NICE LIKE THIS...
AND I'D TRUST AN ILL-INTENTIONED INQUISITOR BEFORE THESE GUYS...
THAT'S FOR SURE!
C'MON SETH, EAT UP!
YEAH, NO WORRIES!
WE'LL PROTECT YOU!
PFFT! WHO? YOU?!
YEAH, ME! MY DAD'S BEAT TWO AND A HALF WIZARDS ALREADY!
AND HE SAYS I'M STRONGER THAN HIM!
A HALF WIZARD?

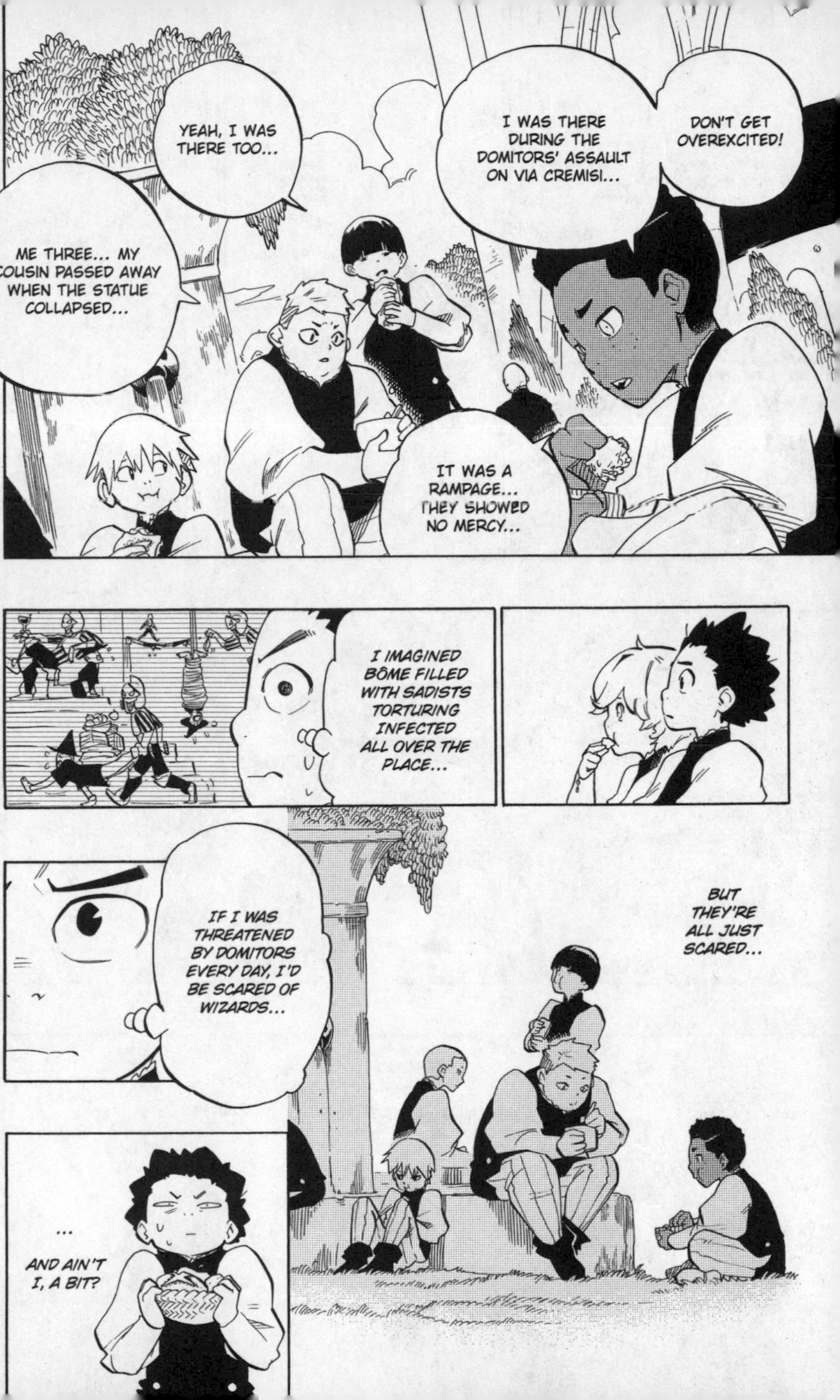
DON'T GET OVEREXCITED!
I WAS THERE DURING THE DOMITORS' ASSAULT ON VIA CREMISI...
YEAH, I WAS THERE TOO...
ME THREE... MY COUSIN PASSED AWAY WHEN THE STATUE COLLAPSED...
IT WAS A RAMPAGE... THEY SHOWED NO MERCY...
I IMAGINED BÔME FILLED WITH SADISTS TORTURING INFECTED ALL OVER THE PLACE...
BUT THEY'RE ALL JUST SCARED...
IF I WAS THREATENED BY DOMITORS EVERY DAY, I'D BE SCARED OF WIZARDS...
...
AND AIN'T I, A BIT?

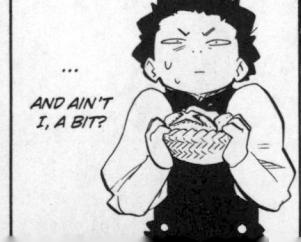

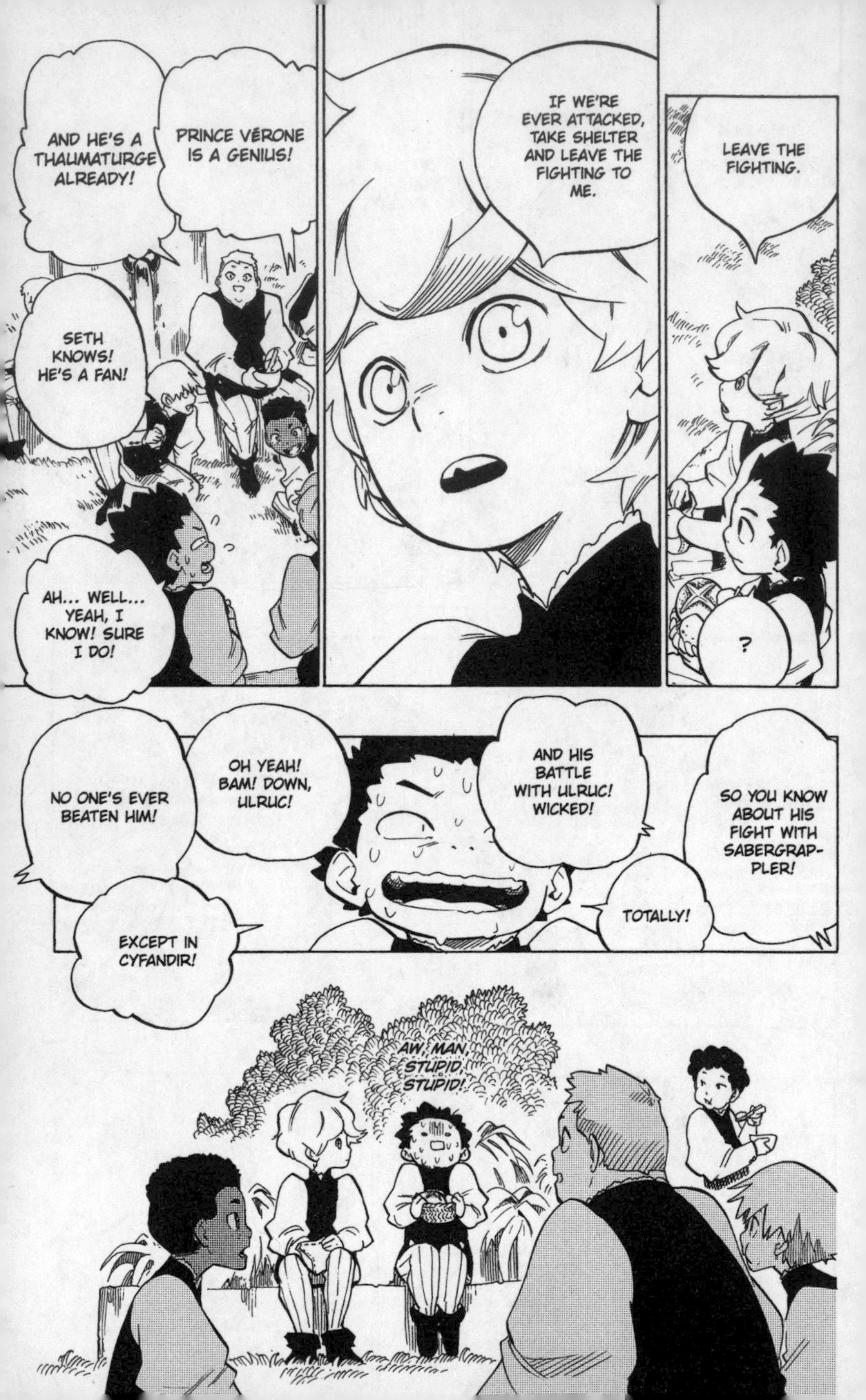

LEAVE THE FIGHTING.
?
IF WE'RE EVER ATTACKED, TAKE SHELTER AND LEAVE THE FIGHTING TO ME.
PRINCE VÉRONE IS A GENIUS!
AND HE'S A THAUMATURGE ALREADY!
SETH KNOWS! HE'S A FAN!
AH... WELL... YEAH, I KNOW! SURE I DO!
SO YOU KNOW ABOUT HIS FIGHT WITH SABERGRAP-PLER!
TOTALLY!
AND HIS BATTLE WITH ULRUC! WICKED!
OH YEAH! BAM! DOWN, ULRUC!
NO ONE'S EVER BEATEN HIM!
EXCEPT IN CYFANDIR!
AW, MAN, STUPID, STUPID!

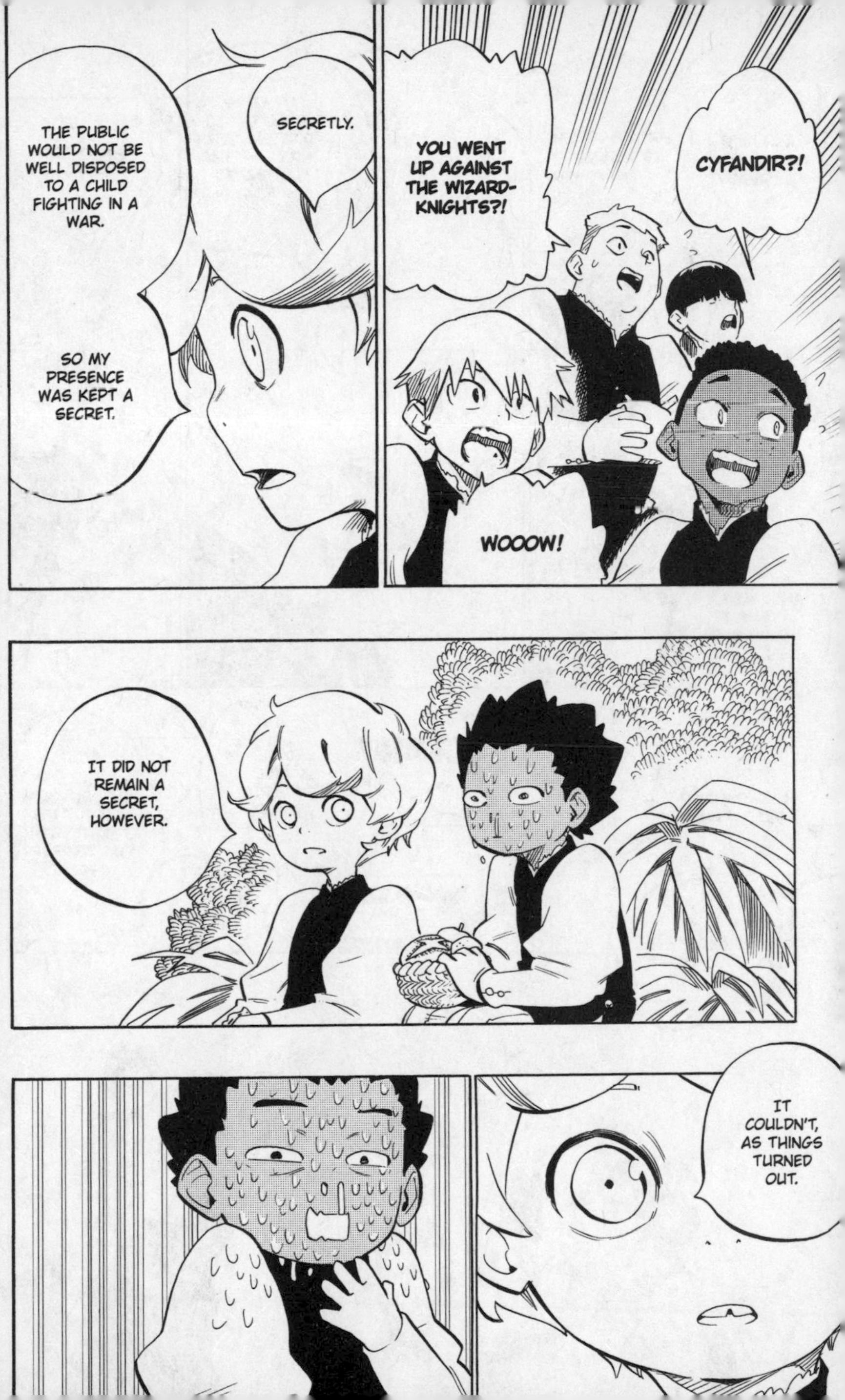
CYFANDIR?!
YOU WENT UP AGAINST THE WIZARD-KNIGHTS?!
WOOOW!
SECRETLY.
THE PUBLIC WOULD NOT BE WELL DISPOSED TO A CHILD FIGHTING IN A WAR.
SO MY PRESENCE WAS KEPT A SECRET.
IT DID NOT REMAIN A SECRET, HOWEVER.
IT COULDN'T, AS THINGS TURNED OUT.

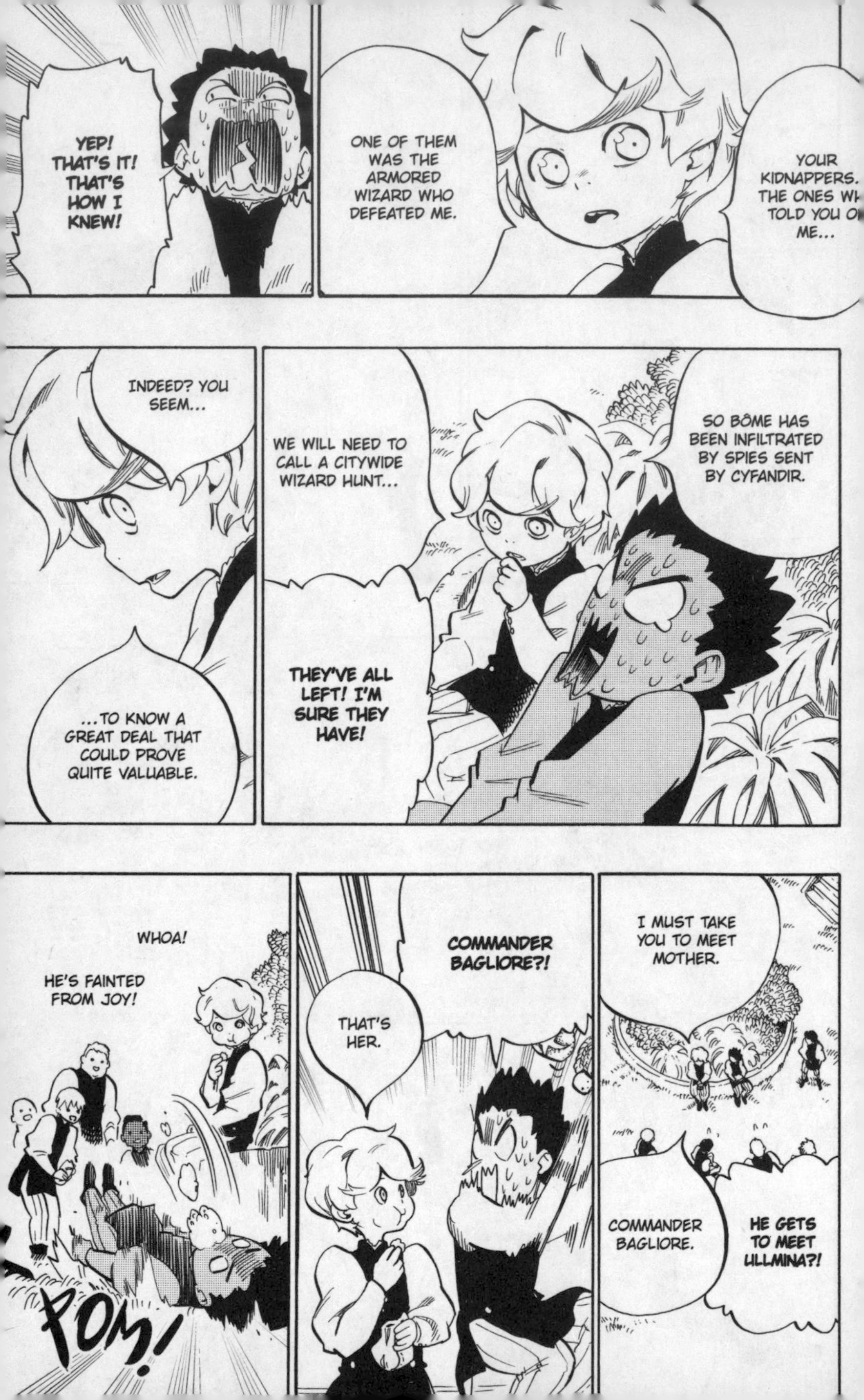
YOUR KIDNAPPERS. THE ONES W TOLD YOU O ME...
ONE OF THEM WAS THE ARMORED WIZARD WHO DEFEATED ME.
YEP! THAT'S IT! THAT'S HOW I KNEW!
SO BÔME HAS BEEN INFILTRATED BY SPIES SENT BY CYFANDIR.
WE WILL NEED TO CALL A CITYWIDE WIZARD HUNT...
THEY'VE ALL LEFT! I'M SURE THEY HAVE!
INDEED? YOU SEEM...
...TO KNOW A GREAT DEAL THAT COULD PROVE QUITE VALUABLE.
I MUST TAKE YOU TO MEET MOTHER.
HE GETS TO MEET ULLMINA?!
COMMANDER BAGLIORE.
COMMANDER BAGLIORE?!
THAT'S HER.
WHOA!
HE'S FAINTED FROM JOY!
POM!

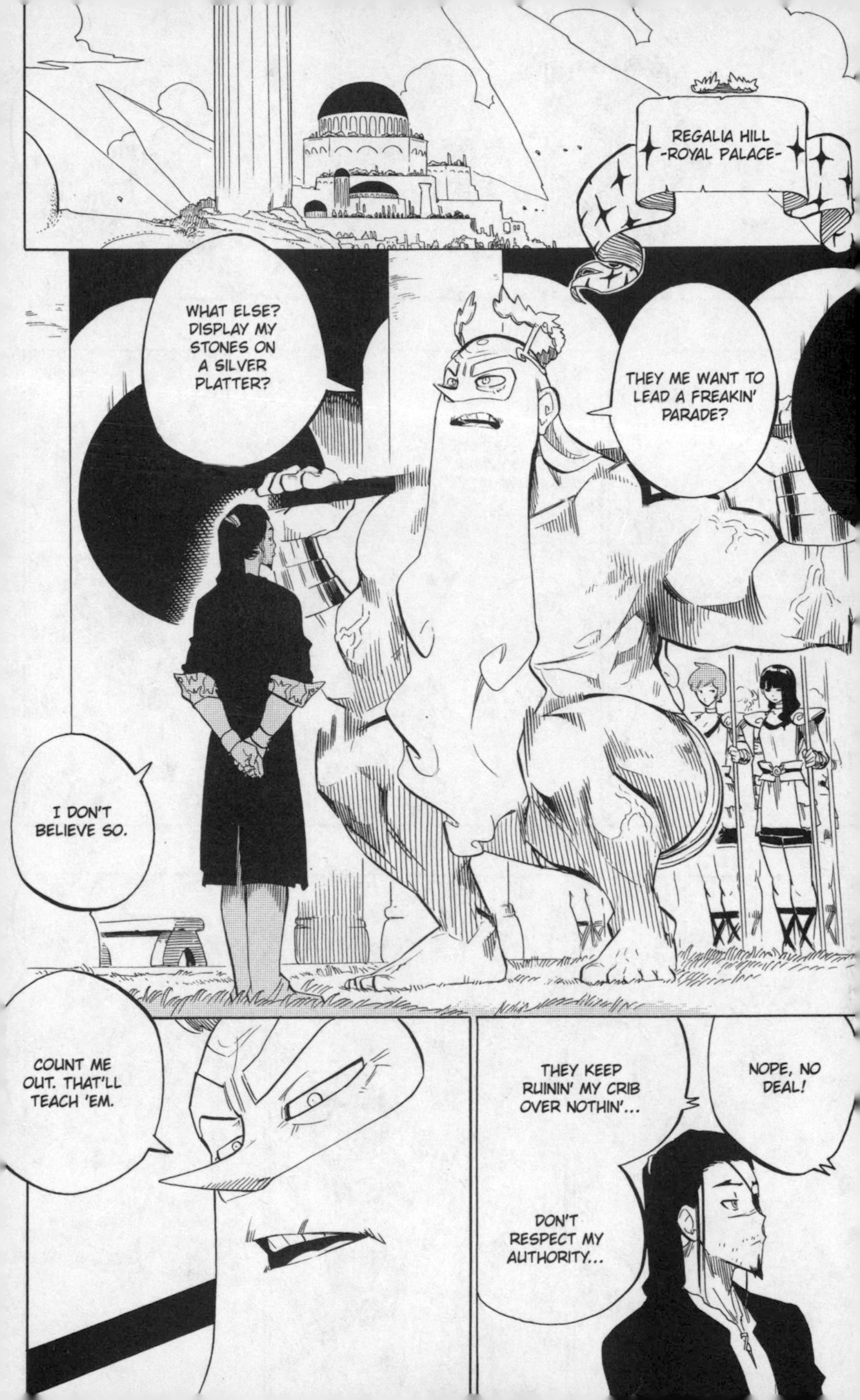
REGALIA HILL -ROYAL PALACE-
THEY ME WANT TO LEAD A FREAKIN' PARADE?
WHAT ELSE? DISPLAY MY STONES ON A SILVER PLATTER?
I DON'T BELIEVE SO.
NOPE, NO DEAL!
THEY KEEP RUININ' MY CRIB OVER NOTHIN'...
DON'T RESPECT MY AUTHORITY...
COUNT ME OUT. THAT'LL TEACH 'EM.

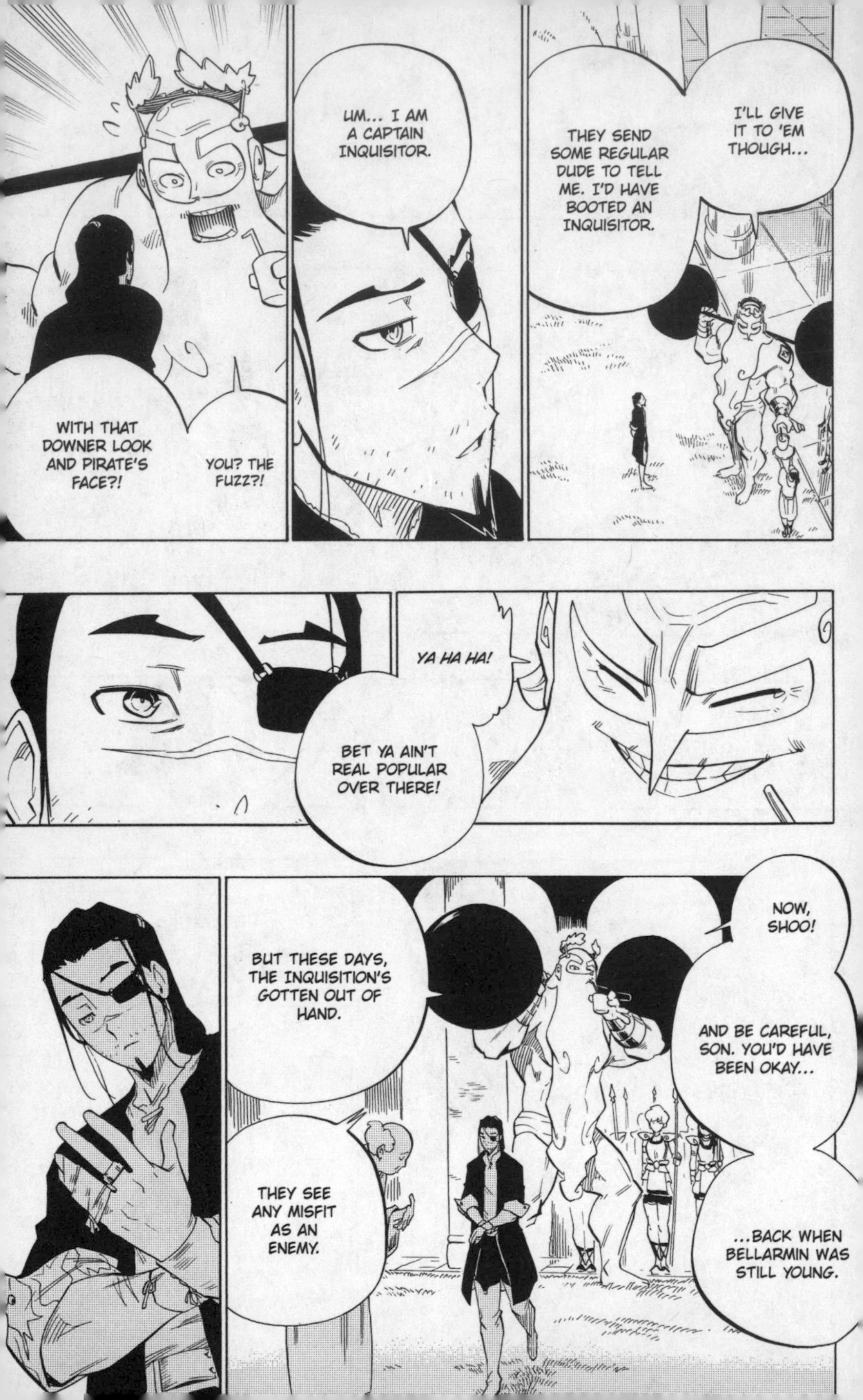
I'LL GIVE IT TO 'EM THOUGH...
THEY SEND SOME REGULAR DUDE TO TELL ME. I'D HAVE BOOTED AN INQUISITOR.
UM... I AM A CAPTAIN INQUISITOR.
YOU? THE FUZZ?!
WITH THAT DOWNER LOOK AND PIRATE'S FACE?!
YA HA HA!
BET YA AIN'T REAL POPULAR OVER THERE!
NOW, SHOO!
AND BE CAREFUL, SON. YOU'D HAVE BEEN OKAY...
...BACK WHEN BELLARMIN WAS STILL YOUNG.
BUT THESE DAYS, THE INQUISITION'S GOTTEN OUT OF HAND.
THEY SEE ANY MISFIT AS AN ENEMY.

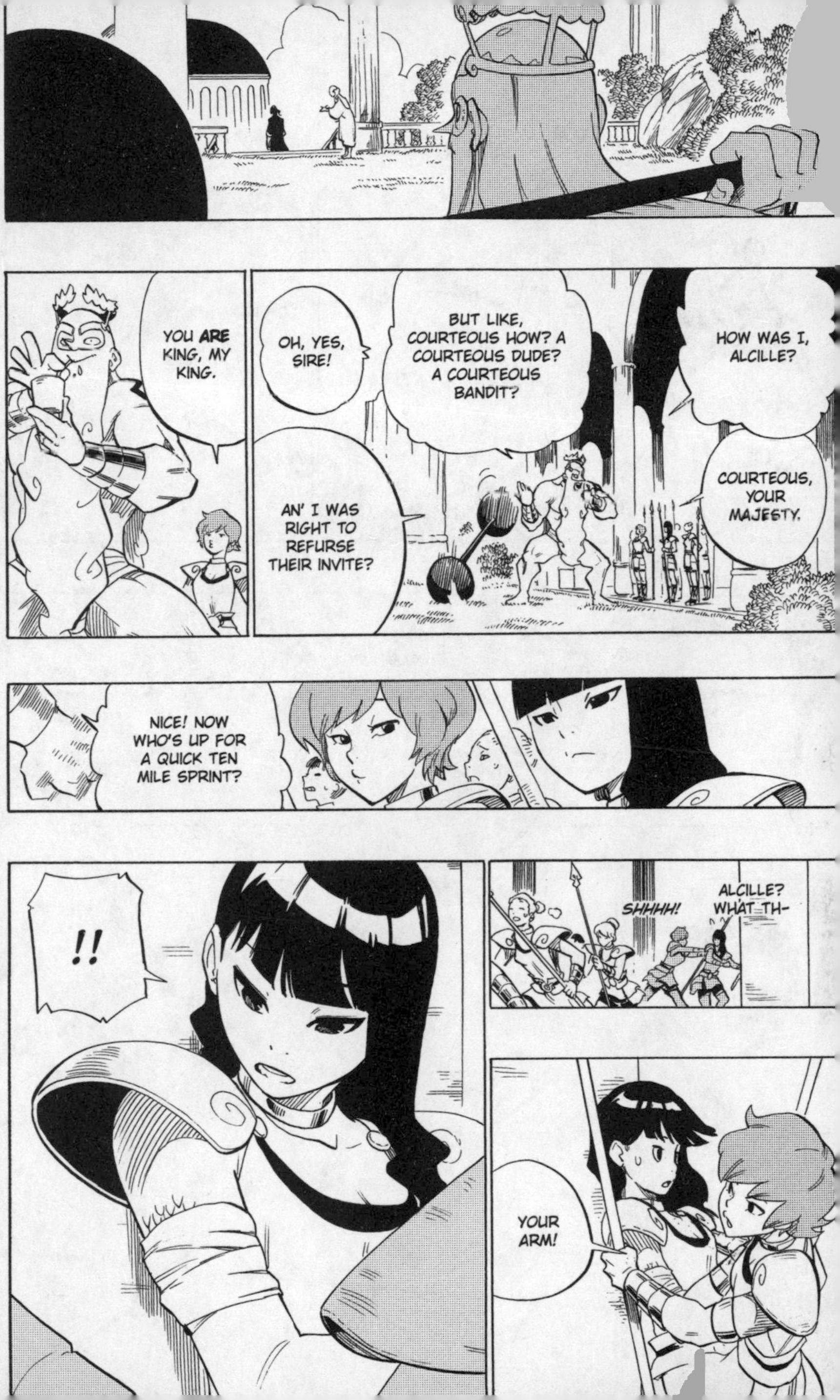
HOW WAS I, ALCILLE?
COURTEOUS, YOUR MAJESTY.
BUT LIKE, COURTEOUS HOW? A COURTEOUS DUDE? A COURTEOUS BANDIT?
AN' I WAS RIGHT TO REFURSE THEIR INVITE?
OH, YES, SIRE!
YOU **ARE** KING, MY KING.
NICE! NOW WHO'S UP FOR A QUICK TEN MILE SPRINT?
ALCILLE? WHAT TH-
SHHHH!
YOUR ARM!
!!

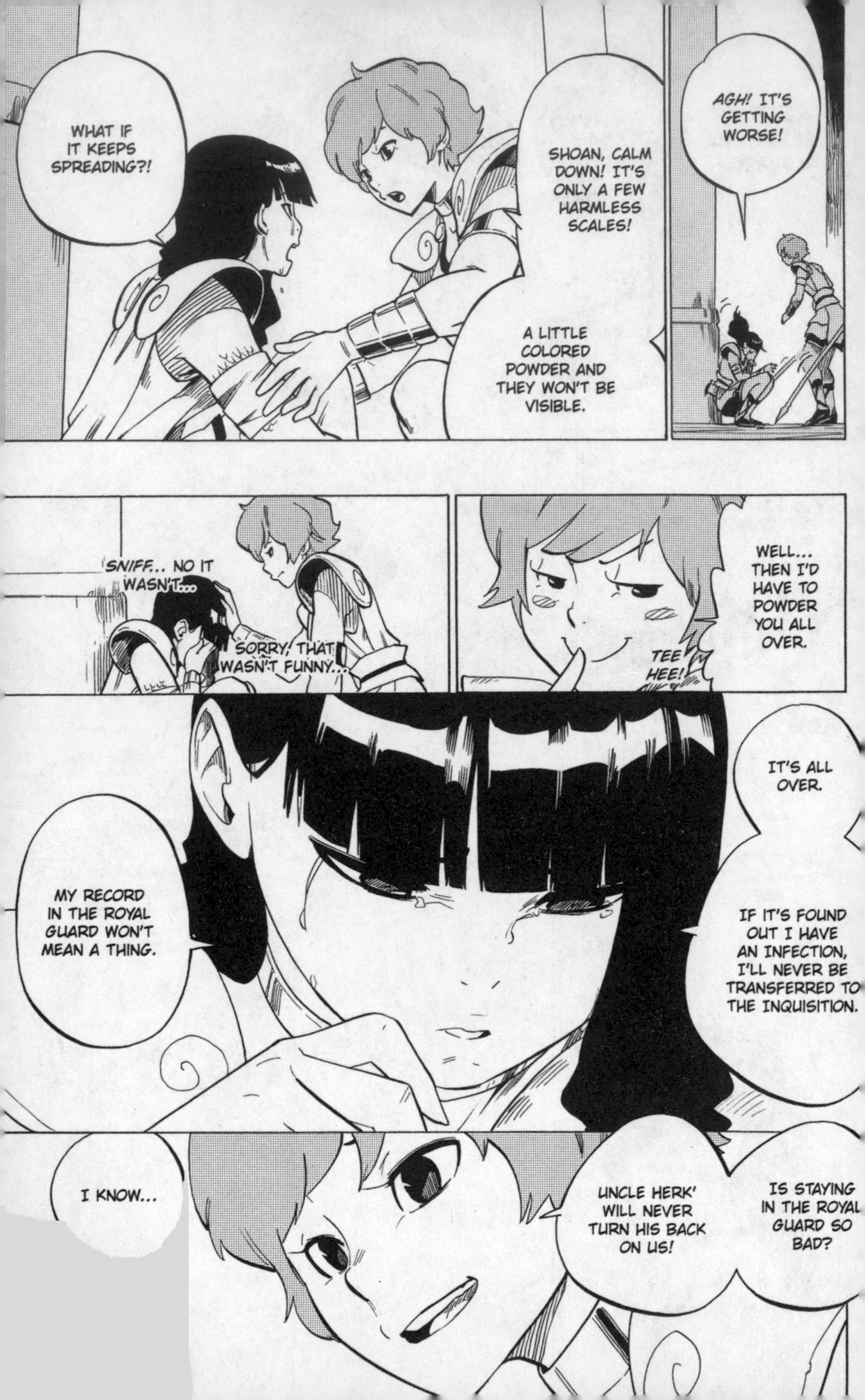
AGH! IT'S GETTING WORSE!
SHOAN, CALM DOWN! IT'S ONLY A FEW HARMLESS SCALES!
A LITTLE COLORED POWDER AND THEY WON'T BE VISIBLE.
WHAT IF IT KEEPS SPREADING?!
WELL... THEN I'D HAVE TO POWDER YOU ALL OVER.
TEE HEE!
SORRY, THAT WASN'T FUNNY...
SNIFF... NO IT WASN'T...
IT'S ALL OVER.
IF IT'S FOUND OUT I HAVE AN INFECTION, I'LL NEVER BE TRANSFERRED TO THE INQUISITION.
MY RECORD IN THE ROYAL GUARD WON'T MEAN A THING.
IS STAYING IN THE ROYAL GUARD SO BAD?
UNCLE HERK' WILL NEVER TURN HIS BACK ON US!
I KNOW...

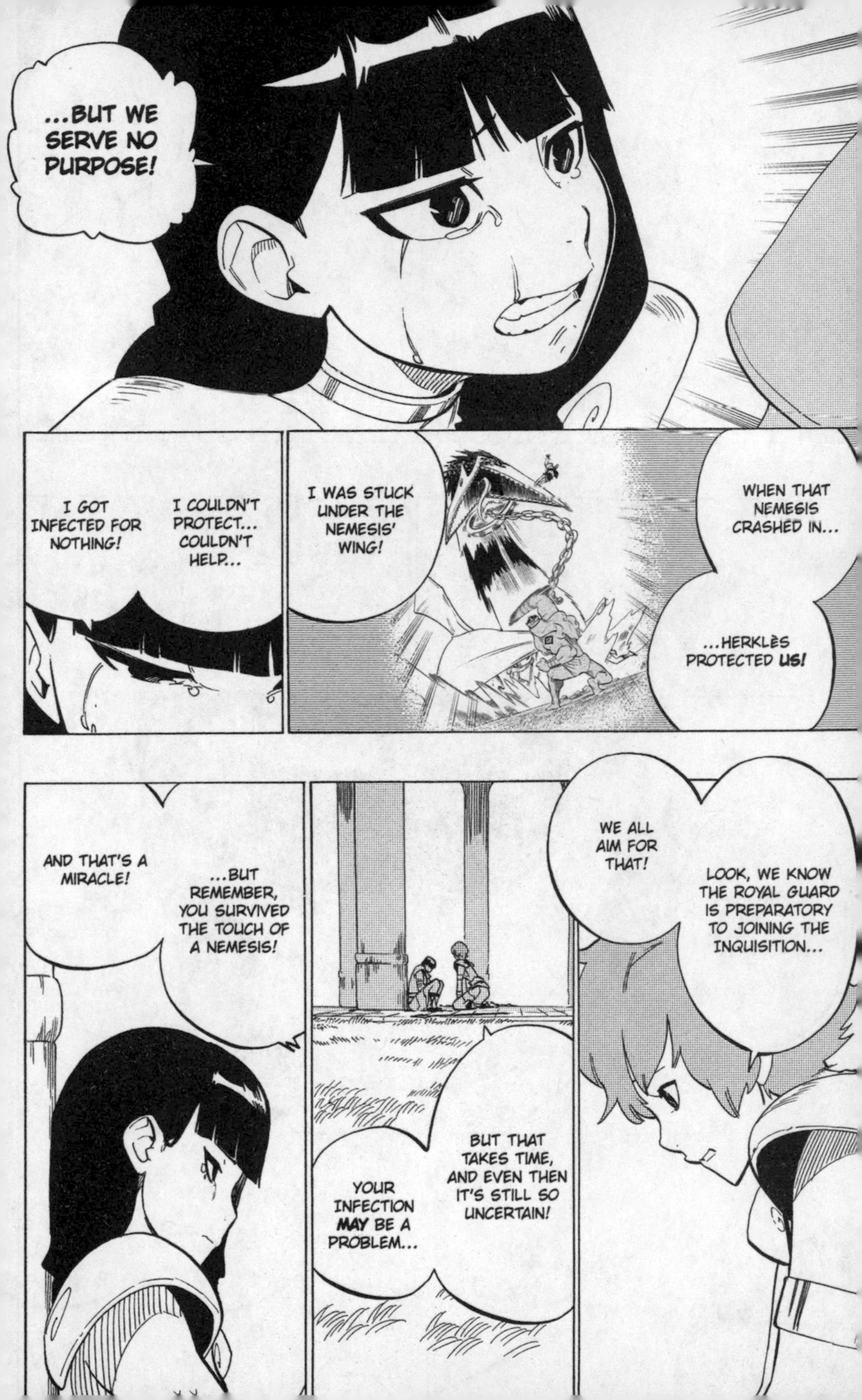
...BUT WE SERVE NO PURPOSE!
WHEN THAT NEMESIS CRASHED IN...
...HERKLÈS PROTECTED **US!**
I WAS STUCK UNDER THE NEMESIS' WING!
I COULDN'T PROTECT... COULDN'T HELP...
I GOT INFECTED FOR NOTHING!
LOOK, WE KNOW THE ROYAL GUARD IS PREPARATORY TO JOINING THE INQUISITION...
WE ALL AIM FOR THAT!
BUT THAT TAKES TIME, AND EVEN THEN IT'S STILL SO UNCERTAIN!
YOUR INFECTION **MAY** BE A PROBLEM...
...BUT REMEMBER, YOU SURVIVED THE TOUCH OF A NEMESIS!
AND THAT'S A MIRACLE!

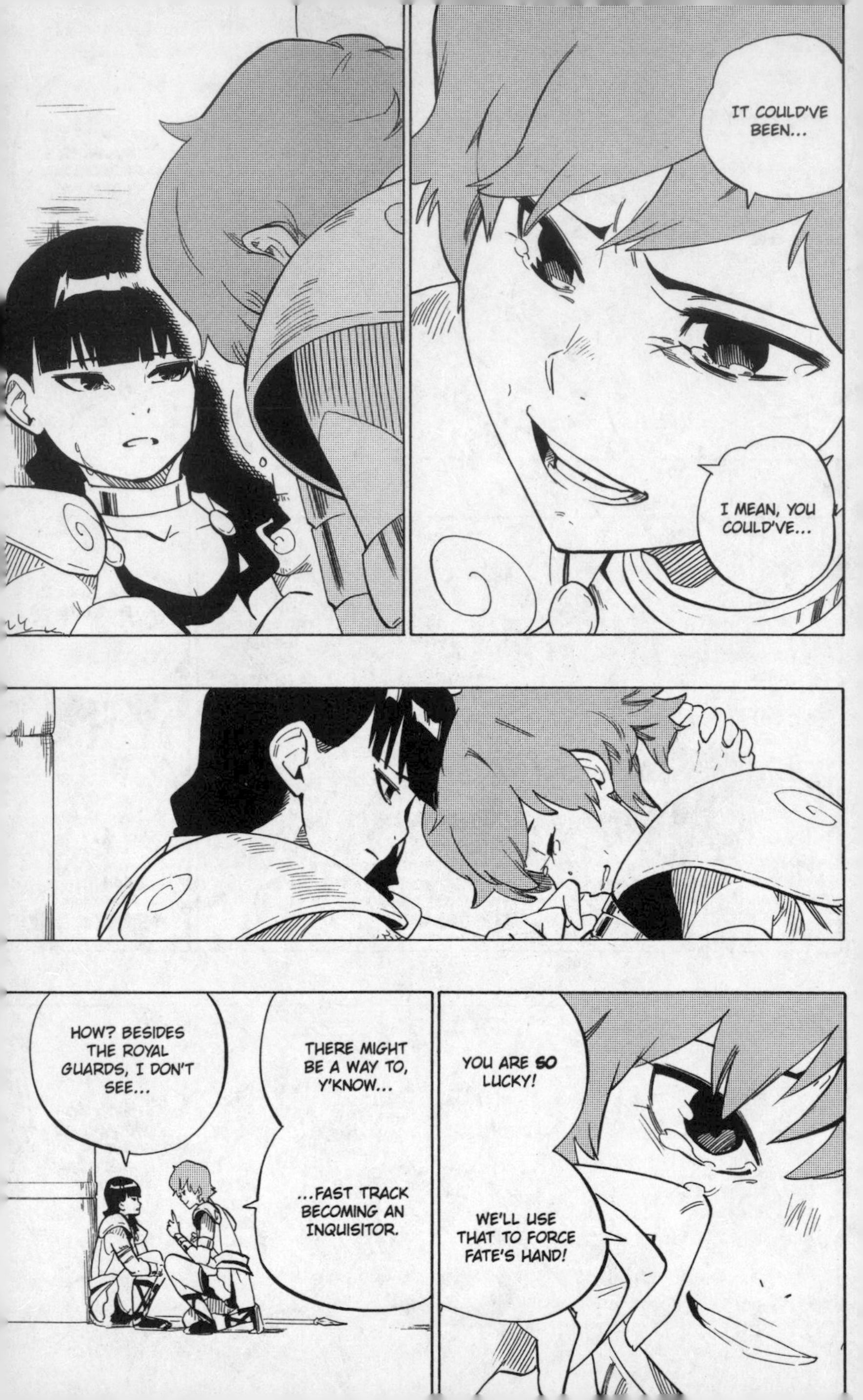
IT COULD'VE BEEN...
I MEAN, YOU COULD'VE...
YOU ARE SO LUCKY!
WE'LL USE THAT TO FORCE FATE'S HAND!
HOW? BESIDES THE ROYAL GUARDS, I DON'T SEE...
THERE MIGHT BE A WAY TO, Y'KNOW...
...FAST TRACK BECOMING AN INQUISITOR.

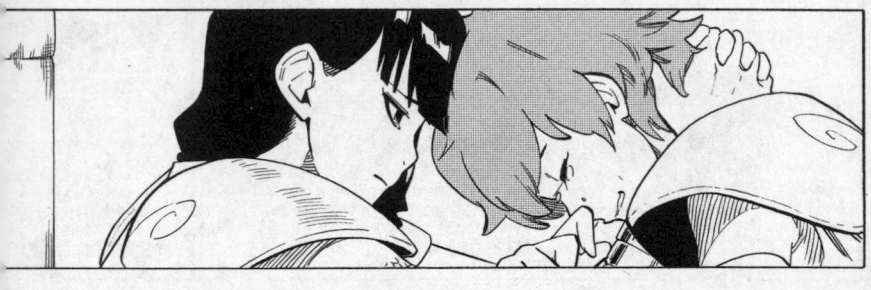

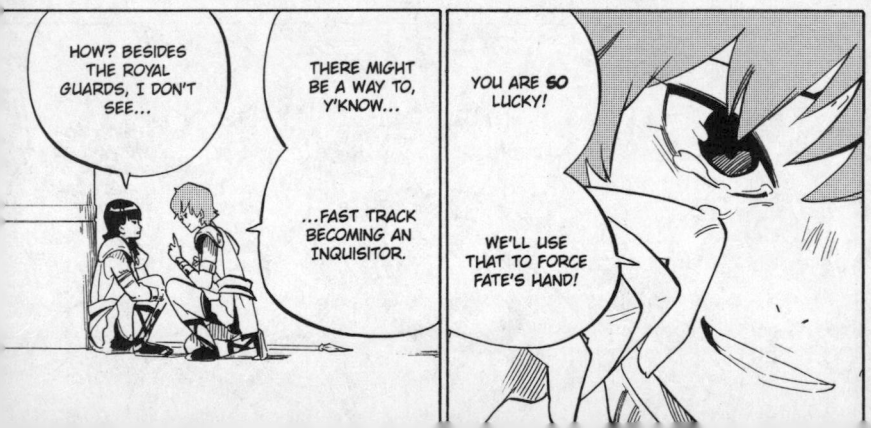

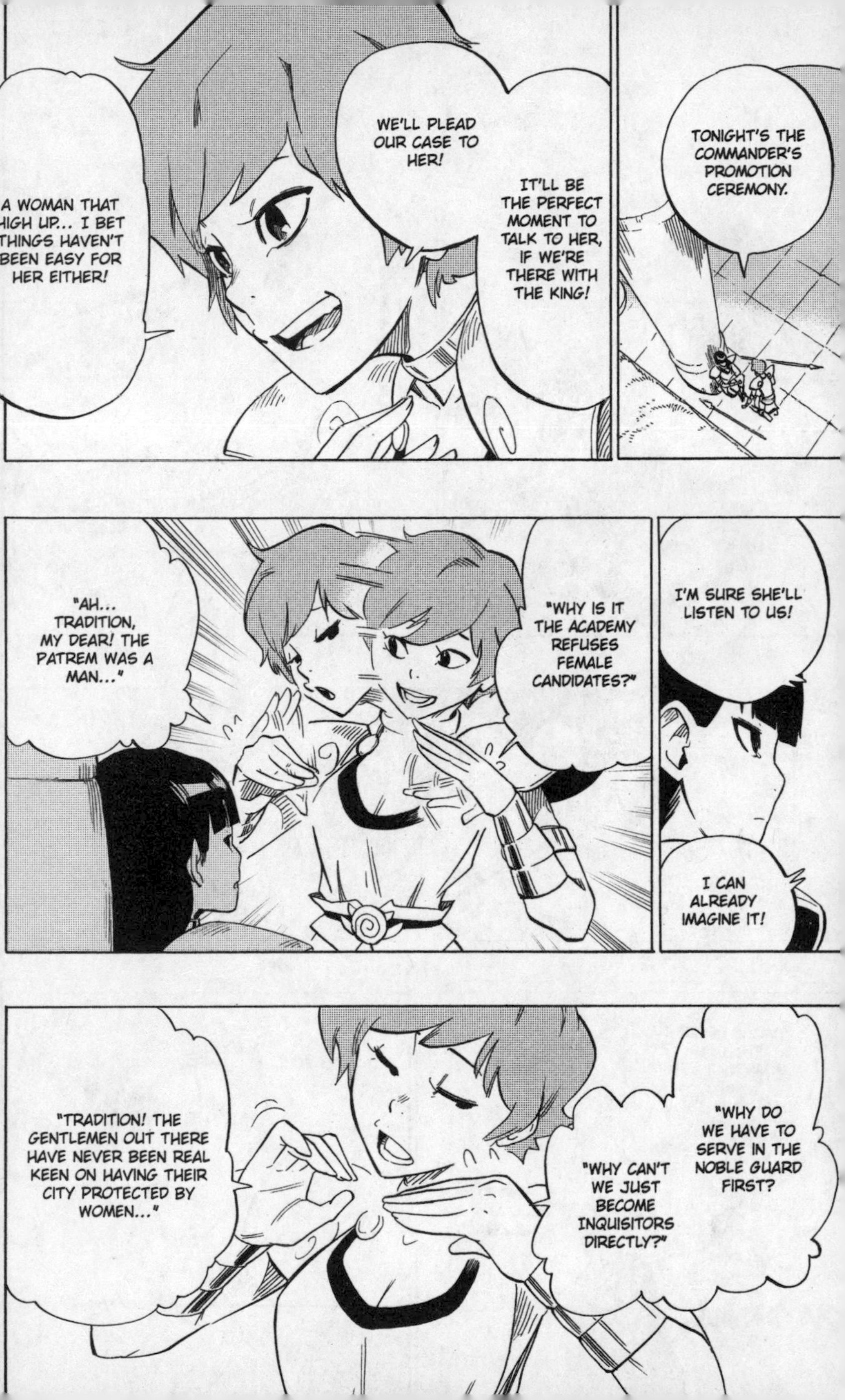

TONIGHT'S THE COMMANDER'S PROMOTION CEREMONY.
IT'LL BE THE PERFECT MOMENT TO TALK TO HER, IF WE'RE THERE WITH THE KING!
WE'LL PLEAD OUR CASE TO HER!
A WOMAN THAT HIGH UP... I BET THINGS HAVEN'T BEEN EASY FOR HER EITHER!
I'M SURE SHE'LL LISTEN TO US!
I CAN ALREADY IMAGINE IT!
"WHY IS IT THE ACADEMY REFUSES FEMALE CANDIDATES?"
"AH... TRADITION, MY DEAR! THE PATREM WAS A MAN..."
"WHY DO WE HAVE TO SERVE IN THE NOBLE GUARD FIRST?
"WHY CAN'T WE JUST BECOME INQUISITORS DIRECTLY?"
"TRADITION! THE GENTLEMEN OUT THERE HAVE NEVER BEEN REAL KEEN ON HAVING THEIR CITY PROTECTED BY WOMEN..."

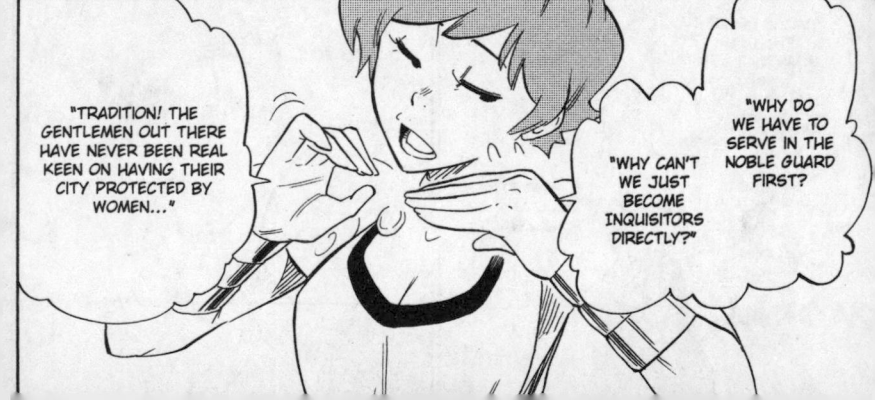

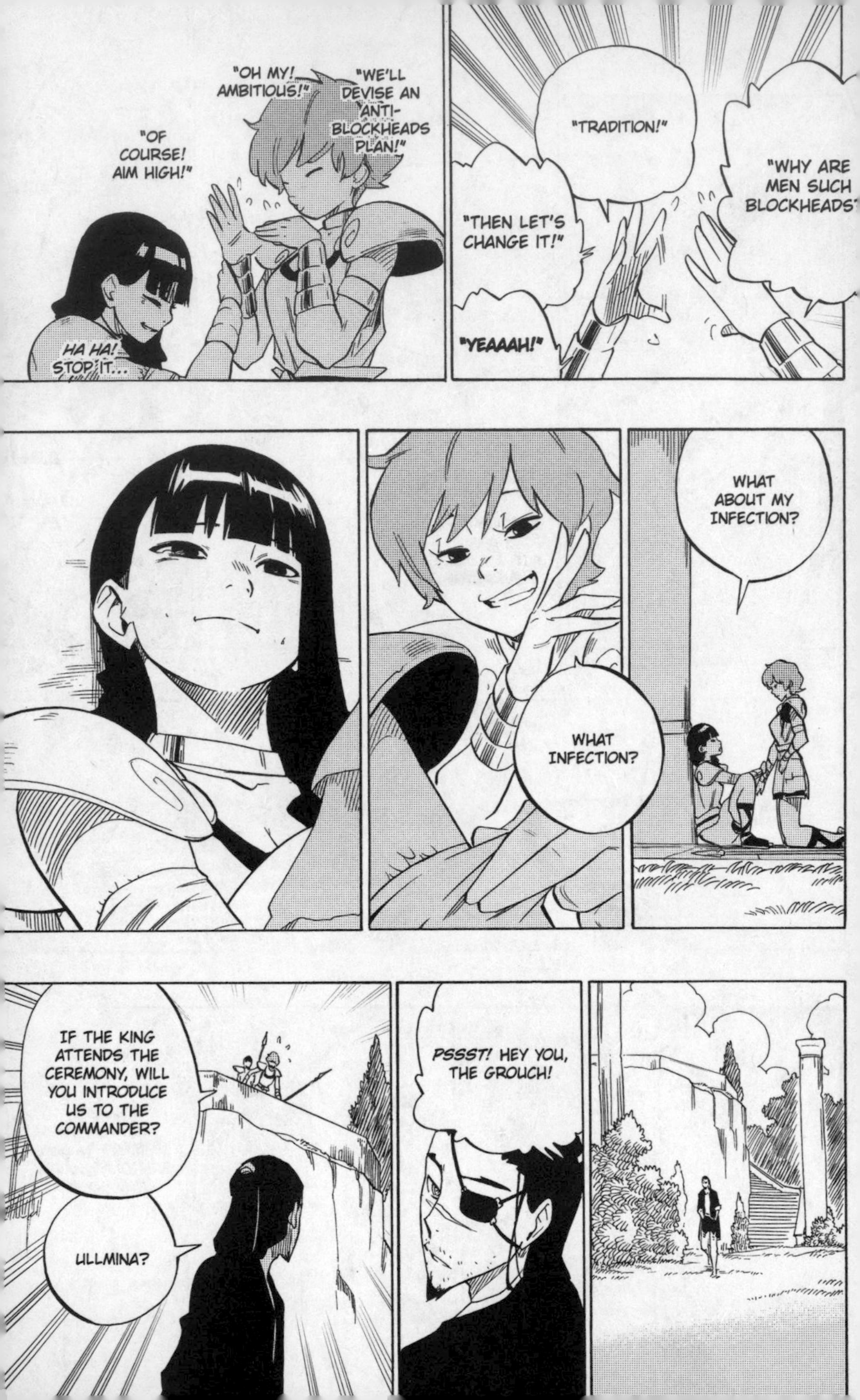
"WHY ARE MEN SUCH BLOCKHEADS
"TRADITION!"
"THEN LET'S CHANGE IT!"
"YEAAAH!"
"WE'LL DEVISE AN ANTI-BLOCKHEADS PLAN!"
"OH MY! AMBITIOUS!"
"OF COURSE! AIM HIGH!"
HA HA! STOP IT...
WHAT ABOUT MY INFECTION?
WHAT INFECTION?
PSSST! HEY YOU, THE GROUCH!
IF THE KING ATTENDS THE CEREMONY, WILL YOU INTRODUCE US TO THE COMMANDER?
ULLMINA?

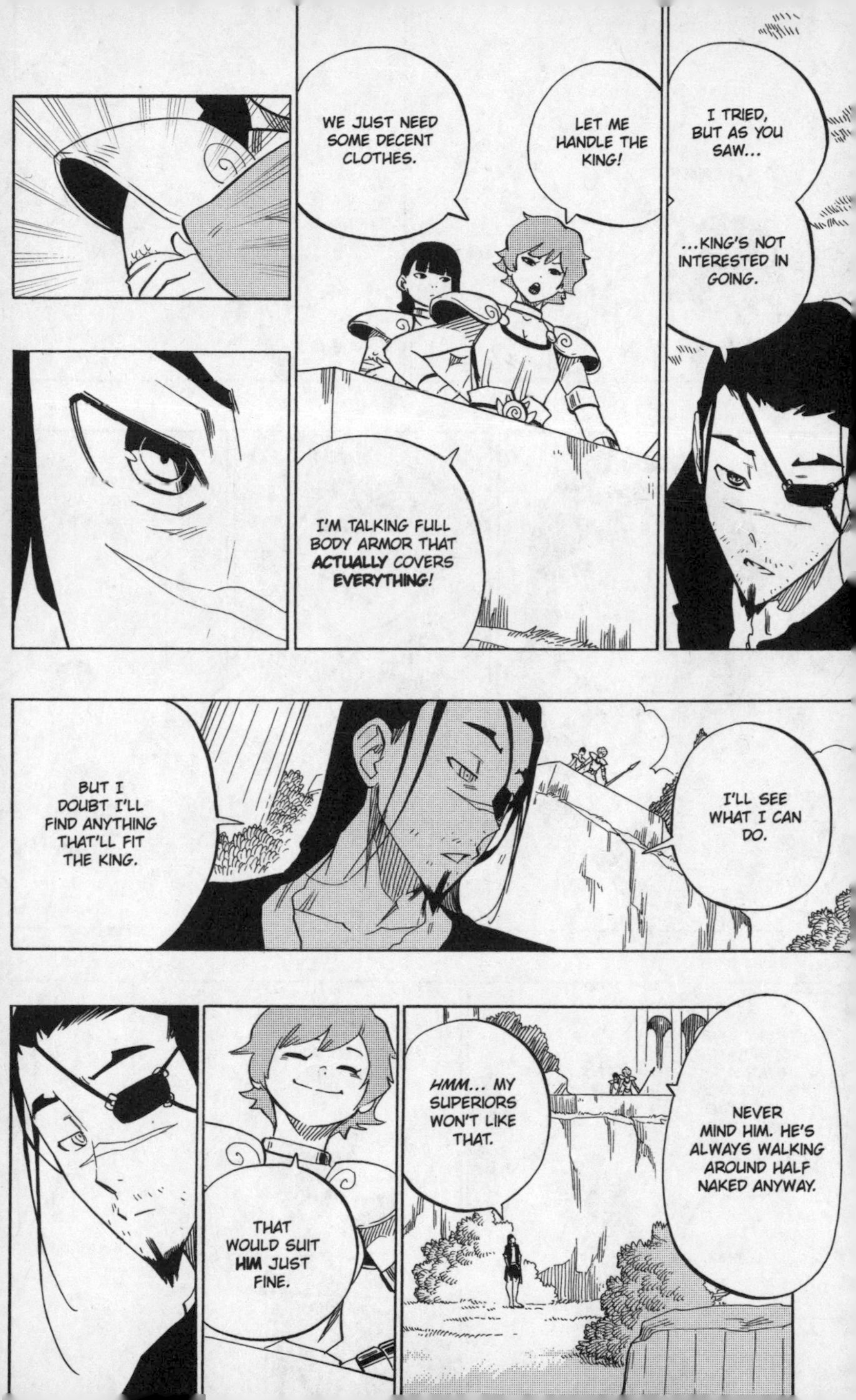
I TRIED, BUT AS YOU SAW...
...KING'S NOT INTERESTED IN GOING.
LET ME HANDLE THE KING!
WE JUST NEED SOME DECENT CLOTHES.
I'M TALKING FULL BODY ARMOR THAT **ACTUALLY** COVERS **EVERYTHING**!
I'LL SEE WHAT I CAN DO.
BUT I DOUBT I'LL FIND ANYTHING THAT'LL FIT THE KING.
NEVER MIND HIM. HE'S ALWAYS WALKING AROUND HALF NAKED ANYWAY.
HMM... MY SUPERIORS WON'T LIKE THAT.
THAT WOULD SUIT **HIM** JUST FINE.

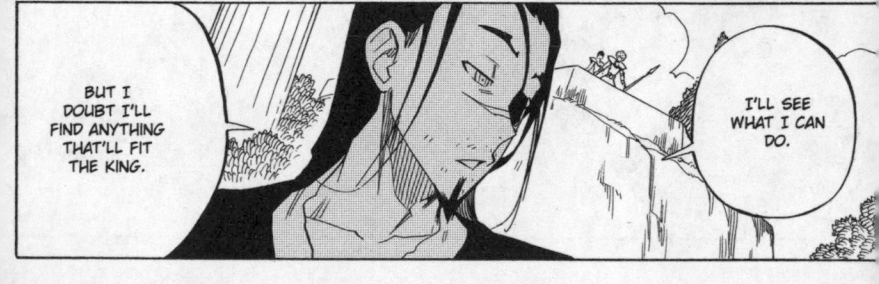

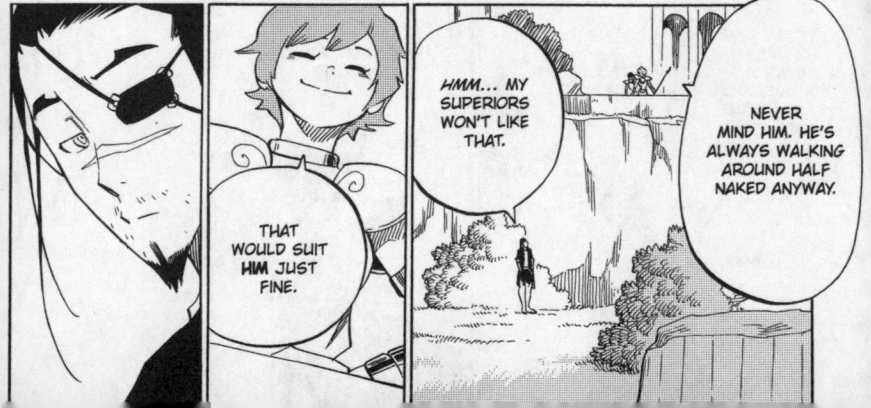

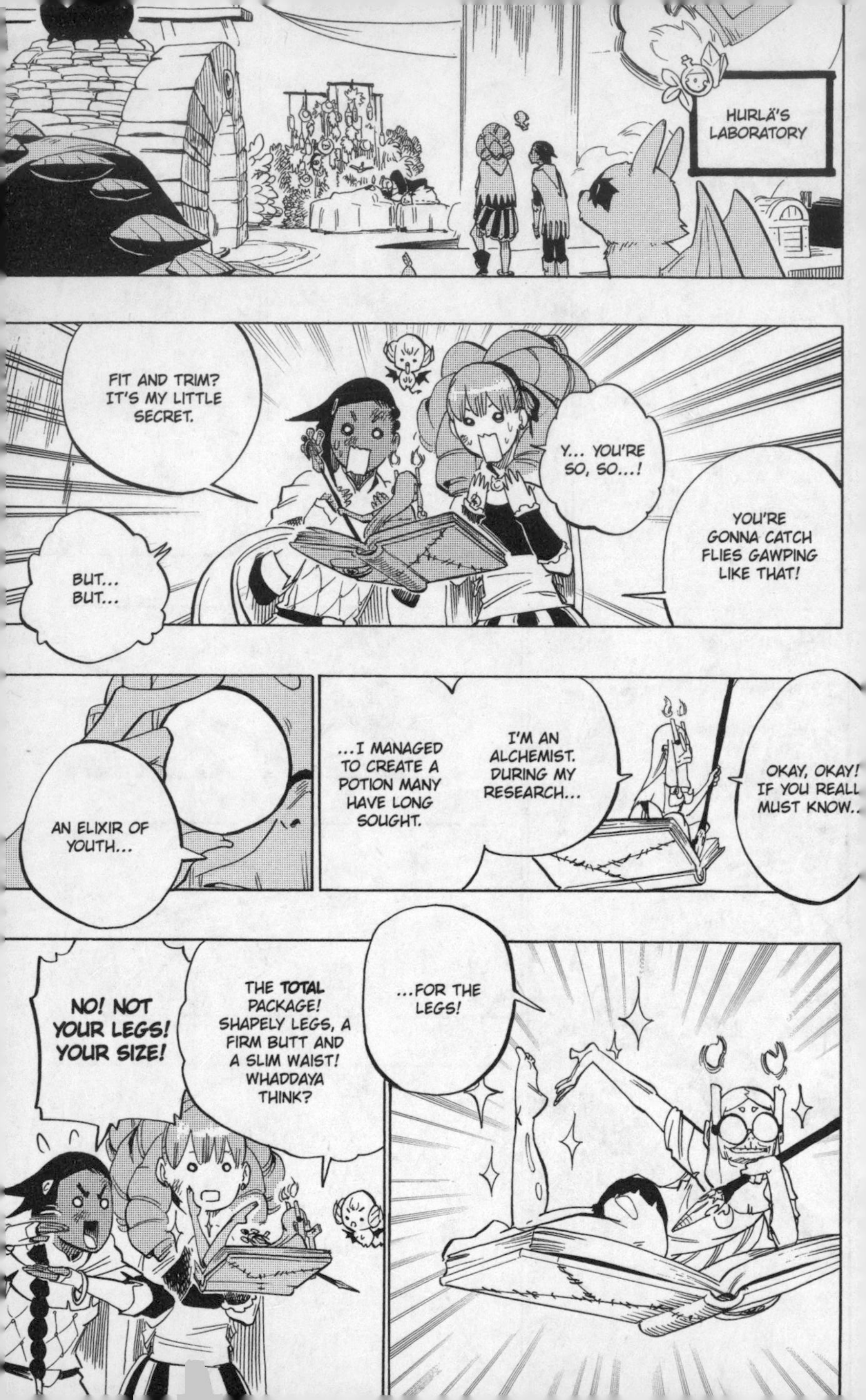
HURLÄ'S LABORATORY
Y... YOU'RE SO, SO...!
FIT AND TRIM? IT'S MY LITTLE SECRET.
YOU'RE GONNA CATCH FLIES GAWPING LIKE THAT!
BUT... BUT...
OKAY, OKAY! IF YOU REALL MUST KNOW..
I'M AN ALCHEMIST. DURING MY RESEARCH...
...I MANAGED TO CREATE A POTION MANY HAVE LONG SOUGHT.
AN ELIXIR OF YOUTH...
...FOR THE LEGS!
THE TOTAL PACKAGE! SHAPELY LEGS, A FIRM BUTT AND A SLIM WAIST! WHADDAYA THINK?
NO! NOT YOUR LEGS! YOUR SIZE!

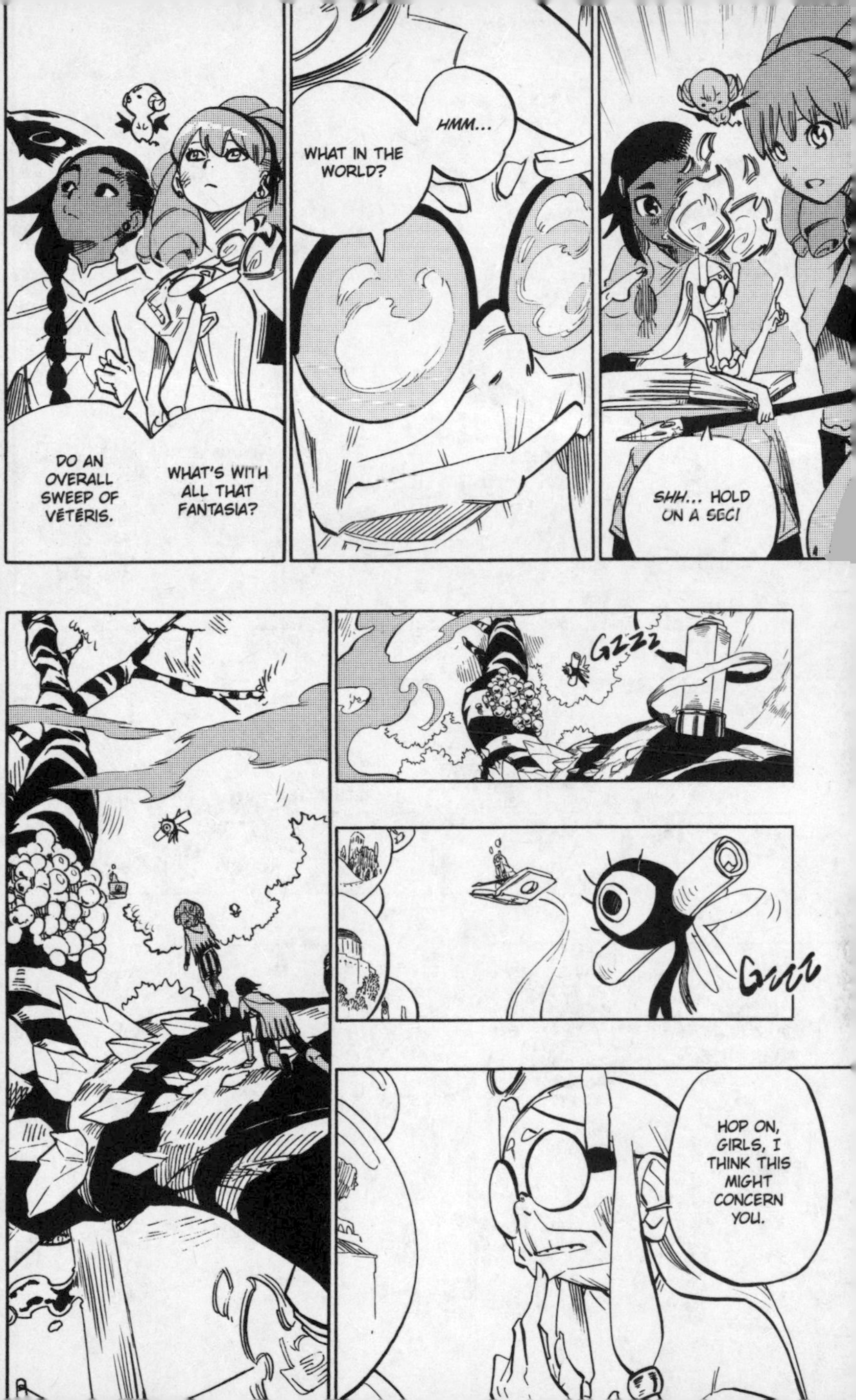
SHH... HOLD ON A SEC!
HMM...
WHAT IN THE WORLD?
WHAT'S WITH ALL THAT FANTASIA?
DO AN OVERALL SWEEP OF VÉTERIS.
GZZZ
GZZZ
HOP ON, GIRLS, I THINK THIS MIGHT CONCERN YOU.

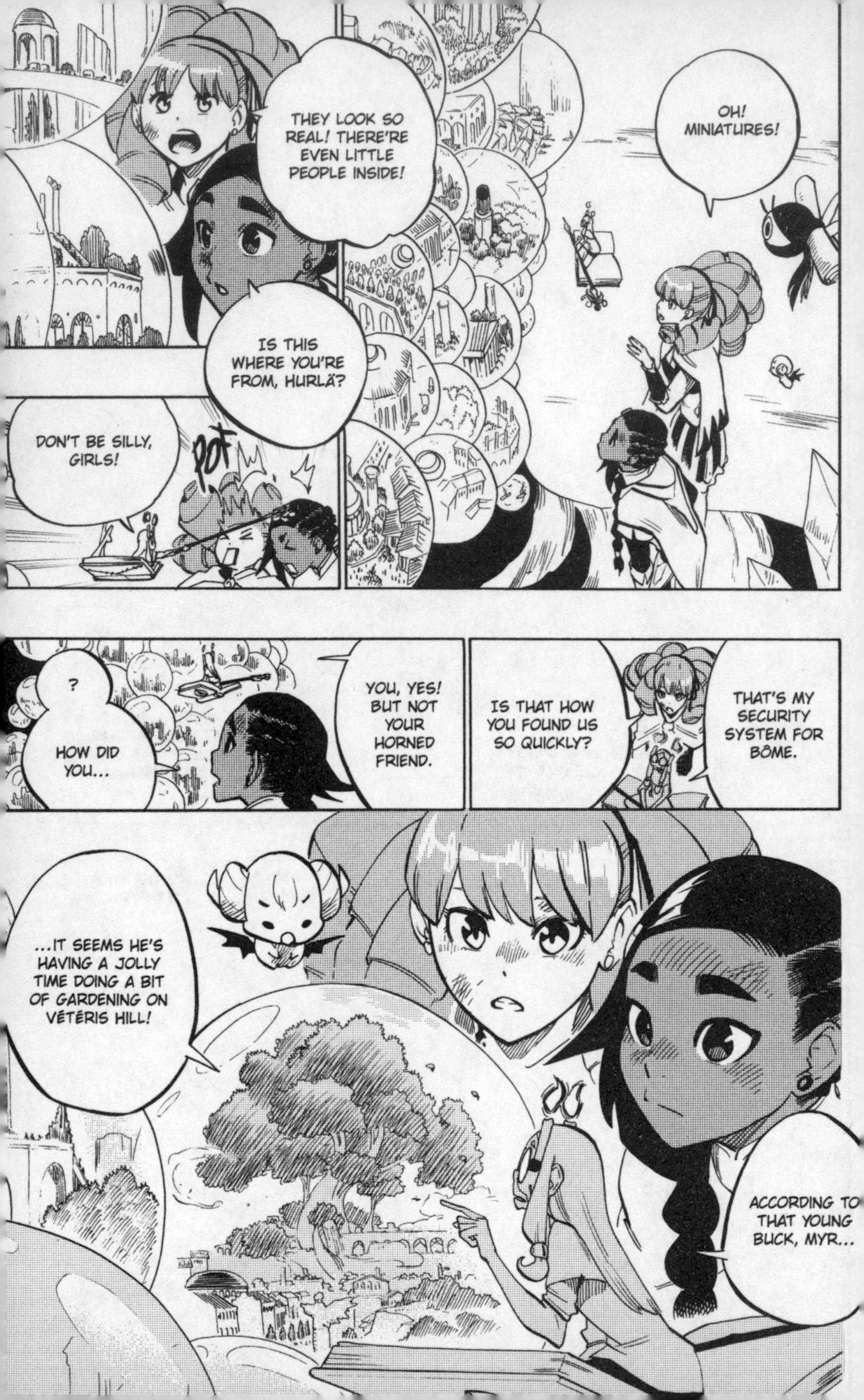
OH! MINIATURES!
THEY LOOK SO REAL! THERE'RE EVEN LITTLE PEOPLE INSIDE!
IS THIS WHERE YOU'RE FROM, HURLÄ?
DON'T BE SILLY, GIRLS!
POF
THAT'S MY SECURITY SYSTEM FOR BÔME.
IS THAT HOW YOU FOUND US SO QUICKLY?
YOU, YES! BUT NOT YOUR HORNED FRIEND.
?
HOW DID YOU...
ACCORDING TO THAT YOUNG BUCK, MYR...
...IT SEEMS HE'S HAVING A JOLLY TIME DOING A BIT OF GARDENING ON VÉTÉRIS HILL!

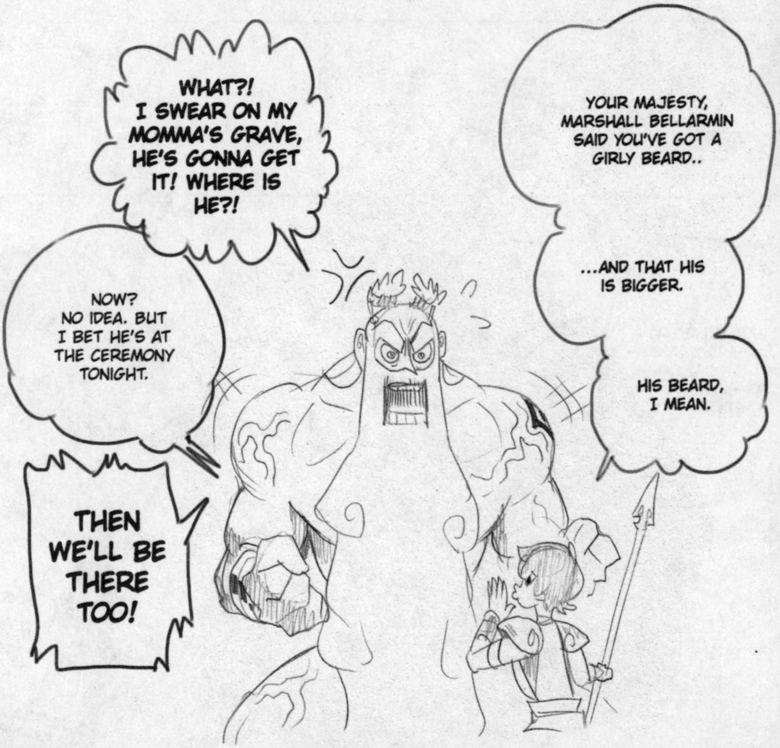
YOUR MAJESTY, MARSHALL BELLARMIN SAID YOU'VE GOT A GIRLY BEARD..
...AND THAT HIS IS BIGGER.
HIS BEARD, I MEAN.
WHAT?! I SWEAR ON MY MOMMA'S GRAVE, HE'S GONNA GET IT! WHERE IS HE?!
NOW? NO IDEA. BUT I BET HE'S AT THE CEREMONY TONIGHT.
THEN WE'LL BE THERE TOO!

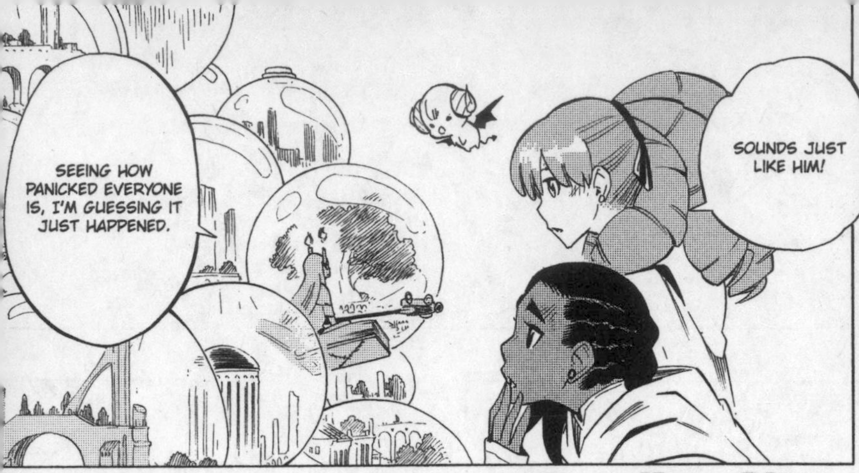
SOUNDS JUST LIKE HIM!
SEEING HOW PANICKED EVERYONE IS, I'M GUESSING IT JUST HAPPENED.

CHAPTER 107 HELP ME

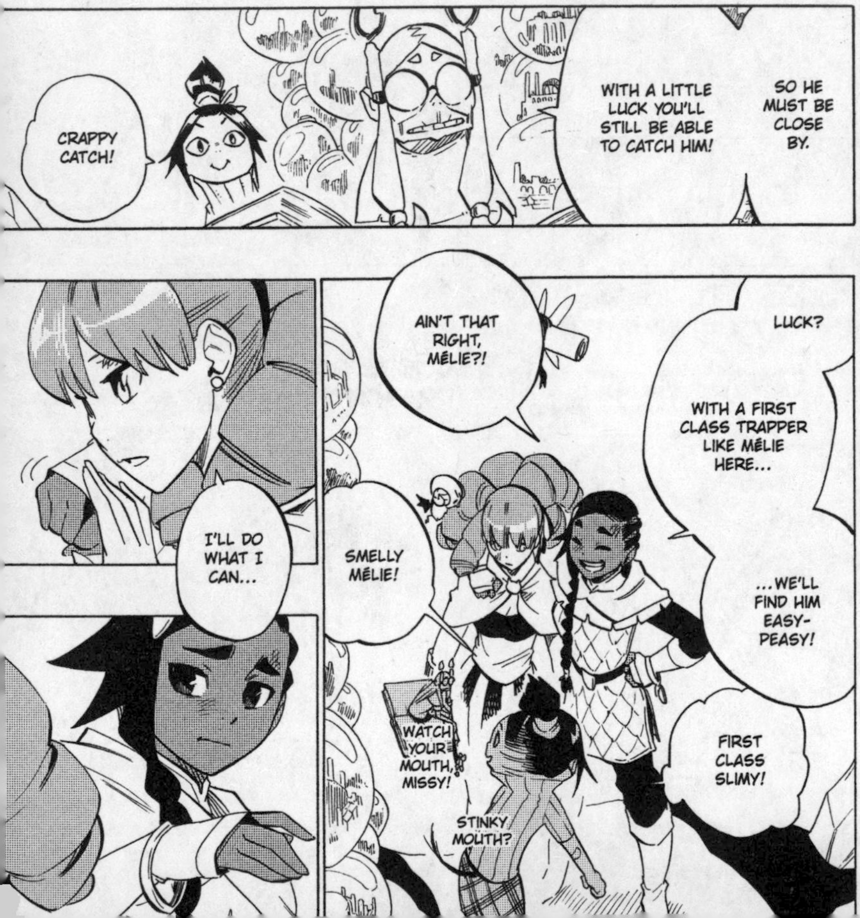
SO HE MUST BE CLOSE BY.
WITH A LITTLE LUCK YOU'LL STILL BE ABLE TO CATCH HIM!
CRAPPY CATCH!
LUCK?
WITH A FIRST CLASS TRAPPER LIKE MÉLIE HERE...
AIN'T THAT RIGHT, MÉLIE?!
...WE'LL FIND HIM EASY-PEASY!
SMELLY MÉLIE!
FIRST CLASS SLIMY!
WATCH YOUR MOUTH, MISSY!
STINKY MOUTH?
I'LL DO WHAT I CAN...

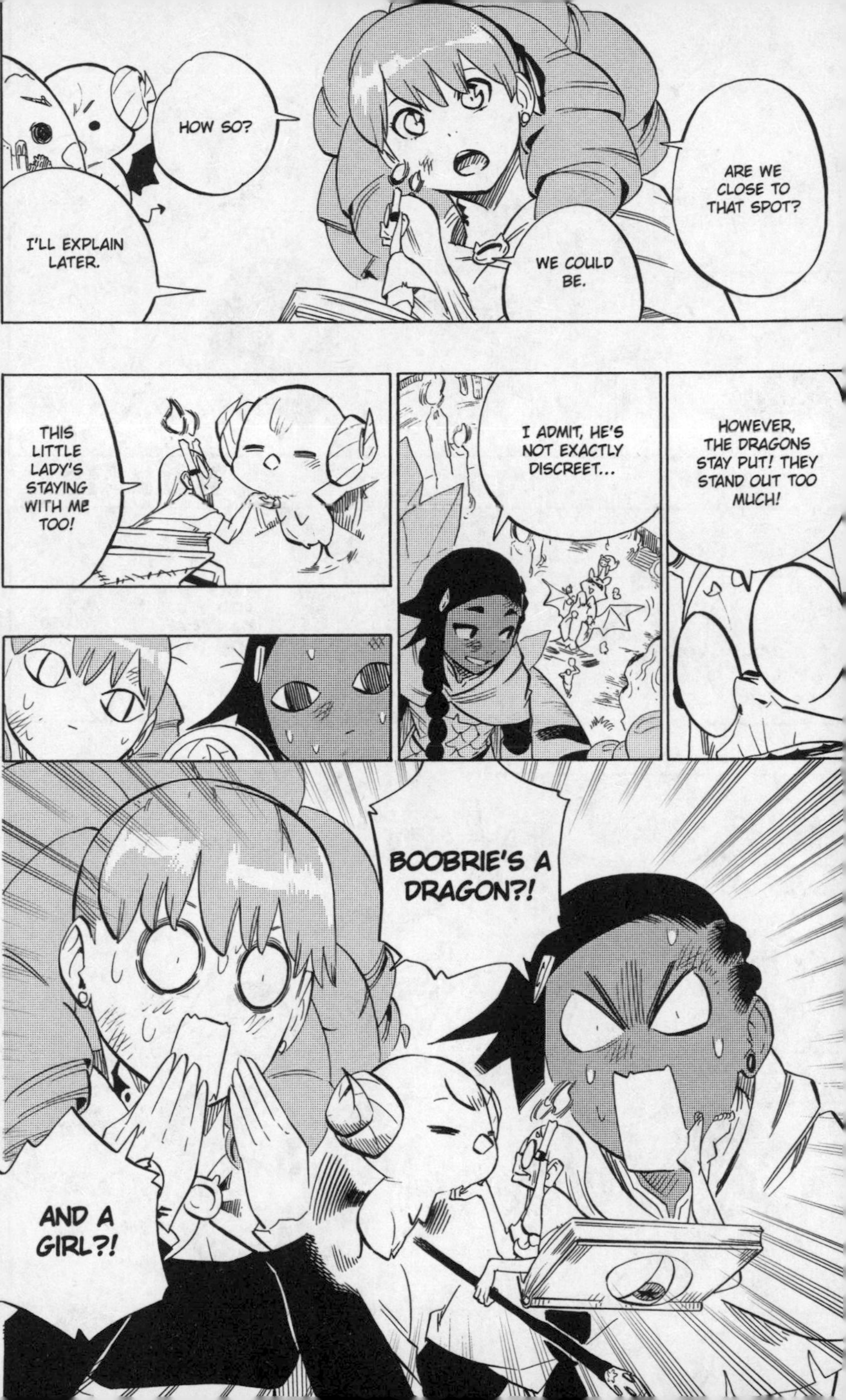
ARE WE CLOSE TO THAT SPOT?
WE COULD BE.
HOW SO?
I'LL EXPLAIN LATER.
HOWEVER, THE DRAGONS STAY PUT! THEY STAND OUT TOO MUCH!
I ADMIT, HE'S NOT EXACTLY DISCREET...
THIS LITTLE LADY'S STAYING WITH ME TOO!
BOOBRIE'S A DRAGON?!
AND A GIRL?!

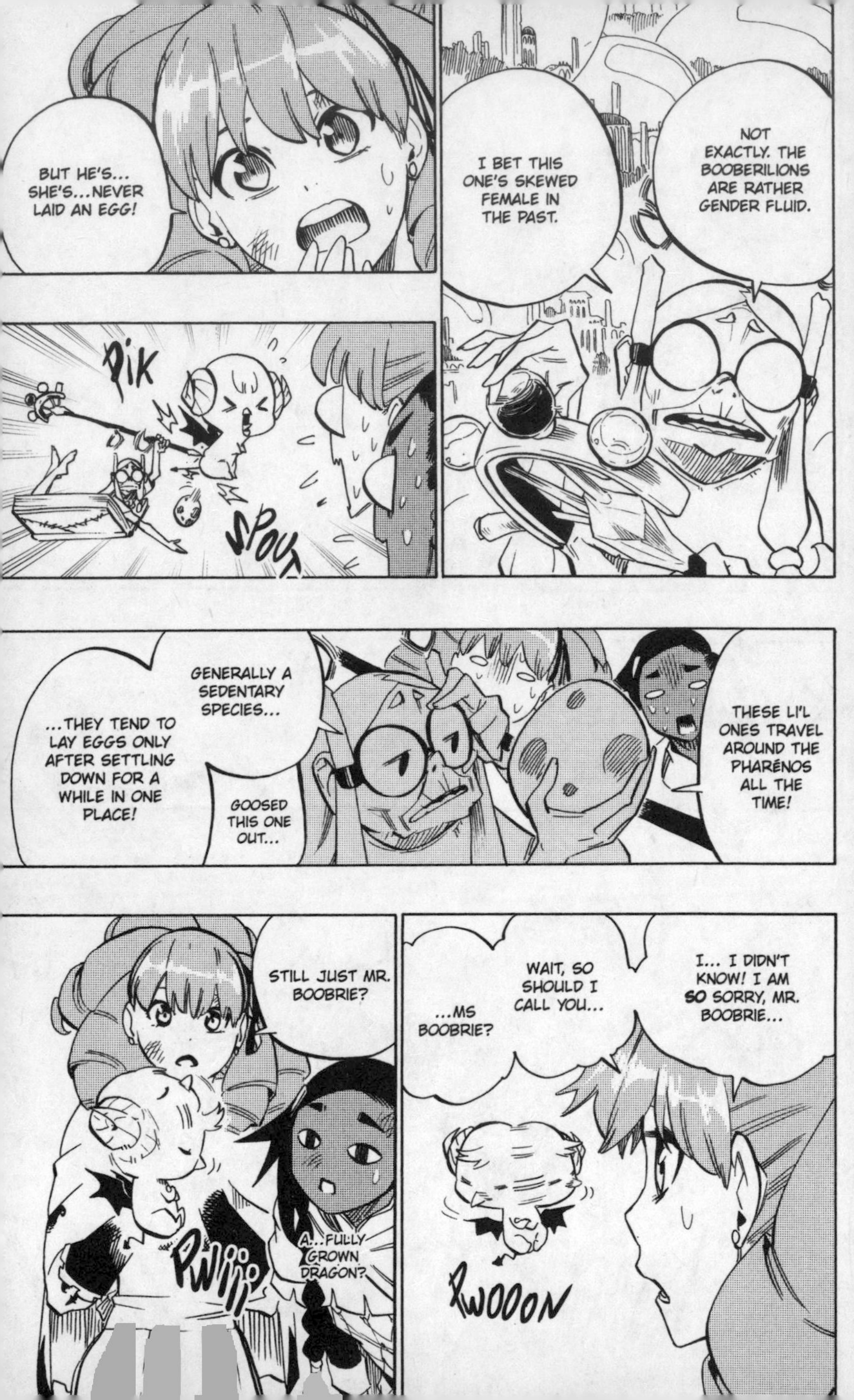
NOT EXACTLY. THE BOOBERILIONS ARE RATHER GENDER FLUID.
I BET THIS ONE'S SKEWED FEMALE IN THE PAST.
BUT HE'S... SHE'S...NEVER LAID AN EGG!
PIK
SPOUT
THESE LI'L ONES TRAVEL AROUND THE PHARÉNOS ALL THE TIME!
GENERALLY A SEDENTARY SPECIES...
...THEY TEND TO LAY EGGS ONLY AFTER SETTLING DOWN FOR A WHILE IN ONE PLACE!
GOOSED THIS ONE OUT...
I... I DIDN'T KNOW! I AM **SO** SORRY, MR. BOOBRIE...
WAIT, SO SHOULD I CALL YOU...
...MS BOOBRIE?
RWOOON
STILL JUST MR. BOOBRIE?
A...FULLY GROWN DRAGON?
PWIIII

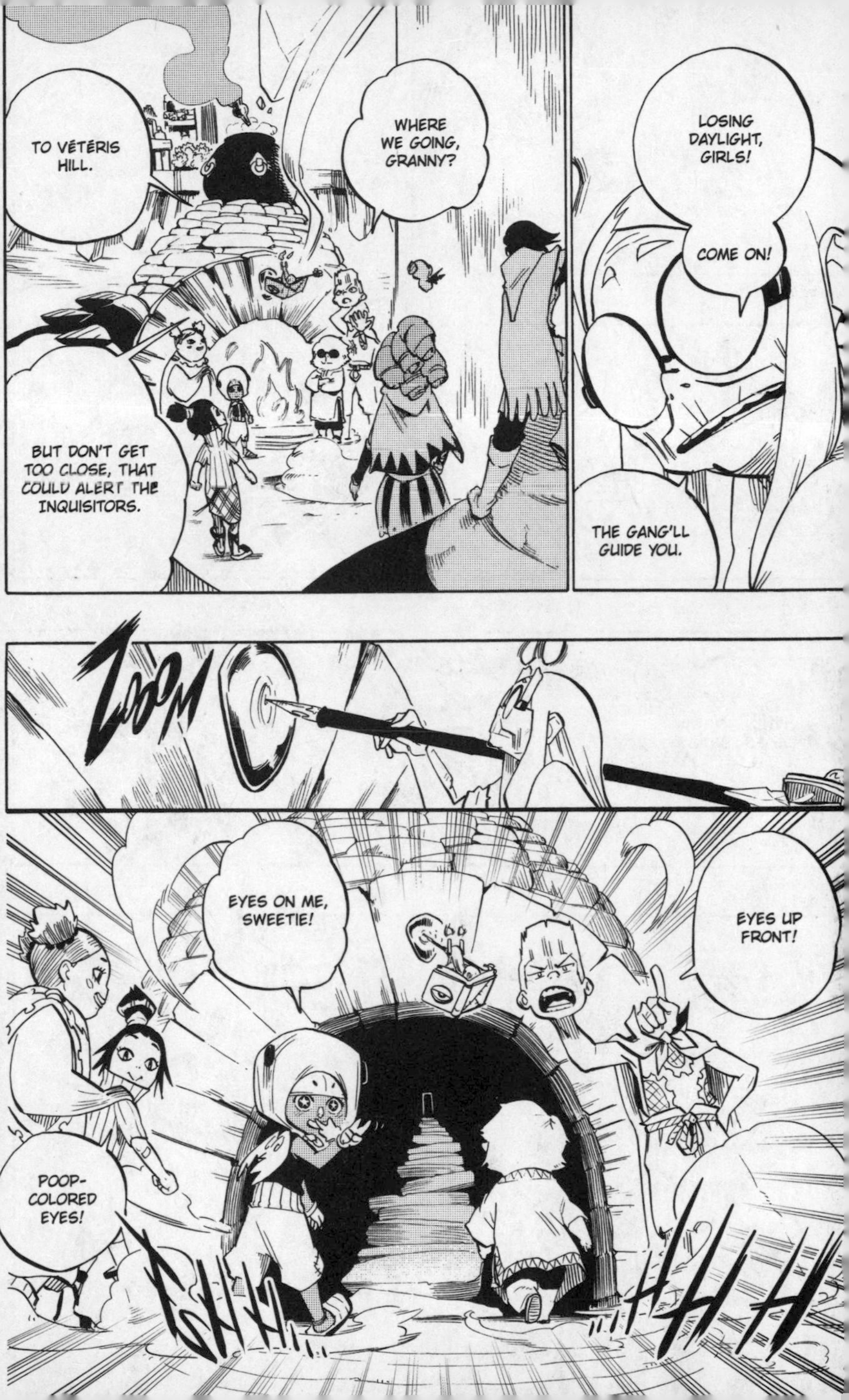
LOSING DAYLIGHT, GIRLS!
COME ON!
THE GANG'LL GUIDE YOU.
WHERE WE GOING, GRANNY?
TO VÉTERIS HILL.
BUT DON'T GET TOO CLOSE, THAT COULD ALERT THE INQUISITORS.
ZOOM
EYES UP FRONT!
EYES ON ME, SWEETIE!
POOP-COLORED EYES!

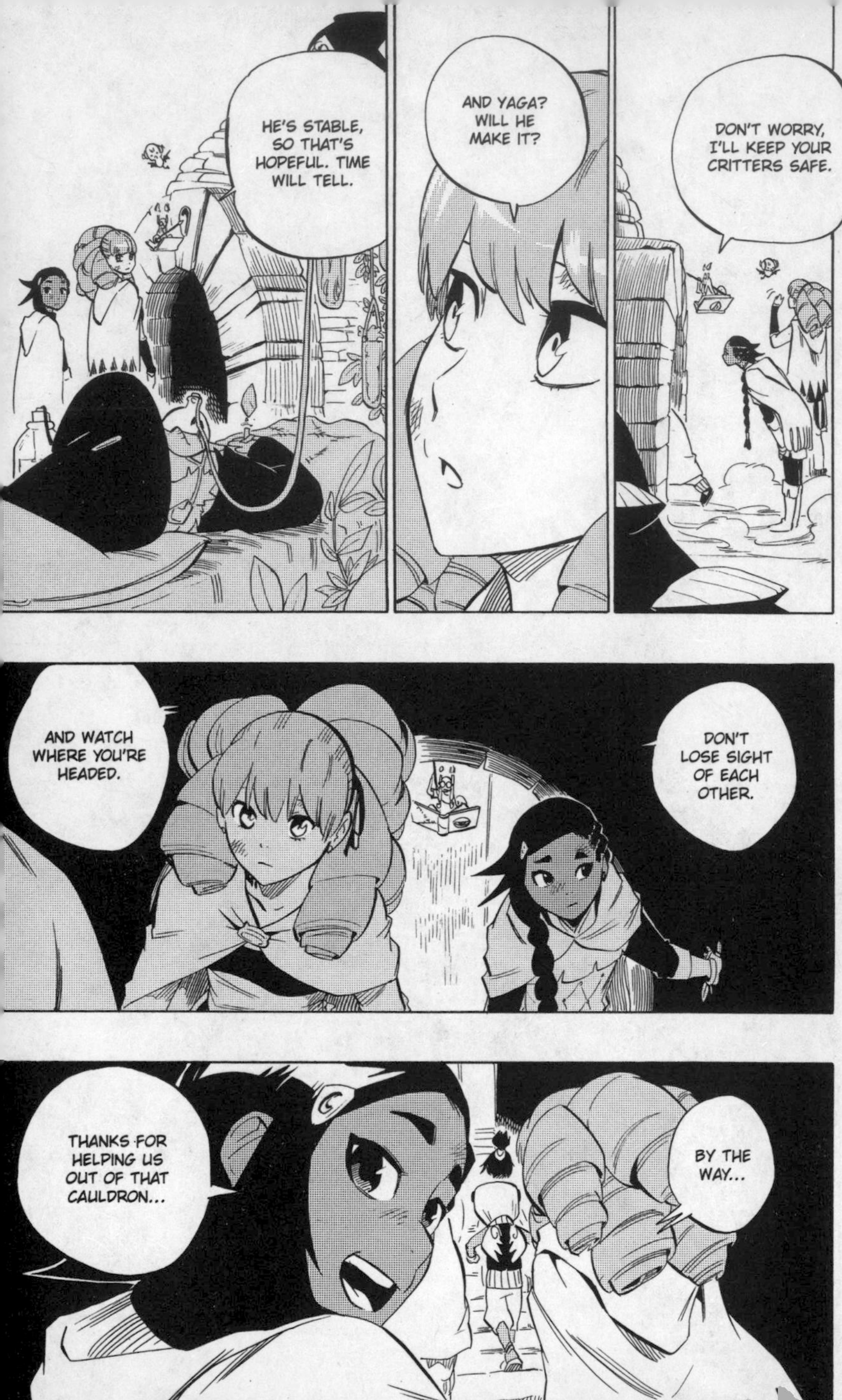
DON'T WORRY, I'LL KEEP YOUR CRITTERS SAFE.
AND YAGA? WILL HE MAKE IT?
HE'S STABLE, SO THAT'S HOPEFUL. TIME WILL TELL.
DON'T LOSE SIGHT OF EACH OTHER.
AND WATCH WHERE YOU'RE HEADED.
BY THE WAY...
THANKS FOR HELPING US OUT OF THAT CAULDRON...

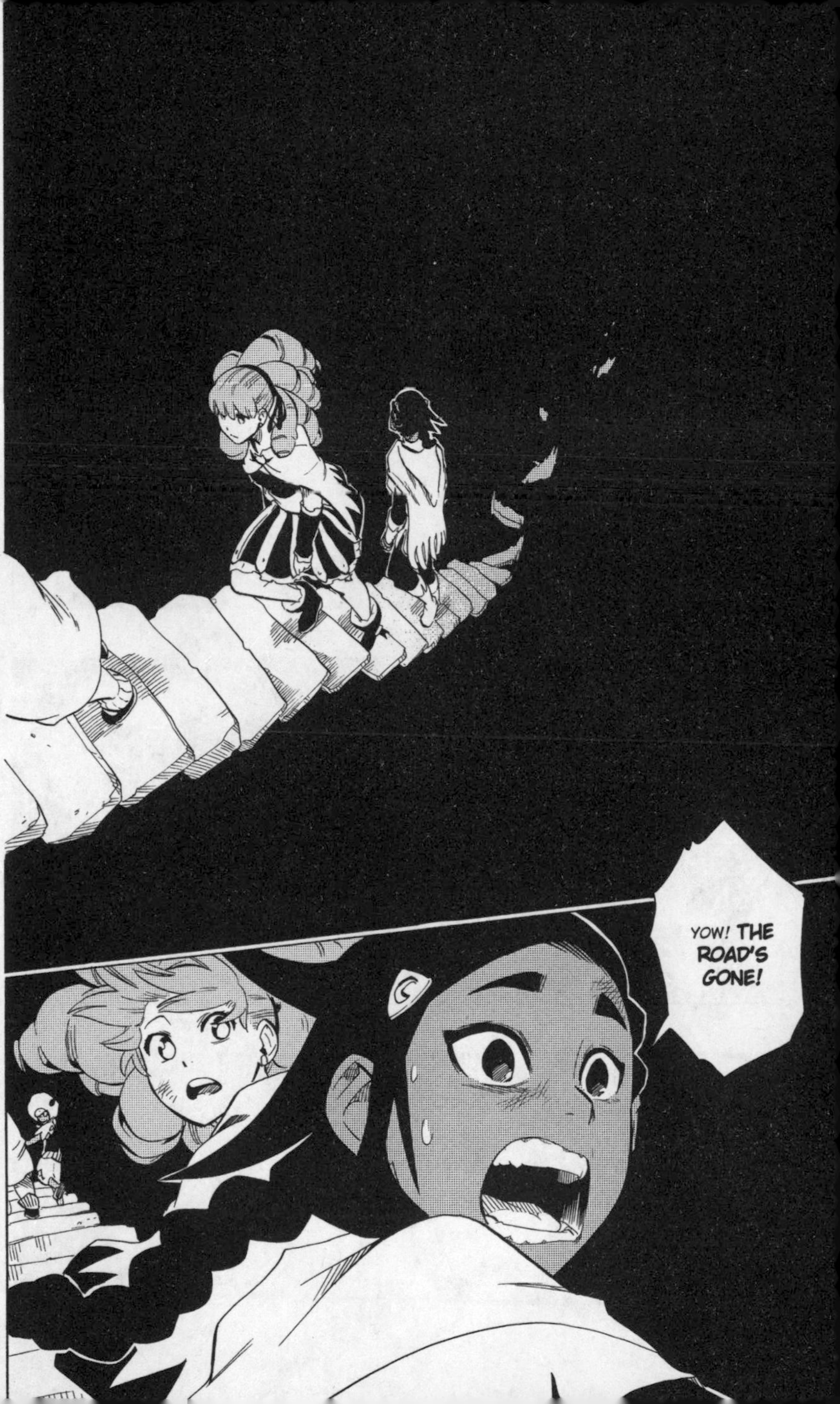
YOW! THE ROAD'S GONE!

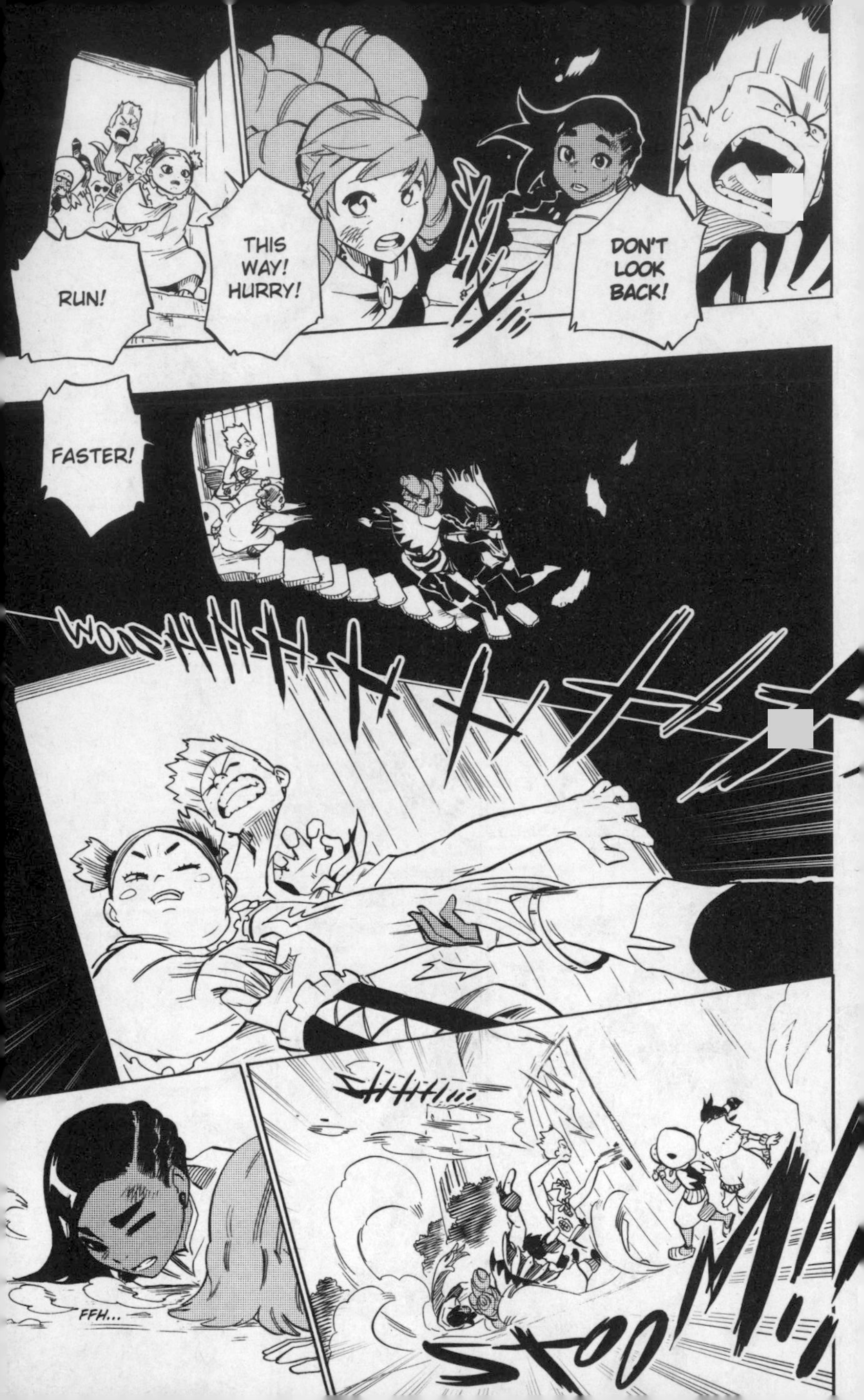

DON'T LOOK BACK!
THIS WAY! HURRY!
RUN!
FASTER!
WOOSHHHH
SHHHH!...
STOOOMM!!
FFH...

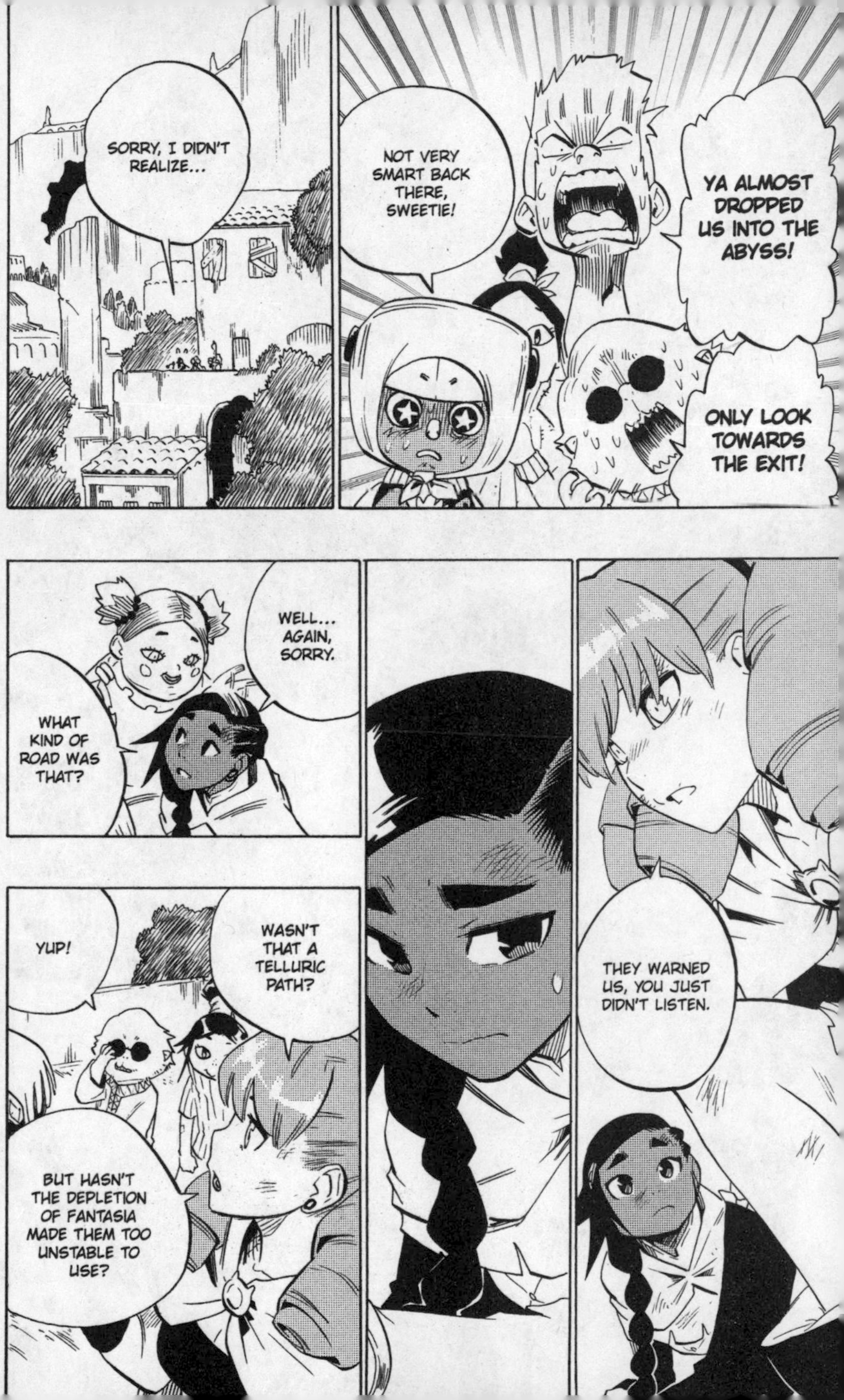
YA ALMOST DROPPED US INTO THE ABYSS!
NOT VERY SMART BACK THERE, SWEETIE!
ONLY LOOK TOWARDS THE EXIT!
SORRY, I DIDN'T REALIZE...
THEY WARNED US, YOU JUST DIDN'T LISTEN.
WELL... AGAIN, SORRY.
WHAT KIND OF ROAD WAS THAT?
WASN'T THAT A TELLURIC PATH?
YUP!
BUT HASN'T THE DEPLETION OF FANTASIA MADE THEM TOO UNSTABLE TO USE?

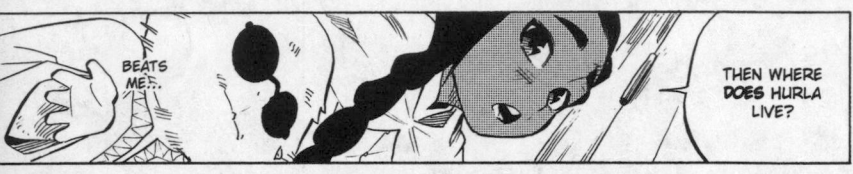

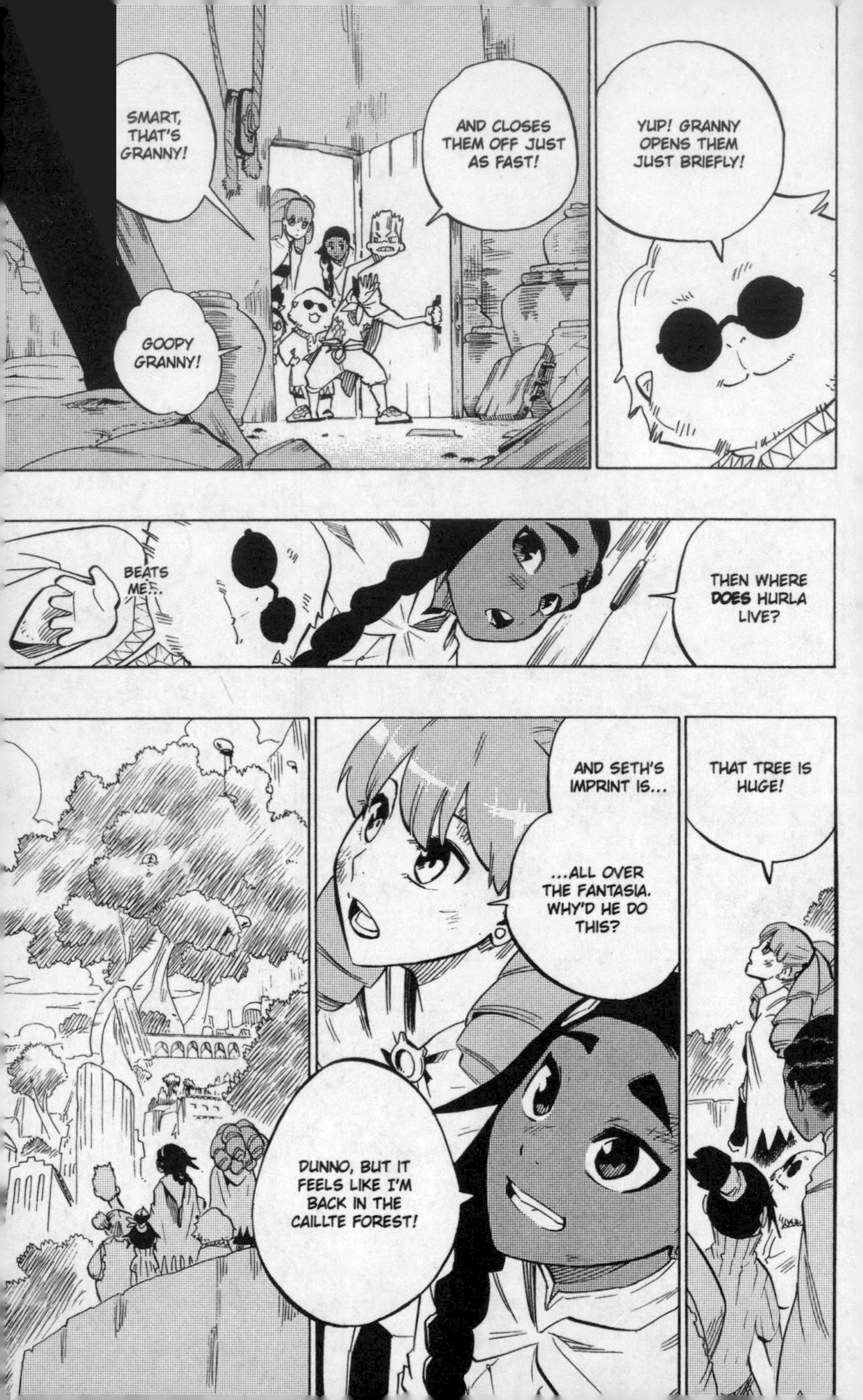
YUP! GRANNY OPENS THEM JUST BRIEFLY!
AND CLOSES THEM OFF JUST AS FAST!
SMART, THAT'S GRANNY!
GOOPY GRANNY!
THEN WHERE **DOES** HURLA LIVE?
BEATS ME...
THAT TREE IS HUGE!
AND SETH'S IMPRINT IS...
...ALL OVER THE FANTASIA. WHY'D HE DO THIS?
DUNNO, BUT IT FEELS LIKE I'M BACK IN THE CAILLTE FOREST!

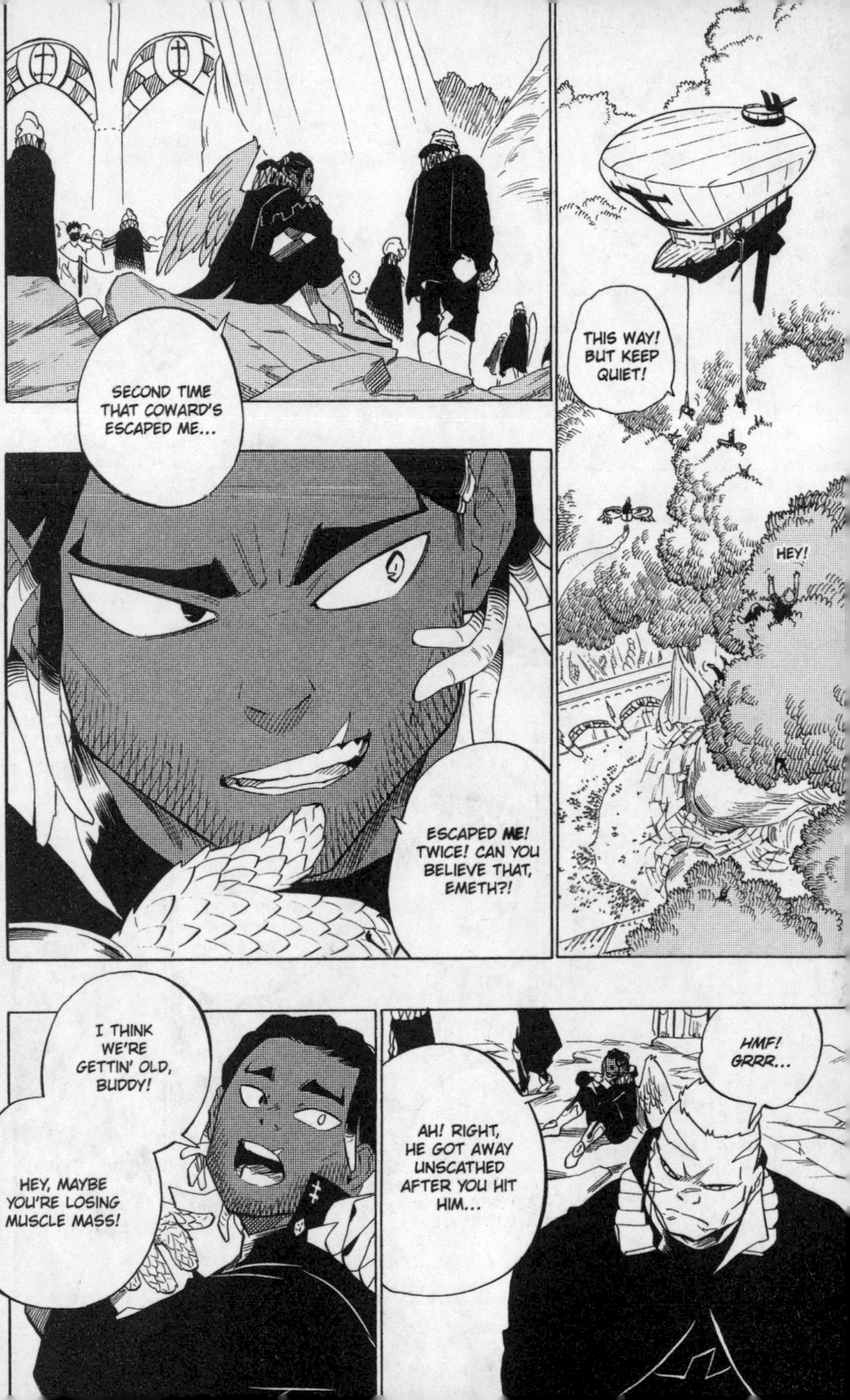
THIS WAY! BUT KEEP QUIET!
HEY!
SECOND TIME THAT COWARD'S ESCAPED ME...
ESCAPED **ME**! TWICE! CAN YOU BELIEVE THAT, EMETH?!
HMF! GRRR...
AH! RIGHT, HE GOT AWAY UNSCATHED AFTER YOU HIT HIM...
I THINK WE'RE GETTIN' OLD, BUDDY!
HEY, MAYBE YOU'RE LOSING MUSCLE MASS!

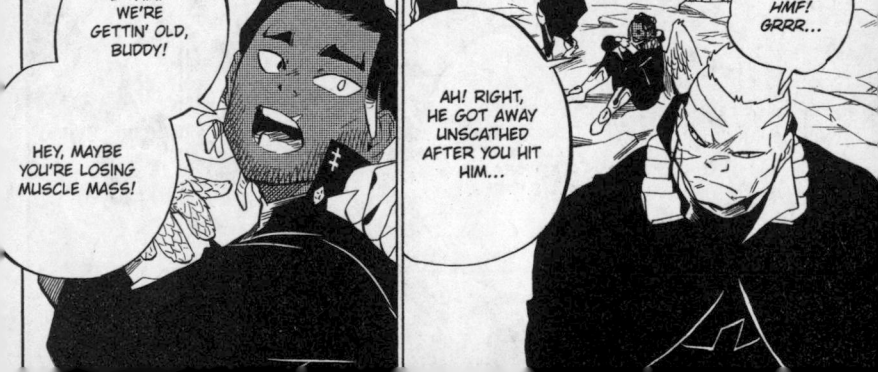

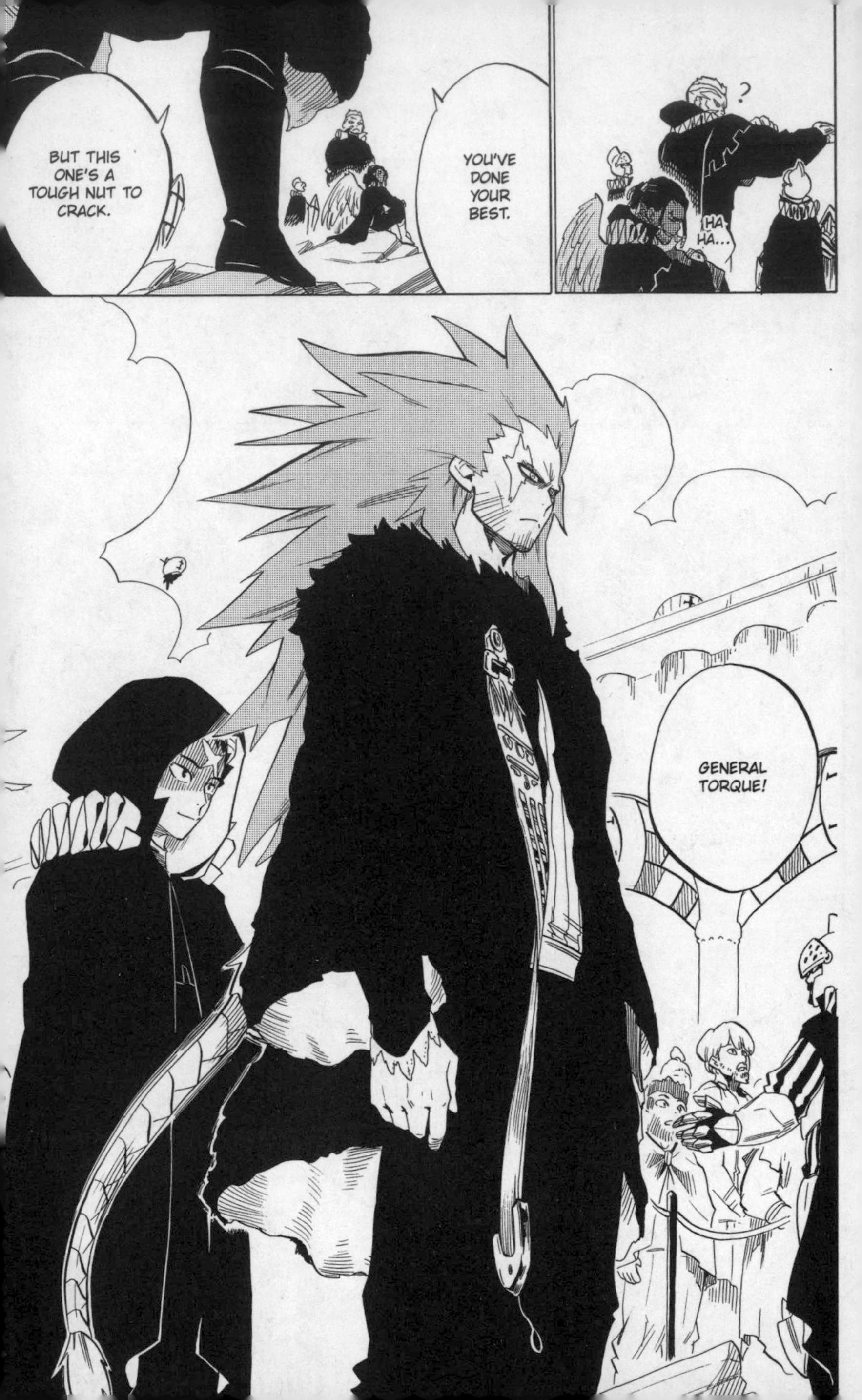
?
HA HA...
YOU'VE DONE YOUR BEST.
BUT THIS ONE'S A TOUGH NUT TO CRACK.
GENERAL TORQUE!

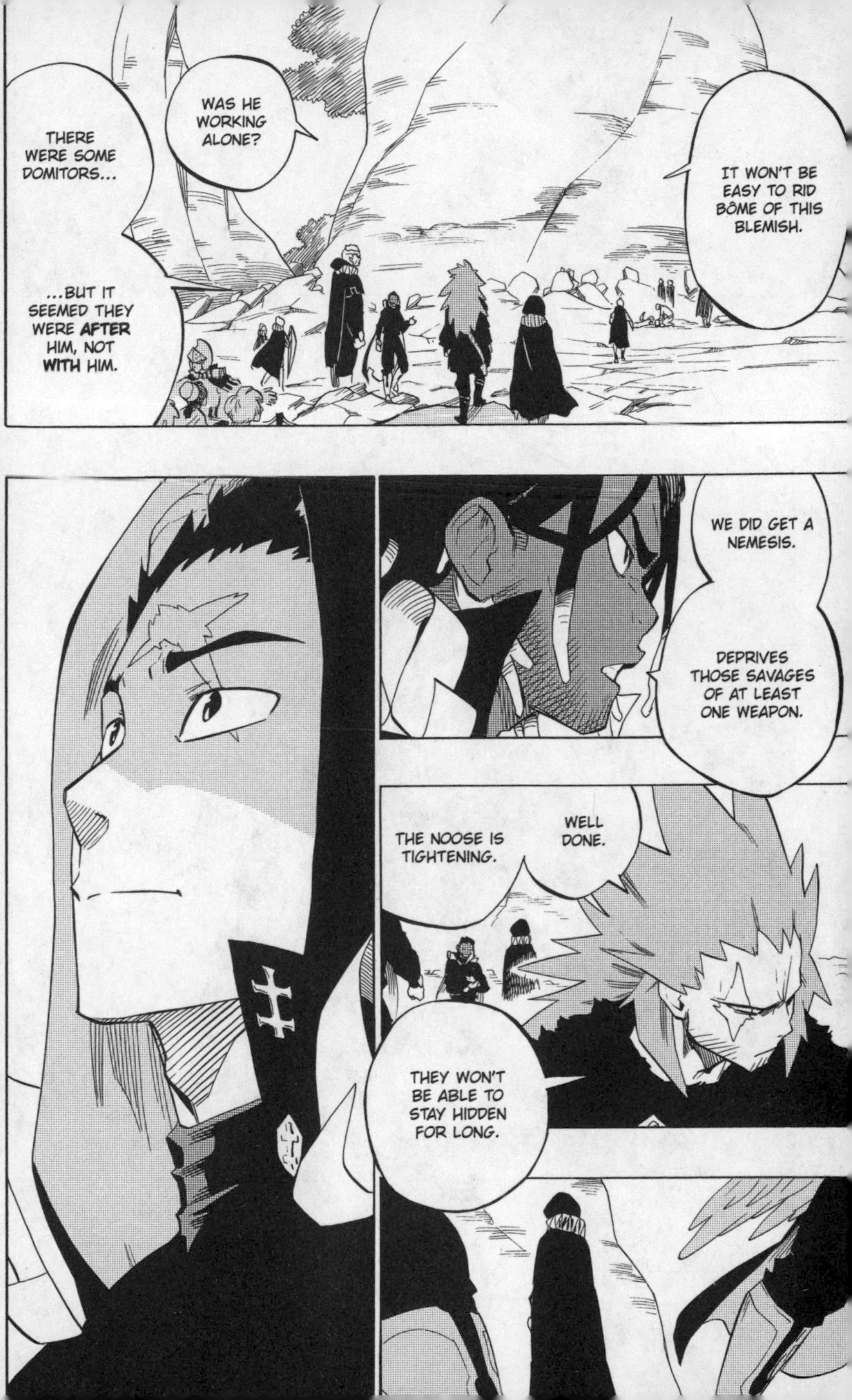
IT WON'T BE EASY TO RID BÔME OF THIS BLEMISH.
WAS HE WORKING ALONE?
THERE WERE SOME DOMITORS...
...BUT IT SEEMED THEY WERE **AFTER** HIM, NOT **WITH** HIM.
WE DID GET A NEMESIS.
DEPRIVES THOSE SAVAGES OF AT LEAST ONE WEAPON.
WELL DONE.
THE NOOSE IS TIGHTENING.
THEY WON'T BE ABLE TO STAY HIDDEN FOR LONG.

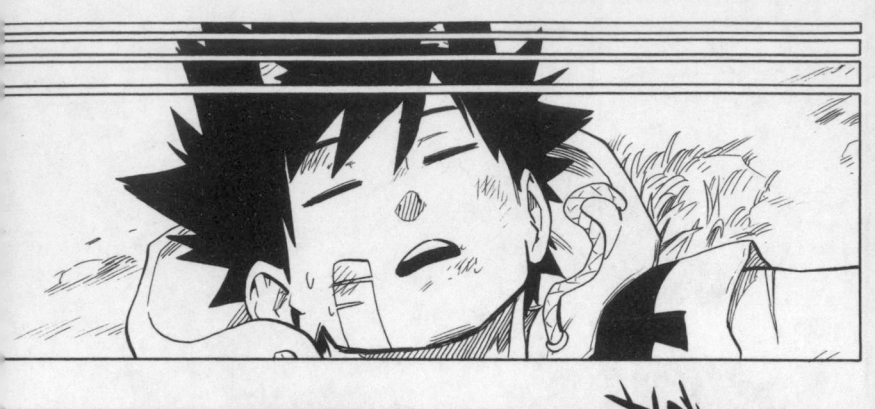

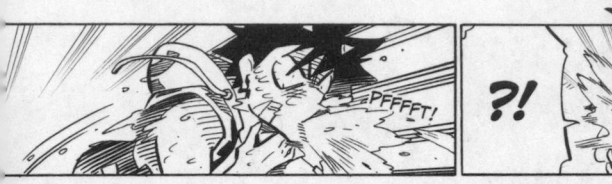

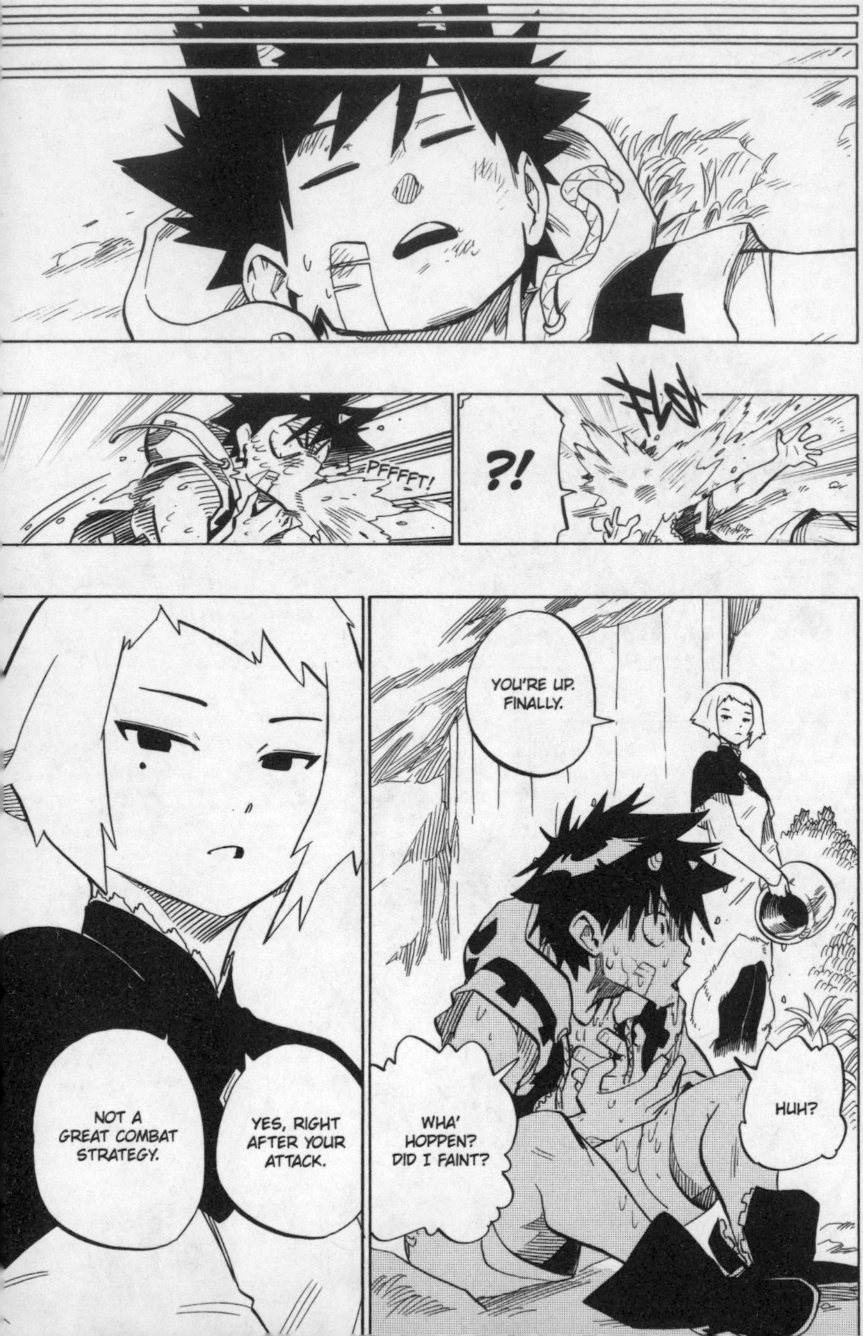
?!
PFFFFT!
YOU'RE UP. FINALLY.
HUH?
WHA' HOPPEN? DID I FAINT?
YES, RIGHT AFTER YOUR ATTACK.
NOT A GREAT COMBAT STRATEGY.

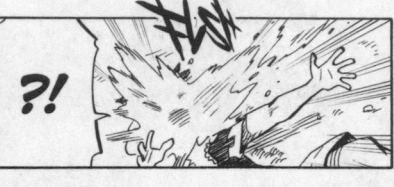

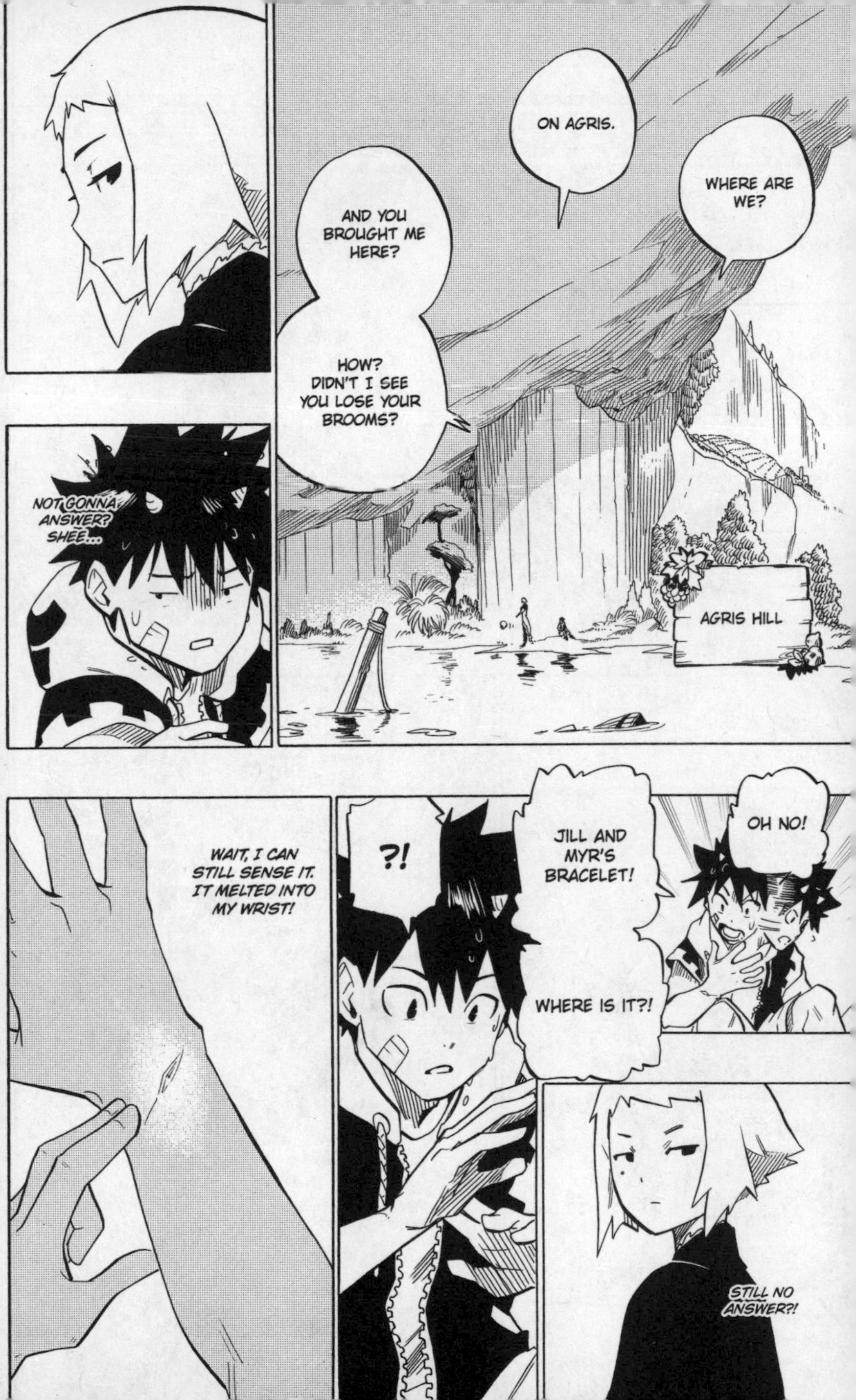
WHERE ARE WE?
ON AGRIS.
AND YOU BROUGHT ME HERE?
HOW? DIDN'T I SEE YOU LOSE YOUR BROOMS?
AGRIS HILL
NOT GONNA ANSWER? SHEE...
OH NO!
JILL AND MYR'S BRACELET!
WHERE IS IT?!
STILL NO ANSWER?!
?!
WAIT, I CAN STILL SENSE IT. IT MELTED INTO MY WRIST!

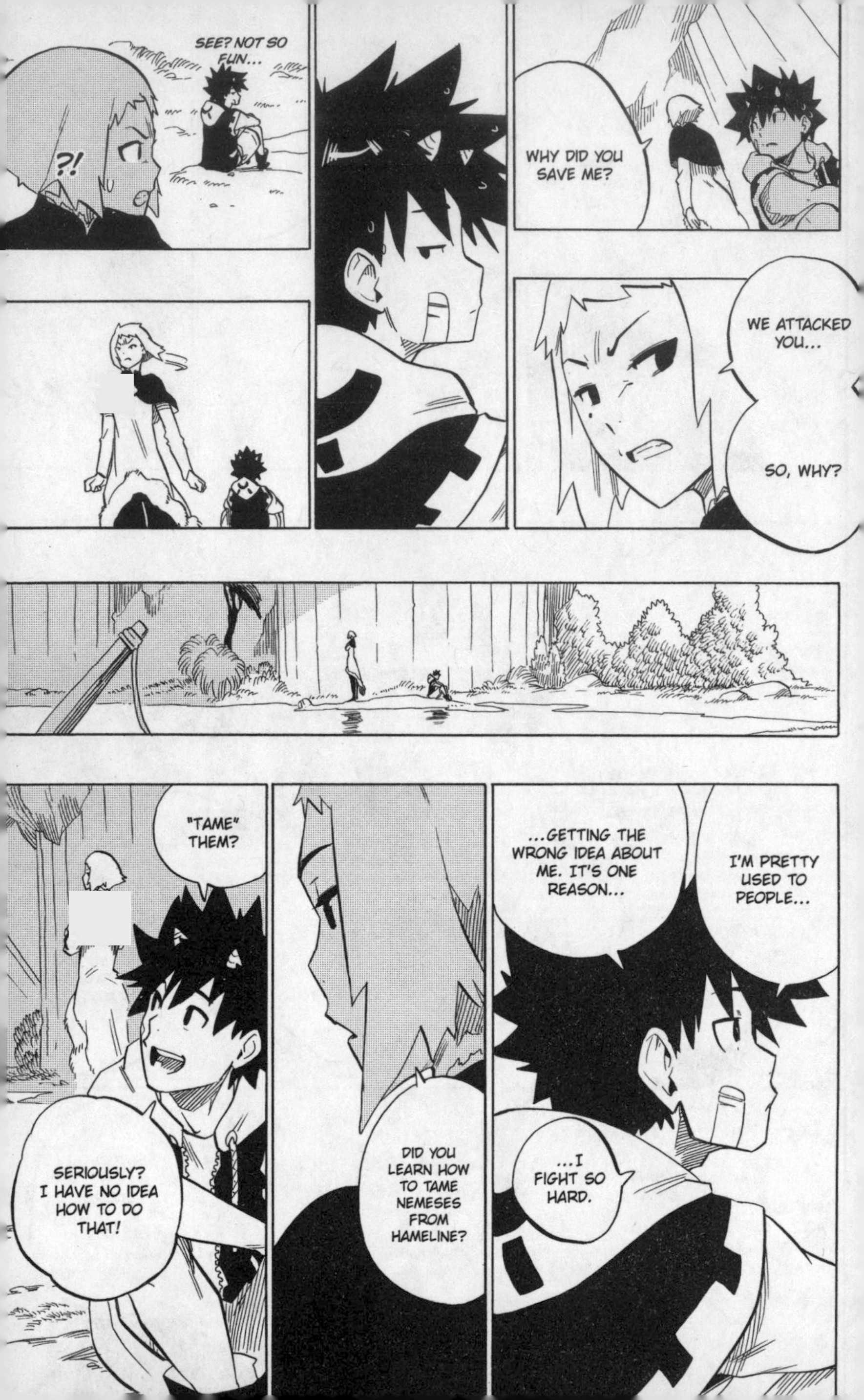
WHY DID YOU SAVE ME?
WE ATTACKED YOU...
SO, WHY?
SEE? NOT SO FUN...
?!
I'M PRETTY USED TO PEOPLE...
...GETTING THE WRONG IDEA ABOUT ME. IT'S ONE REASON...
...I FIGHT SO HARD.
DID YOU LEARN HOW TO TAME NEMESES FROM HAMELINE?
"TAME" THEM?
SERIOUSLY? I HAVE NO IDEA HOW TO DO THAT!

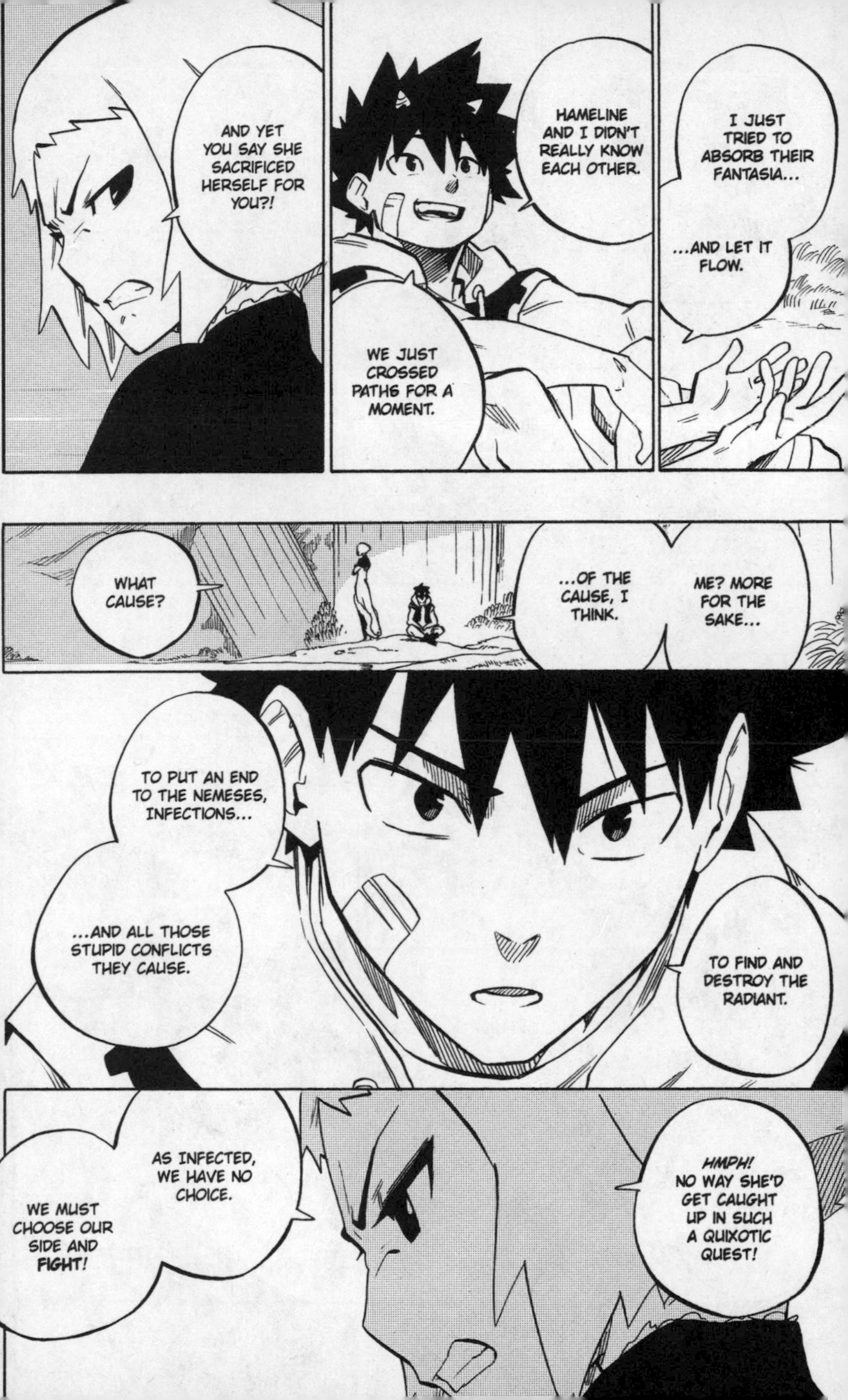
I JUST TRIED TO ABSORB THEIR FANTASIA...
...AND LET IT FLOW.
HAMELINE AND I DIDN'T REALLY KNOW EACH OTHER.
WE JUST CROSSED PATHS FOR A MOMENT.
AND YET YOU SAY SHE SACRIFICED HERSELF FOR YOU?!
ME? MORE FOR THE SAKE...
...OF THE CAUSE, I THINK.
WHAT CAUSE?
TO FIND AND DESTROY THE RADIANT.
TO PUT AN END TO THE NEMESES, INFECTIONS...
...AND ALL THOSE STUPID CONFLICTS THEY CAUSE.
HMPH! NO WAY SHE'D GET CAUGHT UP IN SUCH A QUIXOTIC QUEST!
AS INFECTED, WE HAVE NO CHOICE.
WE MUST CHOOSE OUR SIDE AND **FIGHT!**

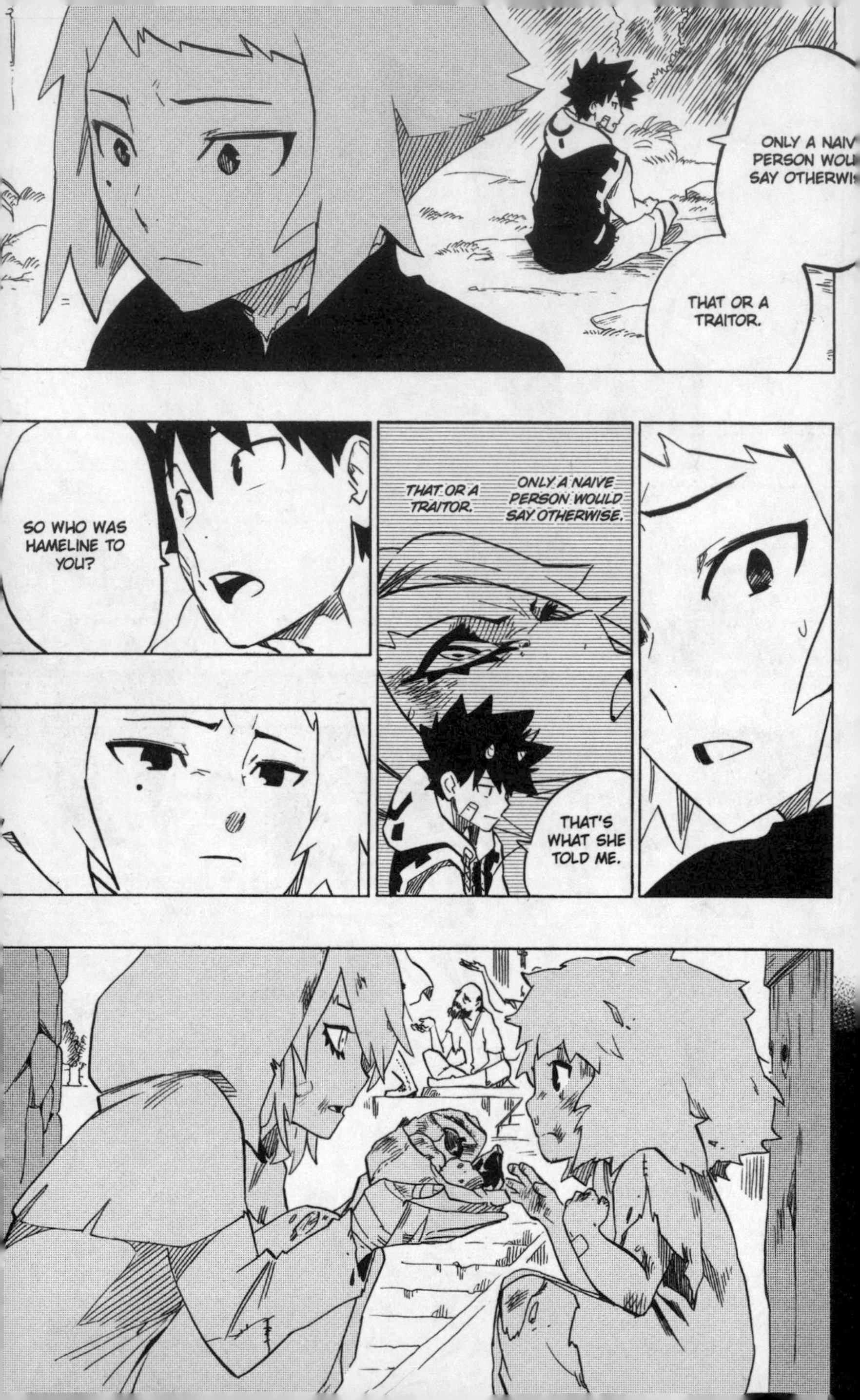
ONLY A NAIV
PERSON WOU
SAY OTHERWI
THAT OR A TRAITOR.
ONLY A NAIVE PERSON WOULD SAY OTHERWISE.
THAT OR A TRAITOR.
THAT'S WHAT SHE TOLD ME.
SO WHO WAS HAMELINE TO YOU?

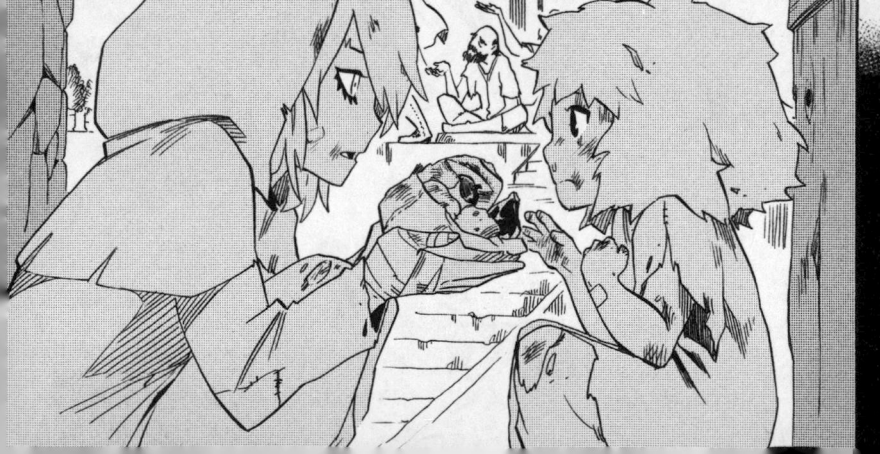

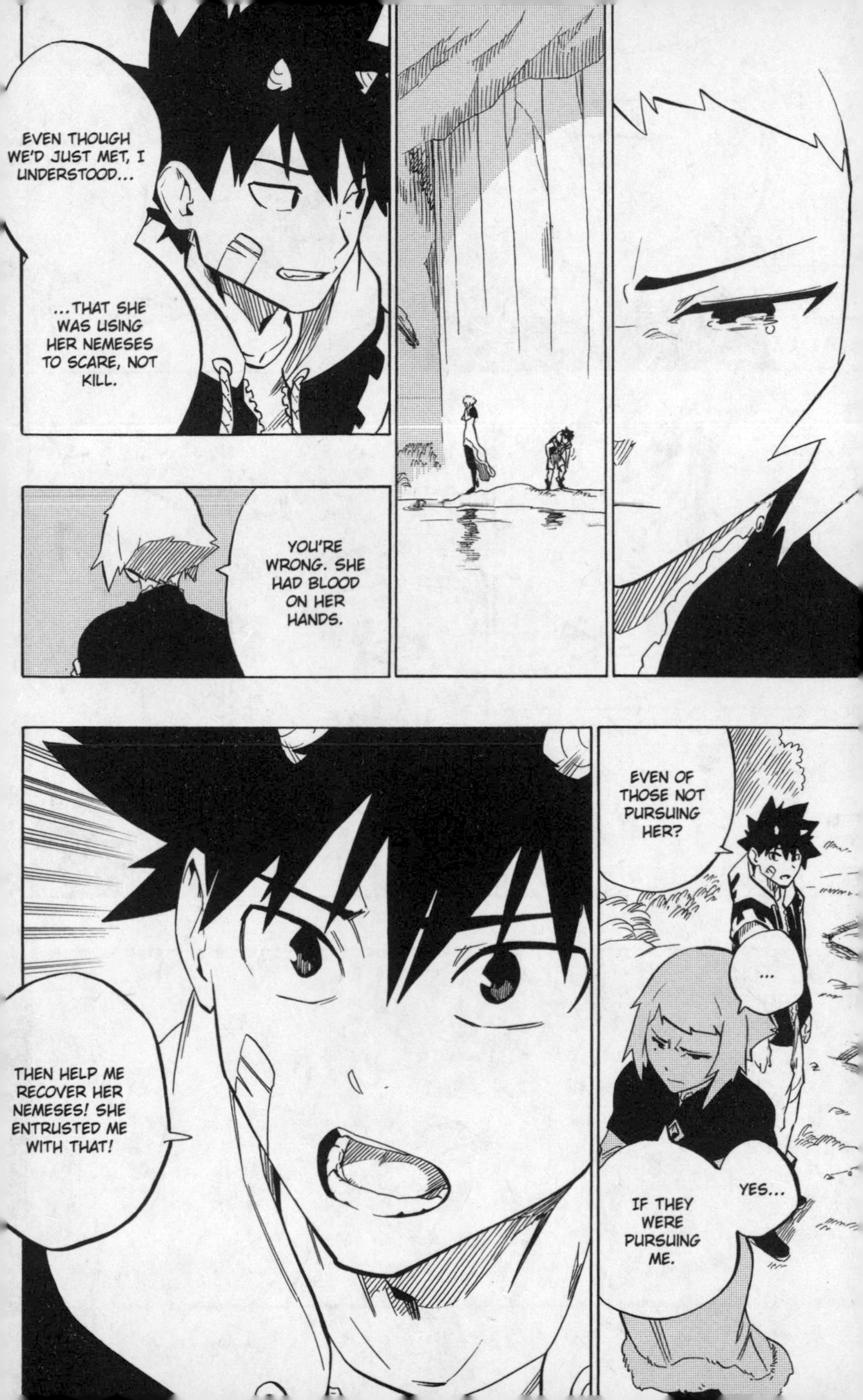
EVEN THOUGH WE'D JUST MET, I UNDERSTOOD...
...THAT SHE WAS USING HER NEMESES TO SCARE, NOT KILL.
YOU'RE WRONG. SHE HAD BLOOD ON HER HANDS.
EVEN OF THOSE NOT PURSUING HER?
...
YES...
IF THEY WERE PURSUING ME.
THEN HELP ME RECOVER HER NEMESES! SHE ENTRUSTED ME WITH THAT!

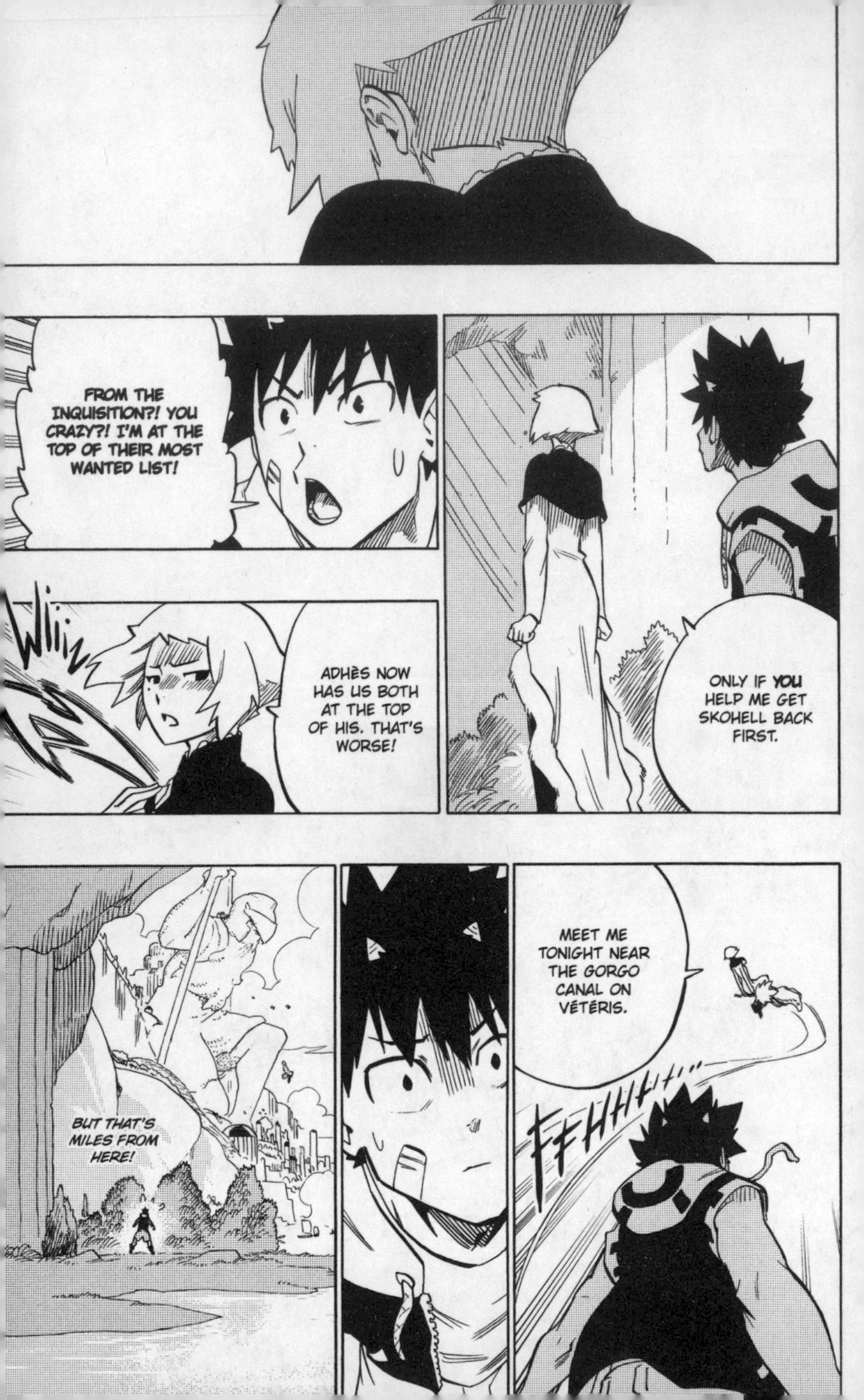

ONLY IF **YOU** HELP ME GET SKOHELL BACK FIRST.
FROM THE INQUISITION?! YOU CRAZY?! I'M AT THE TOP OF THEIR MOST WANTED LIST!
WHIIN
ADHÈS NOW HAS US BOTH AT THE TOP OF HIS. THAT'S WORSE!
MEET ME TONIGHT NEAR THE GORGO CANAL ON VÉTERIS.
FFHHH...
BUT THAT'S MILES FROM HERE!

YÉMITRI

MÉLOPÉE

TAÏNA

PIPOU

BAYTRIL

-THE DROPLET GANG-

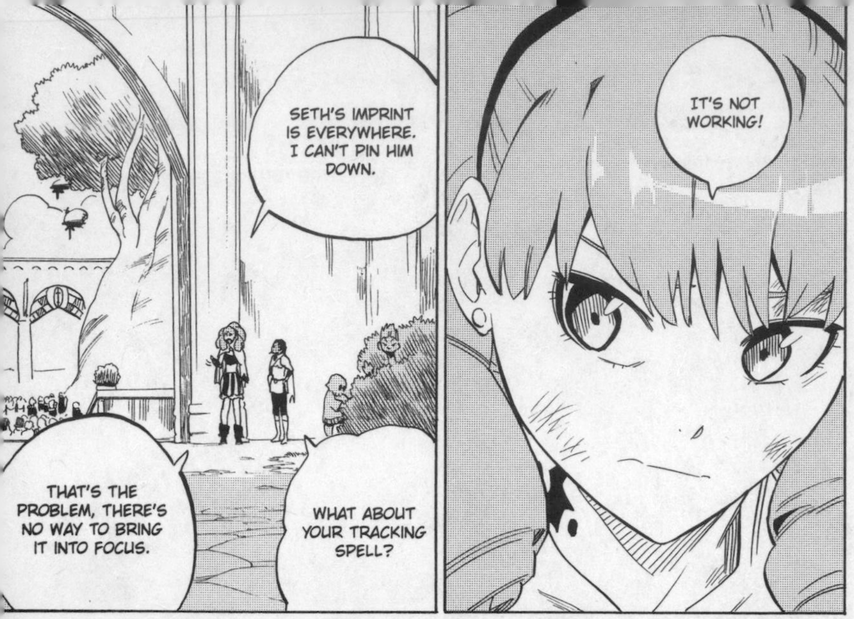
IT'S NOT WORKING!
WHAT ABOUT YOUR TRACKING SPELL?
THAT'S THE PROBLEM, THERE'S NO WAY TO BRING IT INTO FOCUS.
SETH'S IMPRINT IS EVERYWHERE. I CAN'T PIN HIM DOWN.

Chapter 108 Your Own Private Islet

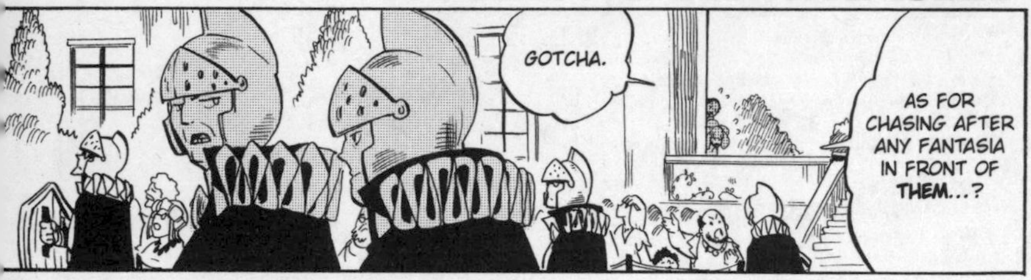
AS FOR CHASING AFTER ANY FANTASIA IN FRONT OF THEM...?
GOTCHA.

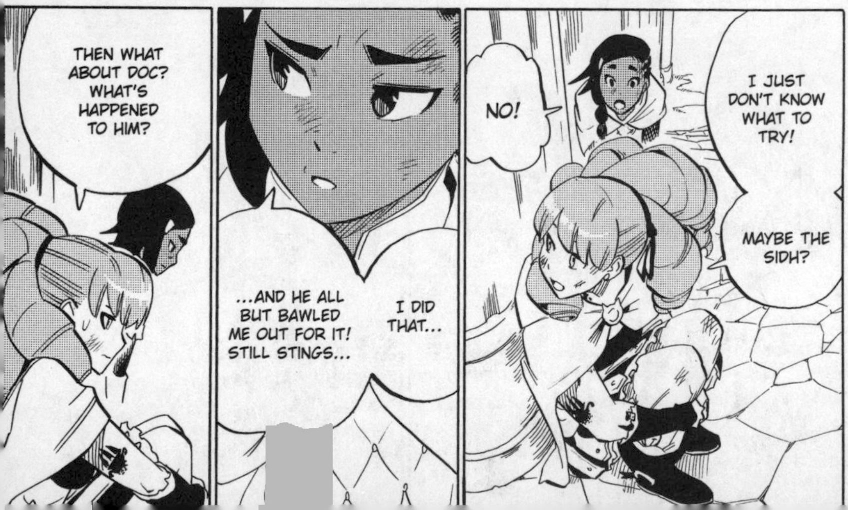
I JUST DON'T KNOW WHAT TO TRY!
NO!
MAYBE THE SIDH?
I DID THAT...
...AND HE ALL BUT BAWLED ME OUT FOR IT! STILL STINGS...
THEN WHAT ABOUT DOC? WHAT'S HAPPENED TO HIM?

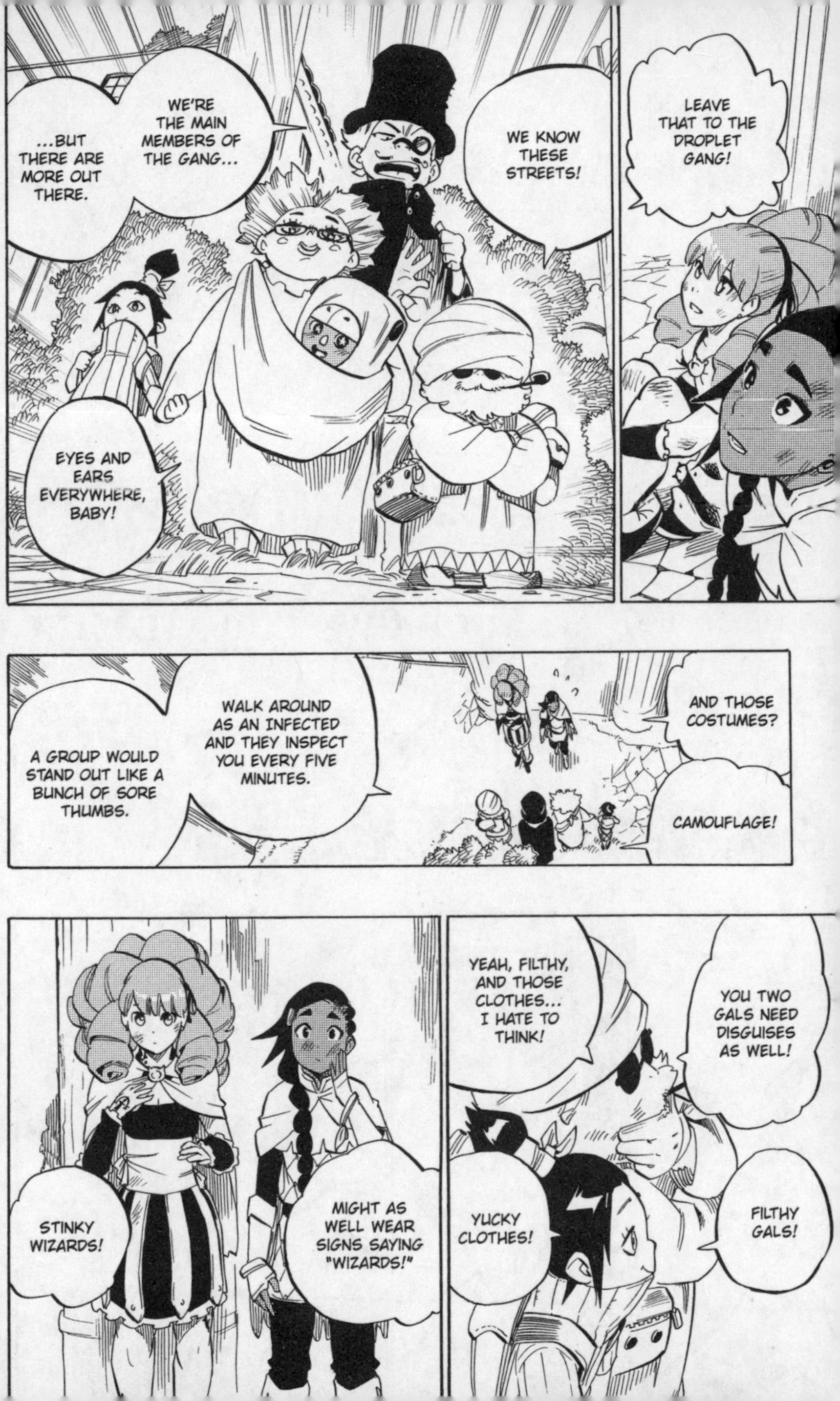
LEAVE THAT TO THE DROPLET GANG!
WE KNOW THESE STREETS!
WE'RE THE MAIN MEMBERS OF THE GANG...
...BUT THERE ARE MORE OUT THERE.
EYES AND EARS EVERYWHERE, BABY!
AND THOSE COSTUMES?
CAMOUFLAGE!
WALK AROUND AS AN INFECTED AND THEY INSPECT YOU EVERY FIVE MINUTES.
A GROUP WOULD STAND OUT LIKE A BUNCH OF SORE THUMBS.
YOU TWO GALS NEED DISGUISES AS WELL!
YEAH, FILTHY, AND THOSE CLOTHES... I HATE TO THINK!
FILTHY GALS!
YUCKY CLOTHES!
MIGHT AS WELL WEAR SIGNS SAYING "WIZARDS!"
STINKY WIZARDS!

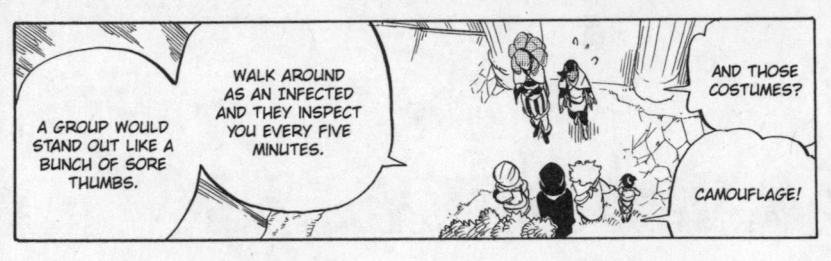

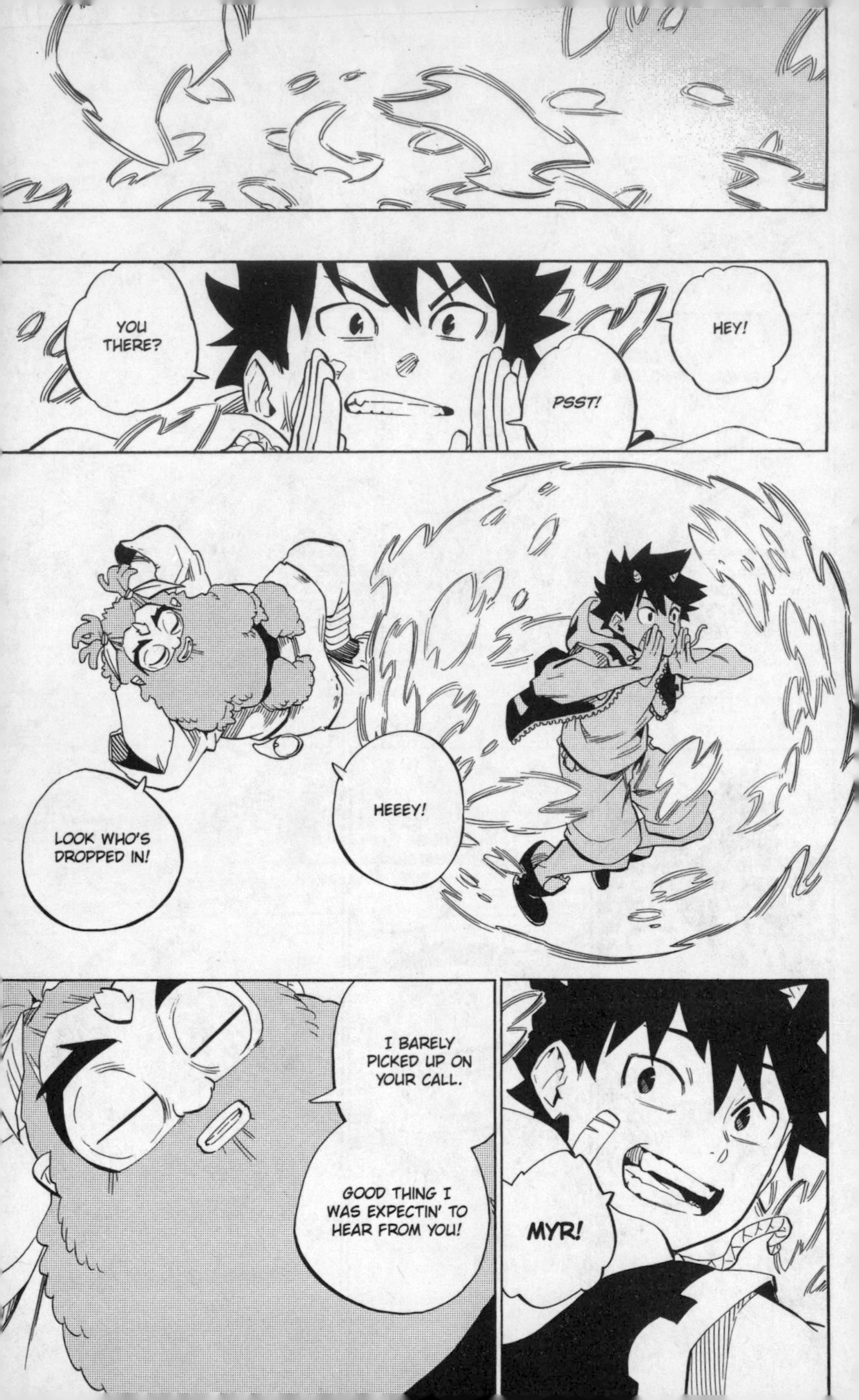
HEY!
PSST!
YOU THERE?
HEEEY!
LOOK WHO'S DROPPED IN!
MYR!
I BARELY PICKED UP ON YOUR CALL.
GOOD THING I WAS EXPECTIN' TO HEAR FROM YOU!

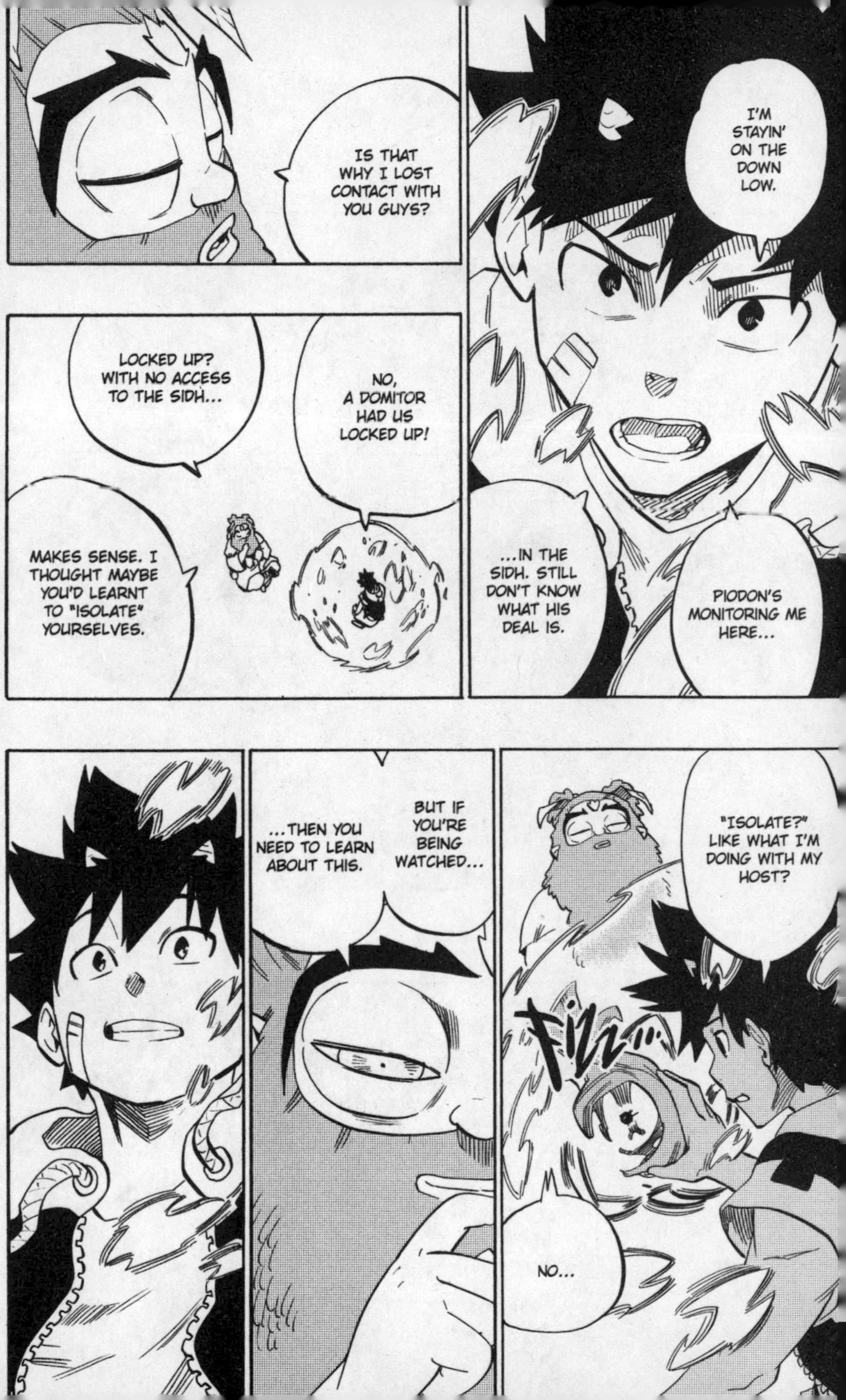
I'M STAYIN' ON THE DOWN LOW.
PIODON'S MONITORING ME HERE...
...IN THE SIDH. STILL DON'T KNOW WHAT HIS DEAL IS.
IS THAT WHY I LOST CONTACT WITH YOU GUYS?
NO, A DOMITOR HAD US LOCKED UP!
LOCKED UP? WITH NO ACCESS TO THE SIDH...
MAKES SENSE. I THOUGHT MAYBE YOU'D LEARNT TO "ISOLATE" YOURSELVES.
"ISOLATE?" LIKE WHAT I'M DOING WITH MY HOST?
FIZZ...
NO...
BUT IF YOU'RE BEING WATCHED...
...THEN YOU NEED TO LEARN ABOUT THIS.

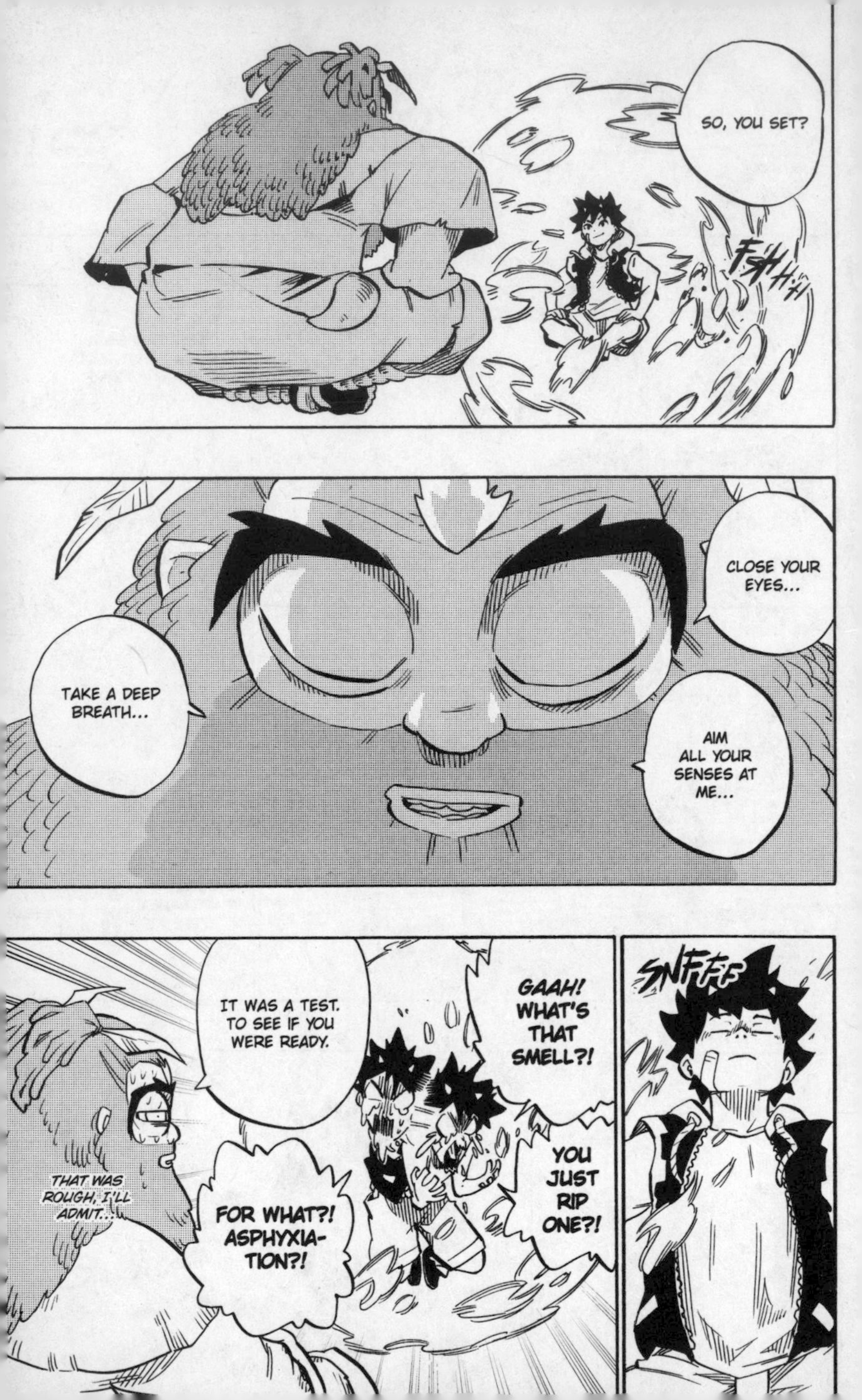
SO, YOU SET?
CLOSE YOUR EYES...
AIM ALL YOUR SENSES AT ME...
TAKE A DEEP BREATH...
SNFFFF
GAAH! WHAT'S THAT SMELL?!
YOU JUST RIP ONE?!
IT WAS A TEST. TO SEE IF YOU WERE READY.
FOR WHAT?! ASPHYXIATION?!
THAT WAS ROUGH, I'LL ADMIT...

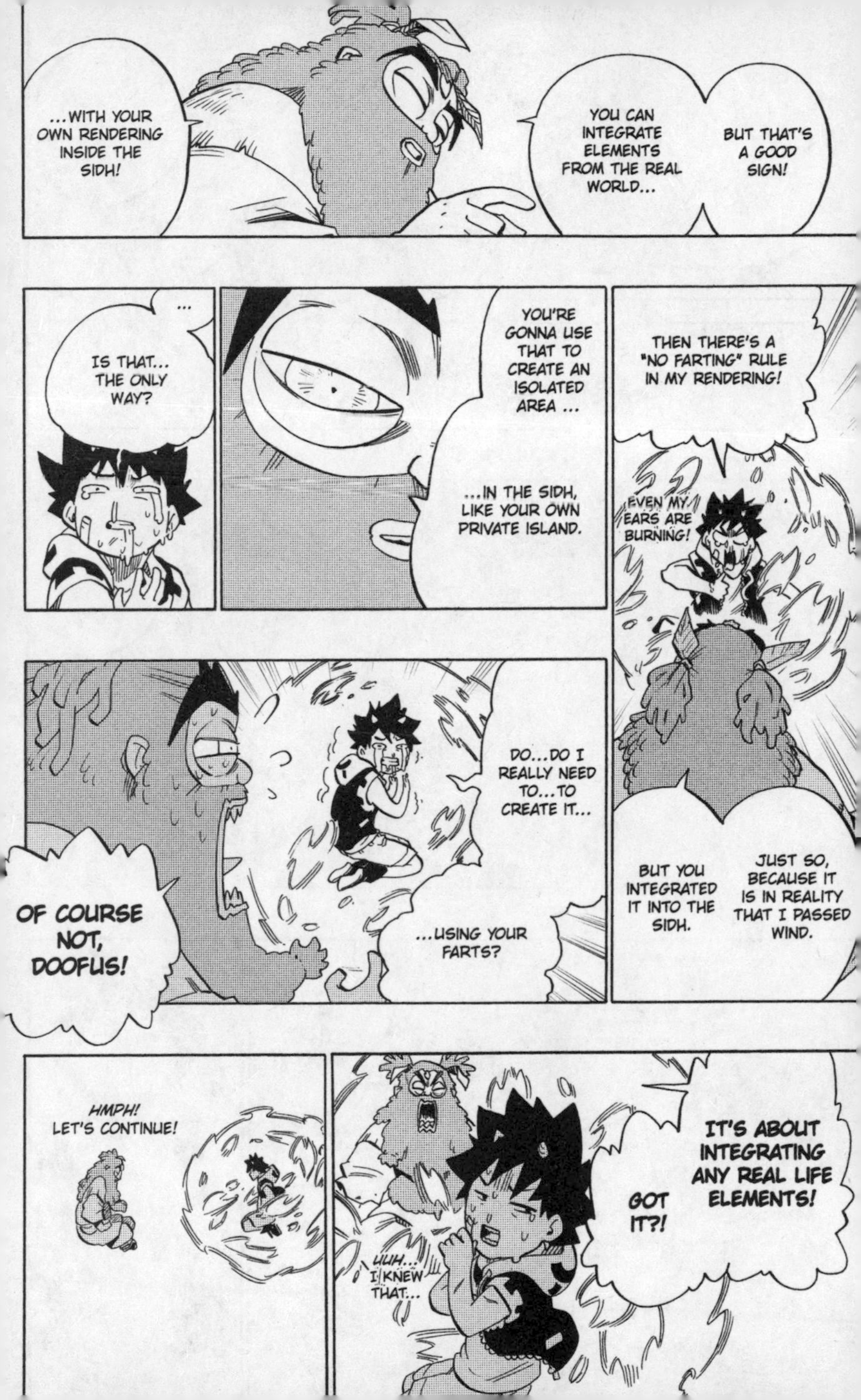
BUT THAT'S A GOOD SIGN!
YOU CAN INTEGRATE ELEMENTS FROM THE REAL WORLD...
...WITH YOUR OWN RENDERING INSIDE THE SIDH!
THEN THERE'S A "NO FARTING" RULE IN MY RENDERING!
EVEN MY EARS ARE BURNING!
JUST SO, BECAUSE IT IS IN REALITY THAT I PASSED WIND.
BUT YOU INTEGRATED IT INTO THE SIDH.
YOU'RE GONNA USE THAT TO CREATE AN ISOLATED AREA ...
...IN THE SIDH, LIKE YOUR OWN PRIVATE ISLAND.
...
IS THAT... THE ONLY WAY?
DO...DO I REALLY NEED TO...TO CREATE IT...
...USING YOUR FARTS?
OF COURSE NOT, DOOFUS!
IT'S ABOUT INTEGRATING ANY REAL LIFE ELEMENTS!
GOT IT?!
UUH... I KNEW THAT...
HMPH! LET'S CONTINUE!

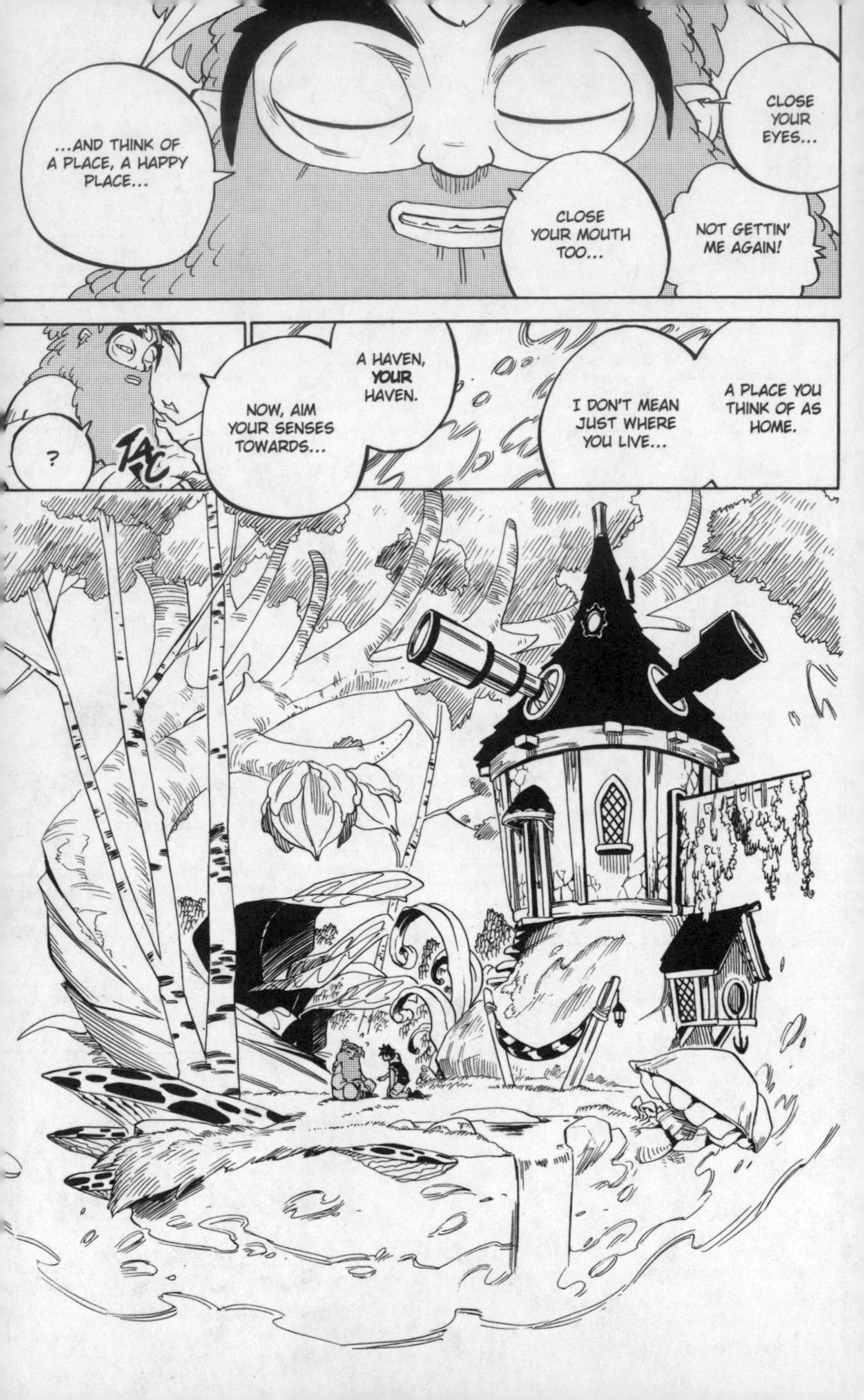
CLOSE YOUR EYES...
NOT GETTIN' ME AGAIN!
CLOSE YOUR MOUTH TOO...
...AND THINK OF A PLACE, A HAPPY PLACE...
A PLACE YOU THINK OF AS HOME.
I DON'T MEAN JUST WHERE YOU LIVE...
A HAVEN, YOUR HAVEN.
NOW, AIM YOUR SENSES TOWARDS...
TAC
?

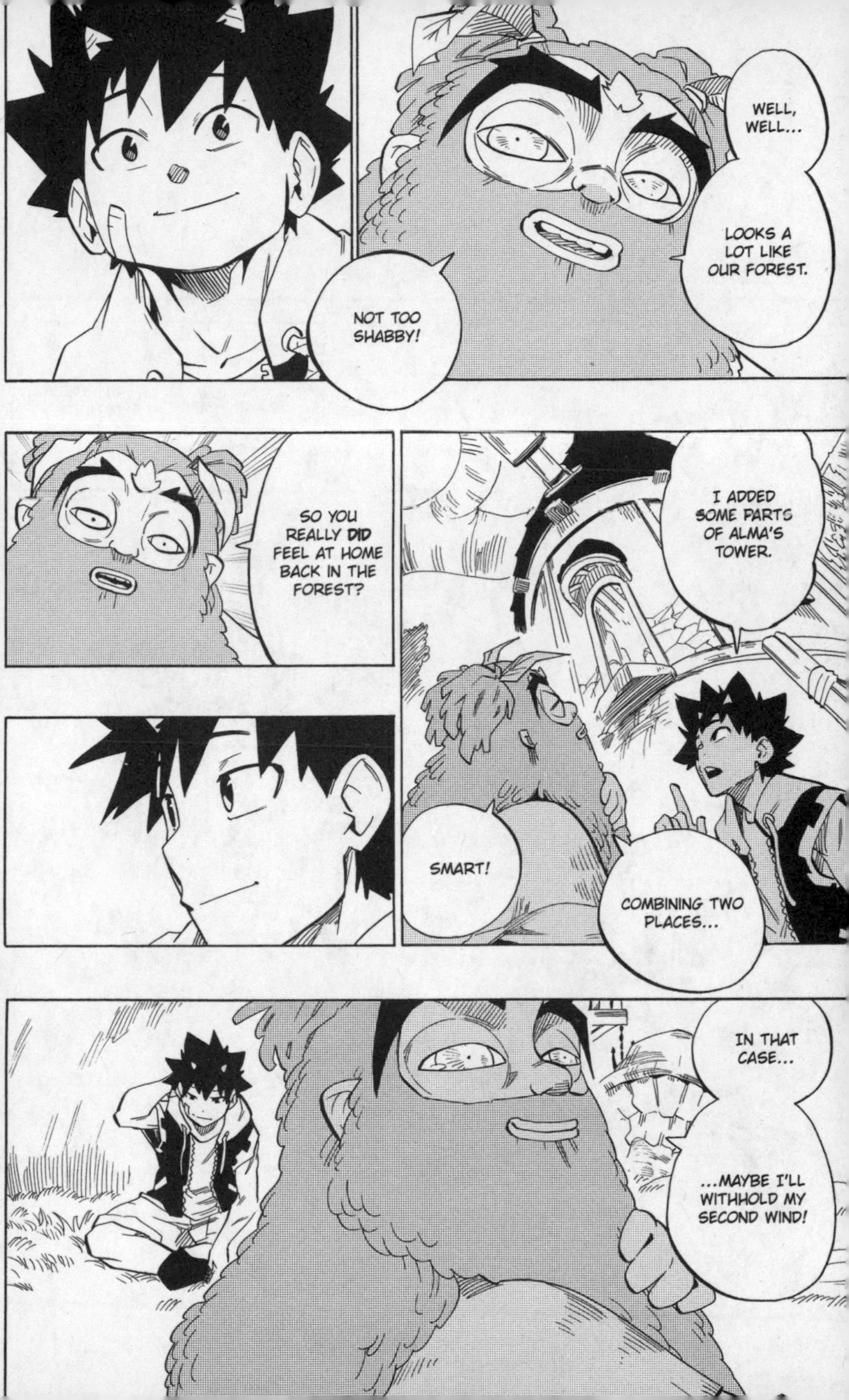
WELL, WELL...
LOOKS A LOT LIKE OUR FOREST.
NOT TOO SHABBY!
I ADDED SOME PARTS OF ALMA'S TOWER.
COMBINING TWO PLACES...
SMART!
SO YOU REALLY **DID** FEEL AT HOME BACK IN THE FOREST?
IN THAT CASE...
...MAYBE I'LL WITHHOLD MY SECOND WIND!

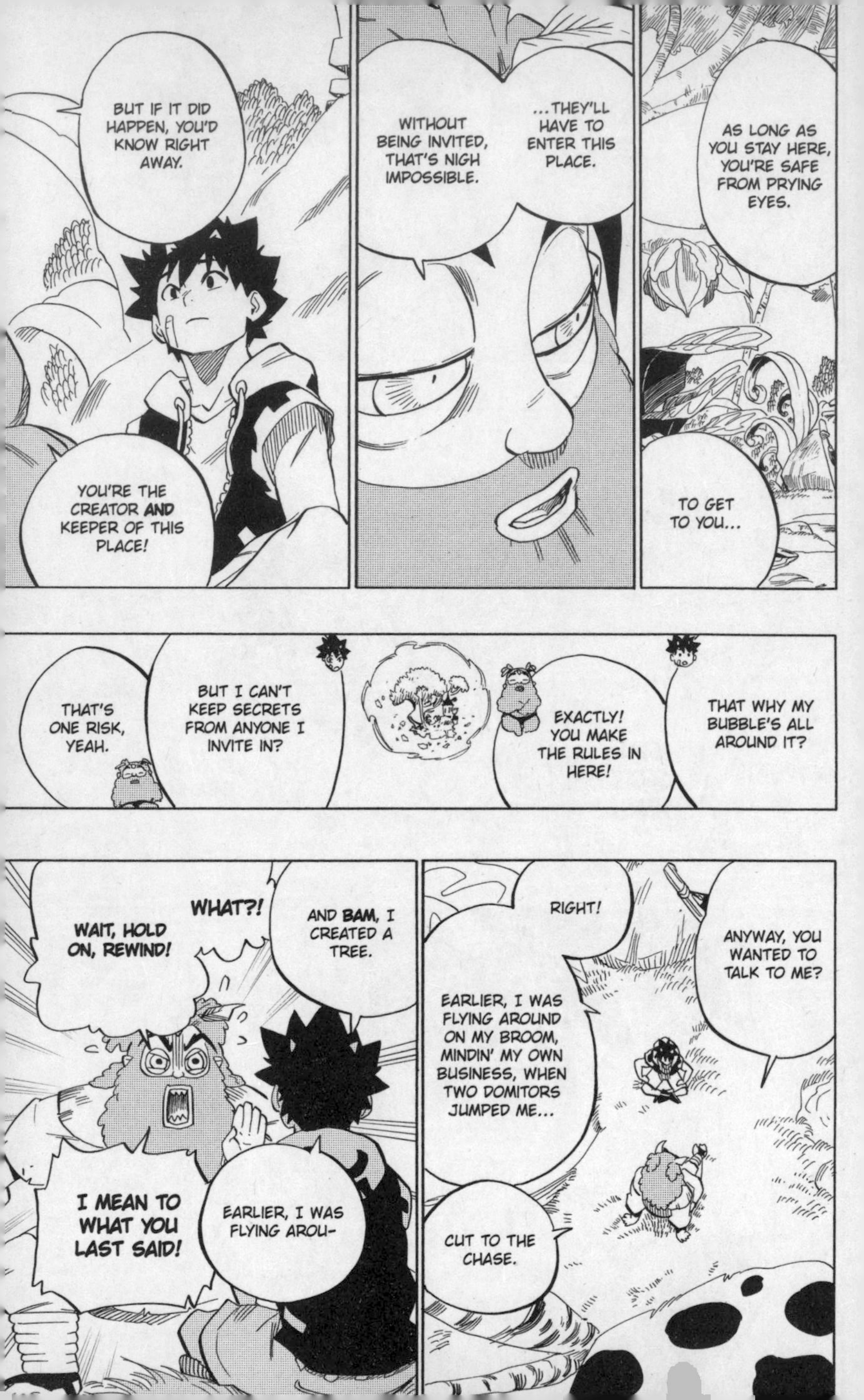
AS LONG AS YOU STAY HERE, YOU'RE SAFE FROM PRYING EYES.
TO GET TO YOU...
...THEY'LL HAVE TO ENTER THIS PLACE.
WITHOUT BEING INVITED, THAT'S NIGH IMPOSSIBLE.
BUT IF IT DID HAPPEN, YOU'D KNOW RIGHT AWAY.
YOU'RE THE CREATOR AND KEEPER OF THIS PLACE!
THAT WHY MY BUBBLE'S ALL AROUND IT?
EXACTLY! YOU MAKE THE RULES IN HERE!
BUT I CAN'T KEEP SECRETS FROM ANYONE I INVITE IN?
THAT'S ONE RISK, YEAH.
ANYWAY, YOU WANTED TO TALK TO ME?
RIGHT!
EARLIER, I WAS FLYING AROUND ON MY BROOM, MINDIN' MY OWN BUSINESS, WHEN TWO DOMITORS JUMPED ME...
CUT TO THE CHASE.
AND BAM, I CREATED A TREE.
WHAT?!
WAIT, HOLD ON, REWIND!
EARLIER, I WAS FLYING AROU-
I MEAN TO WHAT YOU LAST SAID!

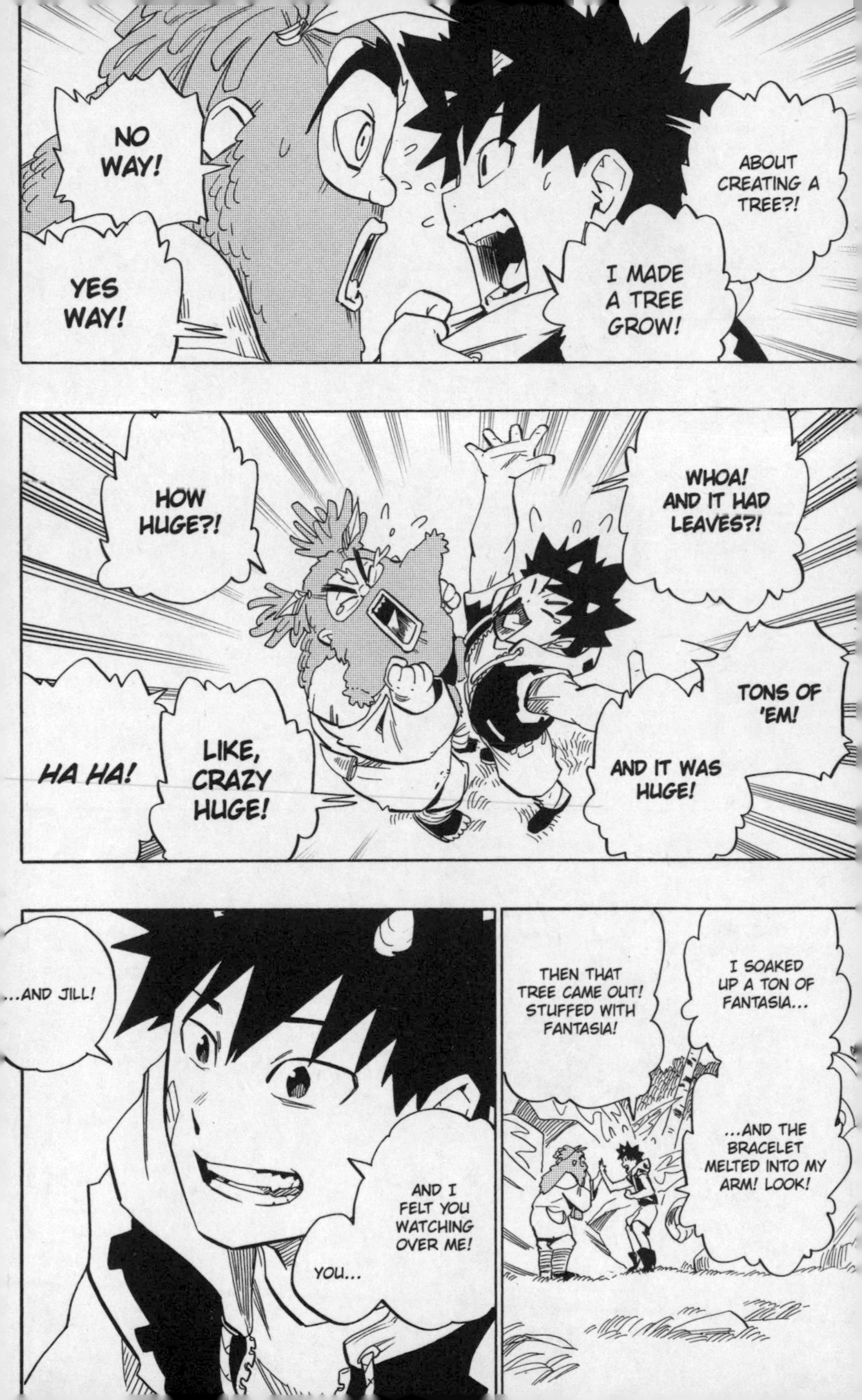
ABOUT CREATING A TREE?!
I MADE A TREE GROW!
NO WAY!
YES WAY!
WHOA! AND IT HAD LEAVES?!
HOW HUGE?!
TONS OF 'EM!
AND IT WAS HUGE!
LIKE, CRAZY HUGE!
HA HA!
I SOAKED UP A TON OF FANTASIA...
THEN THAT TREE CAME OUT! STUFFED WITH FANTASIA!
...AND THE BRACELET MELTED INTO MY ARM! LOOK!
AND I FELT YOU WATCHING OVER ME!
YOU...
...AND JILL!

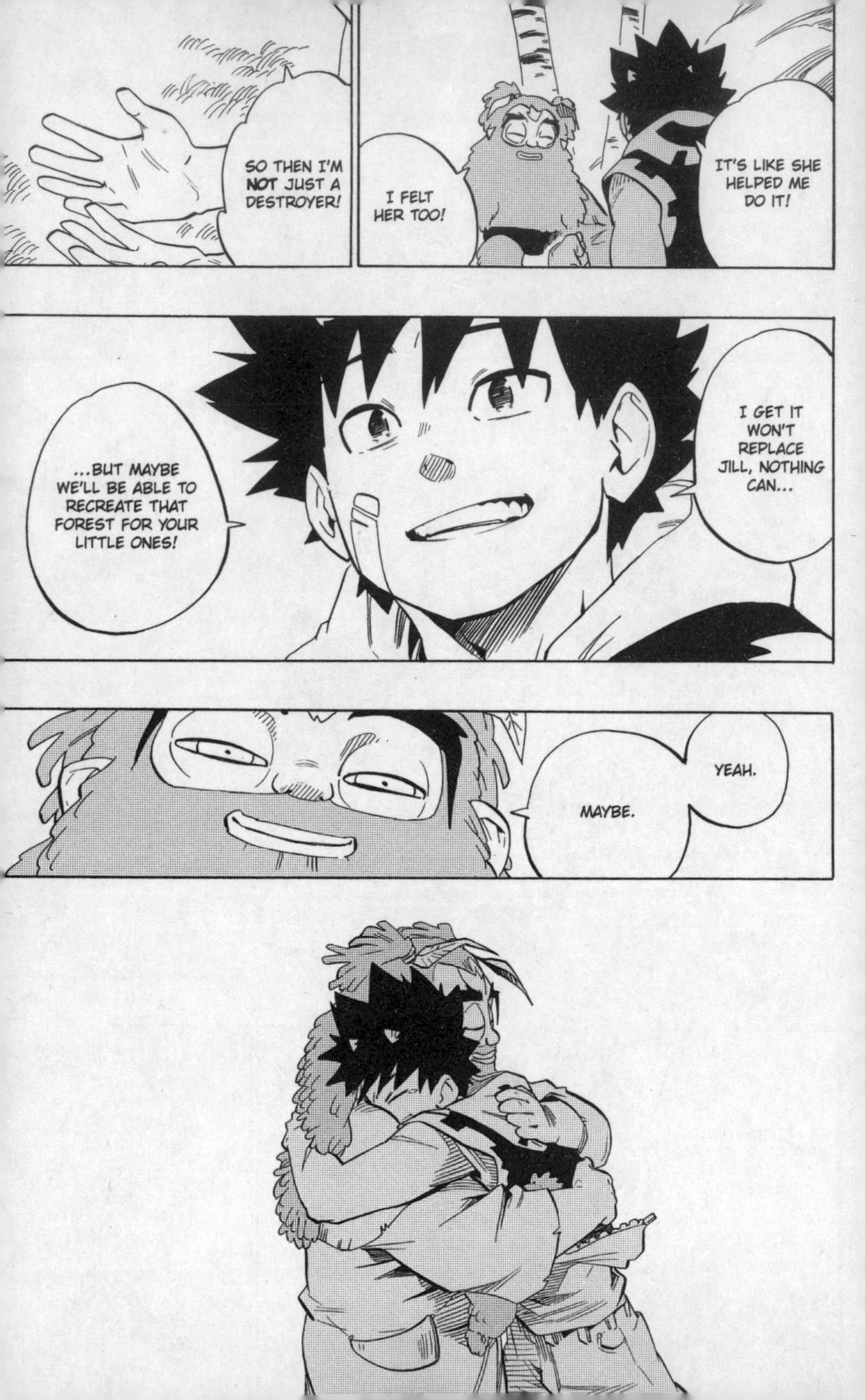
IT'S LIKE SHE HELPED ME DO IT!
I FELT HER TOO!
SO THEN I'M **NOT** JUST A DESTROYER!
I GET IT WON'T REPLACE JILL, NOTHING CAN...
...BUT MAYBE WE'LL BE ABLE TO RECREATE THAT FOREST FOR YOUR LITTLE ONES!
YEAH.
MAYBE.

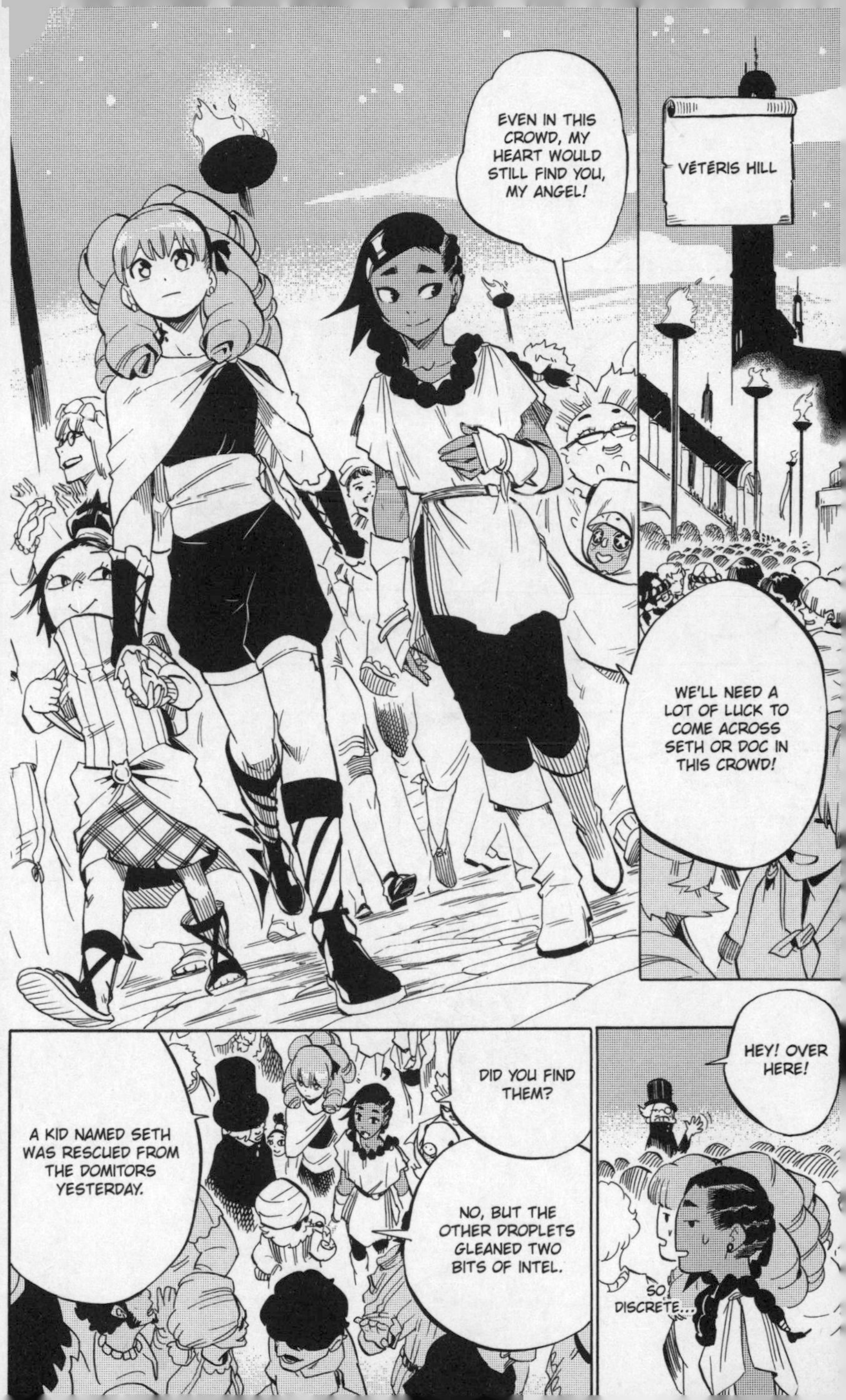
VÉTÉRIS HILL
WE'LL NEED A LOT OF LUCK TO COME ACROSS SETH OR DOC IN THIS CROWD!
EVEN IN THIS CROWD, MY HEART WOULD STILL FIND YOU, MY ANGEL!
HEY! OVER HERE!
SO DISCRETE...
DID YOU FIND THEM?
NO, BUT THE OTHER DROPLETS GLEANED TWO BITS OF INTEL.
A KID NAMED SETH WAS RESCUED FROM THE DOMITORS YESTERDAY.

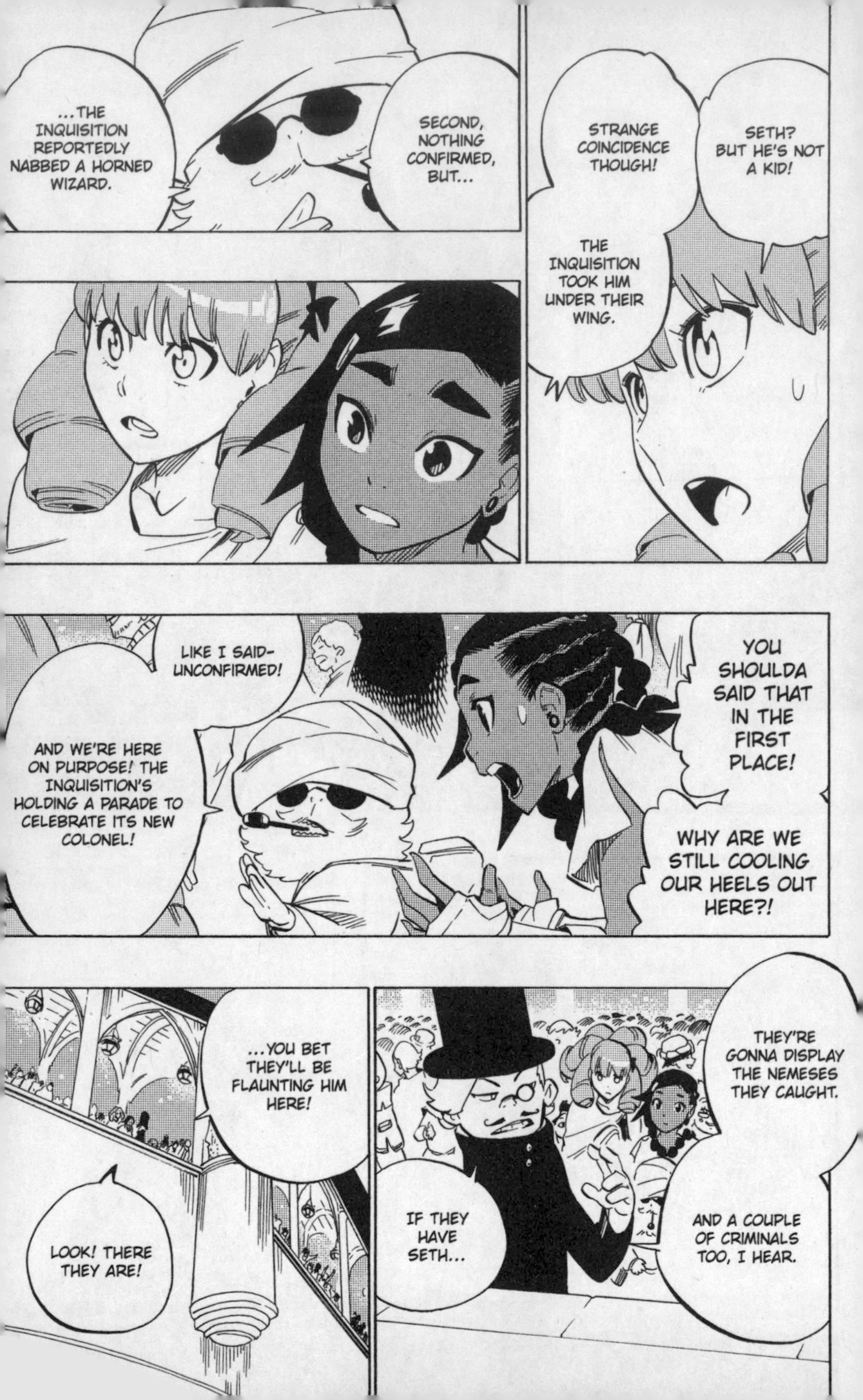
SETH? BUT HE'S NOT A KID!
STRANGE COINCIDENCE THOUGH!
THE INQUISITION TOOK HIM UNDER THEIR WING.
SECOND, NOTHING CONFIRMED, BUT...
...THE INQUISITION REPORTEDLY NABBED A HORNED WIZARD.
YOU SHOULDA SAID THAT IN THE FIRST PLACE!
WHY ARE WE STILL COOLING OUR HEELS OUT HERE?!
LIKE I SAID- UNCONFIRMED!
AND WE'RE HERE ON PURPOSE! THE INQUISITION'S HOLDING A PARADE TO CELEBRATE ITS NEW COLONEL!
THEY'RE GONNA DISPLAY THE NEMESES THEY CAUGHT.
AND A COUPLE OF CRIMINALS TOO, I HEAR.
IF THEY HAVE SETH...
...YOU BET THEY'LL BE FLAUNTING HIM HERE!
LOOK! THERE THEY ARE!

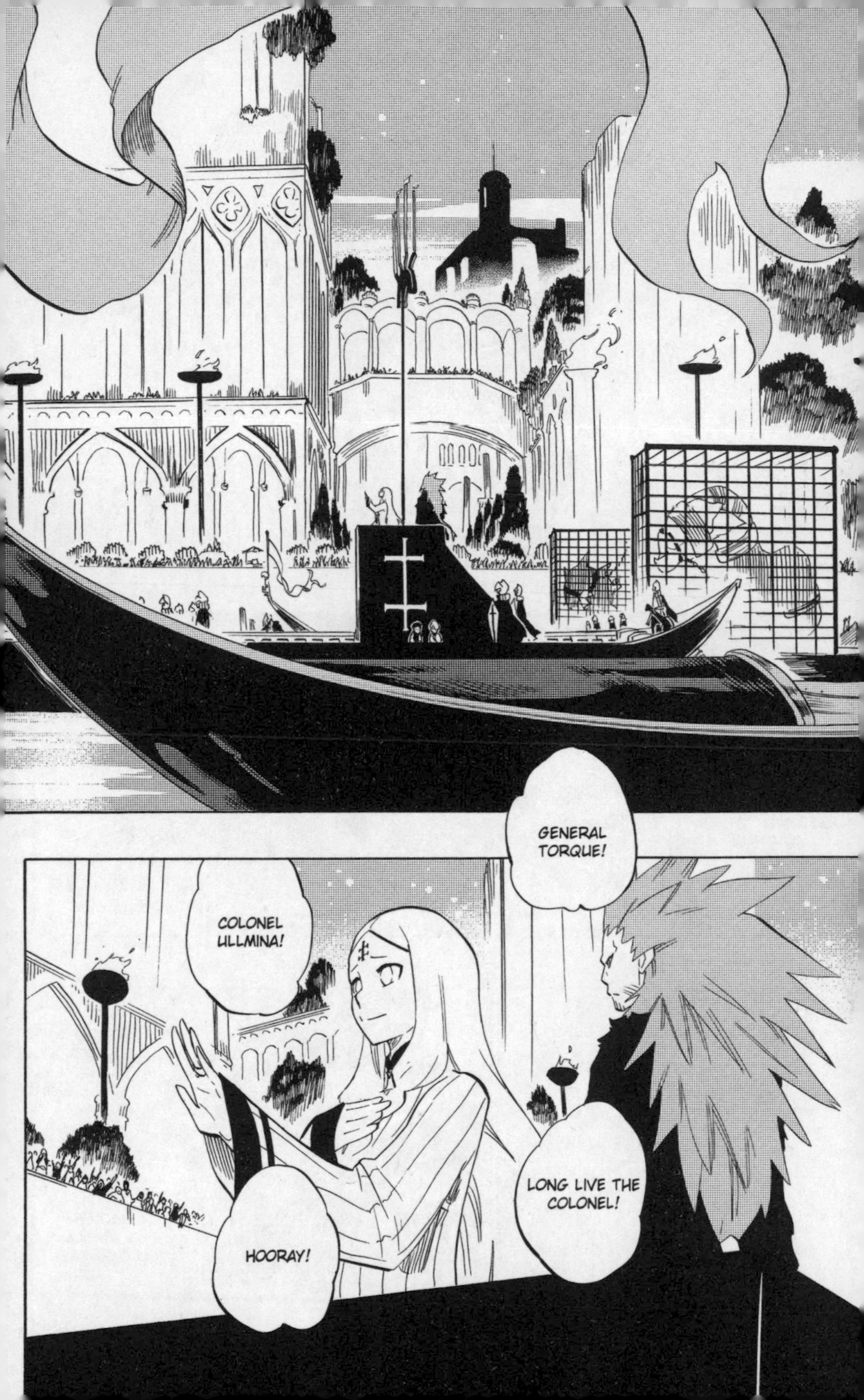
GENERAL TORQUE!
COLONEL ULLMINA!
LONG LIVE THE COLONEL!
HOORAY!

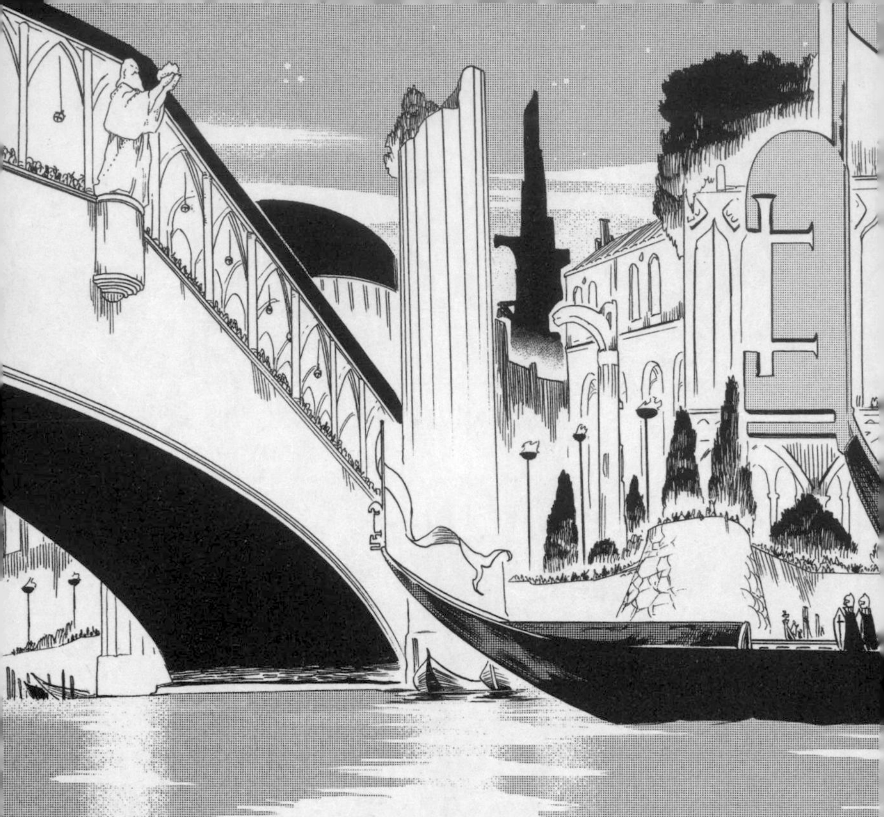
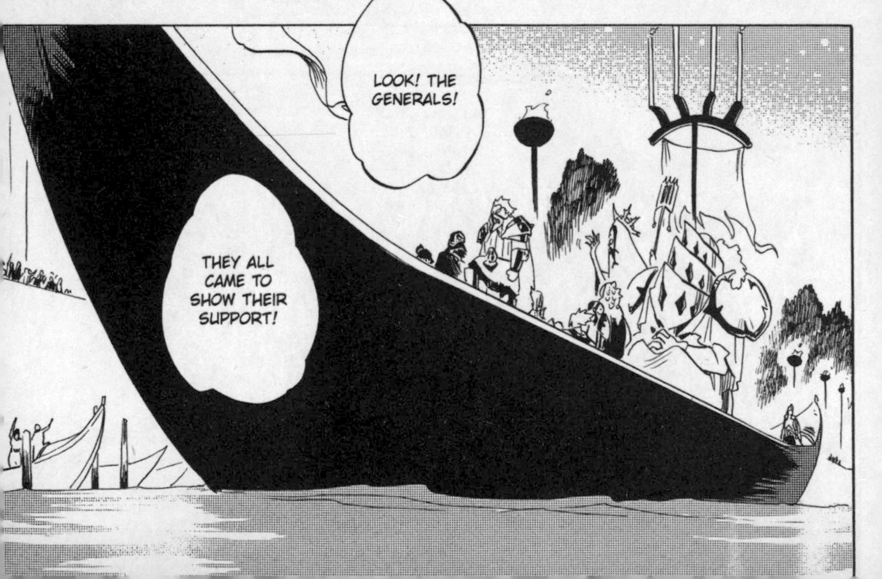
LOOK! THE GENERALS!
THEY ALL CAME TO SHOW THEIR SUPPORT!

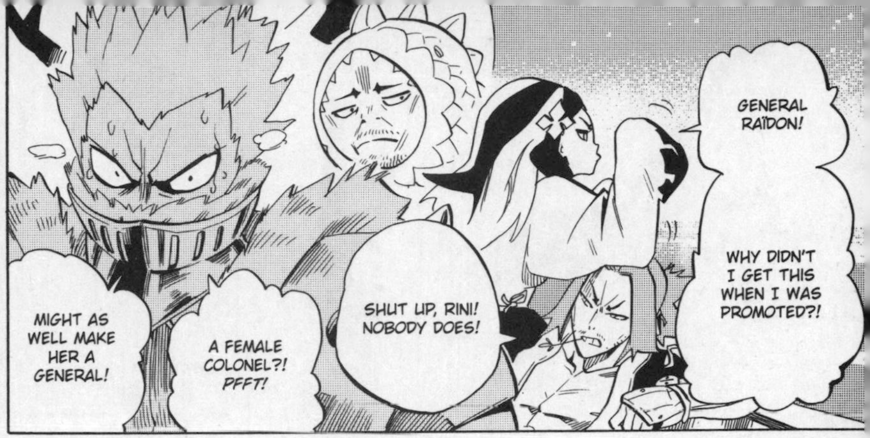
GENERAL RAÏDON!
WHY DIDN'T I GET THIS WHEN I WAS PROMOTED?!
SHUT UP, RINI! NOBODY DOES!
A FEMALE COLONEL?! PFFT!
MIGHT AS WELL MAKE HER A GENERAL!
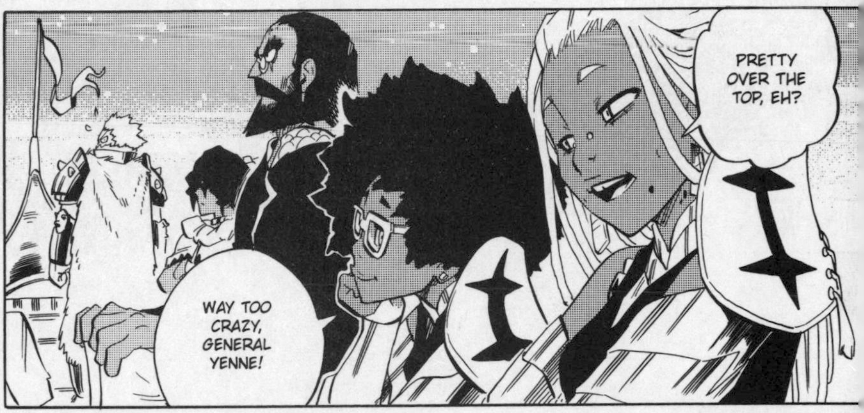
PRETTY OVER THE TOP, EH?
WAY TOO CRAZY, GENERAL YENNE!
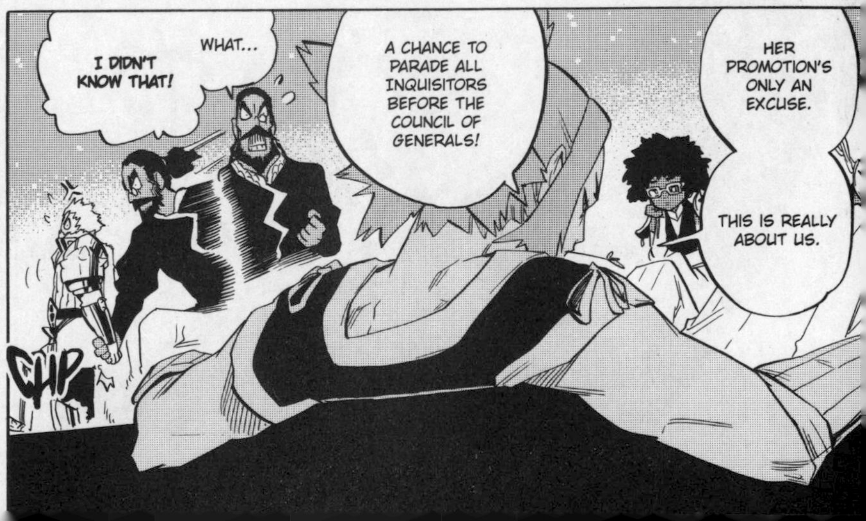
HER PROMOTION'S ONLY AN EXCUSE.
THIS IS REALLY ABOUT US.
A CHANCE TO PARADE ALL INQUISITORS BEFORE THE COUNCIL OF GENERALS!
WHAT...
I DIDN'T KNOW THAT!
CHP

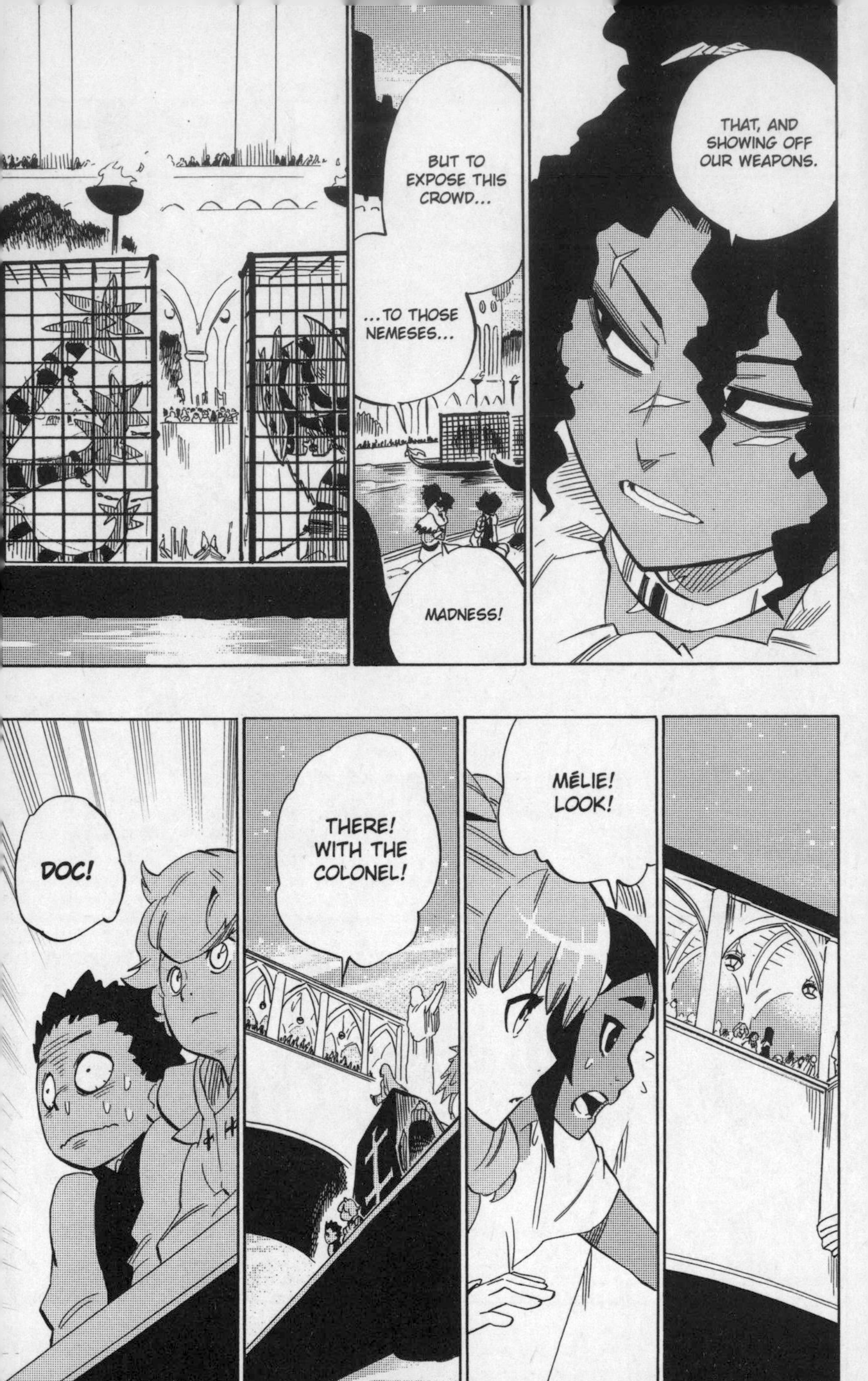
THAT, AND SHOWING OFF OUR WEAPONS.
BUT TO EXPOSE THIS CROWD...
...TO THOSE NEMESES...
MADNESS!
MÉLIE! LOOK!
THERE! WITH THE COLONEL!
DOC!

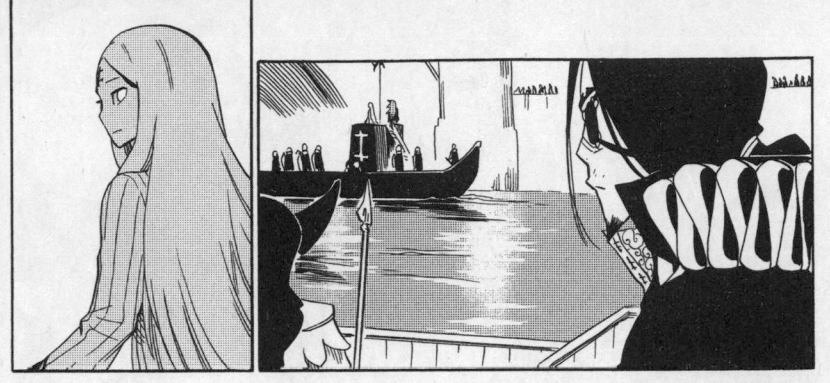

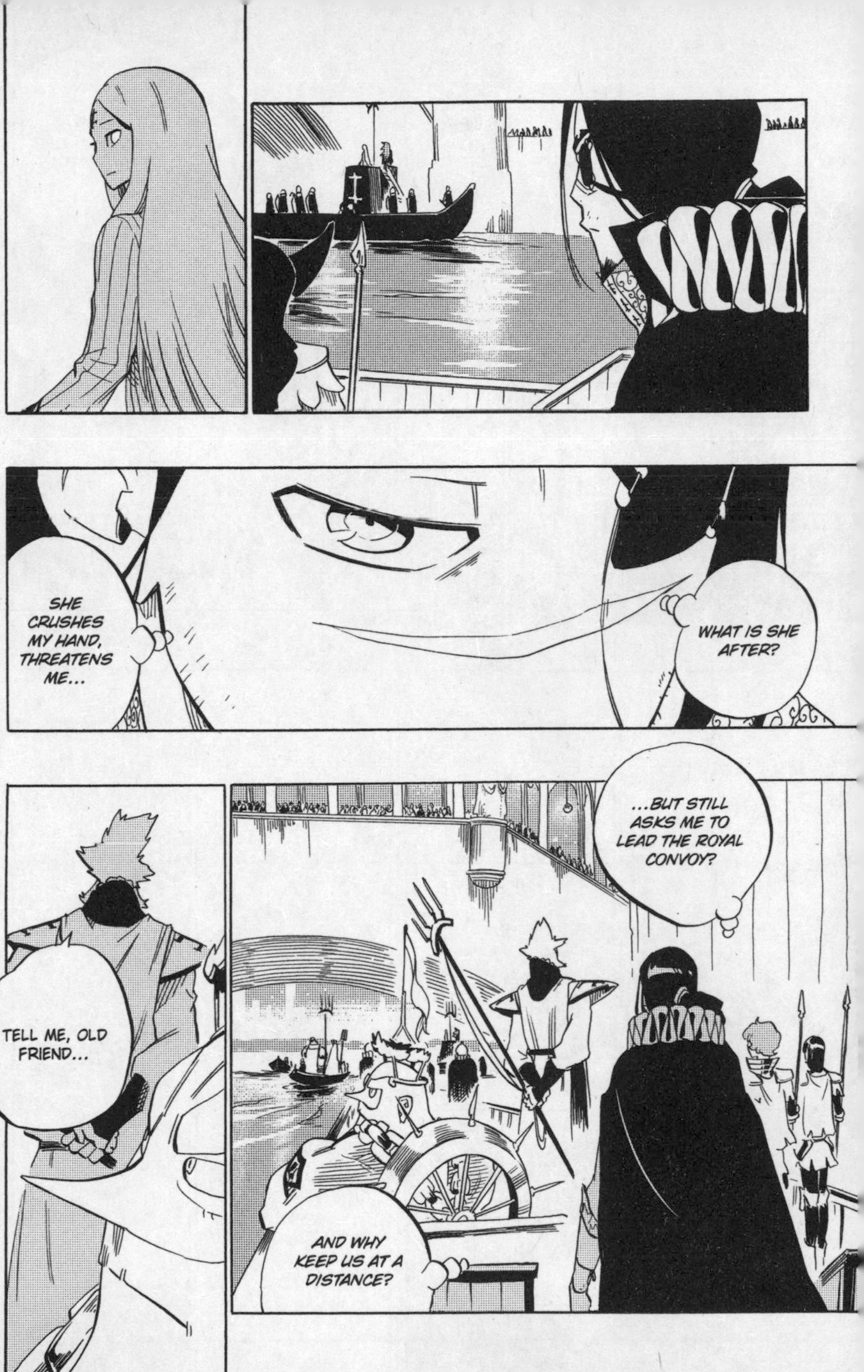
SHE CRUSHES MY HAND, THREATENS ME...
WHAT IS SHE AFTER?
...BUT STILL ASKS ME TO LEAD THE ROYAL CONVOY?
AND WHY KEEP US AT A DISTANCE?
TELL ME, OLD FRIEND...

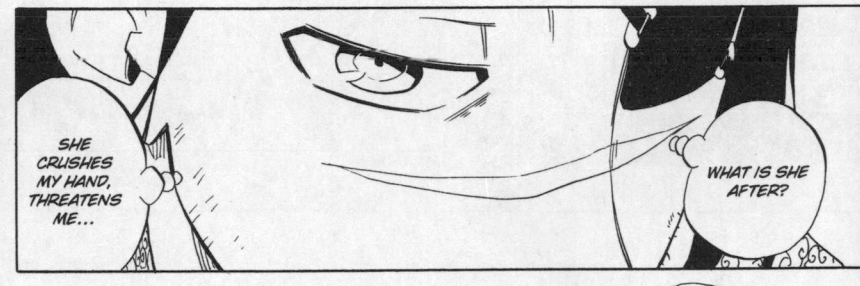

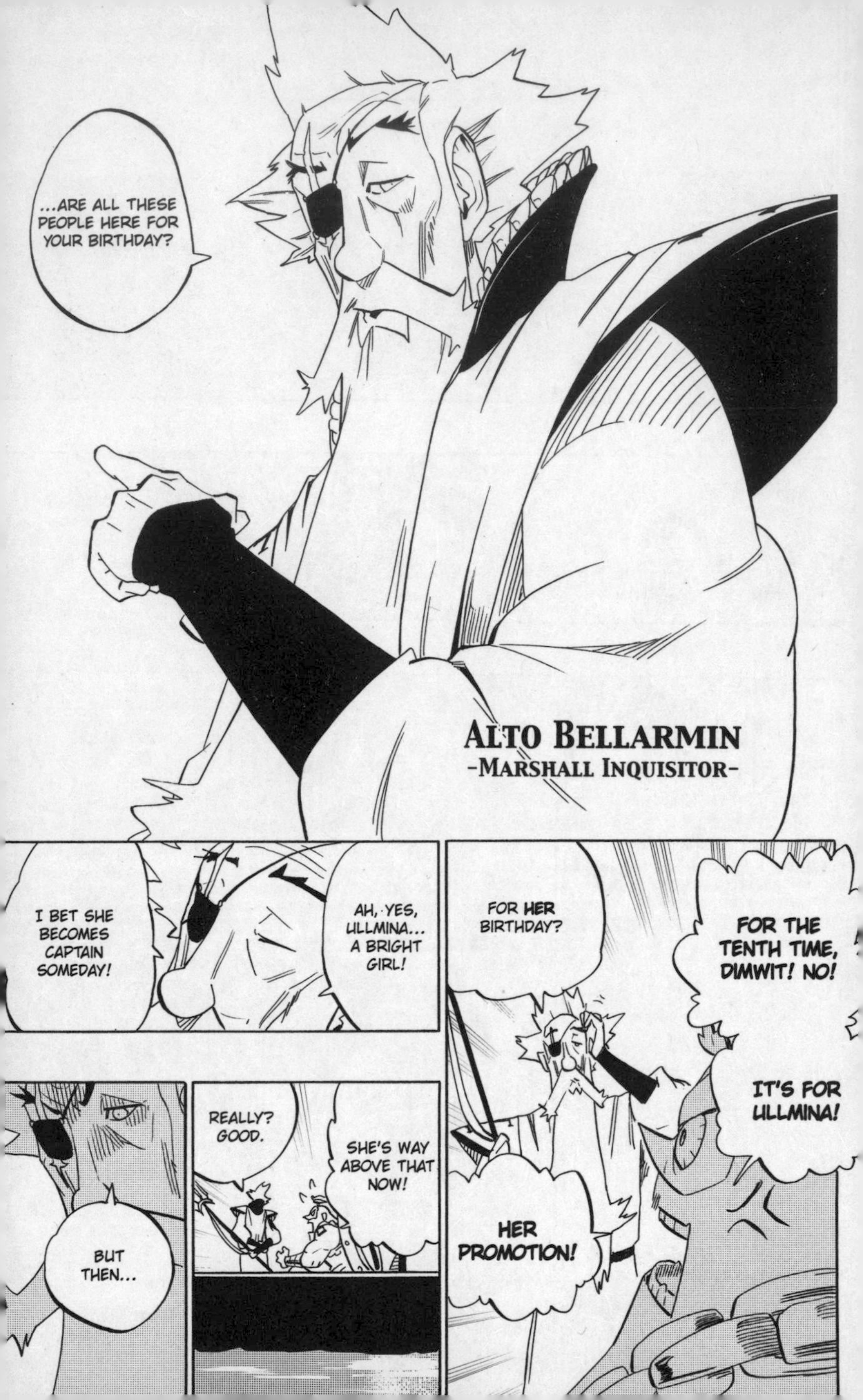
...ARE ALL THESE PEOPLE HERE FOR YOUR BIRTHDAY?
ALTO BELLARMIN
-MARSHALL INQUISITOR-
FOR HER BIRTHDAY?
FOR THE TENTH TIME, DIMWIT! NO!
IT'S FOR ULLMINA!
HER PROMOTION!
AH, YES, ULLMINA... A BRIGHT GIRL!
I BET SHE BECOMES CAPTAIN SOMEDAY!
SHE'S WAY ABOVE THAT NOW!
REALLY? GOOD.
BUT THEN...

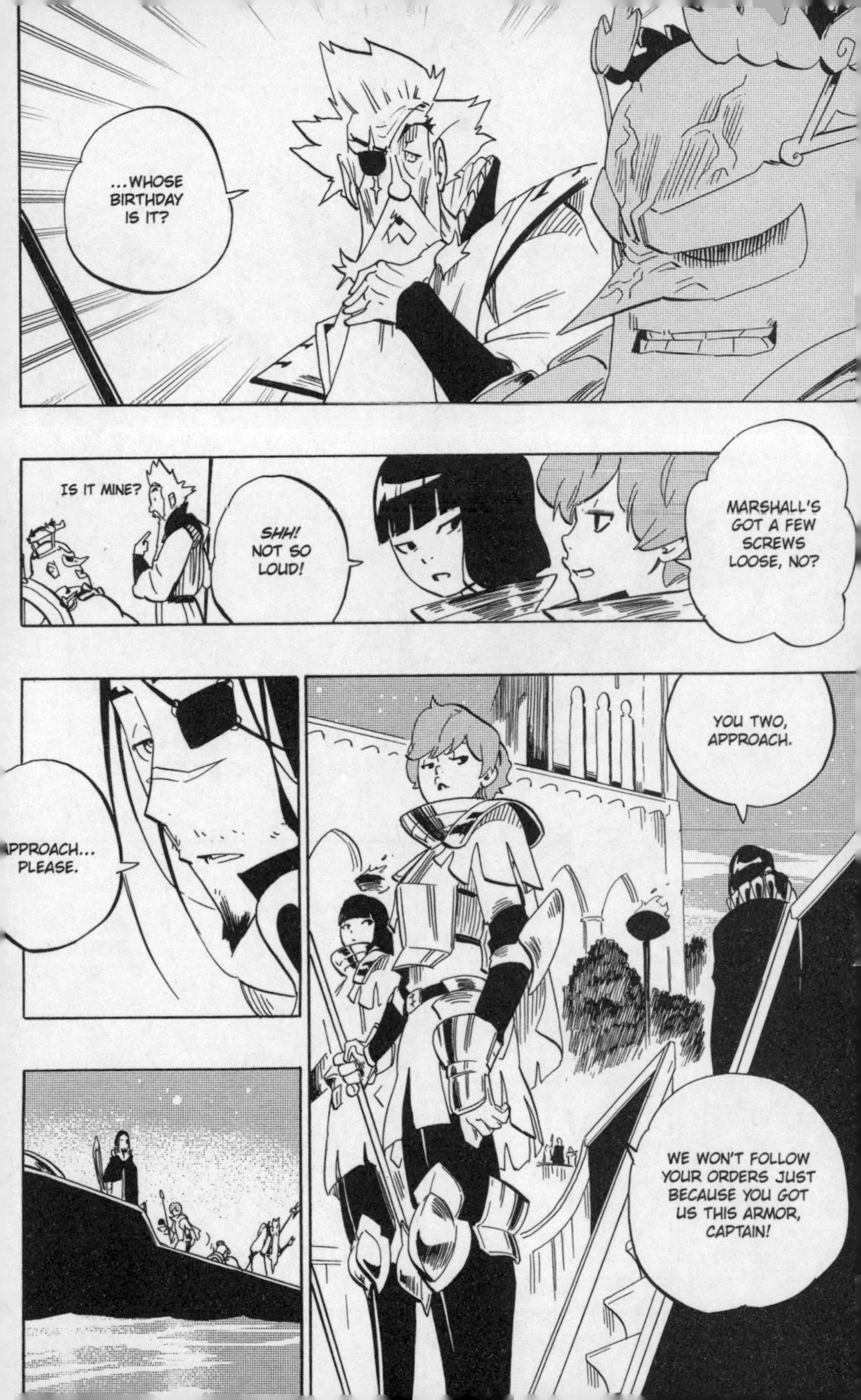
...WHOSE BIRTHDAY IS IT?
MARSHALL'S GOT A FEW SCREWS LOOSE, NO?
SHH! NOT SO LOUD!
IS IT MINE?
YOU TWO, APPROACH.
WE WON'T FOLLOW YOUR ORDERS JUST BECAUSE YOU GOT US THIS ARMOR, CAPTAIN!
APPROACH... PLEASE.

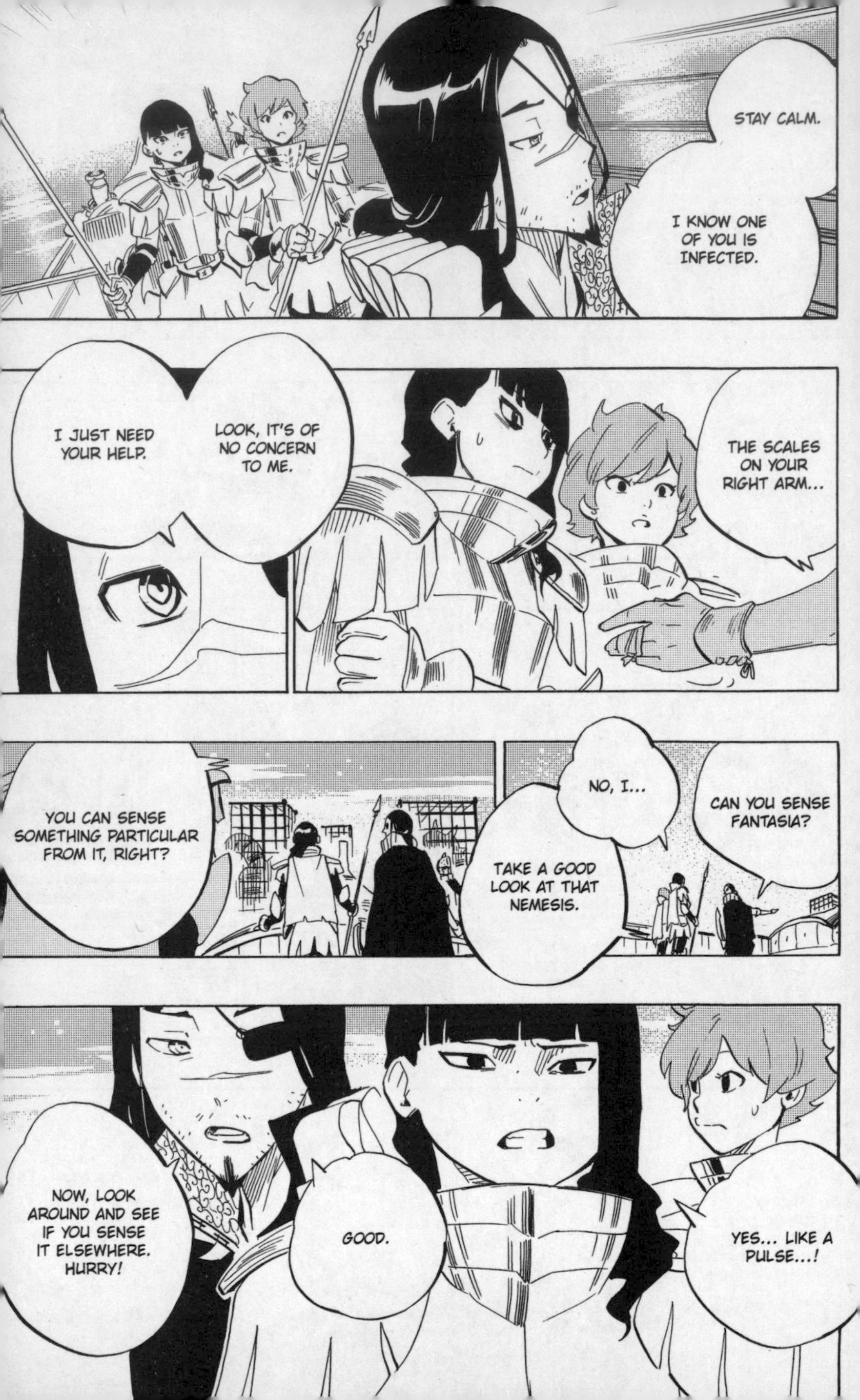
STAY CALM.
I KNOW ONE OF YOU IS INFECTED.
THE SCALES ON YOUR RIGHT ARM...
LOOK, IT'S OF NO CONCERN TO ME.
I JUST NEED YOUR HELP.
CAN YOU SENSE FANTASIA?
NO, I...
TAKE A GOOD LOOK AT THAT NEMESIS.
YOU CAN SENSE SOMETHING PARTICULAR FROM IT, RIGHT?
YES... LIKE A PULSE...!
GOOD.
NOW, LOOK AROUND AND SEE IF YOU SENSE IT ELSEWHERE. HURRY!

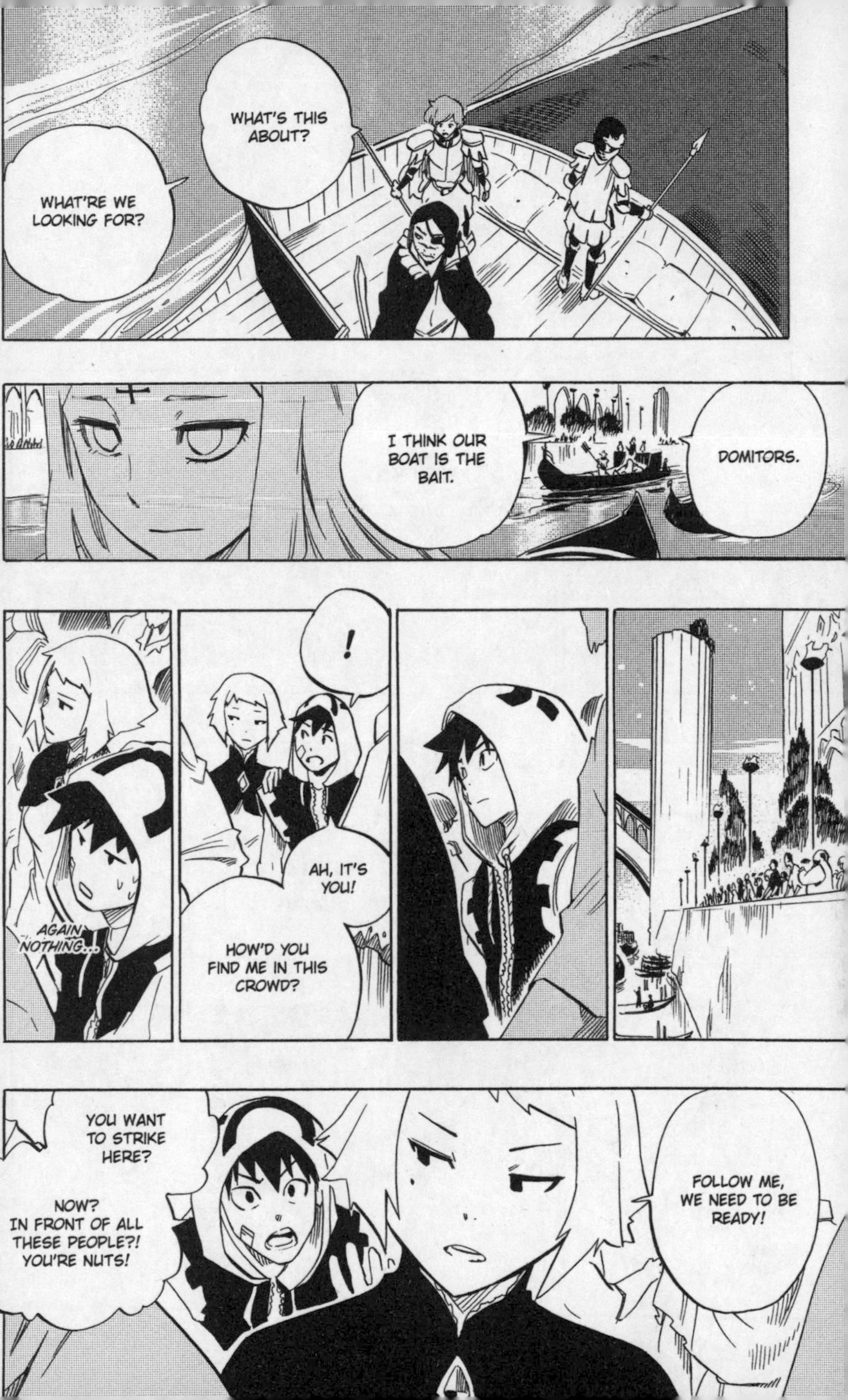
WHAT'S THIS ABOUT?
WHAT'RE WE LOOKING FOR?
DOMITORS.
I THINK OUR BOAT IS THE BAIT.
!
AH, IT'S YOU!
HOW'D YOU FIND ME IN THIS CROWD?
AGAIN NOTHING...
FOLLOW ME, WE NEED TO BE READY!
YOU WANT TO STRIKE HERE?
NOW? IN FRONT OF ALL THESE PEOPLE?! YOU'RE NUTS!

IF **THEY** GET A HOLD OF SKOHELL FIRST...
...THEY'LL UNLEASH HIM **HERE**!
?
WHO, THE OTHER DOMITORS?
HEY! THE PRISON SCOW!
AND THERE'S THE WIZARD THEY CAPTURED!
NOT A CHEERFUL PARADE DISPLAY!
WELL, THEY DESERVE IT!
GLAD TO SEE THEM ALL CHAINED UP LIKE THAT!

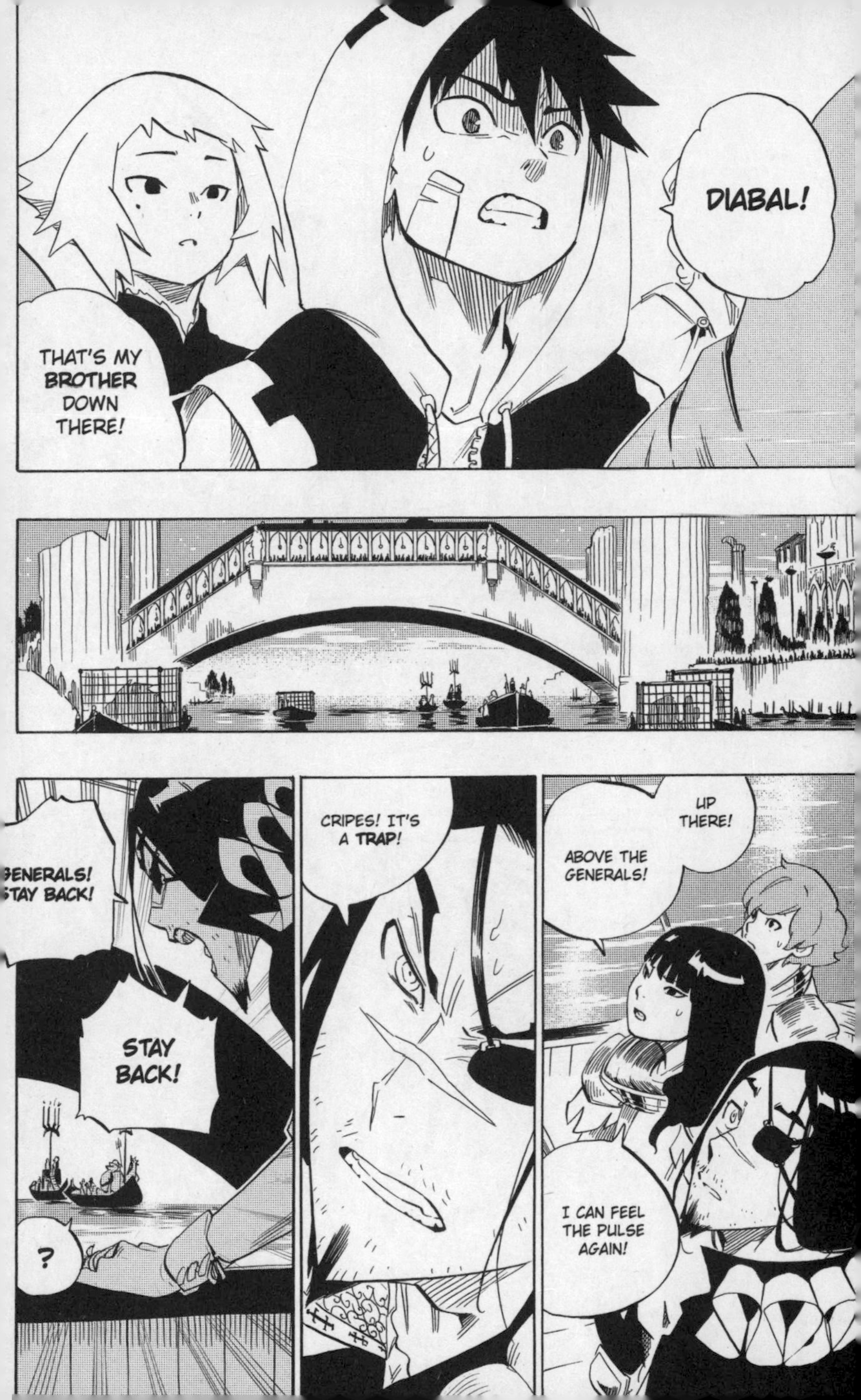
DIABAL!
THAT'S MY BROTHER DOWN THERE!
UP THERE!
ABOVE THE GENERALS!
I CAN FEEL THE PULSE AGAIN!
CRIPES! IT'S A TRAP!
GENERALS! STAY BACK!
STAY BACK!
?

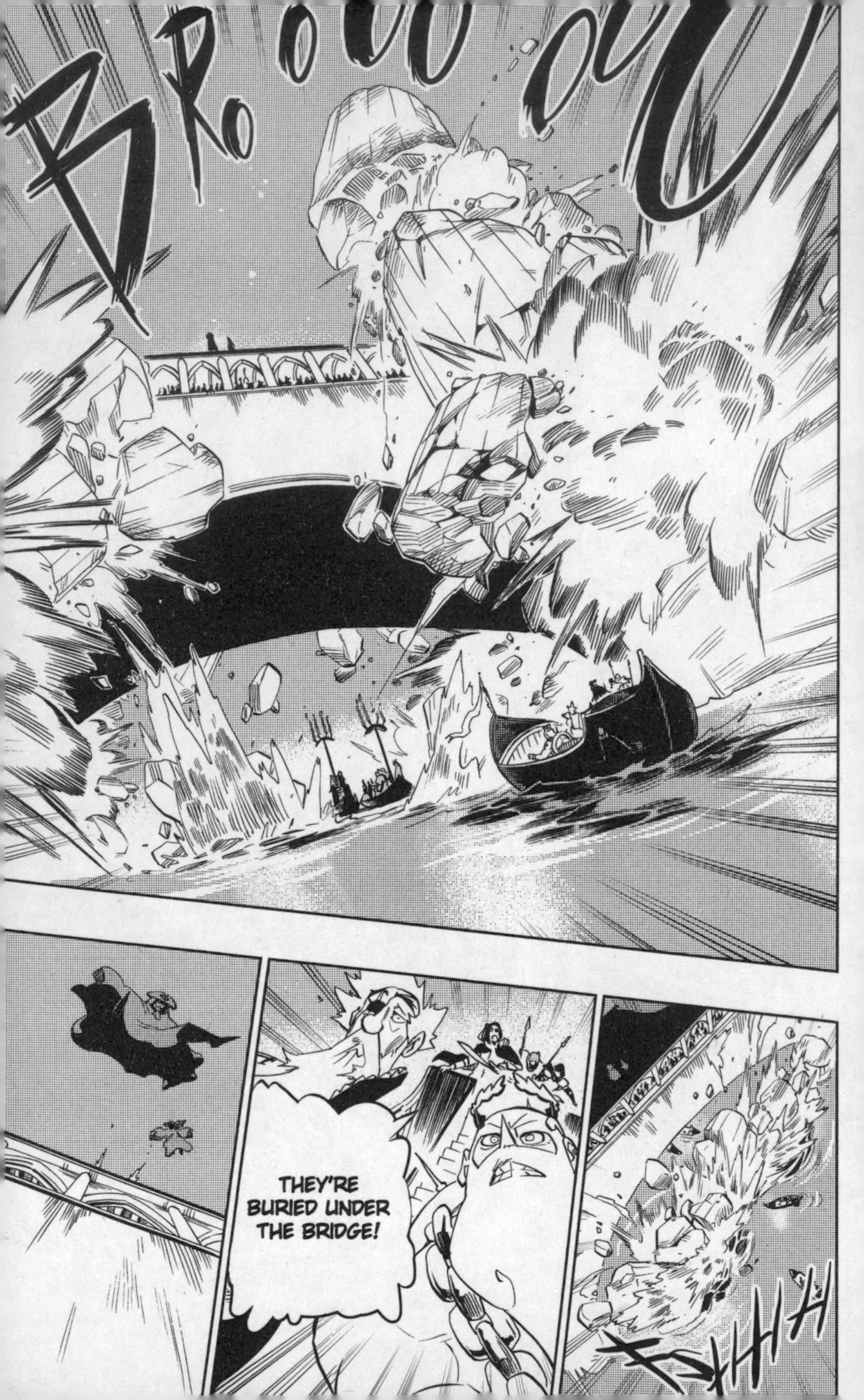
BROOOOOM
THEY'RE BURIED UNDER THE BRIDGE!

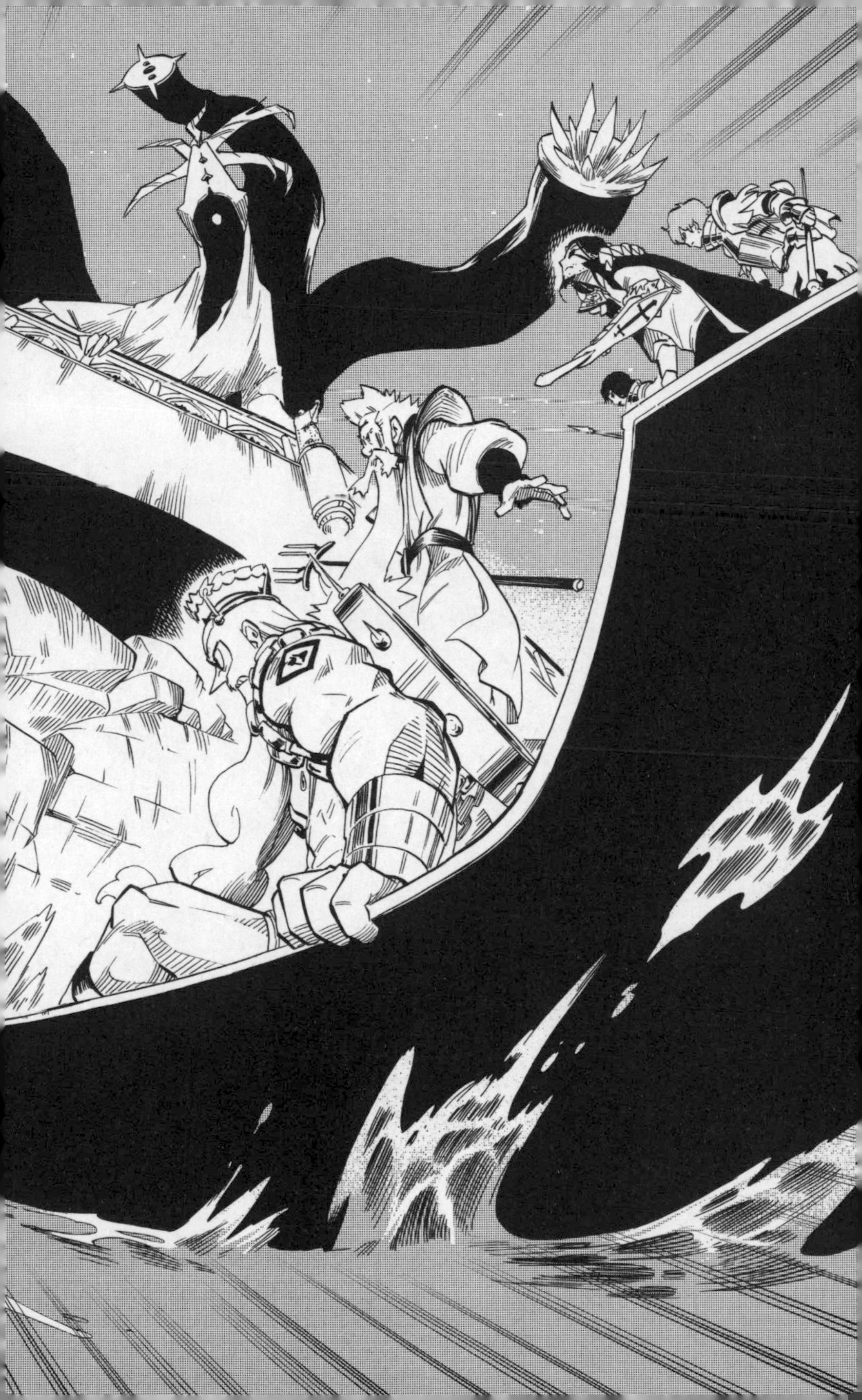

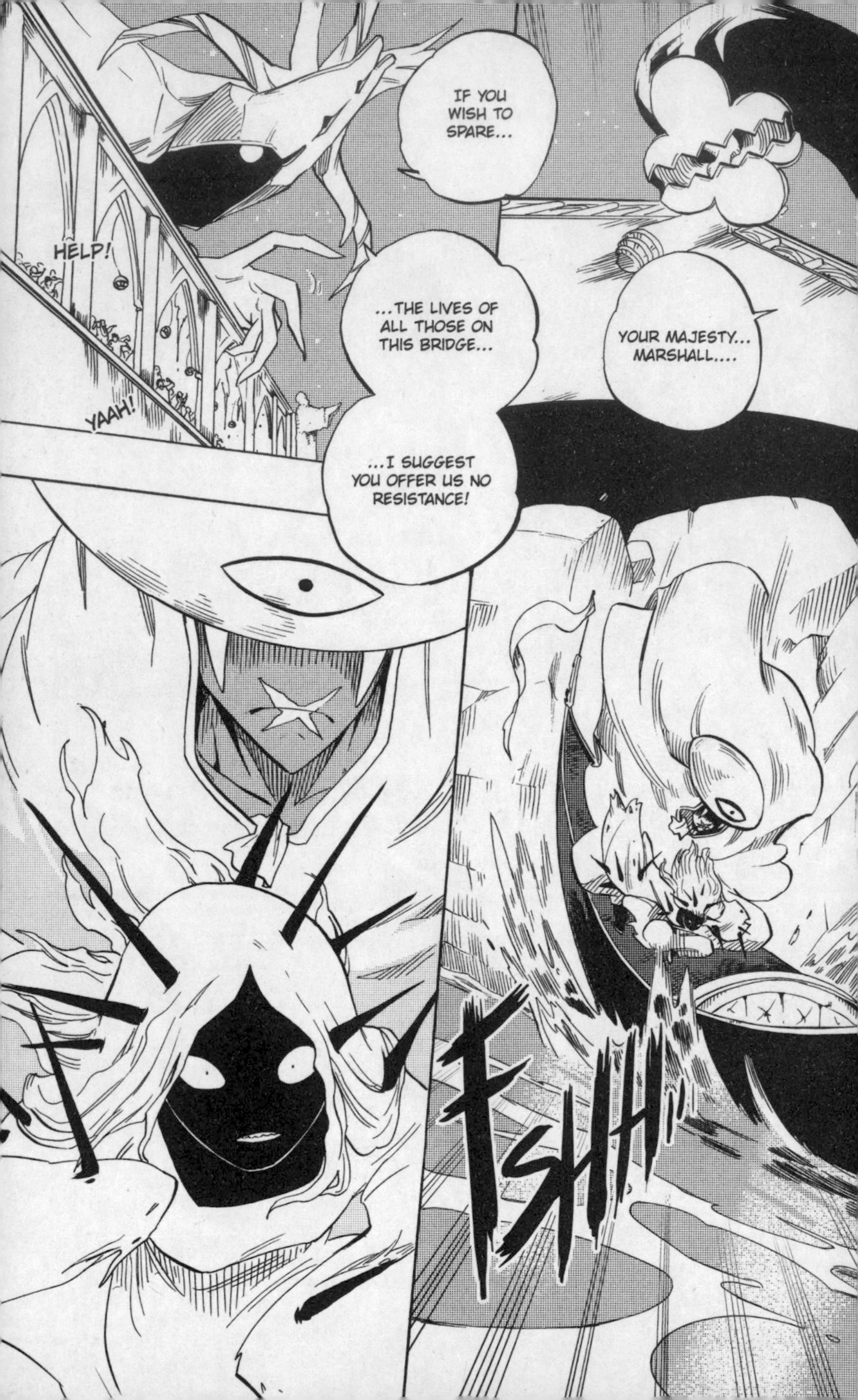
YOUR MAJESTY... MARSHALL....
IF YOU WISH TO SPARE...
...THE LIVES OF ALL THOSE ON THIS BRIDGE...
...I SUGGEST YOU OFFER US NO RESISTANCE!
HELP!
YAAH!
FSHH

TO BE CONTINUED...

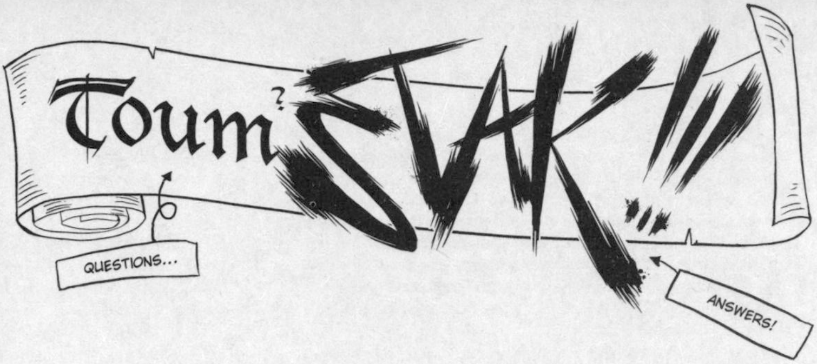
Toum?
STAK!!
QUESTIONS...
ANSWERS!

Claire D.: Good day, good evening and goodnight, how are you, very well thank you, goodbye. Wait, no, not goodbye! First of all, regarding the comment you wrote on the jacket of volume 10, a reliable source of mine (a biologist who also fulfills the role of mother) assured me that the inter-tree communication is a big pile of fake news. Apparently.

Tony Valente: That's weird, I read some articles on the subject written by researchers on the subject of this "Wood Wide Web," or Mycorrhizal network (by L. Gilbert and L. Johnson, I.R. Sanders actually), and it seemed pretty solid to me. They've even started a load of experiments this year to check on the actual range of that trees/mushrooms/re-tree/re-mushroom communication... You know, all that.

-Also, I'd love to know how you found your art style. Did you draw inspiration from other manga artists'?

Among other things, but also by looking at real life, to understand how everything works.

-How much time did it take you to be satisfied with your own drawings?

This might not be the satisfying answer you're looking for, but it's true: even today I rarely am satisfied with what I draw.

-How did your planner look like back in high school? Personally, I create my best art in places where it shouldn't be, and that's why all my notebooks end up getting half their pages amputated. Was that the same for you?

Ha ha, yeah, I also drew a lot in my notes! But I was a little more discreet and never got caught. Almost never. Actually, it did happen. A lot.

-Finally, regarding Diabal (best boy!) and Piodon (second best), we know they fought each other in volume 10, and I was wondering if you had a certain propensity for killing off your characters? If yes, should I be worried about Diabal and be biting my nails? If I were to roll around a field of nettles while eating red ants dipped in tabasco, would that be enough for you to leave him be? I could maybe even start a cult in his name?

You can do all of that, yes. But I won't reveal anything to you. You can definitely do it though.

-Anyway, I wanted to tell you I really think your character designs are amazing. Could we get a color illustration of him?

There's one of him in the second box set that was on sale in France!

-(I'm not worried about Piodon, not only because he's extremely badass, but also because he looks extremely important to the rest of the story). I think that's all... Ah, wait, no! Do you have an idea of how many volumes you'd like to produce?

No idea!

-With the most sincere and utmost respect for your manga which I count among my favorites of all the ones I've read, and Lord knows I've read a ton of manga (including some huge turds, but let's not talk about those)
Signed: Me

Well, thank you for all that!

....

Bohemond Longuedague: Good day, dear friend. I am taking the trouble to write to you to ask you if the events that transpired in Cyfandir aren't reminiscent of the colonization of the Americas by the Europeans, or even the colonization of Africa. Santori (which even gives off an Iberian or Portuguese influence) even said this in volume 9: "Making you and your friends seem like the bad guys to the world will make people more easily accept that we turn all the Infected into slaves." Looks to me like that was exactly the barbaric and monstrous strategy the colonizers used, no?

Tony Valente: Well yes... I didn't have Santori say those lines for nothing. I based it off an episode of the colonization of Great Britain by the Romans (that's where Boadicée's was inspired from), to talk about a much larger topic...

-So aren't the Inquisitors with their turbo nipples and crazy sandals and 5-mile long mustaches reminiscent of those dark events? Also, again in volume 9, you mentioned that you write stories about matters that matter to you!

Exactly right, and I'm going to keep talking about slavery in the next few arcs.

-So? So? What do you mean you need to hear more arguments? Well... Eh... Hyvdeuuufufgzuzeuef... AND DON'T MAKE ME REPEAT MYSELF!

Brangoire! I know it's you, you sneaky guy you!

-Looking forward to reading the next volume and thank you for this magnificent manga series you're giving to the world.

....

Hector: Hello, my name is Hector and I am a huge fan of *Radiant*. Right now, the story's mainly unfolding in the northwestern part of the Pharénos so I had a couple of questions: In the next arcs to come, will Seth and the others travel to the rest of the Pharénos? Is the story between Hameline and Seth over (I hope not)? And why is it called "Pharénos"? Thank you and good luck for the rest of the story.

Tony Valente: Oh, thank you! Knowing you're all there along with me going through this whole world... It just gives me so much energy! There is a chance we might learn more about the Pharénos, yes. Until recently, I was thinking no, but ideas start to fuse together, arcs become more developed... So yeah, maybe we'll see a part of the southern regions! As for the name "Pharénos", I would recommend you to read the Toum? Stak!!! of volume 10 in which I go into more detail!

....

Matis Lauté: Hello Sensei! First of all, I am a very big fan of your manga that I recently discovered, and ever since I can't stop myself from reading all the volumes over and over! Anyway, my question! I think it's been already asked by a lot of people, but you didn't answer it. So I'll ask it again, but in another way: will we someday know in a future volume what's hidden underneath that layer of clouds, because besides the Artemis, the Islets don't fly! Some of them are even swaying around and about to fall. Meaning that they must be standing on top of something...

Tony Valente: You've been reading it over and over?! I am happy to hear that...! I can't go into details on what we'll see, but those clouds the islets are located above comprise one of the pillars of my structure for this whole world. So, yes, I will be talking about it, definitely!

-Another less important question: Where is Grimm's hideout located on the map? It'd be nice to see it indicated somewhere when we actually know where he is... Unless his hideout is hiding underneath a layer of clouds? Again with the question...

Tadaaaaa... Have we already seen him inside that layer of clouds? The answer to that is "yes!" His hideout's in there. Not underneath it. We'll see what's underneath at a later time.

....

<u>Olivier B.:</u> **Mr. Valente, my first question has to do with chapter 74. When Queen Boadicée asks everyone to name their Infection, after Ocoho, Brangoire and herself everyone else also starts to chime in and one person screams out he's got two nostrils and one nose, but how is that even an Infection? It's even more normal than Boadicée growing even more beautiful everyday... Or maybe he was joking?**

<u>Tony Valente:</u> Ah, yes, that was Berthelon Wanhole! Here's his deal: he comes from a noble lineage known for their noses with just one nostril. One beautiful afternoon, as he's walking around at 2:35 p.m., picking some lilacs, BAM! He touches a Nemesis and starts growing a second nostril. With this newly acquired nostril, he becomes extremely unique among his peers, and starts to parade it around... But his father does not see kindly to the way Bertholon proudly flouts the family traditions and decides to disown and ban him. Bertholon runs off to Cyfandir to find refuge with his fellow Infected, proud to be able to finally own his two nostrils... But here, he's normal! His second nostril isn't impressing anyone! His abnormality being rejected by his peers, in fact being invisible due to being totally normal in Cyfandir, he becomes melancholy. But then the war ends and Infections are revealed! Bertholon feels like this is his time to shine and reveals to everyone he's got only one nose but two nostrils! Nobody cares. He falls into a great depression. Poor Bertholon...

With Ocoho becoming the new royal heir, I assume she should have some sort of diplomatic responsibilities outside of Cyfandir if she's going to be traveling around the world. Will we be seeing that in the manga in future volumes? After all, she introduced herself as such to the first person she met after leaving Cyfandir -- Grimm.

She is not officially representing Cyfandir in foreign areas. The Queen sent her to travel around the world to understand how it works, not to represent Cyfandir. We'll of course get references to her new role as heir, but nothing official.

-Finally, are you planning on adding a bit of romance (not talking about the comical kind like at the end of volume 10 with Doc and Miss Melba)? I'm sure it could be interesting to see, even if it doesn't actually turn into anything.

We might, yes. We very well might, actually.

-Finally, my last question concerns Grimm. Will we see his acolyte again, the Frankenstein's monster type of fella Grimm's keeping in his hideout? I'd be interested in seeing them work together.

I don't know about working together, but we'll see Léogon again, yes!

-Thank you

....

<u>Oscar L.:</u> **Hi Tony! I have a question for you, but I'm warning you, it might get kind of long, so I'll give you roughly five seconds to mentally prepare...**

<u>Tony Valente:</u> Okay, let me first quickly go to the bathro–

-Ready?
No, not y–

-Okay, here goes!
Aaaaah!!

-In volume 6, Grimm mentions the long voyage ahead of him to get back to Cyfandir after escaping Dragunov and Liselotte. There, we learn that he needs to go past the Crossing and go up all the way to Cyfandir, which will take him a couple of days. No matter how hard I look, however, I can't seem to find anything that could help me figure out the distance between Grimm's home and Cyfandir, so that's not very helpful. So I looked at the map of North-Western Pharénos to guess where his infamous hideout could be located. Also, as another fan mentioned, his house is somewhere underneath the clouds, _or_ he's not living in that part of Pharénos, but maybe in the South-Western region, in which case it would make guessing his location even harder. It'd really help me out if you could answer this question. But, even if you don't, I'll kick in your teeth and cut off your tongue, as you don't need them to draw manga anyway. So yeah, hope I didn't bore you too much with that f***ing long paragraph worthy to be used in English homework.

To answer your question: you really did your homework on the geography of North-Western Pharénos! I left in those little hints on purpose so people could more or less find where Grimm's hideout's located! Around Agorée... And to answer your threat: my teeth are unbreakable! They're spaghetti teeth, so hit them and they just bend a bit. And my tongue is made of bamboo: cut it off and it grows back. I am OP! Nothing can hurt me! Except for a lack of sleep. And illnesses, sometimes. And back pain. And stress too. And the instantaneous depression that forces me to cut myself off from the rest of the world. But besides that, invincible!

Please send your questions to: radiant@ankama.com

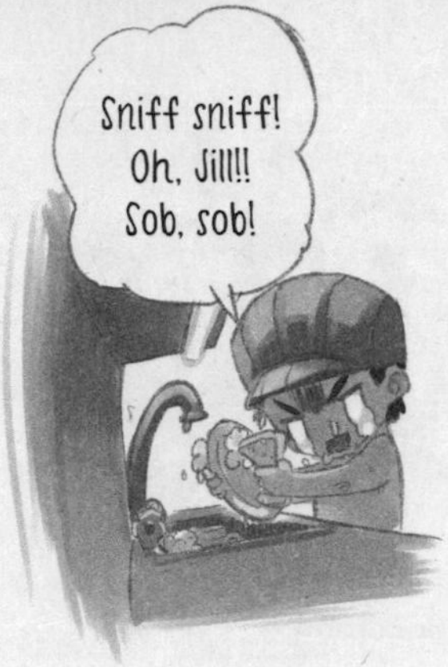
Sniff sniff!
Oh, Jill!!
Sob, sob!

How to find inspiration? Not an easy task! And yet, it's a question that gets asked all too often. So today I decided to share my secret with all of you. This is the secret method that leads me to come up with Hameline's life, Jill and Myr's story, the Battle for Cyfandir, the characters, the folklore and all that...! That secret method is...doing the dishes!

Now that you been bestowed this secret, nothing should stop you from becoming successful!

—Tony Valente

Tony Valente began working as a comic artist with the series *The Four Princes of Ganahan*, written by Raphael Drommelschlager. He then launched a new three-volume project, *Hana Attori*, after which he produced *S.P.E.E.D. Angels*, a series written by Didier Tarquin and colored by Pop.

In preparation for *Radiant*, he relocated to Canada. Through confronting caribou and grizzlies, he gained the wherewithal to train in obscure manga techniques. Since then, his eating habits have changed, his lifestyle became completely different and even his singing voice has changed a bit!

RADIANT

RADIANT VOL. 14
VIZ MEDIA Manga Edition

STORY AND ART BY **TONY VALENTE**
ASSISTANT ARTIST **SALOMON**

Translation/**(´・∀・`)ｻｧ?**
Touch-Up Art & Lettering/**Erika Terriquez**
Design/**Julian [JR] Robinson**
Editor/**Gary Leach**

Published by arrangement with MEDIATOON LICENSING/Ankama.
RADIANT T14

Printed in the U.S.A.

Published by VIZ Media, LLC
P.O. Box 77010
San Francisco, CA 94107

10 9 8 7 6 5 4 3 2 1
First printing, August 2021

VIZ MEDIA
viz.com

ratings.viz.com RATED T TEEN

PARENTAL ADVISORY
RADIANT is rated T for Teen and is recommended for ages 13 and up. This volume contains fantasy violence.

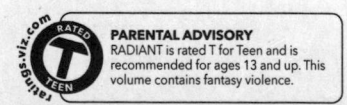

Black ✾ Clover

STORY & ART BY YŪKI TABATA

Asta is a young boy who dreams of becoming the greatest mage in the kingdom. Only one problem—he can't use any magic! Luckily for Asta, he receives the incredibly rare five-leaf clover grimoire that gives him the power of anti-magic. Can someone who can't use magic really become the Wizard King? One thing's for sure—Asta will never give up!

SHONEN JUMP

viz media
www.viz.com

DRAGON BALL SUPER

STORY BY **Akira Toriyama** ART BY **Toyotarou**

Goku's adventure from the best-selling classic manga *Dragon Ball* continues in this new series!

Ever since Goku became Earth's greatest hero and gathered the seven Dragon Balls to defeat the evil Boo, his life on Earth has grown a little dull. But new threats loom overhead, and Goku and his friends will have to defend the planet once again!

RATED **T** FOR TEEN

viz media

viz.com

SHONEN JUMP

DRAGON BALL SUPER © 2015 by BIRD STUDIO, Toyotarou/SHUEISHA Inc.

DEMON SLAYER
KIMETSU NO YAIBA

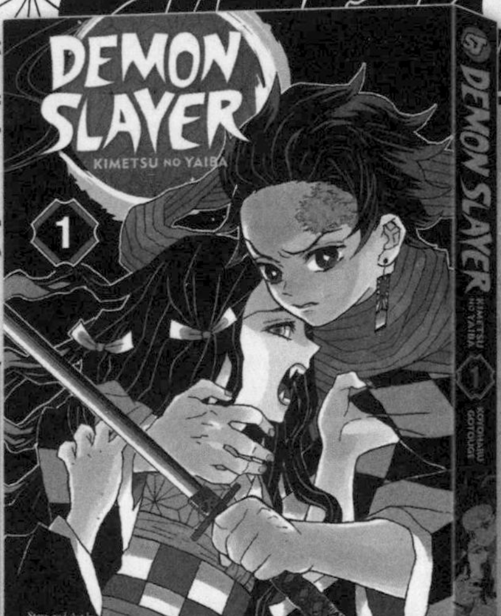

Story and Art by
KOYOHARU GOTOUGE

In Taisho-era Japan, kindhearted Tanjiro Kamado makes a living selling charcoal. But his peaceful life is shattered when a demon slaughters his entire family. His little sister Nezuko is the only survivor, but she has been transformed into a demon herself! Tanjiro sets out on a dangerous journey to find a way to return his sister to normal and destroy the demon who ruined his life.

YOU'RE READING THE WRONG WAY

RADIANT reads from right to left, starting in the upper-right corner, meaning that action, sound effects, and word-balloon order are completely reversed from English order.

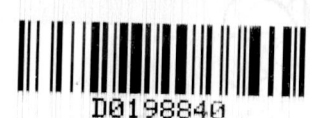

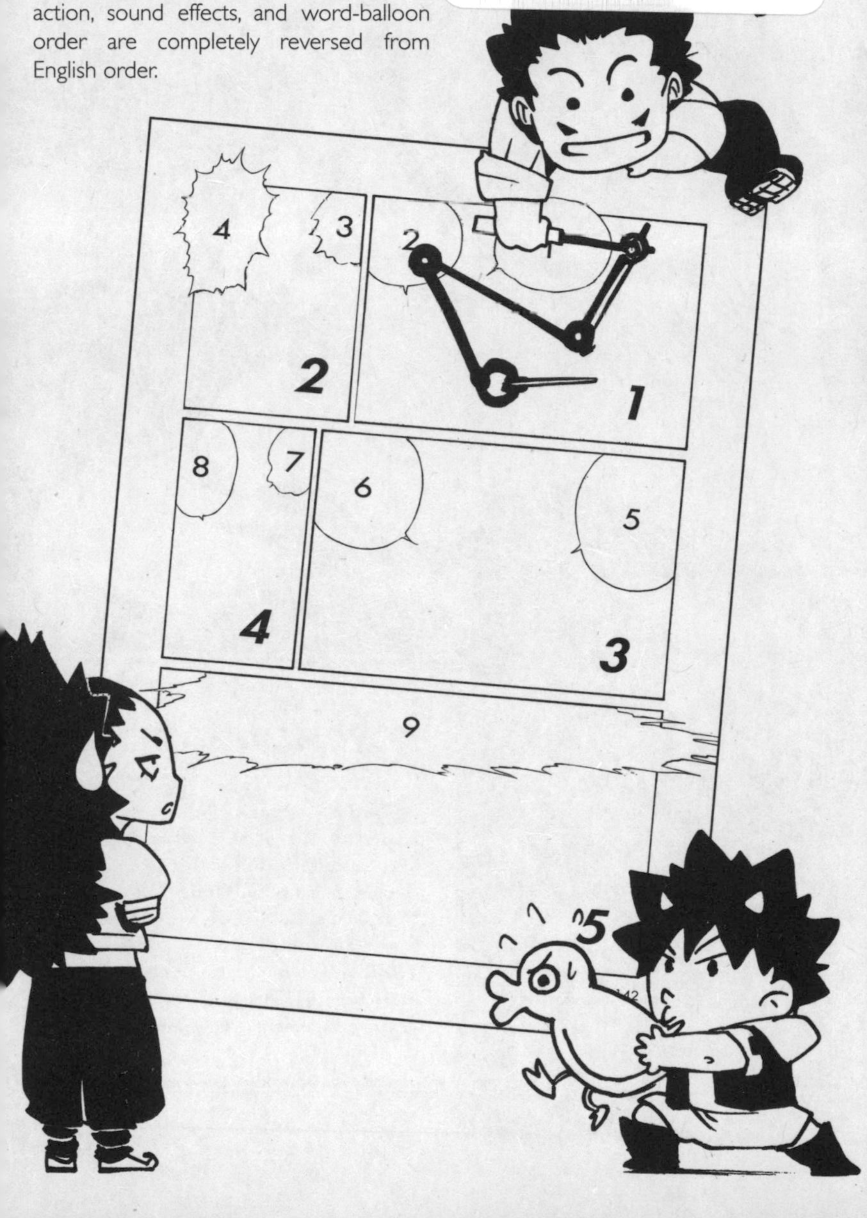

1
2
2
3
4
3
5
6
4
7
8
9
5